CANADIAN CHURCHES

an architectural history

CANADIAN CHURCHES

an architectural history

PETER RICHARDSON & DOUGLAS RICHARDSON

PHOTOGRAPHS BY JOHN DE VISSER

FIREFLY BOOKS

A FIREFLY BOOK

Published by Firefly Books Ltd. 2007

First printing

Publisher Cataloging-in-Publication Data (U.S.)

Richardson, Peter, 1935-
Canadian churches : an architectural history / Peter Richardson and Douglas Richardson ; photographs by John de Visser.
[ ] p. : ill., col. photos. ; cm.
Includes bibliographical references and index.
Summary: Church interior and exterior architecture across Canada from the 18th to the 20th century. Topics include architectural styles and designs, denominational influences and traditions, religious iconography, building materials and stained glass.
ISBN-13: 978-1-55407-239-2
ISBN-10: 1-55407-239-5
1. Church architecture—Canada—History.
2. Church buildings—Canada—History.
I. Richardson, Douglas. II. DeVisser, John, 1930- . III. Title.
726.50971 dc22   NA52971.R534   2007

Library and Archives Canada Cataloguing in Publication
Richardson, Douglas Scott, 1939-
Canadian churches : an architectural history / Douglas Richardson and Peter Richardson ; photographs by John de Visser.
Includes bibliographical references and index.
ISBN-13: 978-1-55407-239-2
ISBN-10: 1-55407-239-5
1. Church architecture—Canada—History.
2. Church buildings—Canada—History.
3. Church decoration and ornament—Canada—History. I. Richardson, Peter, 1935- II. De Visser, John, 1930- III. Title.

NA5240.R52 2007   726.50971   C2007-900831-3

Published in the United States by
Firefly Books (U.S.) Inc.
P.O. Box 1338, Ellicott Station
Buffalo, New York 14205

Published in Canada by
Firefly Books Ltd.
66 Leek Crescent
Richmond Hill, Ontario L4B 1H1

Cover and design by Bob Wilcox

Printed in China

The publisher gratefully acknowledges the financial support for our publishing program by the Government of Canada through the Book Publishing Industry Development Program.

PAGE 1 **Saint-Georges,** *Saint-Georges-de-Beauce, Québec; Roman Catholic. Stone, 1900–1902; David Ouellet. Chancel*

PAGE 2 **St. James' Cathedral,** *Toronto, Ontario; Anglican. Brick and stone, 1850–53; Cumberland & Storm, architects. Last Supper and Ascension window ca 1890 by Franz Mayer & Co., Munich*

PAGE 4–5 **Old Order (David Martin) Meetinghouse,** *St. Jacobs, Ontario; Mennonite. Frame, 1917–18; builders unknown.*

PAGE 7 **St. Dunstan's Basilica,** *Charlottetown, Prince Edward Island; Roman Catholic. Stone, 1914–19; John Marshall Hunter and Charles Benjamin Chappell, architects. Choir*

PAGE 8 **Basilique Notre-Dame de Montréal,** *Québec; Roman Catholic. Stone, 1823–29; James O'Donnell, architect; interior redecorated 1872–88 by Victor Bourgeau, architect. Pulpit*

PAGE 10 **Saint-Charles-Borromée,** *Charlesbourg, Québec; Roman Catholic. Stucco on stone, 1828–30; Thomas Baillairgé, architect. Pulpit*

CONTENTS

Acknowledgements 12

CHURCHES 15

ATLANTIC 29
Terra Nova to Atlantic Canada 30
British and American Colonial Traditions 42
Festive Simplicity 56
New Brunswick Town and Country 63
Deep and Holy Poetry 71
Sublime Newfoundland 78
Rational Gothic 89
Cradle on the Waves 94

QUÉBEC 103
Counter-Reformation to Vatican II 104
L'ancien régime 110
Anglicanism Triumphant 121
Un métissage canadien 124
Notre-Dame-de-Québec 132
Les rivières qui marchent 137
La ville aux cent clochers 143
Québec Modernism 159
Pray and Work 168
Glass Tapestries 174

ONTARIO 177

Loyalists to Modernists   178

Sainte-Marie among the Hurons   188

Unity of the Empire   193

Niagara and Southwestern Ontario   204

Spiritual Fusion   220

Fringe of Settlement   222

Victorian Catholicism   231

Can These Bones Live?   238

Victorian Toronto   241

Church and City   256

Byzantium in Ontario   259

Group Of Seven in Church   272

Resisting Obsolescence   274

WEST AND NORTH 287

Fur Post to Pacific Rim   288

Pre-Confederation Northwest   296

Vancouver's Island and British Columbia   303

Prairie Settlement   310

Bell Towers of the Eastern Rite   328

Late Victorian Gothic Revival   330

The North   336

Modernist Stirrings   340

Western Modernism   347

CHANGES 369

Origins   370

Byzantine   376

Medieval   381

Reformation and Baroque   385

The New World   389

Conclusion   393

Notes and Sources   398

Glossary of Architectural Terms   410

Bibliography   418

Index of Churches
  Name   422
  Location   425
  Denomination   428

General Index   431

DEDICATION

Time present and time past
are both perhaps present in time future.
And time future contained in time past.

—*T.S. Eliot,* Four Quartets

WITH DELIGHT IN OUR GRANDCHILDREN
— SHAPERS OF CANADA'S FUTURE —

JESSE CAMERON
JOSHUA ALESSANDRO
JOSHUA PETER
LÉA JEAN
LUCAS MICHEL
REBEKAH RUTH
ROBIN LILY ISABEL
SAMUEL JAMES
SIMON RAPHAËL
TYLER ALEXANDER
AND OTHERS NOT YET BORN

AND GRATITUDE TO THEIR FOREBEARS
— MAKERS OF CANADA'S PAST —

ROMAN CATHOLICS & PURITANS
ANGLICANS & DUTCH REFORMED
PRESBYTERIANS & INDEPENDENTS
CONGREGATIONALISTS & METHODISTS
BAPTISTS & PLYMOUTH BRETHREN
GREEK ORTHODOX & EASTERN RITE
UNITED CHURCH OF CANADA
AND THOSE WHOSE PIETY IS UNTRACEABLE

For what is the worth of a human life
unless it is woven into the life of our ancestors
by the records of history?

—*Marcus Tullius Cicero,* de Oratore

Architecture has its political use; public buildings being the ornament of a country; it establishes a nation, draws people and commerce; makes the people love their native country, which passion is the original of all great actions . . . . Architecture aims at eternity.
— *Sir Christopher Wren, "Of Architecture"*

ACKNOWLEDGEMENTS

CANADIAN CHURCHES, AN ARCHITECTURAL HISTORY, began with an email enquiry from Firefly Books, in which Michael Worek asked about the possibility of a book on Canada's churches. As it turned out, the idea was Lionel Koffler's. From that first moment Firefly's commitment to the book has not wavered, even amidst worries that they — and the authors — had bitten off more than they could chew. When the list of churches expanded and deadlines came and went, they must have wondered whether they had made the right decision, though they were kind enough not to say so. It was a new experience for two academics to discuss design, layout, colour, cropping, typography and the like with the book's designer, Bob Wilcox. We have been struck by his attention to detail, his concern for beauty and his feeling for "the book." While its heft is the fault of the authors, its design is the result of a cooperative process, driven by Michael Worek and brought to a wonderful conclusion by Bob Wilcox. We are grateful to them.

The opportunity to work with John de Visser was gratifying, for de Visser's productive photographic career includes dozens of books, most related to architecture. Though he had an extensive inventory of photographs of churches, he undertook to photograph our list of buildings afresh. The results are stunning and we are grateful for his fine eye and wonderful sense of light. The work of other photographers, including several who graciously helped out in the rush to make our press date, is acknowledged at the end. Henry Regehr's photographs, especially of interior details, add significantly to the book's visual impact.

There are many persons across Canada who have helped as we have travelled around the country. With almost every building there are persons to thank: priests, ministers, church administrators, heritage organizations, curators, volunteers and friends. There are too many to name them all, and a general thank you for the many kindnesses will have to suffice. But many have made special efforts and have done more than we could reasonably expect: in British Columbia, Rob Destrubé, Father Mark Dumont, Ruth and Simon Harris, Mike Paris, Charles and Anne Paris, and Nancy Richardson; in Alberta, Willi Braun, Colleen Cyr, Brenda Gould, Elef

Christensen, Ron Neufeld, Terry O'Riordan, Dagmar Rais, Lyn Rosenval, David Ridley, Mike Kanigan; in Saskatchewan, Edward and Charlotte Diakow, Bernard Flaman, Gary and Sherry Kish, Frank Korvemaker, David Palmer; in Manitoba, Neil Einarson, Olivier Beck, David Butterfield, Ian Hall, Edward M. Ledohowski, Rowland M. Sawatzky; in Ontario, the late Anthony Adamson, John Barton, Christine Bourolias-Niarchos, Shirley Ann Brown, Angela Kathryn Carr, Peter Coffman, Des Conacher, Margaret English, Vladislav Fedorov, Mark Fram, Sharon Gaudy, Gilbert Gignac and other staff of the Library and Archives Canada, the Rev. Andrea Harrison, Dona Harvey and William Klassen, Ian Howes, Marc Lerman, Marion MacRae, Mary Louise Mallory, Mary McIntyre, Miriam McTiernan and Archives of Ontario staff, the late Pamela Manson Smith, Terry Montgomery, Shirley Morriss, Leona Moses, Stephen Otto, Kent Rawson, Marianna Richardson (who "hopeth all things"), Roy Schatz, Alfred Schrauwers, Malcolm Thurlby, William E. Toye, the University of Toronto Library system (especially Caven Library in Knox College, the Fine Art Library and Thomas Fisher Rare Books Library), John van Nostrand, William Westfall and Ian Wilson; special thanks to Clara Waindubence at Sheguindah First Nations, not only for her assistance but also for suggesting the title of one of the chapters; in Québec, Father Fernando Ferrera, the Rev. Stephen Hayes, Luc Noppen, Claude Paulette, Langis Pitre, Mary Richardson, and Howard Shubert; in New Brunswick, the Most Rev. Harold L. Nutter and George L. Hersey (Yale University, New Haven, Connecticut); in Prince Edward Island, Canon Robert C. Tuck and Catherine Hennessey, as well as George T. Kapelos (of Ryerson University, Toronto) for an introduction to PEI; in Nova Scotia, Tom and Natalie Forrestall and J. Philip McAleer; in Newfoundland and Labrador, Shane O'Dea and Hans Rollmann.

Robert G. Hill has mined his database to help identify architects in cases where our sources did not suffice, so that the data is better than it otherwise might have been. We also thank our research assistants including Ryan Paliga, Daniel Galadza and Maureen Conley.
— *GPR and DSR*

Architecture for churches is a matter of gospel. A church that is interested in proclaiming the gospel must also be interested in architecture, for year after year the architecture of the church proclaims a message that either augments the preached Word or conflicts with it. Church architecture cannot, therefore, be left to those of refined tastes, the aesthetic elite, or even the professional architect.
— Donald J. Bruggink and Carl H. Droppers, 1965

CHURCHES

CANADIAN CHURCHES is divided into chapters covering Atlantic Canada, Québec, Ontario, the West and North and a final chapter entitled "Changes." Within those chapters the material is organized chronologically, thematically or geographically. We have made deliberate efforts to include famous churches alongside less well-known buildings: St. Paul's, Halifax, is juxtaposed with the less well-known but contemporary work of the Moravian Brethren in Labrador; the concrete structure of the Oratoire Saint-Joseph in Montréal is compared with 1950s and 60s concrete-shell churches in Saguenay-Lac Saint-Jean; Toronto's famous Group of Seven art in St. Anne's (Anglican) sits alongside icons by Mount Athos monks in St. George's (Greek Orthodox), also in Toronto; Manitoba's Cathédrale Saint-Boniface is compared with Saskatchewan's often overlooked Silton Chapel.

The challenge was always to limit the number of churches. Lists grew and shrank, grew and shrank again and eventually stabilized. Decisions were rethought. Yet many churches we hoped to include had to be left out because of lack of space, not lack of enthusiasm.

Some denominations may seem over-represented, some under-represented and, regrettably, others not represented at all. There are several reasons for this. Church buildings are not distributed across the country in a balanced way. The different historical, social and religious conditions under which the various parts of the country developed means that Québec is dominantly Roman Catholic while Ontario is strongly Protestant and the Prairies are especially rich in Ukrainian churches. Some ecclesiastical traditions have pursued architectural excellence more consistently and more creatively as they have built for their spiritual needs. Two examples of such creative activity are the important 19th-century developments within the Anglican Church and the late 20th-century implementation of the Second Vatican Council's reforms within Roman Catholicism.

Saint-Isidore, *Saint-Isidore (Dorchester), Québec; Roman Catholic. Stone, 1853–60; Michel Patry and Jean-Baptiste Saint-Michel, architects*

The tin-clad roofs of Saint-Isidore create a striking geometric composition of ascending cones and pyramids, each signalling an important element in the church's plan. First are the roofs of the sacristy and its semicircular apse in the foreground, behind that the semicircular roof of the apse of the church, behind it the roofs of the transepts. The spire marks the location of the altar in the church's apse, and barely visible behind the apse's spire is the main steeple at the front of the church.

ABOVE **St. Luke's**, *Newtown, Newfoundland; Anglican. Frame, 1895; builder unknown*

BELOW **Holy Ascension** (abandoned), *near Sturgis, Saskatchewan; Russian Greek Orthodox. Log, 1905, builder unknown*

FACING PAGE **Sainte-Anne-de-Kent**, *near Bouctouche, New Brunswick: Roman Catholic. Frame, 1890; Léon Léger, designer. Paintings by Édouard Gautreau, 1936*

Authorial preferences, of course, have also skewed the selection. Still, we have aimed to present a representative group of somewhat more than 250 churches, without attempting to shoehorn all denominations into the table of contents. The book reflects different periods, regions, denominations and styles. Our comments are driven by the architecture of the buildings — this is "an architectural history" — but we comment on historical, social, religious, theological and artistic issues as they seem relevant to understanding the buildings as places of worship.

Architecture matters in two fundamental and complementary ways. What architects fashion, and this is especially true of church buildings, both shapes and is shaped. There is a reflexive relationship between a building and its users, between a church and the congregation. On the one hand, a building gives visual form to what is important to a particular religious group and underscores that group's values and priorities. Architecture speaks directly to the relationship between an organization and the society within which it plays its role. To put it the other way around, society and the social order shapes the building. Architecture shapes the values, attitudes and outlooks of the persons who use the buildings. Buildings impose themselves subtly on their users, influencing their emotions, shaping their behaviours and affecting the quality of the activities and relationships within the structure. Each influences the other dynamically and reciprocally.

Style

Architecture is often equated with style, as if the most important decision an architect faces is choosing some historic or modern style. While there were periods when it was possible to choose one among several available styles, particularly when historicism was the dominant mood in the late 18th and the early 19th centuries, this was a passing phase. Architecture is so closely bound up with its immediate

cultural context that the notion of simply selecting a pleasing style from those available cannot be entirely satisfying. Historicism implied that it was the past, especially the styles of the past, which ought to shape the way architecture should be practised. A productive feature of historicism was its emphasis on architectural and archaeological research, especially research in the early Christian, Byzantine and Medieval periods, a process that still continues. This research has resulted in books and articles, often passionately written, along with large archives of measured drawings that are enormously useful.

Though this historical research is still important, it no longer shapes the way in which buildings are planned and executed, as it did for almost 200 years, when the goal was often to revive this or that architectural style from the past. It is this historicist movement that led to the development of the architecture known as Classical Revival, Romanesque Revival, Gothic Revival and so on. Producing faithful extensions of an earlier building style was seen as desirable. Historical precedent was an important matter, particularly in connection with churches. Much serious scholarship went into this matter of style as church leaders and architects sought to identify a style appropriate to the worship of God. The highly influential Ecclesiological Society, whose journal the *Ecclesiologist* (1841–68) was an important organ of Gothic Revival thinking about churches, spread the Gothic gospel among Christians with strong liturgical interests. By the late 19th century, Gothic Revival had become the norm for churches of all persuasions, including even churches that rejected theological systems and any whiff of establishment views, yet who wished to be a part of mainstream culture. These "revival" styles, especially

FACING PAGE **Saint-Joseph**, *Deschambault, Québec; Roman Catholic. Stone, 1835–38; Thomas Baillairgé, architect. Interior 1841–49 by André Paquet*

TOP **St. Mary's Cathedral**, *Yorkton, Saskatchewan: Ukrainian Catholic. Brick, 1913–14; "Coronation of the Virgin" by Stephen Meush, 1939–41*

ABOVE **Saint-Jean**, *Île d'Orléans, Québec; Roman Catholic. Stone, 1734; addition, 1852 by Louis-Thomas Berlinguet. Side altar*

Gothic Revival, influenced church architecture well into the 20th century.

Historicism implied that a range of styles was at the disposal of an architect, that any of several might do for a church building and that designers might choose eclectically from a broad architectural palette. Prior to World War I, however, new building materials, new technologies and a new aesthetic began to outline a different approach, one that took on substance and momentum after the enormous disruption of that war. In its aftermath, society sought a break with the past and looked for an aesthetic appropriate to the new order. By the second quarter of the 20th century, this search for a new aesthetic coalesced around what has come to be called "Modernism," characterized by giving priority to a notion of "functionalism" and the extensive use of steel, concrete and glass. In Canada there were little more than stirrings of Modernism during the 1920s and 30s; it was only following World War II that International Style architecture, as it has come to be called (a term coined in 1932), found a following. Even then the International Style shows up only infrequently in designs of churches. Its geometric forms, straight lines and limited range of manufactured materials were hard for church committees to swallow. Modernism, however, was not so much about replacing historical styles as it was a rejection of historicism. It called for an approach based primarily on first principles and drawing on new technological developments, free from the inherited assumptions of the past.

It was only with the expressionism of the 1960s and later that successful modern buildings emerged from a long period of derivative eclecticism. No one approach came prominently to the forefront in church building, though most designs shared a conviction about expressing the character of the worshipping community in place of adopting some inherited "correct" sense of what churches should look like and which style of buildings expressed "Christian architecture." In the past half-century, while some groups of buildings may be coherently connected by their methods of construction or the idiom in which the architects work, there has been little sense of architectural style as a primary criterion.

Design

Since a basic knowledge of how churches function and what they are intended to point toward can no longer be assumed, we offer some hints on what to look for in understanding, appreciating and interpreting a church building. Is the building extroverted or introverted; does it turn its back on the "world," does it attempt to fit into its surroundings, or is it consciously attempting to make a public statement? Does it dominate triumphantly or sit quietly? How is its presence signalled? Do people walk or paddle or drive or take public transit to their church? Does it complement its location or vie with it for attention?

Inside, does it cocoon its congregation or enable them to connect with their environment? How important are the liturgical features: where is the table or the altar, what does it symbolize and how does it do this? How important is baptism, where does it take place and how is it administered? Is the pulpit located centrally, to one side, near the front wall or pulled forward into the congregation? Is it high or low? What importance is given Scripture and where is it read: from a lectern, pulpit, behind the table or out in the congregation? How are sacraments, preaching, Bible and other liturgical elements related? Is there an ordained clergy? Do others participate? How many leaders are there, where are they positioned, and how much do they move around? Is there a choir and where is it located? Is there a band, organ, piano or musical group? Does the congregation stand or is there seating? What does the seating emphasize: individuals (upholstered seats), families (enclosed pews) or the whole group (theatre seating)? Do people look at each other as they may in curved or circular seating? Do they all look toward a common focus as they would in parallel banks of seating?

Visual cues to a church's theology are plentiful. How, if at all, are the originating events of the faith as a whole or of that particular tradition brought to mind? Are there crosses, and are they large or small, high or low, with or without a figure of Jesus? Is there other sculpture or art representing historical persons (for example, Prince Volodymr, Jean Brébeuf, Martin Luther), animate objects (for example, lamb, lion, eagle) or inanimate objects (for example, a building, a tomb, bread and wine)? How do sculpture and art relate to the architecture and the congregation? Is there a concern for an aesthetic "experience"?

Almost every design element is a complex mixture of architecture, theology, church history and the social circumstances at the time of building. A congregation has an historic lineage — even independent churches do — and consciously or unconsciously the design implies judgments on the importance and significance of that history, even if it is only the church's designation to a canonized saint (for example, Andrew, Peter, Clement) or well-known historic person (for example, Catherine of Siena, John Knox, John Wesley, Pope Pius XII), a sacred place (for example, Mount Carmel, Mount Zion). Sometimes designations express ethnic and historical lineages (for example, African Methodist Episcopal Church, Ukrainian Orthodox Church, Moravian Brethren).

Some person or persons — priest or minister or missionary, building committee or patron, architect or builder — reflected on the theological implications of what they were doing as the building was designed and built. Since architecture is rooted in specific social settings, the design and layout of an 18th-century Roman Catholic church differs from an Anglican or Presbyterian or Moravian church of the same period, and those 18th-century buildings differ from 20th-century churches within the same denominations.

FACING PAGE **Church of the Immaculate Conception of the Virgin Mary**, *Cook's Creek, Manitoba; Ukrainian Catholic. Reinforced concrete and concrete block, 1930–52; Father Philip Ruh, designer. Lady Chapel in transept*

TOP **Church of St. Andrew and St. Paul**, *Montréal, Québec; Presbyterian. Stone, 1931–32; Harold Featherstonhaugh, architect. Memorial window designed by Sir Edward Burne-Jones, produced by Morris & Co. (originally installed in St. Paul's Church, 1885)*

BOTTOM **St. Andrew's**, *Québec; Presbyterian. Stone, 1809–10; John Bryson, builder. Silver communion service, 1839, by William Bellchambers, London*

Churches are for the worship of God and the nurture of his people. In some traditions there are no aids to worship, merely bare spaces and silence. Others use a wide variety of aids: Bible, choral and instrumental music, stained glass, painting and sculpture, candles, lamps and memorials. Simplicity and plainness, whether Quaker or Doukhobor, are just as eloquent an expression of a group's priorities as artistic embellishments. The artistic, however, often attracts comment; a casual glance in these pages shows the enormous attention some congregations have given it. From Stations of the Cross to exquisite silver vessels to sculpture and stained glass, some of history's greatest objects were designed for churches; one cannot ignore the devotion and personal piety that prompted such an outpouring of creative energies. While careful attention to the photographs will disclose many such elements, we wish we could have included more. The fact that these objects have often been carried from one church to another, so that older elements become embedded in newer churches, is mute testimony to the importance of such treasures. Examples include a Russian iconostasis in the Massey College Chapel, University of Toronto; a chandelier in the Ukrainian Catholic Church in Mundare, Saskatchewan; the baldachin in Saint-François-de-Sales in Neuville, Québec; and the Tablets with the Ten Commandments, the Lord's Prayer and the Apostles' Creed in the Mohawk Chapel in Brantford, Ontario; the Mohawk Chapel tablets point, incidentally, to a group whose members had few books of their own.

Change

Though we have valued historic buildings in their as-built form, we have attempted at the same time to show the sequence of steps by which buildings got to their present form. Many structures are the congregation's third, fourth or even fifth building. There is hardly a church here that has not been altered, added to, renovated, changed or rebuilt. There are some brilliant examples of this: Saint-Boniface Cathedral and Saint-Benoît-du-Lac are particularly good modern examples, while St. Paul's, Halifax, and the Cathédrale Notre-Dame in Québec are excellent earlier examples. The changes have a social and religious context, especially in the recent

LEFT **Shiskovichi**, *Saskatchewan; Ukrainian Greek Orthodox (now in Willingdon, Alberta, Museum). Frame; builder unknown*

RIGHT **St. John's**, *Kingnait (Cape Dorset); Anglican. Frame, 1953; builder unknown*

FACING PAGE **St. Peter's**, *Lower Kootenay near Cranbrook, British Columbia; Roman Catholic. Frame, 1887; builder unknown*

ABOVE **Metropolitan Community Church**, *Toronto; Universal Fellowship of Metropolitan Community Churches (previously United, originally Methodist). Brick with cast iron, 1907; Burke & Horwood, architects*

The commonly-called Gay Church in Toronto occupies a distinguished, essentially intact, building by important architects. The vaulted nave has half vaults over the U-shaped balcony and stairs from the balcony to the platform at the front. The educational facilities are on an Akron plan.

FACING PAGE TOP **The Cedars**, *Waterloo, Ontario (Westminster United and Temple Shalom Synagogue). Brick, 1995–96; Charles Simon, architect*

The unique building incorporates both a church and a synagogue, an approach that, given the different calendars of Christians and Jews, makes good sense. The duality is expressed externally by the two skylights, facing each other, each lighting the front of one of the worship spaces. The two congregational facilities form a single space divided by a folding door, so that either community can use the other's space.

FACING PAGE BOTTOM **St. Catherine's Chapel**, *Massey College, University of Toronto; ecumenical. Brick with wood interior, 1962–63; Ron Thom, architect; interior by Tanya Moiseiwitsch, redesigned by Brigitte Shim, architect*

The small 18th-century Russian iconostasis and the Ukrainian cross, silhouetted against the brilliant blue wall, are gifts of Massey's first Master, Robertson Davies.

past, as congregations have found imaginative ways to take on new tasks, seek new participants and express the faith in new ways, thereby maintaining their relevance to the world in which we live.

"Changes," our fifth chapter, discusses evolutionary change in church architecture from the earliest days up to the Baroque period, the point at which the Canadian practice of church building begins. As cultures change and develop, architectural forms do not stand still. Two recent trends are given attention here. First, the late 19th century was concerned to integrate Sunday school activities more fully into Christian worship. The so-called Akron plan was a result of this; it developed a flexible and multi-functional arrangement by using splayed spaces and large folding or sliding doors, in some cases permitting both major spaces to be used as one. Second, large auditoriums have become the preferred style, reflecting changes in leadership and preaching, with the result that megachurches, with theatre-like features and large parking lots, have come to the fore. Just as cultures change and develop, architectural forms do not stand still, and it seems that a new phase of church building has become clearly evident.

On one level, *Canadian Churches* is for anyone interested in architecture and how buildings respond to society's needs. On another level, the book hopes to make the confusing variety of churches understandable to persons with little knowledge of churches or theology. It is also a book for many who are committed Christians, who attend churches regularly, who are familiar with one kind of church and one theology but who know little of the wide range of architectural and theological riches. The book is for all who are interested in churches as buildings, as important pieces of architecture, as documents of history and culture and religion. We hope there will be much in the variety and wealth of Christian traditions displayed here to inform and delight — and even surprise — these several audiences.

Community

Worship occurs within communities. These communities vary enormously: some are amorphous; some are strongly rooted in a religious tradition while others retain a strong sense of ethnic identity, along with their own language and social customs. While writing this book we have been welcomed in monastic communities and native communities. We have explored traditions only faintly familiar to us: Doukhobor, Hutterite, Mennonite, Métis, Moravian Brethren, Mormon, Russian and Ukrainian, to name a few. Some important communities no longer exist, though their buildings remain: Gaelic-speaking Presbyterians, the Children of Peace, Oro's Black settlers and B.C.'s gold miners. Methodists and Congregationalists have disappeared in most places, absorbed into the United Church in 1925. Still, we have been impressed with the way Canada is a myriad of communities from all over the world: whether European, Asian, South Asian, African, Latin American or North American.

We have observed the successes and challenges of many parishes and congregations; to some extent we have shared those joys and trials. We have formed impressions, but only impressions, of the state of Christianity and its various manifestations. While Canadian churches are alive and well, what sociologists and statisticians have been saying for some time is all too apparent: many churches are shrinking and some are disappearing. Christianity is refashioning itself, sometimes willingly but often kicking and screaming, in part as other world religions take root and make their presence felt in Canada, in part as a result of an increasingly secular society. Canada is no longer dominantly Christian. Christianity has to compete, so it is rearranging itself, as it has done regularly through history. One type of refashioning follows an economic model: just as downtown businesses close while malls proliferate in the suburbs, churches follow the same pattern, moving from city streets to suburban highways, often cheek by jowl with malls, utilizing similar architecture and relying similarly on large parking lots to accommodate their far-flung congregation.

We have participated in an architectural reality check of Christian communities across Canada and how they express their beliefs. Some sing and pray in the very buildings their ancestors worshipped in while others worship in buildings and through activities their ancestors would hardly recognize as Christian. The commitments of today's Christians seem the same as the commitments of past generations, even if they are expressed differently. Architecture gives public visibility to these commitments and conveys a clear sense of Canada's religious vitality. We have observed Canada's tolerance of variety, at least in part a product of its encouragement of extensive immigration. Canada has positively encouraged the maintenance of ethnicity, culture, language and tradition, and this has resulted in churches of great diversity in the world's most multicultural country.

Finally, a few words are in order about the First Nations. We have included churches built by or for them in relevant regional sections. We have been deeply impressed by the spirituality of Canada's first peoples and have been struck by their generosity. Canada has not treated indigenous communities well and they have had reason to reject the Christianity brought by Europeans. It has been tragically moving to see the dilapidated condition of some First Nations churches but we have also seen the continued vitality of their piety and worship. And sometimes we have seen remarkable instances of the integration of native spirituality and traditional Christian belief, in creative ways that are wholly satisfying.

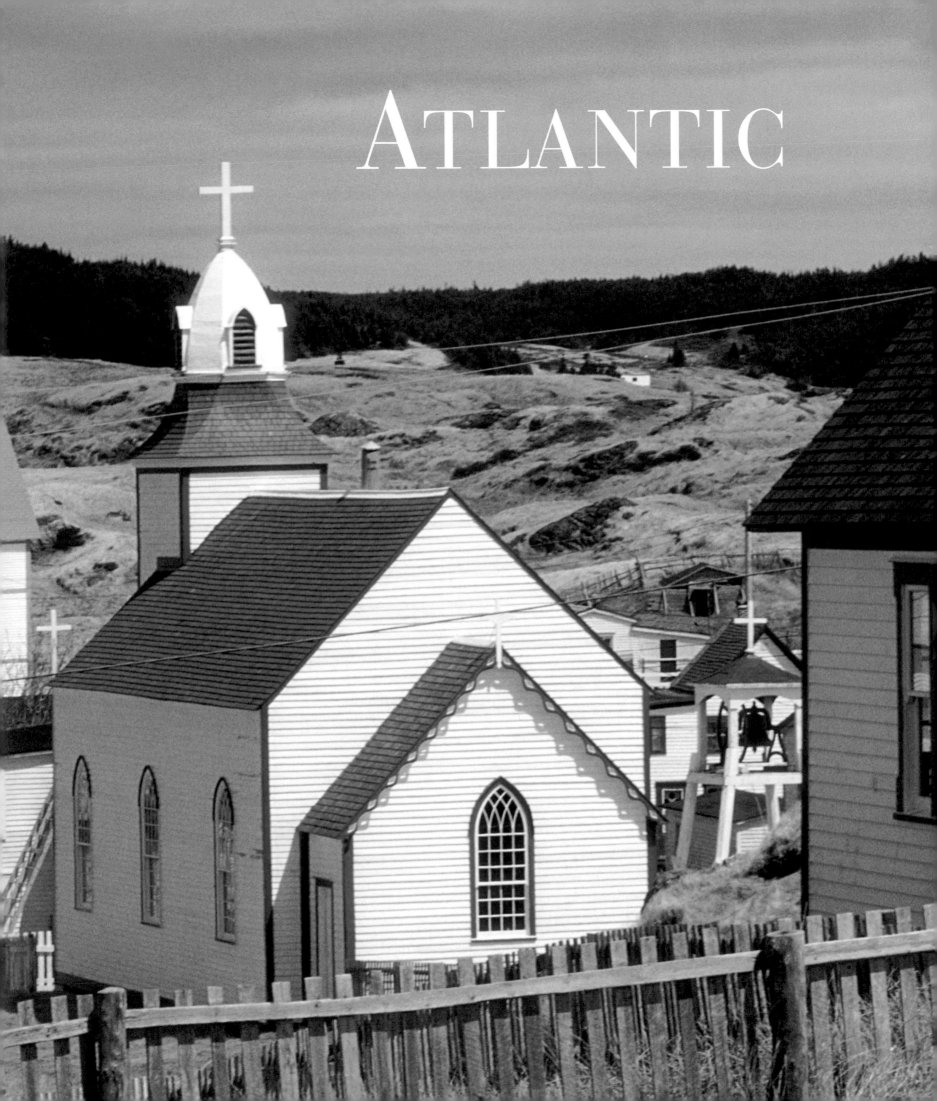

ATLANTIC

Introduction

Terra Nova to Atlantic Canada

By God's will, ... sailing southward amidst the ice [we] discovered a new land, extremely fertile and even having vines .... Eric [Henricus] ... bishop of Greenland and the neighbouring regions, arrived in this truly vast and very rich land, in the name of Almighty God [and] remained a long time in both summer and winter.

— *Vinland Map, ca 15th century*

Terra Nova, THE NEW LAND, IS THE EARLIEST NAME of the region to appear on maps made by western Europeans looking across the Atlantic Ocean. Atlantic Canada was Newfoundland premier Joey Smallwood's term for all the Canadian provinces bordering that ocean. This transition from a Eurocentric view of an exotically distant region to a homegrown political view underscores the changes of half a millennium. The land itself has changed little. It is defined by water, and its deeply indented coastline — about 25,000 miles of it — encourages small, self-reliant, communities. Few areas are easily farmed, with Prince Edward Island the fertile exception. Historically its natural resources are the forest and the sea (especially the Grand Banks), and more recently iron ore, power generation and offshore oil.

First Contact to the Loyalists

Forebears of the Beothuk, Mi'kmaq, Maliseet, Pasamaquody and Inuit occupied Atlantic Canada by 7000 B.C., at the end of the waves of migrations to North America beginning about 14,000 B.C. Its key role in Canada's development stemmed from its being the first land encountered by European fishermen, explorers and settlers. The Norse, working their way across the North Atlantic, were the earliest visitors. By AD 1000 Leif Eriksson had founded L'Anse aux Meadows, with a forge and fishing camps, on the northwestern tip of Newfoundland. By the

PREVIOUS PAGE **The Church of the Most Holy Trinity**, *Trinity, Newfoundland; Roman Catholic. Wood, 1833; builder unknown.* **St. Paul's**, *Trinity, Newfoundland; Anglican. Wood, 1892–93; Stephen C. Earle, architect*
The small wooden church in the foreground, the Church of the Most Holy Trinity, is the oldest Roman Catholic church in Newfoundland. It is located in one of the province's oldest communities, on a large three-fingered harbour that sheltered early fishing fleets. Trinity was the scene of the first court of Admiralty in British North America and also the place of the first inoculations against smallpox (1800) by the local clergyman and surgeon, John Clinch, a friend of Edward Jenner who discovered the vaccine. In the background, the colourful Anglican church, St. Paul's, is the third to be erected on this site.

12th century the Norse had farms on the west coast of Greenland, with a dozen parish churches, a cathedral, monastery and nunnery. European activity in Newfoundland, however, soon ended, probably due to the distances and environment. But not for long.

Portuguese and Basques were fishing on the Grand Banks by the 15th century, while others explored: the Italian John Cabot in 1497 (for England); Giovanni da Verrazzano, another Italian, in 1524 (for France); Esteban Gomez in 1524–25 (for Spain); Jacques Cartier (whose 1534 voyage is the best known of several) for France. By the mid-16th century the new maps showed that the New World had effectively been drawn within the purview and economic orbit of the Old.

The French seized settlement opportunities first. Pierre du Gua (1558–1628), with Samuel de Champlain (1570–1635), created a *habitation* on the St. Croix River in New Brunswick in 1604, which included a small chapel, but in 1605 they moved across the Bay of Fundy to Port Royal in Nova Scotia. Harold Kalman points out that "The community abounded in technical skills...since the artisans included 'numerous joiners, carpenters, masons, stone-cutters, locksmiths, workers in iron,...wood-sawyers...&c.'" that Champlain brought with him from France. Having put so much care into the buildings at Île-aux-Dochets on the St. Croix, they removed all but the largest, disassembling and transporting them for reuse. The new buildings included the first proper chapel north of New Spain.

The English followed in 1610 with a settlement at Cupids on the Avalon Peninsula, and shortly after at Renews, Harbour Grace, St. John's and Ferryland, all in Newfoundland. By the 1690s, although the English occupied parts of Newfoundland, the French held much of its coastline — developing an important administrative centre at Plaisance (Placentia) — as well as holding Île Royale (Cape Breton) and Île Saint-Jean (Prince Edward Island).

War between the French and British resulted in the Treaty of Utrecht (1713) that gave Britain a toehold in Nova Scotia, awarding it much of Acadia. France retained Île Royale and countered by beginning the fortress of Louisbourg in 1717 as the lynchpin of their North American colonies. Military engineers were the first professional designers, with a broad range of skills other than military: town planning, lighthouses, administrative buildings, hospitals and churches. Étienne Verrier

Port Royal Habitation, *near Annapolis Royal, Nova Scotia; Roman Catholic. Timber and planks, 1605–1607; reconstruction, 1938–39*

Champlain's *habitation* at Port Royal, across the river from Annapolis Royal, was reconstructed on the basis of archaeological investigations, descriptions and engravings, using typical French construction methods from the period. It presents a nearly blank outside face, with the buildings grouped around an open courtyard. The high-pitched roof behind the canon platform on the left is the common room. The interior of the simple and rather gloomy chapel behind it is shown above.

Chapelle de Saint-Louis, Fortress of Louisbourg, *Louisbourg, Nova Scotia; Roman Catholic. Stone, 1717–58; Jean-François Verville and Étienne Verrier, military engineers; reconstructed 1961*

Louisbourg was France's supposedly impregnable fortress guarding the entrance to the St. Lawrence River. It included a chapel and provision for priests, so that church services might begin immediately. A parish church was proposed but never built. The reconstruction, based on archaeological remains and hundreds of 18th-century drawings, includes a richly finished interior, a profusion of light, an ample retable and vaulted ceiling.

BELOW **St. Mark's**, *Niagara-on-the-Lake, Ontario; Anglican*

Robert Addison (1754–1829) was born in England and ordained a Deacon of the Church of England. He applied to the Society for the Propagation of the Gospel in Foreign Parts in 1791, was accepted and became the second Protestant clergyman in Upper Canada — the Rev. John Stuart had arrived in Kingston in 1786 — settling in Newark (now Niagara-on-the-Lake) in 1792. He built St. Mark's, the first church in Upper Canada to have regular services, though that stone church, completed in 1809, was burned during the War of 1812, then repaired and subsequently much altered. He ministered to Indians and settlers from Fort Erie to the Grand River, preaching at intervals to the Mohawks in their church near Brantford.

To the memory of the Rev. ROBERT ADDISON, First Missionary in this District, of the venerable Society for the Propagation of the Gospel in Foreign Parts. He commenced his labours in 1792, which, by the blessing of Divine Providence he was enabled to continue for 37 years. Besides his stated services as Minister of St. Marks Church in this Town, he visited and officiated in different parts of this, and the adjoining Districts until other Missionaries arrived. He was born in Westmoreland, England, and died October 6th, 1829, in the 75th, year of his

(1683–1747) arrived at Louisbourg in 1724 as chief engineer and took over supervision of the King's Bastion, combining the governor's residence, chapel (doubling as a parish church *pro tem*), soldiers' barracks and jail, all reconstructed to his surviving plans. Louisbourg fell to colonial Americans with British aid in 1745, was returned to the French in 1749 and fell again in 1758. During this period of uncertainty, the fateful decision was taken in 1755 to deport the Acadian French, precipitated by concern over their refusal to pledge allegiance to the British Crown. Some escaped, some were deported (especially to Louisiana) and some went to France or even England. Eventually many returned to revitalize Acadian culture in the region. The Treaty of Paris (1763) confirmed Britain's hegemony over Atlantic Canada and awarded France only two small islands, Saint-Pierre and Miquelon.

Halifax, founded in 1749 as the British counterbalance to Louisbourg, attracted settlers from colonies along the Atlantic, from Great Britain (particularly the Highlands and Yorkshire), and also from Europe, notably German Protestants (*see* pp. 46; p. 48, and p. 51). The colony also received a huge influx of settlers as a result of the American Revolution (*see* p. 50). Almost 20,000 Loyalists, including substantial numbers of black Loyalists especially in Shelburne and Dartmouth, built new lives in Nova Scotia. Another 11,000 Loyalists settled in New Brunswick, established as a separate colony in 1784. Smaller numbers went to Île Saint-Jean, renamed Prince Edward Island in 1799, and Île Royale (renamed Cape Breton

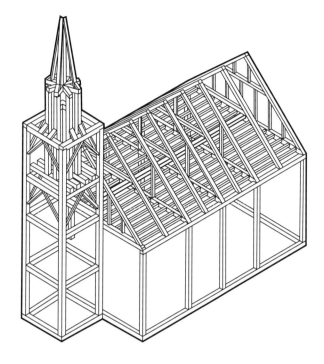

ABOVE LEFT **Typical clapboard church**
This community church near Grand Pré, dating from 1861, is typical of many Congregational, Baptist, Methodist or Presbyterian churches in the Maritimes. Often plain but beautifully executed, this one has spiky pinnacles around the eaves that fit well with the Gothicizing windows and doorframe.

ABOVE **Typical church framing**
This cutaway isometric sketch of the timber framing of the Covenanter Church, Grand Pré, illustrates how different its hewn mortised-and-tenoned timber construction is from later frame construction using two-by-fours or two-by-sixes. The technique is similar to barn construction, though the church is framed to carry the ceiling (instead of a barn's open roof structure) and to support the later tall spire above the tower. The Loyalist builders brought their skills from New England.

Island). The dismal conditions the settlers faced were reflected in a New England quip that called Nova Scotia "Nova Scarcity."

By 1790 Newfoundland had a summer population of about 25,000 but a long-term population of only 10,000, with five men for every woman. The Irish, who worked in the fisheries, already dominated its culture. By 1800 the other Atlantic colonies had almost 100,000 settlers; this included about 7,000 returned Acadians and a small native population.

The British authorities did their best to serve several of the diverse elements of the population. Following a query on behalf of the Bishop of London into the state of the Church of England in the American colonies, the Society for the Propagation of the Gospel in Foreign Parts (SPG) received a Royal Charter in 1701 to "ensure that sufficient mainteynance be provided for an orthodox clergy to live amongst the colonists" and support "the propagation of the gospel in those parts." The SPG initially sent Anglican priests and schoolteachers to work among colonists, then began to evangelize slaves and aboriginals. The earliest missionaries were a colourful lot. The few missions were widely separated and often endured long vacancies owing to harsh conditions, isolation and privation, as well as unsupportive congregations. The first SPG missionary, John Jackson (d. 1717), arrived in 1701 as chaplain to the garrison at St. John's, Newfoundland. He thought the officers tyrannical and oppressive, they thought his "violent temper and scandalous life" disruptive; he

St. James' Chapel, *Long Reach, New Brunswick;*
Anglican. Wood, 1841–43; builder unknown

John Medley, the first Bishop of Fredericton,
consecrated this meetinghouse — of Georgian
proportions, with small panes of glass in rectangular
windows — in 1845. The exterior was Gothicized in
1887, making it more palatable to some.

The interior retains a double-decker reading desk
and pulpit in Neoclassical style, with an Ionic order
decorating its corners and supporting the sounding
board. This is a charming example of common
Georgian practice, of an altar (which is not original)
against the reading desk. One liturgical centre ensured
that the Communion service was visible from all parts
of the building.

was brought back to England in 1705. Richard Watts (1688–1739/40), a Scots-born Presbyterian schoolmaster before he was ordained an Anglican priest in 1727, was appointed garrison chaplain at Annapolis Royal and the SPG's first schoolmaster in Nova Scotia. In 1732 he petitioned for the old French church lands in town (still owned by St. Luke's parish) for Anglican use, the first endowment in Canada for a Protestant church. He found life happier when he moved to Rhode Island in 1737.

Mohawk warrior, diplomat and orator, Theyanoguin (ca 1680–1755), was leader of the "Four Kings," the Iroquois sachems presented at court to Queen Anne in 1710. He converted to Christianity about 1690, becoming a preacher to fellow Mohawks. Their "request for religious instruction resulted in the queen's patronage of missions in America" and a chapel at Fort Hunter, New York, in 1711, precursor to the Mohawk Chapel at Brantford, Ontario (*see* pp. 193–94). When the SPG supplied a missionary, Theyanoguin served as a lay preacher, living near the chapel. In 1770 John Stuart (1740/41–1811) began ministering to both Mohawks and whites at Queen Anne's Chapel at Fort Hunter. Joseph Brant (Thayendanegea) lived for a short time with him in the Mohawk parsonage near the fort and they collaborated in the translation of St. Mark's Gospel into Mohawk, which was finally printed in 1787. In 1785 Stuart settled in Cataraqui (Kingston, Ontario) as rector of St. George's, where a memorial celebrates his SPG connection.

Loyalists to Confederation

Atlantic Canada is mainly British and Loyalist; its provinces — Newfoundland and Labrador, Nova Scotia, New Brunswick and Prince Edward Island — developed separately and were settled by people from varying colonial backgrounds. Almost all communities are located scenically around coves and bays except for areas such as the Saint John River Valley and the Annapolis Valley. As long as fishing and forests supported the population adequately, the Atlantic region thrived.

The first British colony to achieve responsible government was Nova Scotia (1848), followed by New Brunswick (1854), Prince Edward Island (1851) and Newfoundland (1855). When a movement for confederation arose in Canada West and East, it struck a responsive chord in New Brunswick, but less so in PEI, Newfoundland and parts of Nova Scotia. Outside events, however, especially the American Civil War (1861–65) and the 1867 purchase of Alaska by the United States, along with Westminster's strong support for confederation, brought about a new federal state — the Dominion of Canada — with Nova Scotia and New Brunswick as founding provinces. PEI, which had hosted the crucial Charlottetown Conference (1864), joined in 1873; Newfoundland joined only in 1949.

The region's 19th-century religious character seems to have continued unchanged. Wonderful clapboard rural and urban churches range from Presbyterian kirks and Baptist meeting places through more formal Anglican and Roman Catholic churches. The various denominations are not uniformly distributed. Catholics are significantly stronger in PEI, Presbyterians in Nova Scotia and Baptists in New Brunswick, with Anglicans and Methodists relatively evenly distributed. Presbyterians are particularly strong in Cape Breton, Pictou and central PEI, Anglicans in Halifax and Saint John, Baptists in the Annapolis Valley and the

The Book of Common Prayer ... *translated into the Mohawk language ... to which is added the gospel according to St. Mark, translated into the Mohawk language by Captn. Joseph Brant ...* (4th ed., London, 1787).

Theyanoguin and his Mohawk companions are shown at the court of Queen Anne in 1710 in this frontispiece to the *Gospel of St. Mark*, the first complete biblical text published in Mohawk. The translation, by Mohawk chief Joseph Brant and John Stuart of the SPG, was finished in 1774 and published in London, at government expense, in 1787, by which time both Brant and Stuart had settled in Upper Canada with kindred Loyalists after the American Revolution. The 19 engravings in the volume are the work of English and Colonial artist James Peachy.

St. Anne's Chapel, *Fredericton, New Brunswick; Anglican. Stone, 1846–47; Frank Wills, architect*

Frank Wills lithographed a perspective of the chapel's interior, hand-tinting it in watercolour. His combined talents as a leading designer of churches, architectural writer and printmaker were rare. In just a dozen years he designed more than fifty churches (most in the United States). He was just 34 years old when he died at Montreal, in 1857, while working on the Anglican Cathedral there.

Upper Saint John River Valley, and Roman Catholics along the Acadian coastline of New Brunswick, in parts of Cape Breton, at the two ends of PEI and in Newfoundland.

Architectural influences follow this pattern naturally. A strongly British character pervades the ecclesiastical architecture of much of Atlantic Canada, where the established Church of England (Anglican), the Church of Scotland (Presbyterian) and Roman Catholicism (especially Irish) all played important roles. The eastern seaboard was strongly influenced by the United States especially in areas settled by Loyalists. Significant parts of some churches (notably the timber frame and the clapboards) were obtained from New England (*see* pp. 44, 46, 50).

In addition to a vernacular tradition in the American colonies, usually regarded as Georgian Colonial in Canada, British North America drew from the high-style tradition of James Gibbs' Baroque (with its strong Classical undertone), acquired by this Scottish architect during his training in Rome. Gibbsian Baroque appeared in Canada almost certainly because of the influence on designers of Gibbs' celebrated work, *A Book of Architecture* (London, 1728).

Gibbs (1682–1754) could hardly have anticipated, however, that his version of Baroque would be adapted to wooden construction in some cases, such as St. Paul's, Halifax, in 1749 (*see* pp. 42–46). Nearly a century after Gibbs' book first appeared, elements of his style are clear in Greenock Presbyterian Church at St. Andrews, New Brunswick (*see* pp. 63–67). There is also strong evidence of Gibbs' influence, in stone, at Québec City's Anglican Cathedral of the Holy Trinity (*see* pp. 121–23).

In the middle of the 18th century Voltaire made popular a "new awareness of history" in his influential *Essay on the General History of Manners* (1754). Life is not static. Nor are art and civilization, for change, whether gradual or sudden, is characteristic of nature itself. History is a progression, an evolution. And rather than political and military activity, "general cultural progress" fascinated Voltaire. Famously skeptical, he was interested in determining "the authenticity of origins" to the point of idealizing primitive roots and cultures. Concerned with progress, the advance toward rationality and universality, Voltaire became interested in the study of all civilizations (not just Greco-Roman) and all eras; he devoted about a third of his text to the Middle Ages because he recognized its influence on French national character (though England was where medieval studies soon developed most quickly and fully). In effect, such tolerance and breadth of view ushered in an "age of historicism" in literature and the arts (especially in architecture) with an acute awareness of the past and its contributions, real and potential, to intellectual life of the day.

The Gothic Revival emerged as an alternative to the Classical tradition of Georgian and Gibbsian architecture. Gothic appears occasionally from the 1820s, notably in St. Mary's (Roman Catholic), Halifax, Nova Scotia (1820–29) and St. John's (Anglican) in Saint John, New Brunswick (1823).

The great watershed, so far as Gothic in North America is concerned, however, is 1846–47, when Frank Wills (1822–57) undertook St. Anne's Chapel in Fredericton, New Brunswick (*see* pp. 74–75). The first Anglican bishop of Fredericton, John Medley (1804–92), arrived in 1845 from his previous charge in Exeter, England. He brought Wills out to supervise construction of the cathedral Wills had designed on ecclesiological principles for this new see. "Ecclesiology" was thought of as a

St. Stephen's, *Greenspond, Newfoundland; Anglican. Wood, 1857; attributed to The Rev. Julian Moreton*

Remote Greenspond was settled early in the 18th century and was prosperous by outport standards. It had its own clergyman by 1830 and replaced an early church with this larger one in 1857. Slight and widely spaced squared timbers support the gallery and also brace the roof to withstand the heavy winds in this exposed location. The church gives the impression of a spare basketwork filled with light.

comprehensive and exact science of church design in which ancient specimens of medieval style were studied and adapted in imitative but poetic new structures. More than just ensembles of masonry architecture and wooden furniture, they usually included architectural sculpture and other ornament, floor tiles, stained glass, brass furnishings, silver or gold vessels, embroidered vestments and hangings — accompanied by appropriate church music and enriched forms of liturgy — all fused into coherent aesthetic environments and fraught with symbolism. Largely but not exclusively an Anglican pursuit, ecclesiology promoted the more frequent celebration of communion throughout the Anglican Church and was often associated with High-Church interests.

During the early 1840s the Ecclesiological Society in England emphasized three paramount principles of church design: "reality, the absolute necessity of a distinct and spacious chancel, and the absolute inadmissibility of pues and galleries in any shape whatever." St. Anne's steeply pitched roof illustrates "reality" through structural timbers exposed to view, not concealed by a plaster ceiling (as in a Georgian church); thus the open timber roof of the Gothic Revival expresses both its material and its construction in a web of practical but also artful design. Wills and Medley also compensated handsomely for the chancel having been "frequently ignored or misused" over the previous century and a half: in St. Anne's it is both spacious and distinct. Narrower in width and lower in profile than the nave (and with a rising

All Saints', *McKeens Corner, New Brunswick; Anglican. Wood with timber frame, 1861; Edward S. Medley, architect*

All Saints' is Edward Medley's earliest church. Its exposed, structurally expressive frame of massive square-sawn timbers, with inset board-and-batten panels and rational detailing, all derive from R.C. Carpenter's unbuilt design for a prefabricated wooden church for Tristan da Cunha, a treeless volcanic island in the South Atlantic. Probably Medley had studied the design in English architect William Butterfield's office. Butterfield, who published Carpenter's project, had promised designs for wooden churches to Medley's father, New Brunswick's Anglican bishop.

BELOW **Mahone Bay**, *Nova Scotia,* is much loved for its remarkable group of churches. On the right, having lost its spire to a windstorm in the 1920s, is **Trinity United** (1862), built as a Presbyterian church and moved here in 1885. Next is **St. John's** (Evangelical Lutheran), built in 1876; to the left, the colourful **St. James'** (Anglican), built in 1887, to the design of William Critchlow Harris. The fourth church on the left edge is **Mahone Bay United Baptist**.

floor level as well), it is separated by a chancel arch (and eventually by a screen). It was "pues," however, that aroused Medley as nothing else. Back in Exeter, he had written feelingly: "How grateful to a Christian pastor's eye to see the members of one body kneeling together as one body, as all equal in their great Maker's presence." As bishop, he felt so strongly about the social affront and theological implications in leasing pews that he refused to consecrate churches resorting to pew rents. In St. Anne's the seats are open benches (which he thought authorities should *insist* upon), their ends lavished with symbols of the Passion or carved like blind tracery in Geometric style. The planked floors would soon be paved with Minton tiles; the chancel windows were already filled with stained glass of medievalizing character. St. Anne's Chapel was a pioneering work in the architectural history of North America. The Gothic Revival was not only ascendant; it was about to be triumphant, in almost every corner of the Atlantic region.

Just as Baroque and Neoclassical traditions were adapted from stone (or occasionally brick) to wood, Revived Gothic was also a stone language needing translation into wood. Initially the resemblance might be only a strong silhouette — possibly battlemented eaves, a prickly skyline or steeple — and a pointed window-head of some sort (though the straight grain of wood militates against arched forms). Through the mid-19th century, architects tended to reproduce stonework in wood of similar form, in spite of great differences between the materials. Later in the century a builder equipped with a fretsaw, a lathe and a graphic sensibility akin to a folk artist might seek decorative equivalents for the rich sculptural heritage of Gothic, in what has come to be called "Carpenter Gothic." Still later, sensitive architects, such as Edward S. Medley of New Brunswick or William C. Harris of Prince Edward Island, were likely to adopt American board-and-batten cladding because

of its verticality (thought of as the essence of Gothic), in preference to the horizontality of clapboard; combined with neo-medieval planning, liturgical considerations and appropriately detailed furnishings, a happy compromise was often the result.

Confederation to the Present

Following Confederation in 1867, improved transportation, especially the railways, increased the importance of contact and trade with central Canada and the United States. Atlantic Canada, which had been oriented eastward along the shipping lanes to Europe, felt the changes strongly. As other parts of the country turned to manufacturing and exploiting their more promising natural resources, industrialization came more slowly to the Atlantic region. In many areas, natural population increases were more than offset by migration to other parts of the country and the United States.

Canada's crucial ecclesiastical event of the 20th century was church union in 1925. The United Church of Canada was created from most Methodists, all the Congregationalists and about half the Presbyterians (the other half remained in the "continuing" Presbyterian Church). In Atlantic Canada, a strong majority favored church union, though Pictou County, Nova Scotia, was an exception: over 60 percent voted against union and some congregations retained their traditional affiliations. Ironically, church union resulted in more churches, not fewer, especially when congregations split for and against union, and none of the existing churches could accommodate the larger United Church congregation. Methodists and Congregationalists have all but disappeared into the United Church. Of the other denominations, Roman Catholics, Anglicans and Baptists have retained their identity.

FACING PAGE **Saint-Pierre**, *Chéticamp, Nova Scotia; Roman Catholic. Stone, 1892–93; David Ouellet, architect*

This is the fourth church of the Acadian community that settled here after returning from exile in 1782. Built of stone brought across on the ice from Chéticamp Island, the ornately decorated church speaks eloquently to the vitality of Acadian culture and religion. The lofty white double-arcaded nave contrasts with the colourful retable behind the high altar.

BELOW **All Saints'**, *Clifton Royal, New Brunswick; Anglican. Wood with timber frame, 1884–85; William C. Harris, architect*

Seeking work in Manitoba, Harris unsuccessfully entered a competition for Holy Trinity, Winnipeg. The Rector of Holy Trinity visited his own birthplace, Clifton New Brunswick, in 1883 and suggested building a church there, engaging Harris at his own expense. All Saints' combines English ecclesiological ideals and American board-and-batten building technique. It survives untouched, complete with Harris' original furnishings.

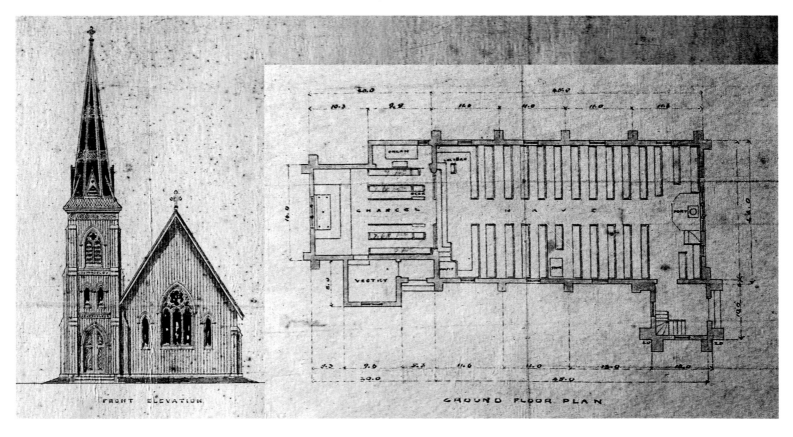

FRONT ELEVATION

GROUND FLOOR PLAN

O Lord! We would not advise; But if, in Thy Providence,
A Tempest should arise, To drive the French fleet hence,
And scatter it far and wide, Or sink it in the sea,
We should be satisfied, And Thine the glory be.
— Thomas Prince

British and American Colonial Traditions

THOMAS PRINCE, MINISTER OF BOSTON'S Old South Church, wrote his unsingable hymn on the taking of Louisbourg in 1746, possibly to the tune of "God Save the King." For New Englanders, winning the war with France was a matter both of Divine Providence and of patriotism; drumming up support for an American militia involved promising "sainthood" to true patriots. Strengthening Nova Scotia with loyal settlers, especially after 1749 when Louisbourg was returned to the French, was crucial to British colonial goals. The earliest surviving British colonial churches in Nova Scotia — whether Church of England or opposed to it — derive from this French–English conflict in the early 18th century.

St. Paul's, Halifax, is the oldest surviving Anglican church in Canada. Its site on the parade ground is a focus of the city's earliest plan, and the building demonstrates a longing for things British. Originally intended for the north end of the square, with a courthouse at the south, St. Paul's was built in fact at the square's south end. Early maps and drawings show Halifax stretching along Chebucto harbor, the long side of the city blocks following the contours, forcing the church into an unconventional north-south orientation with the chancel to the south and the nave's long walls awkwardly at different elevations. When Governor Cornwallis (1712–76) laid the cornerstone on June 13, 1750, he described the setting as a "very gentle" ascent. St. Paul's has been substantially altered over the years: the most important changes occurred when the church was widened in 1868 by adding an extra aisle alongside the original blocks of seating, while the windows were altered

St. Paul's, *Halifax, Nova Scotia; Anglican. Wood with timber frame, 1750–63; after James Gibbs*

The church overlooks the Grand Parade from its south end, almost patronizingly. Compared with Joseph Partridge's view (*see* p. 44), the aisles (added in 1868) give the church a broader aspect and transform it into a more traditional-looking Anglican church. The raking light highlights the deep reveals of the altered windows, now with mullions. The central section is still much as it was, since the added bay and the tower (1812) mimicked precisely the earlier structures.

Joseph Partridge, *"National School at Halifax, Nova Scotia," ca. 1819, watercolour, with pencil and ink*

A Halifax street scene shows St. Paul's across Grand Parade and the west side of Argyle Street; the three-and-a-half-story residence in the distance was St. Paul's Parsonage (1809, demolished in 1984). The view shows the church with the added bay at the front and the re-built tower, completed a few years before the painting, with the original quoins and with windows that were later divided. The windows flanking the earlier porch were later altered and, more important, the building lacks the aisles, added some 40 years later.

by adding central mullions, splitting the round-headed windows into two smaller round-headed lights. The general aspect of the building was less drastically altered when another bay was added at the north end in 1812. At the same time both the facade and steeple were rebuilt to the original design. A chancel was added to the south end in 1872.

The building, said the first incumbent, William Tutty, "is exactly the model of Marybone Chapel" in London — also called St. Peter's, Vere Street, or more informally Oxford Chapel (1721–24) — by James Gibbs. It would have been known through engravings of St. Peter's, Vere Street, in Gibbs' *Book of Architecture*. Governor Cornwallis may have brought the book with him in 1749. In his letter, Tutty adds that the timber frame for a church to seat 900 persons was soon to arrive from Boston. The U-shaped balcony called for a double row of windows, the upper ones significantly larger than the lower, as in Gibbs' design, with matching, handsomely detailed Palladian windows at north and south ends, the whole finished in clapboarding over a nogging of local brick infill. The graceful tower and double cupola over the north end — which reflect the steeples of Gibbs' mentor, Sir Christopher Wren (1632–1723) — signal its dominance. Originally the eaves were picked out with brackets, the corners with quoins and the windows with Gibbs' surrounds. A simple Classical porch with four columns once sheltered the central doorway on the north and doors flanked the chancel on the south facade, details now altered.

The nave's barrel vault is carried on piers in two stages — the upper row fluted and the lower unfluted — supporting the panelled balcony with its flat ceiling, a design more nearly like a London church by Wren, St. Andrew-by-the-Wardrobe, than Gibbs' Chapel. Since the general disposition of nave, aisles and galleries is similar to Boston's Old North Church (1723) and Trinity Church (1725–26) in Newport,

St. Paul's

Some differences are noticeable from the original building. There is a new chancel with appendages for the organ and pipes, and the Palladian window on the original south facade is gone, as the added chancel called for a simpler window.

The beautiful proportions of the nave, with its double arcade, arched at the balcony level with flat balcony ceiling behind, and the simply vaulted ceiling, are reminiscent of Sir Christopher Wren's work.

Little Dutch Church, *Halifax, Nova Scotia; Lutheran,*
Anglican. Originally a house, wood, 1756; builder
unknown

The plain exterior of what was originally a small
Halifax house underscores both its early date and
the uncomplicated role it played as home to "foreign
Protestants" brought into Halifax in the early 1750s.
The 1760 addition of 11 feet comprises the two
windows set more closely together and the steeple.
The building sits on a sloping site within a cemetery,
across the road from St. George's "Round" Church.

Rhode Island, it is not certain that the influence is directly from Wren. New England
influences may have been imported at the same time as the frame (which may have
come from Maine rather than Boston). Although the building's exterior was deeply
influenced by Gibbs, the interior is an amalgam of Gibbs, Wren, New England meetinghouses and later additions. It is truly, as Philip McAleer says, "a Bostonian Wren
building inside a Gibbsian box," a prophetically Canadian compromise.

St. Paul's interior now has six blocks of pews instead of four (two in the nave and
two in either aisle) and an added chancel, resulting in a more amorphous space
than the original. Both alterations revise it from a simple meetinghouse to a traditional Anglican church. At the same time as these alterations came changes in the
liturgical arrangements: originally, as reported in the *Halifax Evening Mail* in 1892,
"the Communion Table stood against the southern wall, with a low railing before
it. The pulpit — a three decker — was a little to the west of the centre passage. On
either side — east and west — were square pews for the officers of the army and
navy. On either side of the centre alley, in front of the Communion Table, were the
pews for the Governor, the Admiral and the Bishop. The Governor's pew was a
miniature drawing room .... The Admiral's pew was equally comfortable. Both
were upholstered in crimson. The Bishop's pew was upholstered in blue." Such
arrangements emphasize the close relationship between church and state, the state
in its military dress, a relationship much altered in the modern period but still sym-
bolized by the royal coat of arms, mounted on the gallery front.

St. Paul's characterizes Halifax's English ruling class, but Halifax was not all
English or even all British. Nova Scotia's social and ethnic mixture is reflected in the
arrival of about 3,000 German, Swiss and French Protestant colonists in 1750–52 as
a part of the Crown's effort to bolster the colony against French raids. The **Little
Dutch Church, Halifax**, served German Lutherans (*Deutsch*, meaning "German,"
became "Dutch"), though many German settlers relocated to Lunenburg before the
church was built. The services were nominally Lutheran but the liturgy was
Anglican. A small house (20 by 29 feet), like many early Haligonian houses, was
moved to a site where it covered a number of graves of typhus victims. The belfry
held the bell taken from Louisbourg after it fell to the British in 1758; the bell was
sold to the Château de Ramezay in Montréal in 1842. Simple bench pews clustered
around a pot-bellied stove add to the building's primitive character.

The Little Dutch Church gave birth to two Anglican daughters. Across the road
is **St. George's (the "Round Church"), Halifax**, home to an expanding German congregation that used German in services until 1827. Queen Victoria's father, Prince
Edward (1767–1820), Commander-in-Chief of British forces in North America,
1799–1800, was deeply interested in the German community because of his German
ancestry (the House of Hanover would not be anglicized as the House of Windsor
until World War I). He commissioned St. George's to serve both the congregation
and his military garrison, after obtaining substantial British government and provincial support. The building follows the views of Andrea Palladio (1508–1580) on
round buildings, a style Prince Edward strongly preferred. Another influence may
have been two circular designs Gibbs prepared for St. Martin-in-the-Fields (1722–26),
London, both published in his *Book of Architecture*. Services were held from 1801,
but the church was not completed until 1812. Though originally strictly circular
and centrally focused, its purity of form was later modified to reflect changing

St. George's, *Halifax, Nova Scotia; Anglican. Wood, 1800–1801; William Hughes, architect*

To appreciate the original "Round Church" later additions must be stripped away, as in the anonymous 1827 watercolour (above right). The building was originally a simple double drum, with two rows of windows in the lower drum lighting the balcony and ground floor, and an upper drum with matching windows, lighting the central nave from above. Its cupola also had round-headed openings. The centralized round form echoes Byzantine fascination with centrally focused churches.

The apparent simplicity of the church's form is belied by modern architectural drawings, showing the complete reconstruction of the building after the 1994 fire. The section underscores the relationship of the balconies to the central circular space, and the way the upper drum and dome cover the nave, with the cupola above. The ground line indicates how the Round Church, like most buildings in Halifax, must contend with its sloping site.

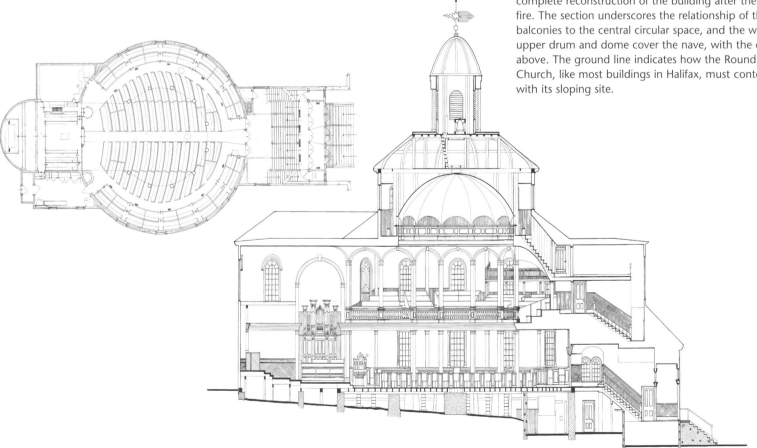

St. George's, *interior*

The original round nave and seating arrangement have been modified by subsequent efforts to give the Round Church a more traditional Anglican character, with chancel, porch and seating all aligned on a strong central axis. But a discerning eye can still catch the excitement of the central focus of the 1800 building, with the circular balcony lending a dynamic feel to the space; a subordinate balcony for servants or slaves rises behind the main balcony.

FACING PAGE **St. John's**, *Lunenburg, Nova Scotia; Anglican. Wood, begun 1753–58; builder unknown*

St. John's complicated building history is barely seen underneath its present thoroughgoing "Carpenter Gothic" style. The tower, added in 1840, includes a choir loft at the balcony level. In the 1870s the church was relocated to make room for a chancel and the nave acquired a sloped ceiling; the side aisles were added in 1892. The photograph was taken before the fire of 2001.

Anglican preferences, with a strong east-west axis, when a semicircular apse was added in 1827, and a vestry, organ chambers and square entrance followed in 1911.

The two-story-high colonnaded space, 60 feet in diameter, supports a 35-foot-diameter drum, whose stylish dome is topped outside by a cupola. The main balcony sweeps around 270 degrees. When the apse was added, the pulpit was moved from its unusual central position to the intersection of the nave and apse, while the communion table was moved from the curved outer wall to the curving apse wall. The church has been lovingly restored to its altered form after a fire (June 2, 1994), reproducing the rich Classical details externally and internally.

The other Little Dutch daughter church is **St. John's, Lunenburg**, southwest of Halifax. When European settlers relocated to Lunenburg from Halifax in 1753, and the church obtained a royal charter, the first church was built around a frame that came from Boston — possibly Old King's Chapel, then being dismantled — in meetinghouse style (ca 1753–58). A 1754 sketch shows a Germanic round tower and an English round-headed window. Although few parts of the original meetinghouse walls survived, its incremental alterations give it a memorable decorative form.

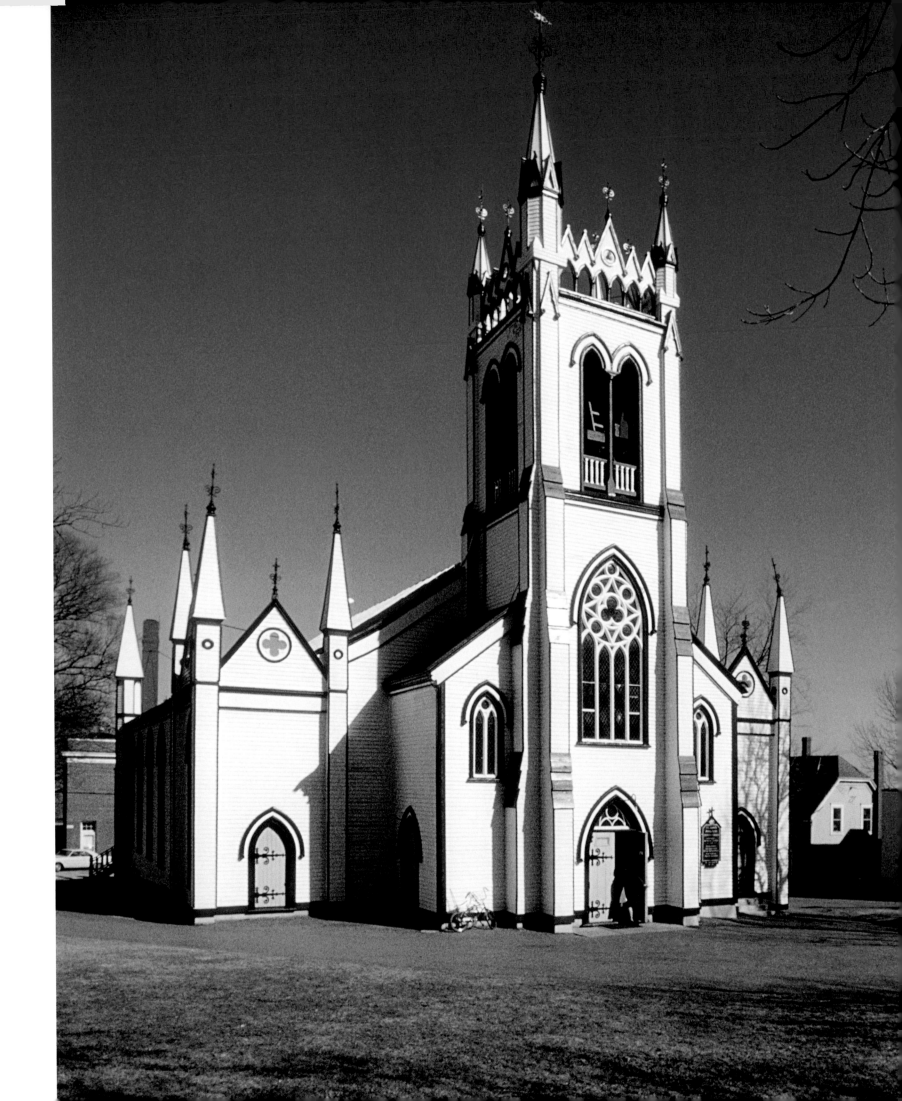

The **Meetinghouse, Barrington**, near Yarmouth, is Canada's oldest dissenting or nonconformist church (the Little Dutch Church was more Anglican than Lutheran). Surviving almost completely intact, though shingles have replaced clapboards, it was built to serve settlers from Cape Cod who arrived in 1761. The township was home to Congregationalist and Quaker whalers — though the Quakers returned home to Cape Cod in 1776. The 30-by-36-foot building is entered in the middle of one long side through a plain panelled door, in classic meetinghouse style. Stairs rise on either side to a U-shaped gallery, oriented to a raised pulpit on the other long side, opposite the door. The pulpit was completed in the 1780s or 90s, along with the panelled gallery front and pews. While some materials were obtained locally, part of the timber frame and some of the sawn boards came from New England.

Meetinghouse, *Barrington, Nova Scotia; Congregationalist and Quaker; later, Methodist, Baptist, Presbyterian, Anglican. Wood, 1765; Joshua Nickerson and Elijah Swaine, builders*

This classic meetinghouse has changed little in almost 250 years. The plain windows set almost flush with the walls and the plain door in the long side's centre could just as well be found in a Georgian residence for the affluent as in a Congregationally inspired meetinghouse.

Barrington's interior is a perfect example of its type, with a beautifully panelled two-decker raised pulpit, panelled pews and U-shaped balcony, all of fine cabinetry. The ship's knees reflect the whaler origins of the building. They brace the timber frame just below the ceiling on either side of the pulpit, curving between the balcony rail and the ceiling.

The **Covenanters' Church, Grand Pré**, epitomizes the strong Presbyterian roots of this part of Nova Scotia, resulting from extensive immigration of Calvinists from Scotland, Switzerland and France. The building encapsulates the Scottish Free Church tradition — the strict covenanting part of that tradition in distinction to the Established Church of Scotland — a tradition burned into the minds and emotions of its followers. Scottish Covenanters were persecuted by the English and martyred through the late 17th century, when several efforts to maintain Presbyterian principles and forms of worship were brutally suppressed and many were "faithful unto death." Though those distant Scottish troubles were long past when the church was built, their inheritance was still remembered vividly when, a generation after the church was erected, it began to be called the Covenanters' Church. It lies along the same road as the historically memorable but architecturally uninteresting Grand Pré Chapel commemorating the Acadian deportation of 1755. Symbolically, even if unconsciously, the Presbyterian kirk reflects dimly the replacement of Acadians with British and colonial settlers a quarter-century later, for it overlooks the landing from which the Acadians were evacuated.

James Murdoch, an Irish Presbyterian clergyman from Donegal, arrived in 1766 to work among the Mi'kmaq. After realizing that earlier Roman Catholic missionary activity had made his missionary task redundant, he gathered a non-native congregation, primarily New England Congregationalists, who had arrived between 1760 and 1768 to take advantage of the colony's promised "full liberty of conscience." The congregation may also have included a few northern Irish arriving about the same time and Highland Scots who arrived in Pictou in 1773. A log building (about 1767) was demolished in 1795, after the arrival of Murdoch's successor, George Gilmore, and eventually the present building was erected. Like the Barrington Meetinghouse, the building mixes British and American influences: a Presbyterian church serving mainly Congregationalists in a New England architectural style, but with a steeple characteristic of a rural Anglican church.

Like St. Paul's, Halifax, and the Barrington Meetinghouse, the frame is made from large timbers prefabricated elsewhere. The panelled door, with a rectangular transom light that is topped by a restrained entablature, faces the road on the long elevation of the church. It is flanked by pairs of windows on the ground floor nearly matching five windows on the second floor. Similar windows wrap around the ends and along the broad rear elevation. The plain details show a little more dash only in the square tower, with its high oculus (bull's eye), projecting crown moulding and octagonal belfry with cupola and spire. This addition transformed the building from what must have appeared to be a typical frame clapboard house in a Georgian idiom into a more clearly recognizable church.

Covenanters' Church, *Grand Pré, Nova Scotia; Presbyterian and Congregationalist, now United. Wood with timber frame, 1804-11; builder unknown*

The church has its long side to the road and a stone wall enclosing the yard and cemetery. As one approaches, its identification as a church is in doubt until one notices the steeple, added in 1818. There is a tension between the expectation to enter under the tower and the more obvious invitation to enter in the middle of the long wall, as expected in an upper class Georgian residence, on which this meetinghouse is modelled.

Comparative Meetinghouse plans

Meetinghouse plans evolved toward traditional church layouts, though usually they retained two-decker or three-decker pulpits — the small square at the open end of the U-shaped gallery in each plan. The earliest meetinghouses were square structures with hip roofs, sometimes entered from more than one side. Then buildings became more residential in appearance, with a wide balcony and the pulpit still on a long wall. Later meetinghouses moved the pulpit to one end and the door to the other, with the balcony turned 90 degrees.

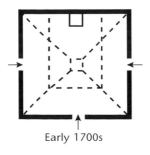

Early 1700s

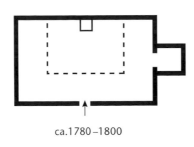

ca.1780–1800

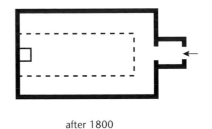

after 1800

The interior's finely executed cabinetry focuses on one of only a few surviving three-decker pulpits. A stepped U-shaped gallery is oriented toward the raised pulpit. Both levels have finely executed pews with matching doors, painted white with natural wood trim. Two woodstoves provide heat from the corners of the ground floor nearest the door. The unostentatious Covenanters' Church strikes a responsive chord among those who look for simplicity and plainness as a complement to their view of worship as a plain and direct response to the Word. The domestically scaled building seems an especially appropriate setting for worship in the pioneer setting of Atlantic Canada (*see also* p. 50).

The Annapolis Valley stretches from Grand Pré near the Minas Basin westward to Digby, just beyond Annapolis Royal. The good agricultural land — available after the expulsion of the Acadians a generation earlier — attracted United Empire Loyalists from the Thirteen Colonies, for it was land that had already been cleared and farmed. The new settlers thrived and established churches, almost uniformly clapboarded. **St. Mary's, Auburn**, is one of the most charming. It was consecrated

Covenanters' Church, *interior*
This three-decker pulpit dominates the interior from all vantage points; it is one of the finest anywhere, a lovely example of Loyalist cabinetry skills. The precentor with tuning fork leads singing from the lowest level, the written word is read from the middle level, and the sermon is preached from the upper level — a good indication of Presbyterian priorities. The upper level puts the preacher almost at the level of those sitting in the gallery pews.

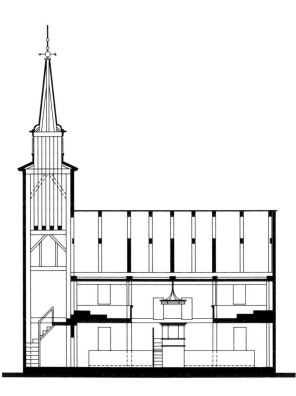

St. Mary's, *Auburn, Nova Scotia; Anglican. Wood with timber frame, 1790; William Matthews, builder*

The stylish west facade of St. Mary's, in a rural setting, gives a sense of repose. Despite its modest size, St. Mary's has an unusually large chancel. The original chancel was cut off and moved eastward, and a new section of building inserted between, a little wider than the original chancel, creating an odd form on the exterior.

Old Holy Trinity, *Middleton, Nova Scotia; Anglican. Wood with timber frame, 1789–91; John Wiswall, builder*

By contrast with St. Mary's, Old Holy Trinity's interior is more coherent and less fragmented. The building's timber frame is visible inside, suggesting an almost modern architectural idiom that prefers to expose the structural elements. The chancel is not as deep, the balcony across the west end has a very transparent railing with spindles, and the pews are more graciously designed. In all, it is light and airy.

FACING PAGE **United Baptist Church**, *Granville Centre, Nova Scotia; United Baptist. Wood; builder unknown*

The quality of the clapboarding in Granville Centre United Baptist is exceptional. The gable and the middle stage of the tower have alternate bands of plain and decorative shingling, while the body of the church is plain clapboarding. The glory of this exterior is the splayed detailing on the tower. This is rare exuberance, not usually associated with Baptists.

by Bishop Charles Inglis (1734–1816) of Halifax, the first Anglican bishop overseas. The building is elegantly plain, with round-headed windows, a projecting tower with an octagonal spire and oculi, and a nicely detailed entrance with pediment. The chancel, following the pattern of St. Paul's, Halifax, has an unusually large Palladian window. St. Mary's was built by William Matthews, at the insistence and with the help of a storekeeper, James Morden.

At **Old Holy Trinity, Middleton**, John Wiswall, the Loyalist rector, constructed much of the building himself. He had arrived in 1782 as a missionary to the Annapolis Valley before settling in Middleton. Though Major Bayard and Captain Ruggles assisted in its construction — presumably because of their expertise — the building is less finely detailed and less pleasing outside than St. Mary's. Such Anglican structures reflected the importance of the Established Church in the first decades of Nova Scotia, but they were joined a generation later by growing numbers of Baptist churches, rooted in Rhode Island's religious freedom and promoted widely during Atlantic Canada's "Great Awakening" by evangelical preacher Henry Alline (1748–84). Nearby, Granville Beach Baptist (1833) is another church that stands out for its plain New England meetinghouse form. Two identical rows of windows light the interior's main floor and gallery, with matching windows on the end walls. **Granville Centre United Baptist** is remarkable for its exceptional clapboard detailing on the tower: the almost *trompe l'oeil* effect of the panelling around the head of the door — which creates a sense of perspective and draws one into the church — is matched by a starburst in the tower's next stage and another piece of patterned clapboarding in the peak of the gable end. All project three-dimensionally in beautifully executed geometric detailing that is consistent with the rest of the fine carpentry details in the church's exterior.

Festive Simplicity

Many of the People of the Church or Congregations called the Unitas Fratrum, or United Brethren, are settled in His Majesty's Colonies in America ... as a sober, quiet, and industrious People; and many others of the same Persuasion are desirous to transport themselves to, and make larger Settlements in the said Colonies at their own Expence, provided they may be indulged with a full Liberty of Conscience, and ... do conscientiously scruple bearing Arms, or personally serving in any military Capacity, although they are willing and ready to contribute whatever Sums of Money shall be thought a reasonable Compensation for such Service....

— *Act of George II, November 10, 1747*

"Festive Simplicity" in Labrador

IT IS SURPRISING THAT KING GEORGE II permitted Moravian — or more correctly United — Brethren to establish themselves in Labrador in 1747, though he seems impressed with their character and peace ethic, while demanding compensation for their exemption from military service. The group's roots reached back to Jan Hus (1372–1415), a Czech reformer who died for his faith a century before Luther's decisive Reformation. It took on new life at Herrnhut in Saxony when Count Nikolaus Ludwig von Zinzendorf (1700–1760) transformed it into a missionary organization working extensively in the Americas.

The first missionaries arrived among the Inuit in 1752, when a small house was established at Nisbet Harbour (Makkovik). Seven Moravian missionaries were killed and the mission was put on hold during the Seven Years' War. After subsequent exploratory journeys, the Moravians obtained a land grant of 100,000 acres and established their first permanent station at **Nain** (1771). The present church (the fifth) still sits solidly on a stone foundation (*see* p. 61).

The buildings at **Hebron** (1830s) are shown in a print of about 1861 as they still are, with a plain church attached to a longer residential building of the same width, the whole pointing to the harbor (*see* p. 59). The buildings are now being restored.

Hopedale, *Labrador; Moravian Brethren. Wood with timber frame, 1865; Ferdinand Kruth, builder*
In addition to a church, the ten Moravian communities usually included other structures: a communal dwelling (usually with a partially hipped roof), a morgue or "dead house," workshops, provisions houses, store buildings, seal-blubber yard, boathouses and gunpowder house. The Hopedale complex of buildings clusters around the 1865 church with its cupola.

Hopedale

In 1897, Hopedale's mission house, on the left (attached to the church), replaced the earlier mission house, which had originally been built in 1782 as a prefabricated structure. The ship with the materials dropped anchor September 2, 1782, the foundations were built on September 5–6, the house erected on September 7, the roof completed on September 9, and on October 5 they celebrated communion for the first time. An enviable record of substantial completion.

The church has a modest, hexagonal cupola in the middle. Simple protruding porches provide some protection from the weather and the windows of both the church and the residential building are covered with heavy shutters. The effect is one of "festive simplicity," as Hans Rollman likes to say.

Early **Hopedale** buildings (a provisions house, 1817; mission house, 1853; church, 1865) have been restored recently by Parks Canada. The church has a similar form to Hebron's, but is somewhat more artistically designed, with doors in the four corners of the long walls and arched windows. It is one and a half stories high with a partially hipped roof of Germanic appearance, topped with an open hexagonal cupola, smaller than Hebron's and with a bell-shaped roof. A wide flat ceiling covers an uncluttered, column-free space that focuses on a small chancel at one end, framed between two side rooms with canted walls to form a semi-hexagon. At the other end, a simple railing with built-in music stands defines the raised platform where the choir and musicians are located.

The communal buildings, designed to accentuate a family approach to Christianity, suit perfectly their setting in Labrador's raw conditions. Inuit have been deeply attracted by the Moravians' emphasis on festive and liturgically sophisticated practices rather than doctrine. There are about 2,500 Moravians in Labrador, a province of the worldwide Moravian Church, which includes other Moravian Brethren in Moraviantown, Ontario, and Bruderheim, Alberta. They express their piety in action and reflect their theology in their hymns. Indeed, singing almost replaces the sermons that are so typical of other Reformation groups. Count von Zinzendorf's best-known hymn is

> The Saviour's blood and righteousness
> My beauty is, my glorious dress;
> Thus well arrayed, I need not fear,
> When in his presence I appear.
>
> Thy incarnation, wounds and death
> I will confess while I have breath,
> Till I shall see Thee face to face,
> Arrayed with Thy righteousness.

"Hebron in Labrador"
This 1860 lithograph by L.T. Reichel (1812–78) shows more starkly than modern photographs the stern conditions under which the Moravians laboured in Labrador, with the lonely Hebron mission station, also built by Ferdinand Kruth, enclosed on three sides by rolling rock hills rising up from the sea.

Hopedale, *interior*

"The new church is neat and friendly in appearance. The good organ is very fairly played by two Eskimos ... Benches without backs are provided for the natives, and the floor is strewn with sand of a dark grey colour. Four helpers of each sex occupy seats at the side, and perform the duties of chapel servants."
L.T. Reichel, on a visit in 1876

The plain interior is directed toward a chancel at one end — lit by a pair of windows — with a platform and a table. At the other end, a generous space with a highly unusual continuous music stand, set aside for the musical leadership of the services, reflects the deep importance of music in Moravian worship.

FACING PAGE **Nain**, *Labrador; Moravian Brethren. Wood, 1925; builder unknown*

This 20th century church building at Nain continues to exemplify characteristic aspects of Moravian buildings: low sidewalls, simple sloped roofs and utilitarian windows. The bell tower is not characteristic of older Moravian church buildings, which usually had a central cupola.

Charles Wesley, the great Anglican and Methodist hymn writer, was deeply indebted to the Moravians. His powerful hymn captures their missionary motivations well:

> O for a thousand tongues to sing
> My great Redeemer's praise,
> The glories of my God and King,
> The triumphs of His grace!
>
> My gracious Master and my God,
> Assist me to proclaim,
> To spread through all the earth abroad
> The honors of Thy name.
>
> Look unto Him, ye nations; own
> Your God, ye fallen race;
> Look and be saved through faith alone,
> Be justified by grace.

What is here presented to the Public was undertaken at the instance of several Persons of Quality and others .... They were of opinion, that such a Work as this would be of use to such ... as might be concerned in Building, especially in the remote part of the Country, where little or no assistance for designs can be procured.
— James Gibbs, 1728

New Brunswick Town and Country

Greenock Church, *St. Andrews, New Brunswick; Presbyterian. Wood, 1821–24; steeple after James Gibbs*
A fine steeple (based on James Gibbs' designs for St. Martin-in-the-Fields, London) is the distinctive mark of Greenock's exterior. In his *Book of Architecture* (1728), Gibbs says "Steeples are indeed of a Gothick Extraction; but they have their Beauties, when their Parts are well disposed, and when ... they ... gradually diminish, and pass from one Form to another without confusion."

FIRST IMPRESSIONS of **Greenock Church, St. Andrews**, are misleading. Although it resembles a mid-Georgian New England meetinghouse, it is late Georgian, and while it derives from Church of England designs it is for the Church of Scotland. A robust tree on the tower suggests the burning bush symbol of Presbyterianism, yet it does not burn. A curious inscription declares conspicuously:

GREENOCK CHURCH
FINISHED JUNE 1824

More than 40 Loyalist families uprooted by the American Revolution settled at St. Andrews in the fall of 1783 on a peninsula jutting into Passamaquoddy Bay. By May 1784 there were "about Ninety Houses up." An Anglican clergyman arrived from Connecticut two years later, and soon a church appeared. The Loyalists included a substantial number of Scots, who subsequently "took the leading part" in the "unplanned pell-mell development" following peace in Europe in 1815. Most Scots were Presbyterian, but in St. Andrews they attended the Anglican church, the only church in town until John Cassilis, a Scottish Presbyterian minister, came as schoolmaster in 1818 and conducted services.

A plain Presbyterian church, begun in 1821, became a monument to disappointment when funds ran out with, according to Melville N. Cockburn, "the frame work erected and boarded in, and the roof partially shingled." An Anglican's dinner

Greenock Church, *interior*

Christopher Scott completed the building to his taste. Internally, 12 extraordinary columns of solid bird's-eye maple (from surrounding Charlotte County) with contrasting capitals of Honduras mahogany carry the long gallery, with elegant fronts in the same woods.

The immense pulpit rises by stages: Doric columns carry the reading desk, which steps to a high pulpit and unites with a Palladian window, in the Ionic order. *The Country Builder's Assistant* (1797), Asher Benjamin's influential pattern book from Massachusetts, shows a simplified version of this scheme, complete with winding stairs on either side. The costly craftsmanship is in the finest quality Honduras mahogany trimmed in figured maple.

jest in November 1822 about the "unsuccessful attempts of the 'Presbyterian Saints' to build a church of their own" initiated the structure's transformation into the most distinguished wooden church in the province. Christopher Scott (1762–1833), a wealthy Scottish resident, struck the table with his fist and swore "in language more forcible than elegant" that he would see to a fine church of their own. He did so, speedily, "according to his own tastes" and at his own expense. Occasional services were being held in the unfinished building in 1823.

Scott was a ship's captain, timber trader, shipbuilder, merchant and banker. One of three brothers in an old Scottish shipbuilding firm, he came to Saint John in 1799 to secure timber for their shipyards at Greenock (Glasgow's harbour) and to establish another shipyard at the mouth of the Saint John River. He brought 50 skilled tradesmen with him, a complete Old World enterprise transferred to the New. Industrious, enterprising and ambitious, Scott became one of the richest men in New Brunswick. By 1820 he had a mansion at St. Andrews, an estate on the Saint John River, the shipyard in Saint John, various partnerships and a highly profitable three-way trade between New Brunswick, the Caribbean and Britain.

A proud Scot's determination and personal identification with the church are

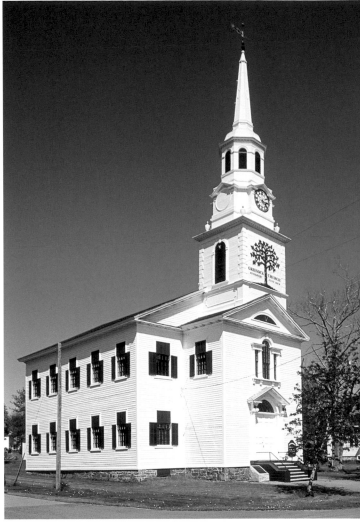

visible everywhere. In contrast to the church's plain but high body with two ranges of tall windows on three sides and a simple rectangular plan, a particularly refined steeple rises above the entry. It transforms gracefully from a square at the base through several octagonal elements, a distant cousin to the steeples of American churches such as First Baptist Church, Providence, Rhode Island (1774). The tower's richness anticipates what awaits within.

What a surprise to view the sanctuary's exceptional materials: no other wooden church is like this. For strength and beauty nothing could rival Scott's lavish use of 12 solid columns of bird's-eye maple with refined Ionic capitals of Honduras mahogany to carry the large gallery. Bird's-eye maple was a specialty of cabinet-makers along the eastern seaboard and the triangle trade made mahogany from the Caribbean readily available; combining the two was favored in New Brunswick and New Hampshire. The church is a large and exquisitely refined piece of case furniture assembled by excellent cabinetmakers working in splendid woods. The ceiling's exceptional plasterwork features a central medallion (related to pattern-book work of the period) and immense Scotch thistles in the corners, symbolizing the Scots' tenacity and prosperity despite adversity.

Free Meeting House, *Moncton, New Brunswick; Baptist; later Methodist, Roman Catholic, Anglican, Presbyterian, Seventh-Day Adventist. Wood with timber frame, 1821; Shepherd Johnson Frost, architect*

The careful spacing of the rectangular windows in pairs around Moncton's Free Meeting House and the repetition of the double-square in those windows (with their double-hung window sash) are typical of Georgian proportional traditions. The height of the round-headed window in the centre of the rear elevation suggests the way the seating is organized about a raised pulpit against that wall in the 15-foot-high interior. The city acquired the building in 1964 and restored it in the 1980s.

The church's design was said to have come from Greenock, Scotland, conceivably a reference to a copy of Gibbs' *Book of Architecture* obtained by the firm of Scott and Company, although a Gibbsian design was old-fashioned by the 1820s. Gibbs was a Scot whose work was reinterpreted in the colonies (*see* p. 42). His London church of St. Martin-in-the-Fields was for a century the most famous and influential church in the English-speaking world. Scott's craftsmen also played major roles in the design. A wooden tower and spire require skilled carpenters and massive timbers: the green oak carved on the steeple was the hallmark of both Greenock and the Scott shipbuilding firm. The elaborate panelling of the gallery in bird's-eye maple and mahogany is Adamesque; the Adam brothers were Scots. The monumental double-decker pulpit — in the same woods and illuminated by a fine Palladian window — reflects the same theology as the Covenanters' Church (*see* p. 52). The pulpit alone is said to have cost £500 (more than the cost of building a small Annapolis Valley church) and two highly skilled craftsmen spent more than a year working on it.

Scott fulfilled his dinner-table promise in 20 months, in what was now called Greenock Church, emphasizing the point with the inscription "finished June 1824." Alexander MacLean, the church's first minister, arrived from Glasgow in time to open it officially on August 1, 1824. The trifling jibe had stung, but the response was swift, the commitment unequivocal and the result resplendent. "One often sees the phrase 'preaching box' used to describe a Scots kirk," writes John R. Hume; as Churchill might have said, some kirk, some preaching box!

New Brunswick's early churches were, like Greenock, wooden, austere and vernacular, reflecting their context and isolation. The **Free Meeting House, Moncton**, is a wonder — for denominations served, churches spawned and uncomplicated beauty. The Bend of the Petitcodiac River, once home to aboriginals and Acadians, was uninhabited in 1766. A "House of Worship to be called and known by the name of the Free Meeting House" was built with donated materials and free labor, and dedicated on September 7, 1821, by Joseph Crandall, a Baptist missionary. Continuing missionary activity resulted in five congregations: Methodists (ca 1822), Roman Catholics (1832), Anglicans (1836), Presbyterians (1838) and the original Baptists. After 1873 it was used by Seventh-Day Adventists among others.

Following the meetinghouse tradition, Moncton's building is rectangular and hip-roofed, with a barn-like timber frame, but delicately beaded siding and a dainty Neoclassical storm-porch. It is perhaps the work of Shepherd Johnson Frost (1788–1853) from New Hampshire, who arrived in 1816.

With settlement and prosperity came architectural monuments resonant of metropolitan culture. New Brunswick's first stone church, **St. John's ("the Old Stone Church"), Saint John**, was among the earliest in revived Gothic style. It was an extraordinary building for this time and place. Boxy and low-pitched — more Georgian than medieval — and centred on a tower-cum-entrance, it was built as a "chapel of ease" for those who could not find (or afford) a seat in the crowded old parish church. Its nearly unknown Irish architect, Lloyd Johnson or Johnston (ca 1767–1842), advertised for "rough masonry" for walls and sandstone for details. In July 1825 (the date 1824 appears over the door) the *Courier* reported St. John's was almost finished and pews were about to be auctioned (a customary Anglican fundraiser): "the elegant structure, which is a design of Mr. Johnson's, is purely Gothic."

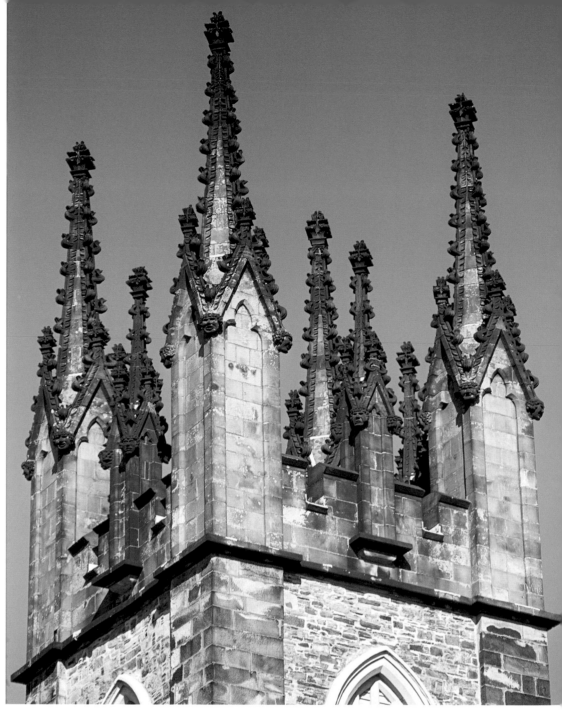

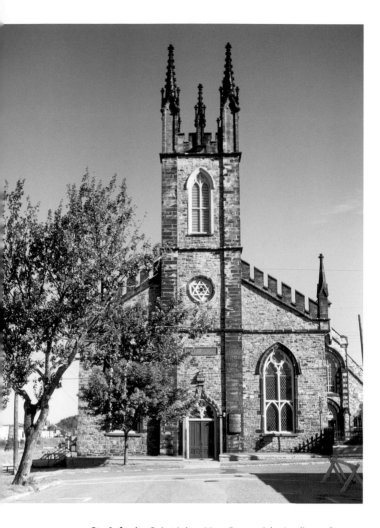

St. John's, *Saint John, New Brunswick; Anglican. Stone, 1823–26; Lloyd Johnson, architect*

The Gothic Revival detailing of "the Old Stone Church" is an astonishingly early colonial reflection of "Commissioners' Gothic," flowing from *An Act for the Building of Additional Churches in Populous Parishes* (1818), which mandated Commissioners for Building New Churches in England. St. John's is set on the axis of Waterloo Row, an echo of Georgian Britain's T-shaped intersections, but found infrequently in North America.

Lloyd Johnson, the Irish architect, set the tone for this Gothic Revival church. Two Scots from Dumfriesshire, however, were responsible for the extraordinary tower: John Cunningham designed it, and Joseph Bell completed the fantastic array of grinning heads where the crocketed pinnacles begin their lacy ascent.

It was Perpendicular Gothic, in fact, and as good as some British churches. Huge lettuce-like foliage arises from the slender *colonnettes* around the door. Clustered columns support the U-shaped gallery in the otherwise plain interior.

The history of Maugerville illustrates early colonial politics. Joshua Mauger settled in Halifax as Navy victualler in 1749, became a distiller, amassed a large fortune and returned to London in 1760, acting as the colony's unofficial spokesman. He assisted more than 200 Massachusetts Congregationalists in securing title to choice land on the east bank of the Saint John River. They extended a call to Seth Noble (also from Massachusetts) in 1774, and built the **Maugerville Meetinghouse** in 1775. Late in 1776 "Noble began to stir up his flock," according to James Hannay, and 27 men, supporting the American Revolution, attacked Fort Cumberland at the head of the Bay of Fundy. It was "a ludicrous failure" and Noble left. When Loyalists arrived in 1783 a Church of England clergyman preached to mixed congregations,

LEFT **Maugerville Meetinghouse**, *Sheffield, New Brunswick; Congregational, now United. Wood, 1775; 1840–42; William Burpee, architect*

William Burpee rebuilt the meetinghouse long after it had been moved downriver from Maugerville in 1788–89. "The resolute plainness of the early Maugerville settlers" and their "old-fashionedness" are so marked in the present building that one feels sure it may almost replicate its predecessor. The tower is deeply engaged in the facade, which is crossed by three round-headed doorways. Battlements and pinnacles bristling on the tower suggest a later attempt to dress the church in Gothic fashion — possibly in the late 19th century.

ABOVE **United Baptist Church**, *St. Andrews, New Brunswick; United Baptist. Wood, 1864–65; architect unknown*

This building was begun in 1864, just as Christ Church Anglican in St. Stephen, 19 miles upriver, was being completed. Christ Church's striking use of board-and-batten construction may have influenced the Baptists. A.J. Downing, a prolific American writer on architecture and horticulture, considered board-and-batten innovative and structurally expressive of the predominantly upright members in frame construction.

but soon conflict arose. The Governor divided the township and the Congregationalists withdrew — with their meetinghouse towed by 50 yoke of oxen — 5 miles downriver to Sheffield in the winter of 1788–89. Reconstructed in 1840, the building's simple Georgian details still dovetail with its fine mid-Georgian communion service — a handsome flagon, a pair of goblets and a plate, all of pewter.

The Baptist Association set its heart on a church in St. Andrews in 1838. When built, the **United Baptist Church, St. Andrews**, had an unexpected source: its striking front is described by Gregg Finley as "a diminutive rendition in wood of the west end of Fredericton's **Christ Church Cathedral**." Board-and-batten's verticality complements the pinnacles and finials of the octagonal turrets, paired lancet windows and arched entrance. The battens end decoratively in arcading, and a yellow-and-white paint scheme enhances the whole effect. Traditional clapboard on the long, low side walls, although inconsistent, is pleasing enough.

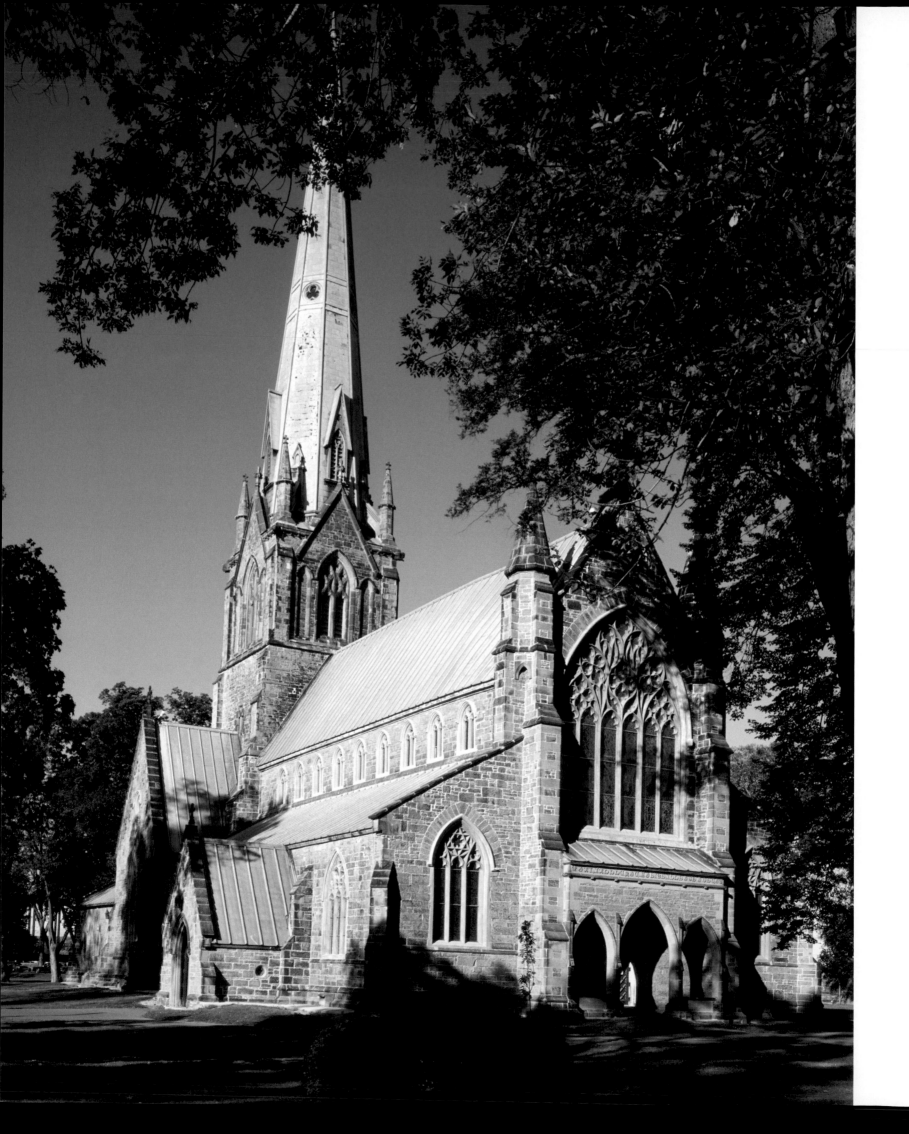

We have no history but that which we make ourselves. But we will ... build with the sword of the spirit in one hand, and the trowel in the other, bent upon reproducing in such ways as God shall lead us, and as the varying conditions of our life permit, England's Church, and England's faith.

— *John Medley, 1878*

Deep and Holy Poetry

VIEWED ACROSS THE SAINT JOHN RIVER, **Christ Church Cathedral, Fredericton**, soars above the New Brunswick capital. A small number of Gothic Revival churches had been built in British North America, all in bland, flat and thin Georgian manner. Fredericton's cathedral was robustly historicist and thus fully Victorian: "the first pure cathedral in the Pointed styles that has ever been reared in a British colony," claimed the *Ecclesiologist* in 1847.

Two Englishmen in the west of England had envisioned this scene in 1844 before either crossed the Atlantic. John Medley, a well-to-do, Oxford-educated scholar and priest, was offered the new bishopric in October 1844. Medley, the first Tractarian to become a bishop, lost no time: appointed on April 25, 1845, and consecrated bishop of Fredericton on May 4, he left England with drawings for his cathedral. Enthroned on June 11, he solicited money, materials, labor and land. Beautiful stone and a splendid 2 1/2-acre riverside site were given, while £4,500 was promised. In August he arranged for excavations and the Governor laid the foundation stone six weeks later. The designer, Frank Wills, from a long line of Exeter builders, likely apprenticed to John Hayward and may have met Medley when the priest commissioned a chapel from Hayward. Medley and Wills shared a fascination with medieval architecture along with a zeal for religious, social and architectural reform.

Hayward and Wills collaborated in the Exeter Diocesan Architectural Society (founded by Medley), part of the Victorian period's ecclesiological movement. Undergraduates had organized the Cambridge Camden Society in 1839 and promoted "the science of Christian Aesthetics" through its journal, the *Ecclesiologist*. Convinced that a church's every part was full "both of meaning and beauty," they were filled with "the spirit of love and admiration for our venerable churches." They proposed "close or mechanical imitation as the only sure way of attaining that excellence which we admire."

Wills and Medley modelled Fredericton's cathedral on St. Mary's, Snettisham, an imposing Norfolk parish church (ca 1340), which Wills measured and drew up.

Christ Church Cathedral, Fredericton, *New Brunswick; Anglican. Stone, 1845–53; Frank Wills, then William Butterfield, architects*

Approached through the city, the cathedral appears abruptly around the river's bend — angular stone cushioned by grassy flood plain and surrounded by large elms. Bishop Medley planted many elms to protect the building's walls from damage by ice floes when the Saint John River flooded its banks in the spring breakup. The site is bounded by two residential streets, while the river forms a curving margin to the east and north on the roughly triangular site.

Medley thought Snettisham was "betwixt an English Cathedral and a Parish Church," and therefore "adapted to [colonial] inhabitants' means." With a central tower and spire on a cross-shaped plan and a triple porch (or "Galilee") at the west end, Snettisham was cathedral-like. Wills thought St. Mary's west window possibly "the finest specimen" of tracery in any English parish church. The central tower left the west end free for this grand Decorated Gothic window with its complex display of sinuously flowing lines, which Simon Jenkins describes as "roses encircling tulips, a glorious summer bouquet in stone." Because Snettisham's chancel was in ruins, Wills called for an extraordinarily extended east end to provide for the choir and a cathedral's liturgical needs.

RIGHT **Christ Church**, *interior*
Because client and architect subscribed to the idea that the Church of England was catholic and reformed, Christ Church Cathedral was in the vanguard of neo-medieval church architecture. In 1847 A. J. B. Beresford-Hope, a leading High-Churchman in London, declared not only that "the same shell which contained the apparatus of medieval worship was, generally speaking, suited to contain that of modern worship," but that the post-Reformation idea of "church-arrangement was identical with the ante-reformational one, and totally opposed to Calvinian bareness." Medley must have agreed.

Christ Church Cathedral, *column*
An octagonal column in the cathedral's nave is one of four such columns with a carving of the head of Christ the King. The number eight was held to allude to the eight days from the entry of Jesus into Jerusalem on Palm Sunday — when he was hailed as "the King of Israel that cometh in the name of the Lord" — through the Passion to Easter Sunday. The heavenly crown is that of the resurrected Saviour, for whom the cathedral is named.

Christ Church Cathedral, *east end and sanctuary window*

William Butterfield, one of England's rising church architects, advised on the east end of Fredericton's cathedral in 1848. The architecturally astute Bishop Medley acted effectively as arbiter between Butterfield and the original (and rather younger) architect, Frank Wills, to achieve an acceptable compromise. Butterfield likely suggested the flowing tracery for the seven-light east window, based on Selby Abbey, Yorkshire (a complement to the six-light west window based on Snettisham). Struck by lightning in 1911, the tower was modified when repaired

The great east window places Christ in Glory directly above the altar. Executed by William Wailes, it fits Medley's description from a decade earlier of "the richest style, in which the figures are numerous, often well drawn, standing under large and splendid canopies" (marshalled rather like figures in a painted Italian Early Renaissance altarpiece). Colours of the rainbow spread kaleidoscopically, except for the reds concentrated on the centre line. White is used extensively as a buffer between coloured pieces, with particularly brilliant effect at morning services.

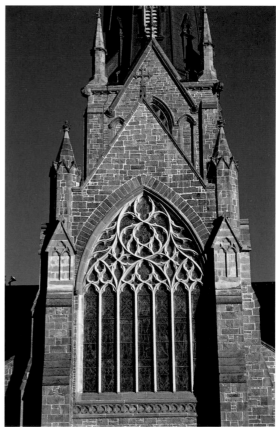

St. Anne's Chapel, *Fredericton, New Brunswick;*
Anglican. Stone, 1846–47; Frank Wills, architect
    With low walls and steeply pitched roofs —
humble yet aspiring — St. Anne's Chapel resembles
contemporary work of the great Roman Catholic
architect A.W. Pugin and his covert Anglican admirers.
A triple bellcote rises at the west end, the well-defined
chancel lies to the east, a sacristy north of that. The
lowly porch offers the only access into the nave. These
discrete forms proclaim clearly the distinct functions
of the parts and the different roles of the participants
(clergy, choir and laity).

Structurally, **Christ Church Cathedral** is a basilica, like Snettisham, with a tall nave and low aisles under separate roofs (*see* p. 77), a work of daring engineering as much as architectural art. Difficulties with the foundation, however, meant that work proceeded haltingly: only the aisle walls were complete (and temporarily roofed) by November 1847. The sandstone in the walls, quarried a mile away, was admirable and looked "as though it had stood there for a hundred years." But Medley was appalled by "the frightful expense of materials and workmen."

Before Medley's frustrating first year in New Brunswick was out (when nothing was achieved on the cathedral except some foundations and outer walls), the Bishop asked Wills to design a chapel of ease in Fredericton's west end. **St. Anne's Chapel** was an instrument of architectural reform, ushering in an era of Gothic church-building throughout the diocese, and of liturgical and choral innovation, too, for the new churches would "ring with music appropriate to the liturgy" with introits, anthems and hymns composed by the Bishop, who was also the first president of the Fredericton Choral Society and conducted the cathedral choir when Christ Church opened.

If the cathedral's progress was glacial, the chapel appeared like a mushroom. Begun at the end of May 1846, it was consecrated in mid-March 1847. Its dedication to Saint Anne (traditionally identified as the Virgin's mother) reflected the Acadian predecessor of Fredericton, Sainte-Anne.

The chapel is of hammer-dressed stone, Early English in style (because of "the impossibility of procuring proper masons to execute stone tracery," according to Wills) and reminiscent of something from the Middle Ages in every detail. Aisleless and small, but very refined, it has a south porch as well as a distinct chancel to the east. Unmistakably, Wills intended St. Anne's to be a model of ecclesiology, overall and in each of its fittings — the font by the door, the handsome free seats, the texts on the walls, and the eagle lectern. Medley welcomed restoration of all "symbolic teaching" (nearly lost under the Puritans) "so that the very pavement of the sanctuary may speak His praises, and the eastern window set forth His passion and sacrifice." St. Anne's heralded more than the cathedral to follow: it was the first church in North America completed on ecclesiological principles. It startled many in New Brunswick and gave pause to those who underestimated Medley. Wills could take particular satisfaction in the outcome and illustrated it in the important book he produced after he moved in 1848 to New York City: *Ancient English Ecclesiastical Architecture and Its Principles, Applied to the Wants of the Church at the Present Day* (1850).

Chris Brooks comments in his book *The Gothic Revival* that "Ecclesiologists were driven by a hunger for meaning, and in gothic found a way of filling the built world with significance—with the Glory of God indeed." Resuming work on the cathedral after St. Anne's Chapel, Medley feared that Snettisham's beautiful compound piers (clusters of half-columns and slender mouldings) were beyond his masons, so he alternated massive octagonal and round columns in Bay of Fundy stone. These are complemented by beautiful carvings representing Christ the King and a cross in a circle, respectively, just above the simple moulded capitals. In Wills' view, every ornament "symbolizes some doctrine or illustrates some truth." This corresponds to a 13th-century manual, published in 1843 as *The Symbolism of Churches and Church Ornaments*, which (with its store of signs and interpretations) offered ecclesiology a key. The translators, John Mason Neale and Benjamin Webb (founders of

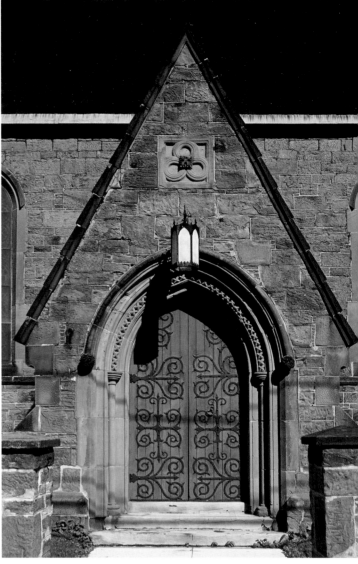

St. Anne's Chapel

The chapel stands at George and Westmorland Streets, behind a low stone wall. It is entered through this porch on the south side, close to the street. Precisely crafted stone, straightforward woodwork and carefully wrought iron prepare the visitor for a thoughtful interior. To the east (beyond the end of the chancel) is the entrance through a lych-gate into the church-yard and the cemetery.

Passing the font (at the entrance to the nave) visitors are reminded of baptismal vows. But the long chancel, prefaced by its beautiful butternut screen, seemed too emphatic in its separation of clergy and laity, and — according to the *Loyalist* (July 23, 1846) — a stumbling block to those who suspected the Bishop's "dark and most insidious design."

the ecclesiological movement), summarize in their preface: a church's "material fabrick symbolizes, embodies, represents, expresses, answers to, some abstract meaning." The theme of Wills' sculpture is fairly clear — the nature of Christ's king-ship revealed in the events of Holy Week and worldwide evangelization.

Carvings and dressed stones, prefabricated in Exeter with French stone from Caen, "arrived with trivial injury" to complete the nave, including the great west window, in the summer of 1848. In the process Snettisham's Decorated roof was changed to a powerful hammer beam of Perpendicular design. Ingeniously, "An air chamber ... between the inside boarding of roofs and its outer covering" was insert-ed to prevent "extremes of heat and cold from affecting suddenly the temperature

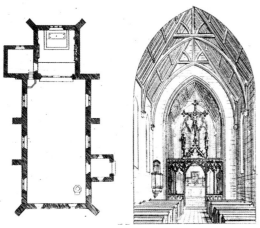

ABOVE **St. Bede's**, *Masborough, near Rotherham, Yorkshire, England; Roman Catholic. Stone, 1841–42; Matthew E. Hadfield, architect*

A West Yorkshire church, St. Bede's, is similar to St. Anne's in general character, plan and details such as the hanging corner pulpit, chancel screen and timber roof (even to the roof's acute pitch, so different from early modern Gothic). If Wills saw this etching of a Roman Catholic church by Matthew E. Hadfield (1812–85) in A.W. Pugin's *Present State of Ecclesiastical Architecture in England* (1843) he shied away from placing a rood on the screen or sanctus bells on the chancel arch. Ecclesiologists accepted "exact imitation" of *"real ancient designs."* Pugin says, "When buildings are derived from a common source, it is very natural that they should greatly resemble each other; ... it is very possible and even probable that two architects may erect precisely the same edifice."

FACING PAGE **St. Mary's**, *Snettisham, Norfolk, England; Church of England. Stone, ca 1340; designer unknown*

Snettisham's tall arcades are carried on elegent compound piers, beyond New Brunswick masons to replicate, while its graceful roof with arching braces gave way to Fredericton's massive hammerbeams, and a deep choir beyond the crossing (*see* p. 72).

of the inside of the Cathedral," reported the *New-York Ecclesiologist*. Evidently, then, mechanical imitation gave way to Modern Gothic as Wills repudiated "slavish literal copying of any particular building." To achieve "the deep and holy poetry of the structure" he now suggested "comprehensive imitation" instead. These changes in the cathedral's arcade and its nave roof transmuted Snettisham's gracefulness into Fredericton's brawny materiality, in keeping with the mid-century's emergent muscular Christianity.

When Medley lost Wills to other projects (more than 50 churches in today's Québec and Ontario and the United States) he appealed to the Ecclesiological Society in 1848 for advice on completing the cathedral. He was referred to William Butterfield (1814–1900), who suggested placing the choir in the crossing, abandoning the transepts, shortening the tower, and curtailing the east end while raising its roof level with the nave. Medley agreed to the choir in the crossing and raising the roof, but held out for rudimentary transepts, a taller tower and a deep sanctuary. The east end, including Butterfield's furnishings, was completed rapidly between May and November 1849.

"The progress of ecclesiological gothic pulled architectural arts and crafts with it," as Chris Brooks points out. Thus, neo-medieval stained glass by three English pioneers of its revival filled nearly every window at Christ Church between 1850 and 1852. In *Elementary Remarks on Church Architecture* (Exeter, 1841), Medley advised stained glass be used "not to create a splendid picture, but a peculiarly rich and solemn light in the edifice itself." He thought it best to strive for "perpetual contrast, no large masses of single colour being allowed," but "a tolerably even distribution of the colours so contrasted over the surface of the window," as in the remarkable seven-light Crucifixion window in the east, above the altar, by William Wailes (1808–88) of Newcastle. The "Snettisham" window to the west, by William Warrington (1786–1869), is a particularly sinuous treatment of parallels between Old and New Testament figures. Different again are the aisle windows, by the Beer family of Exeter, comprising small, strongly coloured panels illustrating biblical scenes, set in almost transparent light grey glass, edged by patterned borders in primary colours. All such glass was revolutionary in the colonies.

When Medley arrived, two-thirds of New Brunswick's scattered settlements had been without priests and even where there was a church, communion was celebrated no more than four times a year. He went to the remotest parts of the province on annual visitations, inaugurating "an era of Gothic church building" and extension. The lapsed and lax he reclaimed "through the preaching of the Word but also through the sacraments administered in the full dignity and beauty of the Anglican liturgy." While tolerating "all forms of Anglican worship, whether high or low, which were reverent," he introduced the chanting of canticles, frequent communion and ritualism. Malcolm Ross emphasizes that the cathedral was vital to this mission, "a symbol of episcopal authority and the model of worship" for the diocese. The spaciousness and the principal axis of the cathedral seem surprising even now and the broad central alley, facilitating processions — which extends from the west doors, past the large font, to the passageway — is indicative of Medley's insistence on "Catholic reverence for the two great sacraments of baptism and the Eucharist." Medley's and Wills' Gothic vision transformed the sacred landscape of New Brunswick. And, beyond that, of Eastern Canada.

Snow and rain with us always comes with a heavy gale; it does not fall quietly as with you at home…. The sudden changes from frost to thaw, the high winds with furious snow drifts, together with the poor materials, render a very simple outline quite necessary. A Newfoundland architect cannot produce all the varieties which battlements, parapets, pinnacles, gabled aisles … give to your English churches, without making his building either ludicrous, or dangerous, or both together.

— William Grey 1853

Sublime Newfoundland

MOST NEWFOUNDLAND CHURCHES, whatever their affiliation, embraced medieval styling through the Victorian era. Openings with pointed arches and towers with battlements continued into the 20th century, even as the rich details gave way to the modern taste for austere geometry, simple profiles and planar surfaces. In the 1790s a general appreciation of the Middle Ages and images of architectural ruins characterized writers of English fiction and British watercolourists and printmakers. By mid-century, Gothic Revival architecture amounted to a national style.

The **Church of the Most Holy Trinity, Trinity**, Newfoundland's oldest surviving church, was built for the Roman Catholic Irish population in 1833. The town lies near the mouth of Trinity Bay. Although it was a prosperous early settlement, Gordon Handcock writes that "outbreaks of mariner rowdyism and drunken brawls remained a characteristic feature" as they had since the middle of the 18th century. The church is as small and sweet as a dollhouse: a neat little Georgian rectangle, with eaves fitting tight to the walls and simple lancet windows; the tower was added half a century later for the new bell (now hanging in a separate metal frame). Slender buttresses barely project from the tower — tokens of Victorian Gothicism added with a mullioned window over the door and fretted bargeboards on the exterior of the shallow chancel (*see* p. 29).

When Sir Thomas Cochrane, Newfoundland's first governor, insisted upon building the present Government House, he obtained a site nearby for a chapel of ease, dedicated to his name-saint and "contingent upon seats being reserved for church-going members of the local garrison." In 1833, Archdeacon Edward Wix raised funds in England for **St. Thomas', St. John's**. Originally it consisted of just the nave and tower built by Patrick Kough (ca 1786–1863) from County Wexford, Ireland. He "came to St. John's about 1804 as a boy with little education" but became a carpenter, successful builder, respected politician and office-holder. Though built of wood, St. Thomas' looks considerable in its stripped-down Gothic

Church of the Most Holy Trinity, *Trinity, Newfoundland; Roman Catholic. Wood, 1833; builder unknown*

This historic small wooden church, Newfoundland's oldest Roman Catholic church, is marked by its bell tower, topped with a candle-snuffer roof and cupola grasped between louvered openings. The cross rising above the assemblage is matched by crosses on the front corners of the building. The bell tower is no longer used, the bell having been hung separately to one side of the entrance in a utilitarian structure, also topped with a cross.

profile, pyramidal spire and pointed windows. It does without the characteristically frail ornaments that pass for Gothic. The acerbic *Ecclesiologist* thought "the intention was certainly better than the effect" but noted Archdeacon Wix had "sent to Italy for a marble altar and font" and pompously supposed these "the only attempts at ritual solemnity" and "decency" in all Newfoundland. When the tone of Anglicanism in Newfoundland changed under Bishop Edward Feild's High-Church views, various strategies nearly doubled St. Thomas' capacity (to 1,300). An emphatic axis reaches from the nave's entrance past the font, through a screen to the end of the deepened chancel in the elongated interior.

The Roman Catholic **Basilica Cathedral of St. John the Baptist, St. John's**, accords with the views of Edmund Burke (1729–97) on the Sublime, specifically that "Greatness of dimension is a powerful cause of the sublime," and also that "the effects of a rugged and broken surface seem stronger than where it is smooth and polished." Burke's *Philosophical Enquiry into the Origin of Our Ideas of the Sublime and Beautiful* (1756) had enormous importance, as James Stevens Curl points out, in shifting 18th-century taste from classically inspired conceptions of beauty (and contemporary Classicism) to Romanticism. Burke associated the Sublime with sensations falling well outside ideas related to beauty. Such impressions as awe, intensity, power, ruggedness and vastness emphasize "Man's relative insignificance in the face of Nature, arousing emotions, and stimulating the imagination." Burke contrasts the

St. Thomas', *St. John's, Newfoundland; Anglican. Wood, 1834–36; Patrick Kough, builder*

The oldest surviving church in St. John's, St. Thomas' was a chapel of ease to the old parish church. It was enlarged by two relatively simple expedients: adding an aisle to either side (after opening the lower part of the side walls) in 1851 and nearly doubling the length of the nave from three bays to five in 1874.

A windstorm in 1846 moved St. Thomas' about 6 inches, and the structure swayed in high winds, but it was stabilized by the addition of the aisles (at which time the original gallery was removed). The chancel was lengthened and a vestry added in 1882–83, and the chancel screen was installed in 1934.

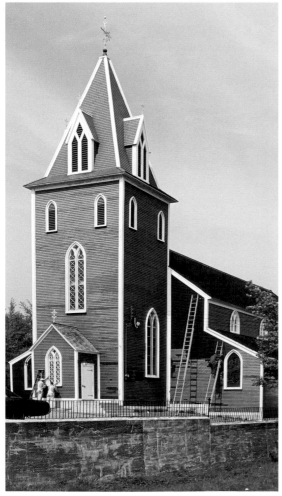

two aesthetics: "sublime objects are vast in their dimensions, beautiful ones comparatively small; beauty should be small, and polished; the great, rugged; … beauty should not be obscure; the great ought to be dark and gloomy; beauty should be light and delicate; the great ought to be solid, and even massive."

St. John the Baptist is majestically silhouetted above the capital — dramatic, independent, challenging, even defiant. And puzzling: why was so large a church required and how was it realized so soon after Roman Catholic emancipation? *Canadian Illustrated News* called the site one of the most remarkable in the world, overlooking the city and facing the Atlantic. Three hundred feet above sea level, "it is at once the most conspicuous object, and the chief architectural ornament of St. John's."

After freedom of religion was proclaimed in St. John's in 1783, Pope Pius VI recognized Newfoundland as a separate ecclesiastical territory and named James Louis O'Donel (1737–1811), a popular Irish Franciscan preacher, its superior. O'Donel arrived in 1784 and altered part of his house into a small chapel. He became bishop in 1795, Canada's first English-speaking Roman Catholic bishop. A plain wooden building (1797) served as cathedral for 58 years, despite rapid growth of the Catholic population: between 1811 and 1816 their number doubled to some 21,000. Michael Anthony Fleming (1792–1850), consecrated bishop in 1829, described the chapel as "a wretched building little better than an extensive stable … now tottering," which left many uncovered in "the pelting of the storm, the freezing winds & drifting snows."

Fleming's vision called for strong clergy and a great church. He recruited 36 Irish priests (compared to nine priests in 1823), priests who had witnessed Daniel O'Connell's successful movement for Catholic emancipation and, as Raymond Lahey says, "could be expected to take a more militant stance than their predecessors in asserting Roman Catholic rights and aspirations." Newfoundland's Catholics gained relief from civil disabilities in 1832 (three years after British and Irish emancipation) with formal recognition in matters as basic as the practice of their religion; the purchase and inheritance of land; the performance of baptisms, marriages and burials; and the holding of public office. In 1834 Fleming begged the government for unused land above Gallows Hill for schools, a residence and a parish church: it was "bleak" but superb, remote yet accessible. After "years of vexation and annoyance," he received 9 acres in 1838. Lamenting that all his churches were "of the most perishable material," Fleming craved a stone church, "a temple superior to any other in the Island — beautiful and spacious, suitable to the worship of the Most High God — a pledge of the permanency of our holy religion, "and an object of pride." Such a church would demonstrate, writes John Edward, that "the Irish finally had arrived in Newfoundland and would have to be accommodated."

In August 1838, the Bishop selected Ole Jörgen Schmidt (1793–1848), a versatile Danish Lutheran and architect to the Danish government in Altona on the Elbe. Now a suburb of Hamburg, Altona was then the second-largest city in Denmark and traded actively with Newfoundland. Schmidt, educated in Copenhagen, knew the architecture of Rome as well as Berlin (he had shown his designs for a church and a cathedral to the celebrated Prussian architect Karl Friedrich Schinkel in 1824). He provided Fleming with plans for a "most extensive cathedral," a house for the bishop and clergy, a convent and schools suited to Newfoundland's climate. He

Basilica Cathedral of St. John the Baptist, *St. John's, Newfoundland; Roman Catholic. Stone, 1841–55; Ole Jörgen Schmidt, architect*

St. John the Baptist was conceived as a national church, with a noble location and grand scale that would engender respect for the Irish and for Roman Catholicism. It was avant-garde in its freely treated Romanesque Revival style and, briefly, the largest church in North America.

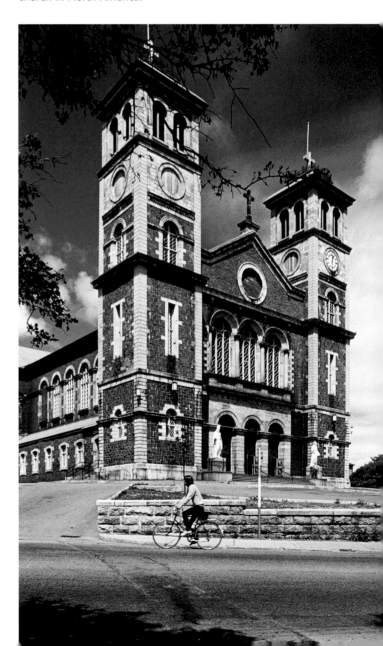

also built a detailed large-scale model of the cathedral to facilitate building without the expense of a supervising architect.

Fleming had Schmidt's plans by November and expressed "entire and unqualified satisfaction at the style of their execution." The design draws mainly on early Christian and Romanesque churches in Italy and Germany: early Christian appealed because of its primitive quality (*see* p. 87), while the "massiveness and strength" of Romanesque had attracted the pioneering British *Architectural Magazine* in 1834. Romanesque also echoed contemporary *Rundbogenstil* (literally "round-arch style") around Hamburg — a "free" architecture based on principle rather than "copyism" — which prizes issues of planning and construction above either formal composition or architectural ornament.

The cathedral evokes sedate North Italian work, which Thomas Hope illustrated in his *Historical Essay on Architecture* (1835). Hope's first illustration, showing the Basilica Sant'Ambrogio in Milan (*see* p. 383), may have provided the cathedral's format: a triple entrance, round-arched, below corresponding windows in the gable, set between tall projecting towers. Sant'Ambrogio's combination of light-coloured stone on all the margins and openings in contrast to darker walls is reflected in St. John the Baptist. This is especially remarkable because two decades would pass before polychromatic schemes became popular in the British Isles. This treatment was almost unknown elsewhere in British North America until mid-century, but apparently was a specialty of Schmidt.

St. John is a basilica in the tradition of ancient Roman administrative buildings

Basilica Cathedral of St. John the Baptist, *interior*
The nave's height is slightly greater than its width. Lavish transepts, however, confer a sense of amplitude. This is enhanced by two decorative features of the moulded plaster ceiling executed with Neoclassical detail: a broad cornice sweeping around the whole church against the flat ceiling and an immense pattern on the ceiling itself, centred on the crossing but spilling into each arm of the church.

and early churches (*see* p. 375): its rectangular nave, with lower side aisles, terminates in an apse the width and height of the nave, which serves as a choir and sanctuary, with no separation other than the freestanding high altar beyond the crossing. The lower nave walls are arcaded, opening into the aisles, which function as an ambulatory around the perimeter with side altars and stations of the cross that permit private devotions even during services. Another arcade rises above the first, framing the windows.

Bishop Fleming was involved at every stage: securing land, approving designs, obtaining materials, organizing the workforce and raising funds. Calling on people outside St. John's to help, because the cathedral was for the whole Catholic population, he used thousands of volunteers for swift "hauls" of materials: to find and erect fencing, gather timbers for scaffolding and, most extraordinary of all, move huge quantities of stone. In the autumn of 1838 he went to Kelly's Island in Conception Bay to supervise stonecutting. He had stone brought to the city off-season, using fishing boats unsuited to such work, involving round trips of some 200 miles. Thousands turned out on May 27 and 28, 1839 to excavate 80,000 cubic feet for the foundations. During three weeks in the winter of 1841 volunteers moved 2,000 tons of red granite donated by the Royal Engineers from Signal Hill.

Ten to twelve thousand attended the foundation-stone laying (May 20, 1841) following a great procession that included Schmidt's model, carried by four bearers. Fleming described the model as "a *cathedral church* in miniature. The whole edifice complete: its aisles, porticos [ultimately omitted], towers, ambulatories, altars, sanctuary, and all." Construction, supervised by sculptor James Purcell from Cork, was rapid at first. Purcell prepared the triple windows, columns and capitals for the front in the winter of 1841–42. Realizing that it was as cheap in the long run and certainly faster to bring stone directly from Ireland than to use local stone, Fleming imported grey Dublin granite and black Galway marble. The walls were finished and roofed by 1845, and the church virtually completed in 1847–49. It opened on January 6, 1850. Fleming, reported the *Patriot*, "preached an eloquent sermon" and celebrated Pontifical Mass, but "seemed quite exhausted at the end." This was his only appearance, in fact; he died six months later. Through his will he made one last offering, a refined memorial to his predecessor, Bishop Scanlon.

Fleming was the island's "most influential Irish immigrant" and the bishop who "effected the most change upon Newfoundland society," writes FitzGerald. No one viewed Newfoundland "less as an Irish colony, and more as its own country." The cathedral was his chief instrument for change and it survives, little altered. It was consecrated in 1855, became a minor basilica (an honorific term given by Rome to selected important churches) in 1955 and is now generally known simply as "the Basilica." Reportedly, Fleming was fond of seeing the cathedral towering above the city as he entered the harbor: it is his memorial.

The **Anglican Cathedral of St. John the Baptist, St. John's**, begun a few years later, stands broadside to Church Hill, within a fenced and sloping green close. The strength of its massive wall of grey-and-tan stone contrasts with the fragility of the colourful wooden houses nearby. Either a simple frame church (1758) or its replacement (1800), called by the *Ecclesiologist* "a wooden shed of the most monstrous description," is visible in period views of St. John's. In 1843 Bishop Aubrey Spencer began an unremarkable Gothic Revival cathedral using stone blocks and carved

Basilica Cathedral of St. John the Baptist, *high altar and choir*
The high altar (1855) — originally an elaborate Renaissance Revival affair in High Victorian taste, framing a sculpture by John Edward Carew (1785–1868) of Dublin — was effectively remodelled a century later (1953–55) with replacement of the sculpture. The simplified architectural framework is now essentially a Palladian motif. Under the front altar rests the idealized third and final version of *The Redeemer in Death* (1854–55), sculpted in Carrara marble by John Hogan (1800–58) of Dublin.

Cathedral of St. John the Baptist, *St. John's, Newfoundland, Anglican. Stone, 1847–1905; George Gilbert Scott, architect*

This view of the east end offers a close-up of Scott's window details — a history lesson in the transformation of Early English into Decorated Gothic. At the top, lancets are grouped to make possible larger openings than single lancets; to either side are windows complemented by patterns cut into flat planes of stone, a technique known as "plate tracery"; the great east window at the centre shows the emergence of large and complex Decorated Gothic windows executed with free-flowing "bar tracery."

The vault over the crossing contrasts with the timber roof over the choir (also meant to be stone-vaulted, as the curving stone shafts suggest). The nave is meant to remain an open timber roof and demonstrates one of A.W. Pugin's greatest principles: *"all ornament should consist of the essential construction of the building."*

details from Cork, Ireland. James Purcell, who was supervising construction of the Roman Catholic cathedral simultaneously, was the designer. Three years later fire swept the city, leaving a mass of useless building materials. Gilbert (later Sir George Gilbert) Scott (1811–78) of London then designed today's austere and stirring cathedral for Spencer's successor, Bishop Feild. Scott was young but had an international reputation as a church architect, having just won the competition (1844–45) for Hamburg's influential Lutheran Nikolaikirche. His office became the 19th century's largest architectural practice, with a prodigious output of some 900 works.

The pyrotechnics of Scott's mature work — colourful, patterned, encrusted, eclectic, even brash — lay in the future. All was gravity and restraint at St. John's due to limitations of environment, material resources and traditions: a "most impracticable climate, no available native materials, an unpliant ritual," complained the *Ecclesiologist*. Scott's cruciform design, massively buttressed from crypt to clerestory, rose dramatically to a central tower and uncomplicated spire. Daring in scale (196 feet long inside but shorter than the Basilica by 50 feet), and as adventurous as any cathedral by the well-known Welby Pugin, it did not please the *Ecclesiologist*, which damned it: "a first-rate University prize poem," with "authority for every detail and phrase; it is learned and dignified, but perhaps cold," displaying "study more than genius." This must have stung Scott, who had deftly combined various phases of Gothic: Early English lancets singly throughout the nave except at the west end, where a grouping steps boldly over the stone-roofed porch; Decorated Gothic in the

transepts and east end; and a full-blown Decorated east window with elaborate tracery. This strategy of combining styles reduced expensive labor yet offered variety.

Scott's grand design started immediately but materialized slowly. William Hay (1818–88), a Scottish architect appointed clerk of the works in 1846, travelled the British Isles to find skilled workers and suitable materials. He arrived in St. John's on May 25, 1847; ground was broken the same day. When the nave was consecrated, in September 1850, Hay moved on to Upper Canada. The choir and transepts followed eventually, in 1880–85, initially under Scott's son, George Gilbert Scott, Jr. (1839–97); but he converted to Roman Catholicism, was confined to Bethlehem Hospital and then fled to France.

St. John's last great fire (July 8, 1892) brought the roof down, demolishing the nave's arcades. John Oldrid Scott (1841–1913), another of Gilbert Scott's sons, began reconstruction. The east end was reconsecrated in 1895, with nave and aisles following in 1902–05. The tower was not continued because of prohibitive costs, but some extraordinary stained glass was installed and long-delayed stone vaulting appeared over the crossing and Lady Chapel. Externally the cathedral epitomizes the Baptist's Judean mission ("one crying in the wilderness"). Internally it is splendid beyond expectations, with its references to prophecy, passion, evangelization and (in the sanctuary window) John's apocalyptic vision: "I baptize you with water but the one coming after me … will baptize you with the Holy Spirit and with fire."

Until recently, Greenspond was approached only across water, and the outline of

Cathedral of St. John the Baptist, *interior*
The interior contrasts rubble masonry with smoothly dressed stone in the arcades and windows. In the choir, shafts rise between the clerestory windows to support stone vaults (still not in place), while a series of pointed openings (the triforium) under the clerestory appear in the wall's thickness — a pleasing exercise in unification and complication. The large stone reredos (by Scott's grandson, Giles Gilbert Scott) behind the altar overlaps the great east window. The stained glass (1911) by C.E. Kempe of London depicts Christ enthroned as the trunk in the "Tree of the Church," with apostles and early saints as branches.

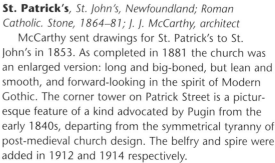

St. Patrick's, *St. John's, Newfoundland; Roman Catholic. Stone, 1864–81; J. J. McCarthy, architect*

McCarthy sent drawings for St. Patrick's to St. John's in 1853. As completed in 1881 the church was an enlarged version: long and big-boned, but lean and smooth, and forward-looking in the spirit of Modern Gothic. The corner tower on Patrick Street is a picturesque feature of a kind advocated by Pugin from the early 1840s, departing from the symmetrical tyranny of post-medieval church design. The belfry and spire were added in 1912 and 1914 respectively.

St. Stephen's, **Bonavista Bay,** was sighted before anything else. Nowadays it is approached from the west shore of Bonavista Bay over a causeway. The white Anglican church with its black roof turns away from the sea, nearly hiding its tower and spire — its western tower and eastern-oriented chancel like a signpost and compass (*see* p. 37 for interior). In Newfoundland it is almost axiomatic that a church silhouette is the unique landmark of the place. In the old outports the shoreline, essential to the fishery for wharves, storage sheds, flakes and warehouses, was claimed long ago and churches were relegated to the settlement's rear. Because St. Stephen's is the tallest structure and sited on high ground, its distinctive profile materializes repeatedly, as footpaths snake among buildings and around erratic rocks: "Winding with the winding shore," as Robert Lowell said of Petersport (his fictional name for Bay Roberts, Newfoundland).

For **St. Patrick's**, **St. John's**, in the city's west end, the Irish community turned to another well-known Gothic specialist. James Joseph McCarthy (1817–82), of Dublin, was Welby Pugin's collaborator, completing several of Pugin's greatest Irish works after his untimely death in 1852. McCarthy apprenticed with a local architect and at 20 began exhibiting work at the Royal Hibernian Academy. A founder of the Irish Ecclesiological Society in 1849, his piety and patriotism suited the time, a period of intense activity for the Catholic Church in Ireland. The London *Builder* (April 1853) announced McCarthy's Early English scheme for a small church in St. John's, with convent and schoolhouse, around three sides of a quadrangle. Two months later McCarthy forwarded his drawings, including a "perspective view in a flat wooden case" and "two models, which I think may be required," perhaps an exterior model and a model of an important detail such as the windows, most of which are paired with trefoiled heads and based on Dunbrody Abbey, County Wexford. He even visited St. John's that October.

Gower Street, *St. John's, Newfoundland; Methodist,*
now United. Brick, 1894–96; Elijah Hoole, architect
    Gower Street Methodist is in a Romanesque Revival
style of Continental origin — smooth in surface, with
scattered details, and vertical in effect. The style is generally associated with primitive roots and early practices, which is perhaps why it was favoured by the
Methodists; there is some irony in the proximity of the
Roman Catholic basilica-cathedral, an early example of
Italian Romanesque.

McCarthy departed from popular Italianate traditions and drew suggestions
instead from Pugin's revived Irish Gothic: a steeply pitched roof, buttresses omit-
ted, Irish window details, outsized plain columns with simple moulded capitals, a
tall and narrow nave and a continuous line over nave and chancel. In *An Apology
for the Revival of Christian Architecture* (1843), Pugin had specifically recommended
ancient Irish models. Those buildings might be "rude and simple; but, massive and
solemn, they harmonized most perfectly with the wild and rocky localities in which
they were erected ... [and] might be revived at a considerably less cost than is now
actually expended on the construction of monstrosities." The laying of St. Patrick's
foundation stone in 1855 (during the Catholic cathedral's consecration) occurred
early in McCarthy's career; the actual foundations and cornerstone came nearly a
decade later (1864), followed by a long pause. The donation of stone in 1875 enabled
construction to continue as long "as funds and materials permitted." St. Patrick's
was completed in 1881, shortly before McCarthy's death.

After the fire of 1892, **Gower Street Methodist, St. John's** (now United
Church), was built conspicuously along an upper ridge where Gower Street meets
Queen's Road. The red-brick church with terra cotta ornaments seems all turrets
and towers mounting to the highest gable: a clamour of layered planes and angular profiles. A rose window rises moonlike in the streetscape of mansard-roofed
wooden houses, quickly rebuilt after the fire. Gower Street Church has round-
arched openings that diminish in almost geometric fashion as they rise. The doorways are moulded and ornamented, while pilaster strips subdivide the facade,
rising to arcaded corbel tables. The English architect, Elijah Hoole (d. 1912), was
not well known, but he had a social conscience (designing settlement housing in
London) and a Methodist pedigree.

A new wooden church ... must show its real construction [and] discard rigorously and unceremoniously all that is essential to stone.
— William Scott, 1848

Rational Gothic

DESPITE GOTHIC REVIVAL'S ARCANE TRADITIONS and symbolism, it focused creative thought on how to adapt European stone architecture to wooden churches logically. In an essay of 1864, César Daly defined Rationalism as the belief that architecture is ornamental or ornamented construction. Peter Collins says the Rationalists "simply believed that architectural form was essentially structural form, however ultimately refined and adorned those basic structural forms might be."

An almost unknown designer, Edward Shuttleworth Medley (1838–1910), rigorously applied this "Rational Gothic" to wilderness ecclesiology in a small group of wooden churches in New Brunswick. Medley came to New Brunswick as a boy and watched the construction of Fredericton's cathedral from the privileged position of the Bishop's son (*see* pp. 70–77). Bishop Medley arranged for Edward to go to London in 1853 and study, probably informally, in William Butterfield's office. At the time Butterfield's most famous London church — All Saints', the model of High-Church ecclesiology — was in progress. Returning in 1856, Edward attended King's College, Fredericton, before he was ordained an Anglican priest. All seven of his churches were Anglican. At 23, Medley had already experimented with the syntax of timber-framed architecture in All Saints' Church (1861), McKeens Corner (*see* p. 38). Two years later, he worked on developing the vocabulary in St. Mary the Virgin, New Maryland, and the emotional expression in Christ Church, St. Stephen.

Small but striking, Medley's aisleless **St. Mary the Virgin, New Maryland**, stands on a lightly wooded site south of Fredericton. Painted white now, it was undoubtedly stained earthy colours originally. An unusually tall porch, which gives impressive scale to the west front and a high-shouldered quality overall, draws itself up into a steeply pitched roof with three gables as if shielding something of great moment. A heavy timber frame protrudes through the surface of wide boards with crisply moulded battens, stout yet upright in appearance. An angular

St. Mary the Virgin, *New Maryland, New Brunswick; Anglican. Wood and timber frame, 1863–64; Edward S. Medley, architect*

The interior of St. Mary the Virgin houses exceptionally beautiful woodwork. Light floods through the largest windows under broad blind arches. Small windows illuminate the pulpit and lectern. Boarded-in hammer-beam arches arise from the window-framing to make a chancel arch, visually reinforced by an open chancel railing. The chancel walls display the jagged rhythms of an angular blind arcade, which is followed by the soft embrace of the trefoiled curves rising in the sanctuary.

drip-moulding zigzags around the building at windowsill level; in the apsidal east end, it climbs under three windows that rise progressively. In the tradition of French Gothic, the spaces within are unified, the nave flowing into the chancel without changes in wall-plane or roofline. The belfry, straddling chancel and nave, distinguishes and unites both.

Although small, the nave seems expansive, thanks partly to two small but clear side windows. The south window lights the chancel seat and lectern while the pulpit hugs the wall beside the north window. These windows are massively framed (inside and out) to support a trefoiled arch that frames the chancel and carries the

St. Mary the Virgin, *exterior*

The south side of St. Mary the Virgin is a hybrid of techniques: ancient European half-timber construction that exposes the frame and innovative American board-and-batten technology of the period, used here in place of whitewashed infill. The gaps between the vertical planks are covered by battens to keep the weather out. Two of the heaviest posts are very closely spaced, framing the smallest window; joined internally to a pair on the north side, they carry the belfry.

A detail of the south porch (below) shows three characteristic features: the sturdy framework of large timbers, the board-and-batten membrane cladding it and the angular drip-moulding that here zigzags over the doorway. All are structural. The doorposts are beveled with the simple chamfer of the joiner and the barn-framer, more to prevent injury to the opening than for any workmanlike elegance. Only the carved leafy crop on the peak of the doorway is truly decorative and even it has a rationale, capping a vertical joint in the drip that might be susceptible to rot.

belfry. A low chancel railing and altar rail maintain open sightlines while they further define the volumes. The sanctuary woodwork reprises the trefoil motif around the stained-glass windows beside and above the altar. The arching head of the east window breaks through the woodwork and rises into a gable. The altar is as thoughtfully designed and straightforward as that by Butterfield in Fredericton's Christ Church Cathedral. The spare and elegantly crafted benches, reflecting a light touch, are exceptional (the antithesis of Wills' massive seating in St. Anne's Chapel at Fredericton, *see* p. 75). The whole ensemble is Medley's High Victorian Gothic masterpiece in miniature.

Christ Church, St. Stephen, on the St. Croix River (upstream from St. Andrews and across from Calais, Maine) is Edward Medley's most ambitious work. Still a deacon, he was curate at the predecessor church when it burned in 1863. He turned adversity to opportunity, however, designing the new church and contributing heavily toward its cost. (When Bishop Medley consecrated the new church in 1864, he ordained his son.) The new church, together with its Sunday school and rectory, occupies a whole block in a residential area, dominating its magnificent site toward the crest of the hill against which the town is built. Regrettably, a high tower of idiosyncratic profile beside its south aisle was felled by a gale early on. Medley had tried unsuccessfully to persuade the vestry to build a brick church, but in the end Christ Church's distinction rests on its being a timber one.

"On Wooden Churches" (1848) by the Rev. William Scott of Oxford was sympathetic in approach, arguing that originally wooden churches were built "in poor places, deficient in materials, quarries, and roads, … just as they are required in Canadian forests, or at Newfoundland fishing stations." In 1848 Bishop Medley asked the Ecclesiological Society for suitable designs — specifically "small, plain wooden models for wooden churches in the country"— because even though few could read architectural plans, "if they had a model, they could walk round it, and examine it, and see what it was made of and how it was made." Butterfield promised designs, but nothing came of this. By 1851, an American ecclesiologist urged wood "for our rural neighborhoods, and throughout our vast interior." Young Medley, undertaking his first church, profited from a design for a prefabricated wooden church (*see* p. 38). The *Ecclesiologist* had already cautioned North Americans against "too rigorously adhering to English types alone" except in the central states, suggesting that "citizens of Michigan or Maine might not unprofitably seek inspiration even from Sweden or Norway." They meant the ancient stave churches like the Norwegian Church of St. Mary at Hitterdal (ca 1242) — small but soaring structures, framed with vertical logs. Arguing that a wooden church "must show its real construction," discarding all that is essential to stone, Scott also turned for inspiration to timber-framed English barns, for they too "consist of nave and aisles." This provided a final ingredient in Medley's eclectic Christ Church.

Christ Church is exceptionally tall even without its tower. Though it seems to show its real construction in large timbers picked out in darker paint than the board-and-batten panels between, in fact planking is applied to the surface of the large timbers, suggesting the underlying frame while shielding it from the elements. The sense of assurance externally is matched in the well-lit interior, which echoes barn framing. Large octagonal posts carry the clerestory posts. Between these uprights, curving braces and spandrels turn the post-and-beam structure into

St. Mary the Virgin, *sanctuary*
The sanctuary's windows reflect Pre-Raphaelite influence in their pungent colouring and bold design. They depict the Crucifixion, Resurrection and Ascension in almond-shaped fields between circular pieces. Christ is lifted up in each scene, forming a cycle that Medley must have worked out in conjunction with the elevated character of the architecture. They appear to be the work of London-based Clayton & Bell, the most prolific Victorian stained-glass designers (in partnership since 1855).

Christ Church, *St. Stephen, New Brunswick; Anglican. Wood and timber frame, 1863–64; Edward S. Medley, architect*

Christ Church was a major undertaking in High Victorian style: big-boned, with tall profiles, variously inclined roofs and unfamiliar details juxtaposed with linear ornament, originally in a variety of colours. It owes some debt to large brick churches of the 1850s in cities throughout the British Isles. Barns provided suggestions for wooden churches beginning in the late 1840s. The nave of Christ Church follows much the same pattern as the famous tithe barn at Harmondsworth in England (built about four centuries earlier). Instead of naturally bent pieces from tree limbs and a hand-hewn character, as in the barn, the church is framed with straight and regular members from the sawmill with a strong and purposeful character.

an arcade. Other braces spring transversely below the clerestory windows to support the roof's tie-beams, while the rafters rise to the ridge in a unique rooftruss. The chancel aligns with the nave and a chancel arch is embellished with tracery resembling a rose window. Handsome yet almost delicate screens (like decorated windows) rise on either side of the chancel, complementing wooden tracery in the east window that follows a type used by Medley's mentor, Butterfield, whether or not supplied by him specifically for this project. The stained glass is an exciting example of Clayton & Bell's work at the end of their best period, the early 1860s.

Christ Church glows with the warmth of beautifully aged wood: pine, cherry and walnut produce a subtle polychromy. Although Medley's work ranges from wilderness vernacular through High Victorian, his churches are the most refined of all Canadian Gothic churches in wood.

Christ Church, *St. Stephen, New Brunswick. Chancel window*

Clayton & Bell's chancel window groups seven scenes from the life of Christ in separate lights of animated composition and lively colour: his birth and baptism to the left with the Last Supper above, his crucifixion and ascension to the right with the Garden of Gethsemane above these, while the resurrection fills the tallest light in the middle. The energy of the whole comes to a still centre around the image of Christ in glory in the wheel-like head of the window.

In the early communities the church evolved as the most ornate and substantial of all the buildings, ... the dominant architectural form. In the lush, rolling Prince Edward Island landscape, and in contrast to the other more utilitarian buildings, the church stands out as a fine jewel.
— H.M. Scott Smith, 1986

Cradle on the Waves

St. John's, *Belfast, Prince Edward Island; Presbyterian. Wood with timber frame, 1823–26; Robert Jones, builder*
St. John's is withdrawn, above and back from Belfast Cove, on a broad treed site nearly surrounded by its cemetery. The oldest Presbyterian church in PEI, it bears little relationship to any Scottish kirk except that it is gaunt and plain. It is a striking North American example of unembellished profiles and openings that we might call Stripped Gothic on account of its suggestive silhouettes and voids.

"MOST ORNATE" is a relative term, for most Prince Edward Island churches are small and unassuming, yet well-preserved and poignant. Their pristine geometric forms are like pieces in a Monopoly game, not unlike the little white churches of Cape Breton, Nova Scotia, described by American poet Elizabeth Bishop as "dropped into the matted hills like lost quartz arrowheads." Especially engaging in such buildings when painted white are the shifting patterns of light and shade, through the hours of the day and the months of the year.

Lord Selkirk's initial group of 800 Highland Scots settlers came to Hillsborough Bay, in the southeast corner of Queen's County overlooking the Northumberland Strait. **St. John's, Belfast**, is their kirk. In 1792, young Thomas Douglas (1771–1820) had witnessed the Highland clearances and in 1801 (as fifth Earl of Selkirk) he had observed Ireland after the 1798 Rebellion. These experiences prompted him to "restore hope to dispossessed people and strengthen Britain overseas." He arrived with his settlers in August 1803 (*see also* p. 290). "By the time he left in late September 1803 his people were well on the way to being happily established," writes John Morgan Gray. Traditionally Highlanders raised cattle, tilled small plots part-time and harvested kelp; in PEI timbering, although unfamiliar, took kelp's place. In J.M. Bumsted's view, "The settlers and the Island were ideally suited to one another" and PEI was vastly more successful than Selkirk's other schemes.

St. John's congregation was organized immediately by Dr. Angus Macaulay (schoolmaster, physician, Presbyterian lay preacher), who recruited and came with Selkirk's settlers. He erected a chapel at his own expense near his house on nearby

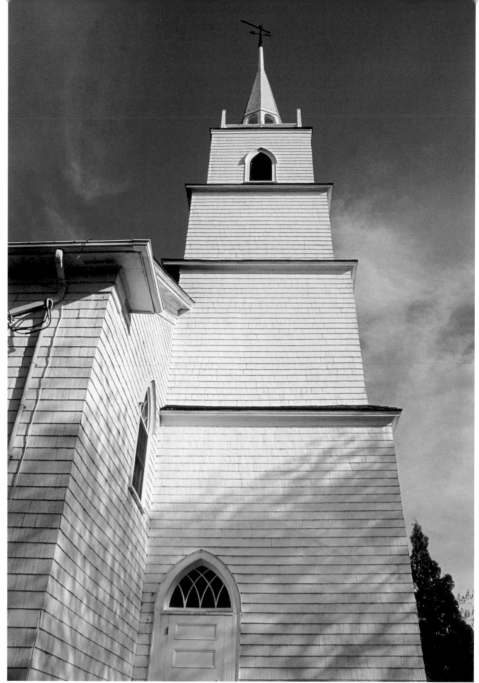

ABOVE AND RIGHT **St. John's**, *Belfast*
A view of one corner of the church shows the intersecting tracery of Gothic Revival in the windows, the returned cornice on the eave of the roof in Georgian tradition, and the hardwood shingles split by hand and fastened with iron nails hand-forged by the local blacksmith.

A view inside the tower reveals the overlapping construction of its successive stages, drawn up into position like a telescope opened for use.

BELOW **Church at Cross Roads**, *Cross Roads, Prince Edward Island; Baptist, now non-denominational. Wood, 1836; builder unknown*

In the Church at Cross Roads one can clearly make out a few square-headed windows at the gallery level that were filled in later. So important was the matter of style and the meanings attached to it, however, that the windows on the lower level were given arching Gothic Revival heads. The window sashes, though, retained their conventional rectangular windowpanes.

Point Prim, teaching school in it and preaching regularly in Gaelic from 1804, pending a minister's arrival. Being predominately Gaelic-speaking, however, Selkirk communities were largely isolated until 1823, when the energetic Church of Scotland minister John MacLennan accepted their call and "identified the need for a commodious, centrally located church."

St. John's square tower of four diminishing cubical stories looks wonderfully like a child's series of gigantic graduated blocks. Such a tower is constructed like a telescope: the frame of the second story is about as tall as the first and built at ground level, within the first stage, then drawn up into position — the lower part of its timbers overlap the upper portions of those in the first story, to which they are secured — and so the work proceeds. If the Gothic windows (with heads like pointed arches and upper sashes with intersecting tracery) are original, they are contemporary with the "Old Stone Church" in Saint John, Notre-Dame in Montréal and old St. Thomas', St. Thomas, Ontario (*see* pp. 67, 144, 204).

The Scottish-born designer, Robert Jones (1778–1859), was versatile: he spent seven years studying cabinetmaking and drafting in the London area before emigrating in 1809. A builder, merchant, farmer and militia officer, he held many public offices. Being also a joiner, surveyor of timber and mill operator may have distinguished him from others when he responded — although "a devout Baptist" — successfully to an Island *Register* advertisement in 1823; the result is his masterpiece. After St. John's was completed in 1826, Gaelic- and English-speaking parishioners held separate services as late as 1910. The tipi-like spire was added in 1860 and the interior considerably altered in the late 19th and early 20th centuries.

The **Church at Cross Roads**, east of Charlottetown, was begun by Scotch Baptists, who were influenced by movements in Scotland but were not official members of the Baptist Church. As neat as a small oatmeal loaf, this stripped-down Georgian church — such as one might see wherever Baptists, Methodists or Presbyterians were strong in the British Isles — was carried out in wood rather than brick or stone. It documents the common but little-known practice of "Gothicizing" plain churches at a later date. With numbers dwindling, the church became non-denominational and has been Cross Roads Christian Church since 1925. On the other side of the island in northeast Prince County, **Princetown Presbyterian (now Malpeque United) Church** overlooks the bay known to the Mi'kmaq as "the big water" (*makpaak*). It is an elaborate Late Victorian Carpenter Gothic church from a period characterized by developing technology and a degree of prosperity: the church is lightly framed with milled lumber rather than hand-hewn heavy-timber construction. The decorative fretwork in the bargeboards and skeletal mouldings, as

Princetown, *Malpeque, Prince Edward Island; Presbyterian, now Malpeque United. Wood, 1869–70; builder unknown*

The Charlottetown *Patriot* described Princetown Presbyterian in 1870: "The internal arrangements of the building are neat and comfortable. There is an end gallery, and the pews and pulpit are of the modern style. An arched recess behind the pulpit has a fine effect besides relieving the darkness of the windowless wall. Altogether it is a handsome church … at a cost of $1800." The interior was refurbished in 1976 and the steeple restored in 1984.

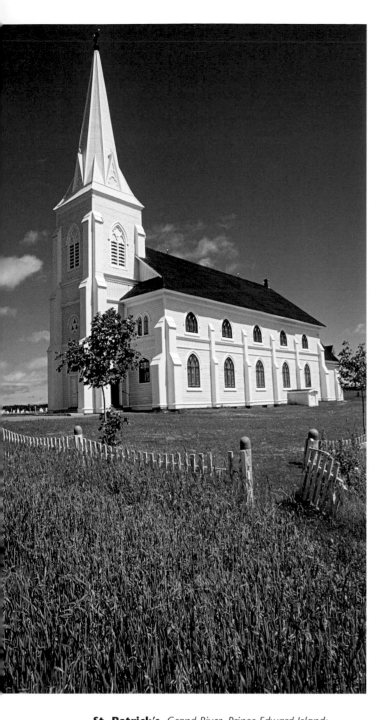

St. Patrick's, *Grand River, Prince Edward Island;
Roman Catholic. Wood, 1836–44; builder unknown*

St. Patrick's stands beside the Grand River as it flows toward the Gulf on the west side of Richmond Bay. In the middle of Prince County, the church is visible at a considerable distance in this low-lying area. William C. Harris' tower, part of his 1890 additions and alterations, almost looks as though it was subsiding, but presumably he kept this addition short for stability.

crisp as a pen-and-ink drawing, resemble fringed linens. The church could not be mistaken for a masonry building. Farther west, **St. Patrick's, Grand River**, grew from smaller churches of 1810 and 1818, and was extensively renovated in 1890 by William Critchlow Harris (1854–1913). Harris enlarged it, accommodating a U-shaped gallery — the interior (completed in 1844) he left unchanged — and arching the heads of the divided windows. He added stout angle buttresses at the corners, with slender versions between, and a buttressed tower of three stories in the west end. Most of these features originate in stone construction and are considered "secondary forms" when executed in wood, a fact clearly indicated by the agreeable two-tone scheme of ochre paint with white trim.

All Souls' Chapel, Charlottetown, attached to the north wall of St. Peter's (Anglican) Cathedral, is described by Robert C. Tuck in his book *Gothic Dreams* as "numinous and mysterious." It is also rarefied, otherworldly and intensely personal, as befits "an outpost of the Tractarian Movement." William Harris and his older brother, portraitist Robert Harris (1849–1919), cooperated on this memorial to George Hodgson, the first incumbent of the church their family helped found. The focus in this place of shades is a circle of diffused luminosity: Robert's painting of the Ascension of Christ shows Christ enthroned on clouds, "hands outstretched and palms turned downward in an act of consecration over the altar and communicants." We view this insubstantial vision through the weighty chancel arch carried on massive groups of enriched columns (surely a deliberate contrast). Below the painting, statues of Christ and the Apostles fill niches in the sanctuary wall. Beneath those, the dark walnut altar has three smaller roundels (to complement the circular altarpiece) on communion themes: Christ with communicants, the Crucifixion and the Supper at Emmaus. Robert's small roundels are behind glass, so they appear now to echo St. Paul's epistle: "At present we see only puzzling reflections in a mirror, but one day we shall see face to face." The themes of his murals include Christ's leave-taking, the stoning of St. Stephen, and early Fathers of the Church (some of the features memorialize Harris family members). Encaustic tiles in the geometric and floral patterns of the Esthetic Movement form a unifying band around the upper walls. Harris' churches "were to be 'thin places,' where the veil between this world and the next seems to be penetrable," writes Tuck. It is a concept particularly suitable to the brothers' collaboration in this shrine.

Just south of Malpeque on the Gulf side of the Island is **St. Mary's, Indian River**. The Mi'kmaq called PEI *Abegweit* ("cradle on the waves"), apparently likening it to a papoose's cradleboard, caressed by the sea. St. Mary's Church is like a cradleboard too, nurturing the spirit. It rises on a gently sloping grassy plain within view of the bay and the river, which flows through the kind of choice land that inspired the Island's unofficial motto, "Garden of the Gulf." It is wooden and painted white, except when windblown reddish-brown dust lends it a pink cast, though originally it was painted in "masses of dark colour," according to Tuck. Black trim and red roofs make the various parts legible. Because St. Mary's is shingle-clad — a favourite regional treatment — flat walls turn corners and transform into octagonal or cylindrical portions (capped by gables or cones) with apparent ease. This strongly textured skin hints at the spaces within. The rural church is very visible, owing to its isolation as much as its sheer size, elephantine in the best sense: it is a gentle presence and has a beauty that is *sui generis.*

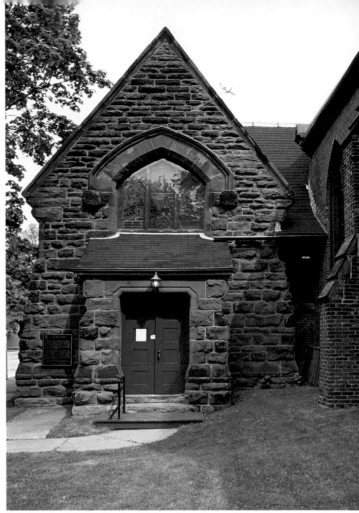

All Souls' Chapel, *Charlottetown, Prince Edward Island; Anglican. Stone, 1888–89; William Critchlow Harris, architect and Robert Critchlow Harris, artist*

The chapel is built of red rock-faced sandstone and seems very much of the earth, particularly by comparison with the smooth red-brick walls of St. Peter's Cathedral to which it is attached. Its form almost suggests a mausoleum, so petite is the building, so small are the windows, so dark is the interior.

The interior is extensively decorated with architectural sculpture, stained glass, a painted and carved altarpiece and murals. The ensemble is a complete work of art (a goal of High Victorian architecture) in the service of the High Church. Here daily mass and eucharistic vestments were introduced at St. Peter's.

Although culturally the most homogeneous province of Canada, the Island now has the largest percentage of Catholics among the Atlantic provinces. Acadians have been strengthened by a steady influx of Roman Catholic immigrants from southern Ireland and the Highlands of Scotland who settled Indian River in the 1790s. In August 1896, as the priest was saying his rosary nearby on his verandah, the previous church (1843) was struck by lightning and burned to the ground. Monsignor D.J. Gillis made plans for a new church: "Yes, yes, build it like Kinkora, only bigger and better," he told William Harris (the architect of St. Malachy's, Kinkora, PEI, 1899). Thus, St. Mary's became the largest wood church in the province.

Harris' churches, "although of timber frame construction, seem to have been

St. Mary's, *Indian River, Prince Edward Island; Roman Catholic. Wood, 1900–1902; William Critchlow Harris, architect*

Viewed from the southeast, St. Mary's reveals much about the interior. The church is planned on a Latin cross with a transept on either side of the nave housing a side altar. (The tall semi-polygonal apse at the north end is not visible in this view.) In addition to the doors at the south end there is another entry (with a porch) in the bell tower to the left. The semi-octagonal tower to the right is a baptistery.

The bell tower at the southwest corner houses stairs to the gallery and the belfry. It rises in four bands, each defined by a dark belt, a tapering profile and a change in shingle pattern: a drum houses the west porch and several windows, scaled to the main front; then a shorter stage whose small windows light the stairs; a tall bell-story; and an ornamented spool-like circlet that breaks out into a group of sculpture niches with figures of the Twelve Apostles crowned by gablets, followed by a tall conical spire.

designed with stone in mind," including their ceilings "reminiscent of French Gothic vaulting," says Tuck. After 1894, he adds, they also "followed French precedents in respect to the unity of nave and chancel." The chancel is apsidal, not rectangular, extends the same width and height as the nave and is ceiled with a half-dome that cups the space and rises to meet the nave ceiling, an uncomplicated scheme that is flexible liturgically. There is an especially strong family resemblance among a dozen designs for churches with asymmetrical two-towered fronts that Harris prepared between about 1898 and 1911. Only half were built — for Roman Catholics, Presbyterians, Methodists and Anglicans — but Harris' formula tended to smooth out denominational differences. St. John's (Anglican) in North Sydney, Nova Scotia, was almost a mirror image of St. Mary's. Harris adapted the plans and interiors, however, to each congregation's budget and liturgical needs.

Harris' energetic wood-vaulted interiors are uniquely satisfying, whatever the denomination, and dynamic even in a straightforward axial view. Ribs spring from clustered columns and individual *colonnettes*, dividing the ceiling into a series of cells that seem to rotate and vibrate overhead. St. Mary's interior is particularly lofty and light-filled, the centre axis focused on the high altar, with side altars in the transepts approached almost axially along the aisles. The choir and organ are in a rear gallery. The tradition of ribbed and groined vaulting originates in stone (as in Scott's Cathedral of St. John the Baptist, St. John's; *see* p.84). The *Ecclesiologist* had

dismissed plaster-on-lath ceilings in imitation of stone vaulting as sham, insisting that "in GOD's house everything must be *real*." Almost certainly it would have condemned ribbed vaults of wood — billowing like a spinnaker here in the nave, with uplifting effect — but Harris' elaborate ceilings, crafted meticulously by boat builders, are more than a delightful illusion.

The architect not only created "music of the eye" through these lush wooden ceilings, but also redoubled his efforts to improve the quality of sound. Acoustics may be a physical science, but it requires empirical experiment. Though Harris' ceilings resemble inert stone vaults visually, they are analogous to shaped wooden instruments of the violin family — he was "an enthusiastic fiddler" himself — that resonate, amplifying and reflecting sound. In 1896 Harris explained his avoidance of "abrupt square surfaces at right angles" and other strategies against echoes at St. Paul's Anglican Church, Charlottetown. Instead, he cultivated curving surfaces that reflect and "add to the intensity and clearness of either speech or music." He thought "the resonant qualities" of smooth spruce boards valuable and designed "a series of large sounding panel boards, similar to the body of a violin, having a face of very thin spruce, a sounding air space, and a back of very thin maple boards" to give "marked resonance to the sounds produced in the chancel." The "unnerving" result is "almost too good," reported the Charlottetown *Examiner* in 1896. St. Mary's acoustic qualities are equally outstanding.

St. Mary's, *interior*
The interior shows a characteristic range of form and colour for a Harris church from the turn of the century. The chapels are in rib-vaulted apsidal recesses. They are like diminutive versions of this big-boned, gabled and pinnacled church itself. Their bold simplicity extends to the massive altar-enclosure (where a railing might normally suffice). The aisles give access to seats on the margins of the nave but are essentially passages, vaulted like the nave, to the transepts and chapels.

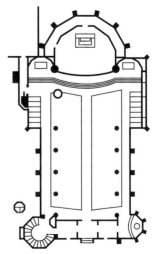

QUÉBEC

Introduction

Counter-Reformation to Vatican II

Architecture is the most complete and most complex of all the arts, and hence the most representative of the mind of a race and the civilization of a period.... Redeemed humanity expresses itself in the Christian arts. First of these ranks religious architecture, with the material temple as its primary object. The facts show that ... the Christian arts have produced supremely human works of art.

— Dom Paul Bellot, 1933

PREVIOUS PAGE **Saint-François-de-Sales**, *Neuville, Québec; Roman Catholic. Stone, 1761–73; nave rebuilt 1854; school of Baillairgé*

The so-called Solomonic columns of Neuville's baldachin, part of the oldest and most important sculptural composition in Canada, frame the High Altar (*see* p. 111). This very architectural altar, by François Baillairgé, dates from 1800. In its centre is the tabernacle to hold the consecrated Host. The side altars, also by François Baillairgé, date from 1802.

Québec during the French Régime

New France was initially relatively small, but at its height it was a huge territory stretching from the Atlantic Ocean to the Gulf of Mexico. The province of Québec is three times the size of France. Four-fifths is Precambrian Shield, whose lakes, rivers, forests and mines have created its wealth. Québec's cultural traditions and sophisticated creativity — not to mention political factors — have given *la belle province* a crucial place in modern Canada. Its churches reflect New France's traditional roots in France, British influences after 1763, 19th-century urban developments and 20th-century experimental modernism.

Native peoples settled Québec about 10,000 years ago, while European contacts go back just over half a millennium to Norse exploration and slightly later fishing on the Grand Banks. Jacques Cartier landed on the Gaspé coast in 1534; he returned the next year to explore the St. Lawrence as far as Hochelaga (Montréal).

In 1608 Samuel de Champlain established a settlement, at Québec. He soon saw the strategic advantage of missionaries who would spread "the peace-loving Gospel" through the wilderness. The Récollets arrived first (1615), followed by the Jesuits (1625) and soon thereafter by two women's groups, the Augustines de la miséricorde de Jésus and the Ursulines, led by Marie de l'Incarnation; both came in 1639. The "peace-loving Gospel" was not very peaceful as the politics of colonization impacted upon native groups. Dutch exploration in the Hudson Valley began

LEFT **"Building a new chapel"**
This modern re-creation of a sketch — "On bâtit la première chapelle," ca 1686, by Claude Chauchetière (1645–1709) — puts the priest and the master builder, with a carpenter using a square, in the foreground. The frame of a church hardly more than the size of a modest house has been erected, with the posts, main beams, rafters and ridge in place. The spaces between the uprights will be filled in the Québec area with vertical timbers mortised; in the Trois Rivières area with horizontals, and in the Montréal area with logs. No such wooden church survives in Québec.

ABOVE **Processional chapel**, *Île d'Orléans, Québec*
Roadside shrines, processional chapels and Calvaries were common in the earliest settled parts of Québec, and many still survive in such areas as Île d'Orléans and the Chemin du Roy. In the background is the St. Lawrence River and Mont-Sainte-Anne.

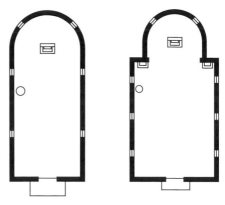

The Maillou plan   The Récollet plan

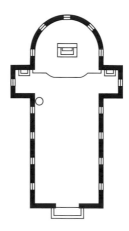

The Jesuit plan

Québec church plans

Three commonly used church designs differed
primarily in the relationship between the nave and
the chancel. The Maillou plan (top left) was the
simplest, making no physical distinction between
nave and chancel. The Récollet plan (top right) defined
the chancel by narrowing it. The Jesuit plan (bottom)
made the nave and chancel the same width, but
amplified the liturgical centre by using a Latin cross
plan with transepts, allowing for larger side altars.

Saint-Charles-Borromée, Charlesbourg, Québec; Roman Catholic. Stucco on stone, 1828–30; Thomas Baillairgé, architect

English influence is apparent in the church's west
facade — punctured by an English Palladian window
and an oval window above — while the side elevations
are more typically Québécois. The church is located in
the centre of the Trait-Carrée, an experimental 17th-
century urban layout with a square central tract and
radiating roads, which is still visible in Charlesbourg.

in 1609 and settlement in 1624. Their alliance with the Iroquois, who had withdrawn to the Finger Lakes region in western New York, rivalled the French alliance
with the Huron. New England settlement began in the Massachusetts Bay colony in
1620. For half a century three European nations competed in converting the native
people to their form of Christianity and, through them, to control colonization,
trade and transportation. Guns and baptism went hand in hand.

None of the earliest wooden churches built in Québec survives. By the late 17th
century stone churches were being built (*see* pp. 110–19), using an architectural
vocabulary drawn from France but adapted to frontier needs and materials. Three
main plans came into use in these uniformly Roman Catholic churches: Récollet,
Jesuit and Maillou. Pulpits were pulled forward into the nave of the church, often
raised to the gallery level; altars, with the priest facing away from the congregation,
were provided for the Mass; communion rails created space for the faithful to
receive the sacrament. Piety was fostered through confession, prayer, Stations of the
Cross and statuary, often depicting the suffering Jesus and his sorrowing mother.

In 1658 François de Laval (1623–1708) was consecrated bishop of Petra in Jordan

because there was no diocese of Québec yet. He arrived in New France in 1659 and was named bishop of Québec in 1674. He refused to consecrate churches not built of stone. Some important *ancien régime* furnishings and art exist from the late 17th century and some churches from the early 18th century (*see* pp. 110, 124–25). Their importance is out of all proportion to their numbers in demonstrating the forceful leadership of parish priests and religious in orders, as well as colonists' fidelity and devotion to their faith.

British Colonialism

The British gained New Netherlands after defeating the Dutch in the Second Anglo-Dutch War (1664). The French and British then clashed as the speedily growing English colonies to the south and the newly formed Hudson's Bay Company (1670) to the north hemmed in New France. Peace of a sort came in 1713 with the Treaty of Utrecht, but the Seven Years' War (1756–63) was decisive in determining the future of North America. The British under General James Wolfe defeated the

"View of the Place d'Armes, Québec," *Adolphus Bourne, 1832*
Place d'Armes, though now treed, still retains the same form and a similar relationship to the surrounding buildings as seen here, especially the Cathedral of the Holy Trinity. Its distinctive rear facade with four monumental Ionic pilasters appears prominently in Bourne's view. The comparative height and prominence of its steeple and the steeple of the Basilique-cathédrale was clearly of interest to Bourne.

St. Michael's and St. Anthony's, *Montréal, Québec;
Roman Catholic. Brick with concrete shell, 1914–15;
Aristide Beaugrand-Champagne, architect*

Beaugrand-Champagne's splendid structure was
one of Canada's earliest churches to be built in
concrete, a form of construction especially suited
to Byzantine Revival style. Its dome spans 75 feet,
creating an arresting interior that has much the same
character as Byzantine churches of 1,500 years earlier.

Marquis de Montcalm on Québec's Plains of Abraham in 1759 and Montréal
surrendered in 1760. The Treaty of Paris (1763) granted Britain New France,
including Québec, Cape Breton, the Great Lakes Basin and the east bank of the
Mississippi River. Freedom of worship was guaranteed and the French language
continued to be used.

After the Conquest, church buildings may show both British and American
influences — whether stylistically, aesthetically or denominationally — but French
and Roman Catholic influences remained dominant (*see* pp. 124–35). The armed
struggle's end brought no dramatic break with Québec's French Catholic past, nor
did the influx of a substantial number of United Empire Loyalists following the
Declaration of Independence in 1776 and Britain's loss of the American colonies in
1783. New France's religious life was as strong and vibrant as it had been before
the war, stronger, perhaps, because religion became a cohesive factor in Lower
Canada's cultural and social makeup, resulting in vigorous campaigns of building
and rebuilding.

Still, English, Scots and American Loyalist influences — strongest in the
Eastern Townships and in the main cities — brought new architectural influences
and new denominational organizations. French Catholic buildings were influenced, too, as in the Palladian window in the main facade of Saint-Charles-
Borromée in Charlesbourg (*see* pp. 127, 129). The British ruling classes worshipped in their own manner. In the city of Québec an Anglican cathedral (1799-
1804) and a Presbyterian church (1809-10) both visually rival Notre-Dame (*see* pp.
120–23, 127–28, 132–35). The Cathedral of the Holy Trinity, because of its location,
style and a steeple marginally higher than that of Notre-Dame, symbolizes the
English community's preeminence. Two blocks away, the secondary importance
of the Scottish Presbyterians is marked by a less generous site, a less prominent
building and a lower — but still Gibbsian — steeple.

Montréal, the country's fur-trading centre, gradually became the centre of
Québec society and religion; by the 1820s its population outnumbered Québec
City. The 19th and early 20th centuries saw the Gothic Revival style adopted in
many Montréal churches, both Catholic and Protestant, though it was less commonly used among Catholic churches in other parts of the province.

The Rebellion of 1837, centred in the Richelieu Valley, was partly a result of
shifting demographics and increased tensions between the French-speaking
majority and the rapidly growing English-speaking minority. A parallel rebellion
in Upper Canada was less vigorous, but both underscored the need to give more
power to the locally elected representatives, an important step toward responsible government. The British government in London took the opportunity to combine Upper and Lower Canada into one colony in 1841.

A second wave of immigration from Europe, particularly of Irish Catholics,
began in the 19th century. From 1815 on, and especially after the Famine of the late
1840s, their numbers grew astonishingly. In rural areas, many Irish Catholics were
assimilated into French Catholic communities, though in large cities English-
speaking Irish Catholics retained a strong sense of identity (*see* pp. 150–51). In 1867
the British North America Act gave the country new self-confidence. This was
marked by a new architectural ambition, prompting the education of Canadian
architects in the United Kingdom and at the École des Beaux-Arts in Paris.

Confederation to the Present

Sporadic immigration continued to transform Québec's religious and social makeup after Confederation. Today French-speaking Catholics from Haiti and Vietnam and Spanish-speaking Catholics from Latin America form important urban communities. Québec has shifted from a rural to an urban industrial society, based in Montréal. The influence, authority and power of the Catholic Church was eroded by the social, political and intellectual changes of the 1960s' Quiet Revolution, which also led to a separatist movement that looked for an end to Canada's "colonial" control over Québec. The most significant developments followed Paul-Émile Borduas' cultural manifesto "Refus global" (1948), which called for an end to social, political and religious authoritarianism: "We are a small and humble people clutching the skirts of priests who've become sole guardians of faith, knowledge, truth and our national heritage," wrote Borduas. The call was heeded in a variety of ways.

Though traditional religious convictions eroded, openness to new architectural ideas surged ahead, beginning in the 1910s (*see* pp. 158–71, 174–75).

After fledgling experimental steps in the 1920s under the leadership of Ernest Cormier and in the 1930s under Dom Paul Bellot (*see* pp. 159–63, 168–70), there was a flood of imaginative work in the 1950s and 60s embracing modernist ideals, experimentation with new materials and methods of construction, and radical liturgical rethinking. These developments coincided with the theological, liturgical and organizational changes before and during the Second Vatican Council (1962–65). While the vast majority of churches in Québec are still Roman Catholic, there is startling variety in church buildings in the past half-century, especially in rural areas. But then, the first surge of exciting churches on Île d'Orléans and along the Chemin du Roy was also spawned in rural areas more than 200 years ago.

Cathédrale Saint-Jean-Baptiste, *Nicolet, Québec; Roman Catholic. Concrete, 1961–62; Gérard Malouin, architect*
   Though more startling than most, this cathedral is typical of the exciting surge of modern churches utilizing recent technological developments, in this case thin-shell concrete in intersecting parabolic forms, allowing large clear spans. "Frightening in its modernity," says one Québec guidebook. The chancel window (*see also* pp. 163–66) is by Éric de Therry, a monk at Taizé, France.

Now and then we perceived churches on both sides of the river, the steeples of which were generally on that side of the church which looked toward the river, because they are not obliged here to put the steeples on the west end of the churches .... Each church, it is true, has a little village near it; but that consists chiefly of the parsonage, a school for the boys and girls of the place, and of the houses of the tradesmen, but rarely of farmhouses.

— Peter Kalm, 1749

L'ancien régime

Saint-François-de-Sales, *Neuville, Québec; Roman Catholic. Stone, 1761–73; nave rebuilt 1854; school of Baillairgé*

This 1695 baldachin is one of the treasures of Québec's *ancien régime*. It was modelled on one in a Paris church, Val-de-Grâce, but the glorious quality of the canopy's design and carving stands on its own merits.

TWO GROUPS OF CHURCHES, furnishings and art provide direct insight into the ethos of the *ancien régime* and the enthusiasms of the religious authorities. Île d'Orléans and the Chemin du Roy — the one an island in the St. Lawrence a few miles northeast of Québec City and the other the main road southwest from Québec to Montréal — have retained a rural ambience that conveys something of the character of pre-Conquest Québec. Île d'Orléans has long been hailed for its traditional farms, sugar bushes, apple orchards and vineyards. There are six parishes on the island, each with a small village: Sainte-Pétronille in the western, most developed part of the island; Saint-François in the eastern, most rural area; Saint-Pierre and Sainte-Famille, overlooking Sainte-Anne-de-Beaupré from the north shore; and Saint-Laurent and Saint-Jean, overlooking the main shipping channel to the south. Four of the six churches are pre-Conquest.

Saint-Pierre is Canada's oldest surviving parish church. Begun about 1715 and constructed in earnest from 1717, it was finished by 1719, with the steeple added in 1720. The interior and furnishings were completed later. Now a museum, it speaks compellingly to New France's piety and attachment to the Church. The fieldstone building is more than twice as large as the wooden church it replaced (1673–76). Bishop Laval insisted on more permanent stone structures to serve the needs of the population and might withhold funds provided by Louis XIV for building parish churches or refuse to consecrate a church not to his liking.

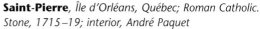

Saint-Pierre, *Île d'Orléans, Québec; Roman Catholic. Stone, 1715–19; interior, André Paquet*

The high west wall of Saint-Pierre is extremely plain in its geometry, with a simple pair of doors and fanlight set into a round-arched opening, and with a matching oculus, or bull's-eye, of the same width directly above. It is almost reductionist in its simplicity.

On the side (above right), one gets a better impression of a typical Jesuit-plan church, with its transepts rising to the same height as the nave, under steeply pitched roofs. The regularly placed windows with round heads, the semicircular apse and the tall, gently curved octagonal spire above the square *clocher* complete the archetypal French regime church.

Saint-Pierre's geometry is breathtakingly simple. The gable is an equilateral triangle, and the fieldstone facade is punctured only twice. The *clocher*, or belfry, a replacement of 1834, is a wooden cube pierced by openings recalling the doorway. The tower supports an open octagon of slender columns carrying a candle-snuffer spire. A pair of windows in the nave is matched by a pair in the transept, and a single window in the apse. Most of the exterior is original: the roof was damaged by British soldiers in 1763 and the apse, rather than the nave, was extended in 1817–18.

The Latin-cross Jesuit plan, with a deep apse as wide as the nave, creates a light and gracious space. The impression of spaciousness is enhanced by the curved rail embracing both transepts and their side altars, so the combined areas — chapels, choir, sanctuary and area in front of the railing — amount to about half the church's length. A semi-elliptical vault over the nave and choir intersects a similar vault over the transepts on a gently curving line of intersection. When one is not under the low-hanging balcony, the whole space seems an uncluttered fluid entity.

The strikingly rich but restrained interior is the work of André Paquet (1799–1860), a skilled 19th-century artisan. He was dependent on plans of the renowned Baillairgé family of sculptors and architects, François (1759–1830) and his son Thomas (1791–1859); Paquet had been apprenticed to Thomas. In 1830,

Saint-Pierre, *interior*

Looking back to the entrance, the plain walnut pews on a mustard-coloured floor contrast with the white, cream and gilt interior; the oval vaulted ceiling rises from a Classical cornice. The pulpit is pulled into the middle of the congregation, well above the floor. A finely detailed, curving altar-rail defines the sacred space clearly and makes generous allowance for the liturgy. The vertical pipe in the middle is a heater.

André Paquet carried out the Neoclassical interior. He organized the sanctuary rhythmically with paired Corinthian pilasters supporting an ornate architrave, and made the apse continuous with the transepts' eastern wall. The altar by Pierre Émond is in *tombeau* form and stands on its own raised platform, surrounded by clerics' seats.

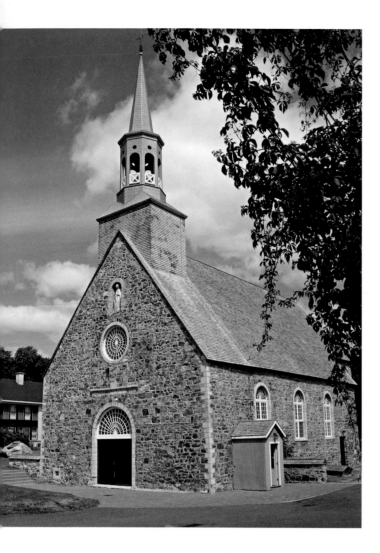

Saint-François-de-Sales, *Île d'Orléans, Québec;
Roman Catholic. Stone, 1734–36; rebuilt 1992, Yves
Gagnon and Jean G. Grondin, architects*

Saint-François-de-Sales has the most rural setting of
the Île d'Orléans churches, at a corner of the road that
circles the island. At first sight it seems similar to Saint-
Pierre, but it adopts a Récollet plan (without transepts)
and its west wall is more complex, with doors and fanlight, an oculus and a niche with a saint's statue.

before undertaking Saint-Pierre's ambitious scheme, Paquet installed the elaborate
high altar and tabernacle that Pierre Émond had carved in 1795 in the *ancien régime's*
Baroque style, as well as Émond's two plainer side altars of 1800, all with their tabernacles. All are in the classic 18th-century French *tombeau* form, an inverted S-curve,
gilt on white, with the central altar displaying the papal tiara and St. Peter's keys.

Paquet's Neoclassical work of 1832–35 and 1842–48, when the all-important
retable (the decorative work behind and above the altar) was installed, frames
Émond's altar with a kind of triumphal arch that forms a backdrop for the altar and
its tabernacle. Gilded clouds of glory cap the central arch, inscribed with the tetra-
grammaton (four Hebrew letters, YHWH or *Yahweh*), representing God, within a
triangle that symbolizes the Trinity. The nave lacks the chancel's pilasters and has
simpler classically detailed mouldings than those over the altars, but ribs in the
vault create similar bays. The vault has a circular sunburst surrounded by stars over
the crossing and fleur-de-lis-like motifs elsewhere. The paint scheme is cream,
ochre and gold, while details are highlighted in pale blue.

The replacement pulpit (1872), whose steps rise up the transept wall with open
risers as if free-floating, contributes to the church's airiness. Its raised panels mimic
the shape of the windows; the front panel represents the Ten Commandments with
Roman numerals I to X. Facing the pulpit is the *banc d'œuvre* (churchwarden's seat),
part of Paquet's final improvements. Its Ionic pilasters are surmounted by another
segmental pediment, repeating the central motif of the retable. The congregation
had panelled walnut pews arranged in three blocks. Centred above the pews, a
heater hangs dramatically between the ceiling and the worshippers.

When early settlers scrabbled a living out of the soil they must have been struck
by the contrast between daily life and life associated with the church, with God. The
promise of a life beyond this life was mirrored in the church's liturgy.

Saint-François-de-Sales, like Saint-Pierre, has a high gabled west elevation. The
end wall has three openings under an octagonal *clocher* and spire on a square base.
The church's Récollet plan has a narrower chancel than nave. A speeding car hit the
church in 1988, setting it alight. The fire destroyed the roof and André Paquet's early-
19th-century interior. The original walls survived and the interior has been rebuilt in
an almost Scandinavian style, with plain, naturally finished floors, vault, pews and
woodwork, showing the influence of liturgical reform following Vatican II.

Saint-Jean, whose parishioners were involved in fishing, shipbuilding and
piloting, is squeezed between the river and the road, overlooking a large cemetery.
The main facade differs markedly from those of Saint-François and Saint-Pierre. It
appears more Baroque, due to an 1852 addition, modelled on Thomas Baillairgé's
renovation of Cathédrale Notre-Dame de Québec (*see* pp. 132–35). Its Récollet plan
features a five-window nave and narrower apse, with a sacristy and presbytery
behind. The west elevation's central bay with two flanking recessed bays focuses on
a central Palladian window, with circular windows in the side bays and a central
elliptical window in the upper gable. The *clocher* has a square base and three-stage
octagonal tower with matching spire.

The interior is typical of the *ancien régime* — bright, open and chaste. A projecting hexagonal sounding board crowned by consoles carrying an urn overshadows
the projecting pulpit on the left, matched on the right by a projecting square canopy

Saint-Jean, *Île d'Orléans, Québec; Roman Catholic. Stone, 1734; addition, 1852, Louis-Thomas Berlinguet, architect*

Saint-Jean's chancel is more elaborate, though more pinched, than Saint-Pierre's, largely because this is a Récollet plan with a narrower apse. It has similar pilasters, but Saint-Pierre's half-columns are replaced with full columns beside the altar, the arch is more nearly a triumphal arch, and the altar is more strongly architectural. The crowned pulpit and the churchwarden's seat balance each other and frame the altar.

Of the six Île d'Orléans churches, Saint-Jean, on the island's south shore, has the closest connection with the river (just visible in the background) that sustains the town.

Sainte-Famille, *Île d'Orléans, Québec; Roman Catholic. Stone, 1743–47; interior, 1812–25, Thomas Baillairgé and Louis-Basile David*

Sainte-Famille, with Sainte-Anne-de-Bellevue in the background across the St. Lawrence, has a Latin-cross Jesuit plan with transepts. As the name suggests, it is dedicated to the Holy Family, with the infant Jesus in the top position high in the gable, Mary and Joseph in the next positions, flanking the central window, and Joachim and Anna, Mary's parents, beside the main door. The church's size, the elaboration of the facade and the more regular masonry detailing suggest this parish was wealthier than that of Saint-Pierre, only a few miles away, a generation earlier.

crowning the churchwarden's seat, the only surviving instance of this form. These twin elements frame the liturgical focus, the high altar and the two side altars, executed by David Ouellet in 1876; the altarpieces behind are the work either of Jean Baillairgé in 1773 or of Louis-Basile David in 1810–13. The organ loft occupies the upper of two galleries, both with fine carved detail over a Classical cornice. The lower balcony passes beyond the first window in the nave, while the upper one stops short of the window.

The main elevation of **Sainte-Famille** is unusually broad. Its two boldly projecting corner towers (with two spires added in 1807) are punctured by oculi and by side entrances in the inner sidewalls. Above the wide main door, capped by a fanlight, is another round-headed window, which lights the balcony. Within the facade are five niches, the topmost of which holds the central figure, the infant Jesus with hand raised in blessing, holding a book. The transepts have balconies above the side altars, the north balcony giving access to the projecting pulpit with its hexagonal sounding board finished with an angel sounding a trumpet. The interior is coral, cream and white, picked out extensively with gilt.

The Chemin du Roy, the King's Highway, joins Québec and Montréal along the north shore by what was then the oldest (1660–1737) and longest (about 160 miles) major road north of the Rio Grande. Its villages are among Québec's earliest; when Acadians were deported in 1755 a number of families settled in the Portneuf area. **Chapelle Sainte-Anne, Neuville** (mid-18th century), is a typical processional chapel. Such chapels are especially associated with Corpus Christi celebrations when parishioners stopped at them while making their way to church. Like all processional chapels, Sainte-Anne's looks like a miniature church. Nearby is the parish church **Saint-François-de-Sales, Neuville**. While the church is early (1761 onward), its much earlier baldachin of 1695 (*see* p. 111), brought from Québec's Episcopal palace, is one of Québec's most remarkable treasures. It was exchanged "for wheat

ABOVE **Sainte-Famille**, *sculpture*
A flamboyant trumpeting angel stands atop the pulpit's hexagonal sounding board. Behind, the rich cornice with its serpentine vegetal band separates the sidewalls — part of a Corinthian pilaster can be seen flanking the pulpit — and the patterned vaulted ceiling.

Chapelle Sainte-Anne, *Neuville, Québec; Roman Catholic. Stone, mid-18th century; builder unknown*
Sainte-Anne's roughly plastered stone construction, round-headed openings and *clocher* mirror in miniature the typical forms and materials of parish churches, though in several respects — the niche in the facade and the flat rear wall — it differs from most other processional chapels.

Saint-François-de-Sales, *Neuville, Québec; Roman Catholic. Stone, 1761–73; nave rebuilt 1854; school of Baillairgé*

The attractive 19th-century nave of this parish church hides genuine treasures inside: a 1695 baldachin (*see* p. 111) and 1802 side altars by François Baillairgé. The choir is from 1761, the time of the Conquest. The rebuilt nave comprises three vaulted spaces carried on tall columns through its full height.

BELOW **Sainte-Famille**, *Cap Santé, Québec; Roman Catholic. Stone, 1754–58 and 1763–67; interior, 1773–1809; architect unknown*

Prominently situated on Cap Santé, overlooking the St. Lawrence River, Sainte-Famille's traditional Récollet plan has, for the first time, transepts added. The Levasseurs provided three sculptures of the Holy Family for its west facade, and Louis-Amable Quévillon undertook the retable, ca 1803.

for the poor people of the town [Québec] who were suffering from a food shortage," writes Madeleine Gobeil-Trudeau. This sole surviving example of a carved wood baldachin was inspired by the Église Val-de-Grâce in Paris (1666): its six Solomonic columns with rope-like shafts support a circular entablature and a crown topped with a cross.

On a point projecting into the St. Lawrence River, **Sainte-Famille, Cap Santé**, has an overpowering high-peaked west front, flanked by slightly projecting square towers. Its facade focuses on three round-headed niches that hold sculptures (ca 1775) by the Levasseur family of sculptors (*see* p. 124). Inside, a Neoclassical retable fills the width of the choir and projects upward into the vault. But of the Chemin du Roy churches, none takes advantage of its site as well as **Saint-Joseph, Deschambault**, on Cap Lauzon. Thomas Baillairgé drew plans for a new church in 1833 in his signature Neoclassical style; its execution utilizes a Jesuit plan, but with transepts that are half octagons and an apse that is part circular and part square. The double row of nave windows is similar to the design of the Cathedral of the Holy Trinity in Québec City.

Saint-Joseph, *Deschambault, Québec; Roman Catholic. Stone, 1835–38; Thomas Baillairgé, architect; interior, 1841–49, André Paquet*

This church's rather ornate interior focuses on a statue of Saint Joseph incorporated in the retable. The nave and aisles are separated by a strong arcade that is repeated more grandly at the gallery level; the various parts are held together by a continuous cornice that wraps around the apse.

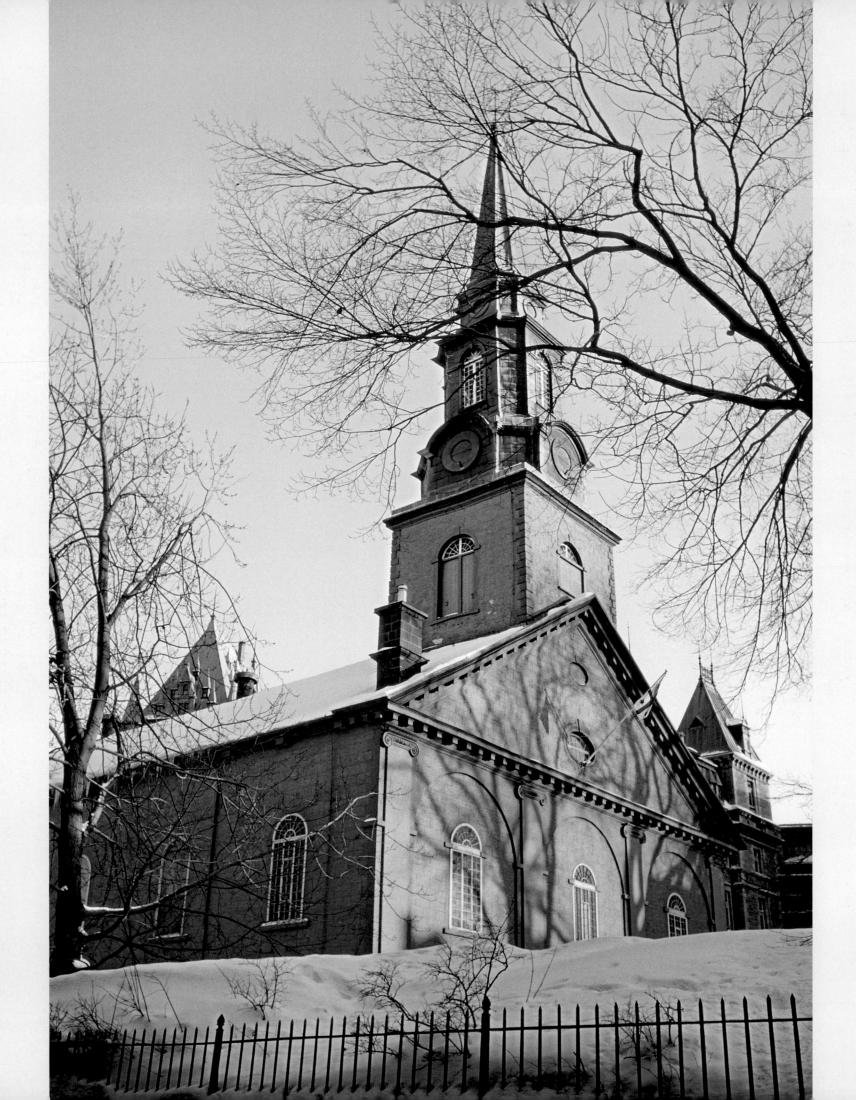

The Place d'Armes, or Grand Parade, in front of the Château, though not extensive, is hand-some, and may be termed the court end of the town, surrounded by the most distinguished edifices in the capital, and having in its centre an enclosed space, confined by chains and wickets, and laid out into walks. The Episcopal Church is neat and commodious, having extensive galleries on the front and sides. It is furnished with a powerful organ of sweet and melodious tone. It is erected on the west corner of the Place d'Armes.

— *Joseph Bouchette, 1832*

Anglicanism Triumphant

Cathedral of the Holy Trinity, *Québec City, Québec; Anglican. Stone, 1799–1804; William Hall and William Robe, architects*

In the centre of Québec City, with the Chateau Frontenac in the background, Holy Trinity's blocky silhouette sits within an English-style cathedral precinct, or close, behind a low stone wall with an iron railing. The scale of the pilasters is very grand, and the details still sharp after some 200 years, rescuing the rear facade facing Place d'Armes and the main facade on a side street from being bland (*see* p. 107).

ANGLICAN CHURCH BUILDING had lain dormant for nearly four decades when, after using the Récollet and Jesuit chapels since 1763, they erected the **Cathedral Church of the Holy Trinity** in Québec City, the first Anglican cathedral outside Britain. When the Récollet monastery burned in 1796, its beautiful central site passed to the Church of England. Bishop Jacob Mountain sought funds from the British government to build the cathedral; estimated to cost £5,000 in 1799, it had cost about £18,000 when consecrated in 1804. It was like nothing in the province: an astonishing church with a simple rectangular plan, a facade with colossal pilasters and broad pediment, a blind arcade on both ends and a bell tower combining height with complexity.

Holy Trinity emulated James Gibbs' St. Martin-in-the-Fields (1722–26) in London. Gibbs had innovatively combined a Roman temple exterior, a high steeple and a Baroque interior; the steeple's "decorum" was especially admired and imitated. He illustrated St. Martin's lavishly in his *Book of Architecture* (*see* p. 390). Captains William Hall of the Royal Artillery and William Robe (1765–1820) of the Royal Engineers, together responsible for Holy Trinity, had some training in design, since military engineers functioned as architects and civil engineers. Robe acknowledged his dependence on St. Martin's, but points out that "materials and workmanship in Canada made a plain design necessary," adding that "The designs within the Church are all my own, as well as the construction of the roof." Robe's reliance on

Cathedral Church of the Holy Trinity, *Québec; Anglican. Stone, 1799–1804, William Hall & William Robe, architects*

The massive Ionic order and blind arcades of the two main facades contrast with the plainer side walls of the nave, though the round-headed windows carry around all sides, on the sides with smaller arched windows below to light the main floor. Above a classically detailed pediment, a low-sloped roof carries a tall Gibbsian steeple, that rises slightly higher than the steeple of the Catholic basilica.

Detailed photographs show the base and the capital of the majestically scaled Ionic order on the blind arcades. Those on the rear of the building, shown here, are similar to those framing the doors on the front.

Italian Renaissance architects Alberti and Palladio probably accounts for the Ionic order's monumental scale.

The Canadian climate posed severe difficulties. Unlike steep-roofed Québécois churches, Robe's shallow pitch allowed moisture to penetrate and necessitated rebuilding the roof more steeply in 1816–18. Hall and Robe always intended a tall building; they emphasized its height and found a precedent in the Roman Pantheon "to give more boldness to the pilasters for the intended height of the building." The cathedral's timber-framed spire was given a glorious peel of eight bells (the first in this country) in 1830.

The side walls might have been enriched with the same giant order except for the expense involved and the quality of the stone available. The Pointe-aux-Trembles stone was expensive and difficult to quarry in large pieces, but Robe thought it "the only stone near Québec which bears the Chizzel and resists the weather." Two tiers of windows along the plain side walls imply the U-shaped gallery. The interior order

is Ionic, like the exterior. Robe's pine barrel vaulting and apsidal half-dome may be responsible for the perfect acoustics. The fretwork is his own original design, inspired by Québécois tradition rather than Neoclassical fashion: "the idea was taken from the common mode of ceiling rooms in Québec with board and batten, which I thought, if crossed diagonally might have a good effect." The network of interlaced lines arches overhead, white-on-white (and in smaller and smaller diamond shapes in the semi-dome). The whole is a model of clarity and lucidity.

By tradition, an elm toppled in a storm supplied the wood for the bishop's throne in 1846. The throne is designed like a fine Georgian doorway, panelled, with fluted Ionic columns carrying a segmental pediment, and bearing the Episcopal arms. King George III gave a handsome, simple chalice and patten of silver in 1766, and a sumptuous gilded 10-piece service in 1808. The cathedral also has an important collection of altar frontals (cloths), one of which derives from George III's coronation in 1760.

Holy Trinity, *interior*
A conventional layout, with cathedral choir, has replaced the earlier triple-decker liturgical arrangement — clerk's desk below, reading desk in the middle and pulpit above. Following Gibbs, Robe used giant columns on pedestals (fully visible above the box pews) to carry balconies and arches supporting the nave's barrel vault. The nave is connected seamlessly with a semicircular apse of the same width and order, focusing on a large Palladian window. The ceiling is Robe's own design.

In several places which we visited we found images and paintings, and candles which burned in front of some of these. The nuns explained that these pictures and images were not kept here for worship, for God alone is to be worshipped, but only to arouse piety through them.

— *Peter Kalm, 1750*

Un métissage canadien

La Chapelle des Ursulines, *Québec City, Québec; Roman Catholic. Stone; interior, 1730, the Levasseur family; structure, 1900–02, David Ouellet, architect*

The interior of the convent's public church has some of the most important carved work to be found in New France, much of it by the Levasseur family. The main altar on the right was installed between 1730 and 1736 by Pierre-Noël Levasseur.

FRENCH CATHOLIC TRADITIONS dominate Québec City and its environs but in many small villages English and Scottish church traditions are also found. Sometimes they are blended in an architectural merging unique to the region. Québec City's historic lower town, centre of French culture since 1608, has grown up around the much rebuilt Notre-Dame-des-Victoires, but the most important churches are within the walls of the Upper Town and in nearby towns such as Charlesbourg.

The **Ursuline Convent** has occupied the same site since 1641–42. The order was founded by Marie de l'Incarnation (1599–1672), a mystic from Tours, whose husband died in 1619, leaving her with an infant son. She pursued a life of meditation and penitence, entering a cloister when her son was 12. Reading the Jesuits' *Relations*, she decided to found a seminary for aboriginal girls in New France. With two other nuns and a wealthy widow as patron, she landed in 1639 and began her small community. Her letters describe the inhospitable realities of life in New France. She says the first chapel was "the finest and largest there can be in Canada," though it was only 17 by 28 feet: "the cold is too great to permit the building of vaster rooms. There are times when the priests are in danger of having their hands and ears frozen." The present chapel, which comprises a nuns' choir and attached church, completes an almost industrial-style complex of buildings, a factory for reflection, prayer and charitable works.

The masterpieces of the chapel — pulpit, tabernacle and retable — are by Pierre-Noël Levasseur. The Levasseur family dynasty of skilled artisans included some of Canada's most noted 18th-century sculptors, beginning with two brothers who settled in New France. The hexagonal pulpit, with matching sounding board crowned by intricate ornament and a trumpeting angel who seems to help project the sermons below, dates from 1726. The Levasseur workshop supplied a magnificent carved wood retable (1732–36), which fills the front of the square sanctuary, the sole surviving example of a widely diffused type. Four elaborate columns carrying a deep entablature and an attic story with segmental pediment comprise an *arc de triomphe* against the flat wall. This ensemble, resembling a Louis XIV church front, frames a central panel with altar, tabernacle and altarpiece. Niches display statues of Saint Augustine

La Chapelle des Ursulines, *exterior and nuns' choir*

David Ouellet's dressed stonewalls and eclectic ornament anticipate the lacily domed chancel of the Ursuline Convent. One wall of the church runs parallel to the street — the projecting wing that looks like a transept actually houses the Sacred Heart altar, which is used in connection with the nuns' choir — and hovering over the view in the distance is Québec's Anglican cathedral.

The nuns' choir contrasts starkly with the public church, which is at right angles to it. The arrangement provides privacy for the nuns as they and the public participate in services. Galleries on three sides wrap the Byzantine-style nave.

and Saint Ursula, the attic story houses a statue of Saint Joseph and the infant Jesus.

David Ouellet (1844–1915) rebuilt the public church simply in deference to the Levasseurs' retable. The nuns' choir, however, is dainty and filled with light; its focus is the Altar of the Sacred Heart on the axis of the choir but on the side wall of the chapel, from which it is separated by a screen. The church and the nuns' choir form an L, in whose angle is a small chapel from 1870 by Joseph-Ferdinand Peachy, where Marie de l'Incarnation's austere black-marble tomb fills the space as her spirit fills the convent. The Ursuline Convent is a "staunch guardian in a place that is only thirty-four years younger than the city itself," writes William Toye.

At the heart of the **Séminaire de Québec** is **Monseigneur Jean-Olivier Briand's private chapel**. Bishop Laval founded the seminary in 1663. In the next century Bishop Briand commissioned an extraordinary chapel to be built into a room about 18 feet square. Pierre Émond (1738–1808), who carried out the commission in 1784–86, was a joiner, timber framer, sculptor, cabinetmaker and architect, a range of vocations that speaks to the social mobility of the industrious craftsman in the New World of the 18th and 19th centuries.

One windowless wall is a backdrop for an altar and retable, flanked by figure sculpture, panelling and cupboards below. Baroque opulence shows in the vegetal motifs in the frieze and Neoclassical rigidity in the taut profile of the slender shafts. Instead of a painted altarpiece, Bishop Briand used a fine engraving after Rubens' *Marriage of the Virgin*, a subject suggestive of self-denial and dedication. The tangled branches of an olive tree (*olivier*) above the tabernacle play on the patron's given name and mix formalism and naturalism rather nicely. The retable uses an economy of means to transform a plain room into an expressive, self-referential and devotional chapel, without being lavish.

St. Andrew's, Canada's oldest Presbyterian congregation (founded in 1759), occupies an awkward triangular urban site. To suit it, John Bryson designed in 1809–10 a T-shaped building (about 39 by 89 feet) with the vestibule in the stubby leg of the T and the sanctuary in its wide top. The original spire disappeared a century ago but has been rebuilt; dormers, added in 1875 to light the balconies, break the gently sloped hip roof. The windows are beautifully scaled with round heads, some divided by a mullion into two round-headed sashes. The T-shaped plan is a Scots tradition, with a high pulpit on one long wall and curved balconies across the two ends. The banks of panelled pews focus on the raised pulpit. A vestry (1900) serves as a small museum; it contains a copy of George III's deed and the harmonium (1856) that was used before an organ was acquired in 1900 (*see* p. 23).

A nearby town, Charlesbourg, was laid out in 1665 as a square with triangular plots radiating from a smaller square at the centre, known as the Trait-Carré. **Saint-Charles-Borromée** is the focus of the town. The twin towers of the almost square west elevation dominate the silhouette and terminate in octagonal open belfries and curving spires. The facade's openings include central doors with fanlight, a Palladian window (an English influence) above these and an oval window in the pediment, all with concentric glazing bars. Niches in the towers repeat the arching elements, as do the nave windows (*see* p. 106).

The interior decoration, mainly from 1833 to 1849, blends the Baroque traditions of the *ancien régime* with the Neoclassicism of Thomas Baillairgé. The broad nave is uncluttered by columns (except under the double gallery), producing a sense of

La Chapelle de Monseigneur Briand, *Québec City, Québec; Roman Catholic. Wood interior, 1784–86; Pierre Émond, sculptor*

Pierre Émond's interior consists of one wall of unpainted pine woodwork, aging gracefully to a honey brown, in the small room set aside for a chapel. Two Corinthian columns with pedestals project to form a partial canopy over the altar, and pilasters terminate the panelled wall.

spaciousness and light. André Paquet carved the pulpit, following a prototype by Baillairgé at Saint-Louis de Lotbinière (1833), featuring Moses with the tables of the law. Its stair winds around two walls of the left transept; an intricately fretted piece of woodwork imitates Baroque wrought-iron railings (*see* p. 10). Across from the pulpit is the churchwarden's pew, with a bas-relief of St. Charles Borromeo that is framed with details like those in the choir. The east wall, treated like a triumphal arch, is far more than a retable; it has evolved into something truly monumental, based on a design published in Paris in 1669 by Claude Perrault. The focus of the whole building was to be a new tabernacle on the high altar by a follower of Baillairgé, but influenced by his uncle's design nearby on a side altar, carved by Paquet in 1854, the new tabernacle recalls St. Peter's in Rome. Altogether, the interior is a stunning masterpiece of consistency.

Charles Baillairgé's (1826–1906) large but plain church, **Saint-Jean-Baptiste**, was destroyed by fire (with much of the Saint-Jean-Baptiste quarter outside the old walls) on June 8, 1881. The next day the parish council of Notre-Dame-de-Québec (which included Saint-Jean-Baptiste) decided to replace it with a larger church. Three days later Baillairgé's former pupil, Joseph-Ferdinand Peachy, produced an eclectic scheme for rebuilding on the foundations. He received the commission; the

St. Andrew's, *Québec City, Québec; Presbyterian. Stone, 1809–10; John Bryson, builder*

St. Andrew's triangular site, donated by George III in 1802, is now hemmed in by civic buildings. To suit the site, Bryson (who worked on the Anglican cathedral) designed a T-shaped building. The magnificent spire is based on one of Gibbs' designs for St. Martin-in-the-Fields, London.

The traditional Scottish interior has a high pulpit on the long wall opposite the entrance, with curved balconies across the two ends and a loft, now used for an organ, over the vestibule, reached by a finely designed spiral stair.

design and specifications were ready in August; work began in October and the church opened in July 1884.

Standing on steep ground above Lower Town, Saint-Jean-Baptiste is a towering (240 feet), conspicuous, overreaching monument typical of the 1870s and 80s. Baillairgé's foundations suggested Peachy's general conception on this very constrained site. Inside, as outside, Peachy followed closely the detailing of La Sainte-Trinité in Paris (1861–67), though not closely enough, as Saint-Jean-Baptiste lacks its plasticity and integrity.

The lavish interior, like the exterior, is highly eclectic. Clustered *colonnettes* stand on squat marbleized columns that become soaring arcades. The aisles tunnel through the mass of the building, carrying a lofty gallery. The furniture followed (1922–26) in Late Renaissance or Baroque style, by the Daprato Studios and Michele Rigali (an Italian sculptor in Québec). Like fountains, these furnishings rise, spike and fall away, in clusters of marble columns and cupolas and cascading bases. Although almost cloying, Saint-Jean-Baptiste expresses national, cultural and religious aspirations, like Paris of the Second Empire (1852–70) or Ireland in its post-Famine celebration of Catholic Emancipation. It underscores Québec's own intertwined ethnicity, spirituality and *nationalisme*.

Saint-Charles-Borromée, *Charlesbourg, Québec; Roman Catholic. Stucco on stone, 1828–30; Thomas Baillairgé, architect*

Some of the furnishings from the previous church — an 1808 tabernacle by Pierre-Florent Baillairgé and two magnificent gilded statues by Pierre-Noël Levasseur from 1742–43 — are incorporated in the new building. Levasseur's agitated St. Peter and majestic St. Paul are in arched recesses above the doors. A symphony of white and gold in the unencumbered all-wood interior transfixes the observer.

FACING PAGE **Saint-Jean-Baptiste**, *Québec City, Québec; Roman Catholic. Stone, 1881–84; Joseph-Ferdinand Peachy, architect*

Saint-Jean-Baptiste is a hall church, with aisles almost as high as the nave and larger than usual windows, on a rectangular plan. The design is closely identified with La Trinité (1861–67) in Paris, which Peachy had visited in 1879, a design blending late Gothic and early Renaissance elements. The high vaulted nave is carried on columns that soar past the side balconies.

Saint-Jean-Baptiste, *view to north* Given the church's rather constrained site in the Saint-Jean-Baptiste quarter, just outside the walls of old Québec, the most remarkable feature is the way it can be seen from Québec's Lower Town. The reason for this is its high steeple and the extremely sharp drop just to the north of the building, which can be appreciated in this photograph looking off in the distance toward Charlesbourg.

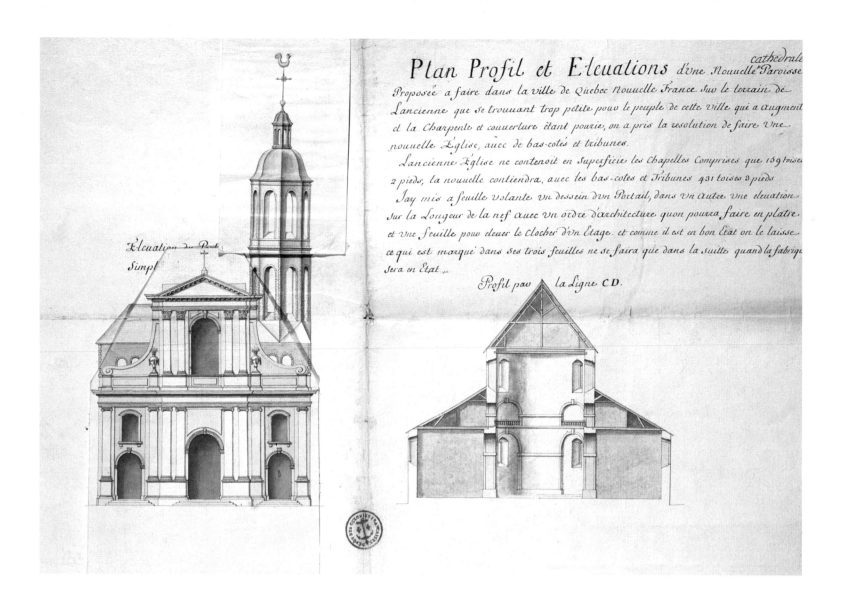

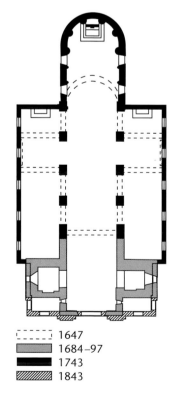

1647
1684–97
1743
1843

Notre-Dame de Québec

At the core of much the most important church in Québec, **Basilique-cathédrale Notre-Dame de Québec**, is the earliest stone church in New France. It was customarily referred to simply as "the parish church" (*la paroisse*) even after Laval was appointed the first bishop of Québec in 1658. Its predecessors were small wooden mission chapels; when the second church burned down in 1640 the community rebuilt it in stone with Jesuit help. *La paroisse* was largely completed in 1647–50 and dedicated to Our Lady of Peace, commemorating peace with the Iroquois. About 38 by 80 feet, with transepts for side chapels, a wooden *clocher* over the crossing and an apsidal east end, it had a planked floor and possibly panelled walls — a simple church that exceeded Laval's expectations, for he called it "large and magnificent" on his arrival in 1664. In 1674 it was consecrated a cathedral (the first north of Mexico). Today's building, a national icon of high style, still reflects its original footprint, which was half the length and one-third the width of the present building.

That Laval hired craftsmen in Paris in 1671 to teach carpentry, sculpture, painting, gilding for church decoration, masonry, and woodworking in an École des arts

et métiers now seems doubtful. Claude Baillif (ca 1635–98) arrived in 1675, "the best, if not the only, qualified master-builder in Québec at the time," according to Alan Gowans. However, his project for enlarging the church in 1683 was only partly completed when he drowned at sea. The military engineer, Gaspard Chaussegros de Léry (1682–1756), proposed structural, spatial and formal transformations far surpassing Baillif's vision. In drawings dated 1743 and 1745, he conceived a tall interior with low, wide-spreading aisles, fronted by a "Jesuit facade" with superimposed pilasters to express the low aisles and high nave. His proposal must have appeared a work of high style, even though his 17th-century models were now *passé* in Europe. The first basilican interior of its kind in North America, it was completed in 1745–49. The elaborate front could only be built at a later date when funds were available, so the authorities resorted to a plain facade ("Portail Simple"), unarticulated and lumpen in appearance. Even so, Notre-Dame was transformed from a small vernacular church into something large and lofty.

On a visit to Québec in 1749–50 Swedish botanist Peter Kalm noted the church was being ornamented and its organ improved, though he found roadside shrines

FACING PAGE **Basilique-cathédrale Notre-Dame**, *Québec City, Québec; Roman Catholic. Stone, 1647; altered 1684–97, by Claude Baillif, master builder; altered 1744–49, by Gaspard Chaussegros de Léry, military engineer; burned in shelling of Québec, 1759; rebuilt 1766–71, by Jean Baillairgé; baldachin 1787–93, by François Baillairgé; burned 1922, rebuilding completed in 1930*

Chaussegros de Léry's transformations, approved in 1744, outshone Baillif's vision. On paper, his heightened nave, lengthened choir and wide-spreading aisles were fronted by a "Jesuit facade" with superimposed pilasters. A plain version of this first basilican church in North America was constructed in 1745–49, omitting all ornamental elements, "to be built at a later date."

ABOVE **Basilique-cathédrale Notre-Dame**, *lithograph view by Robert Sproule, 1834*

The British bombardment of Québec City in 1759 reduced the cathedral to a shell. The ruins of Chaussegros de Léry's church, with its plain facade, were rebuilt with few variations in 1766–71, by Jean Baillairgé, a French woodworker who had emigrated to New France. Decades later, Robert Sproule's 1834 lithograph documents Notre-Dame's still-provincial appearance.

Basilique-cathédrale Notre-Dame, *interior view with baldachin*
Jean Baillairgé's son François, a painter and sculptor, designed the baldachin in 1787. It was completed over the next six years, in connection with Jean's retable.

FACING PAGE **Basilique-cathédrale Notre-Dame**, *exterior*
In 1843, Thomas Baillairgé (François' son) designed a twin-towered front of cut stone, around a severe triumphal arch. The revision to the towers proposed at the same time was not completed. After Notre-Dame was gutted by fire in 1922 the towers were rebuilt in the same form and completed in 1930.

and processions more interesting (*see* p. 117): bells, banners, crucifers, friars, a silver crucifix, clergy in vestments, a priest swinging a censer, a silver image of the Virgin in a silver shrine, acolytes with candles, more clergy and the bishop in full dress with crozier. Marie de l'Incarnation had commented on the love of beautiful ceremony a century earlier: "The music never ceased" during one procession with 47 ecclesiastics, at which the viceroy, the governor and two noblemen assisted by carrying a canopy over four reliquaries.

On July 23, 1759, the British bombardment of Québec reduced the cathedral to a shell. Services were transferred first to the Ursulines' chapel, and then to Monseigneur Briand's chapel in the seminary. The simplified rebuilding of Chaussegros de Léry's design (1766–71) made the architectural reputation of Jean Baillairgé (1726–1805). Said to have apprenticed with an architect, he is described by Luc Noppen as "a craftsman who became an architect by necessity." He sent his son François to the Royal Academy in Paris for training as a painter and sculptor in 1778–81. François' artistry secured the new commission for extraordinary improvements to the choir, redefining the tone of the whole interior. Altogether four generations of Baillairgés worked on Notre-Dame.

François' drawing for a baldachin, submitted to the churchwardens on April 15, 1787, was approved a week later. It was completed over the next six years in connection with his father's retable, and crowned the sanctuary with otherworldly splendour. Six saints, each standing in front of a pilaster, correspond to angels directly above, each angel bearing a console from which arches rise to meet at the focus of the apse. The scrolling arches of foliage connected by floral swags compose a giant Baroque-Rococo tiara. The Saviour is at the crown's summit, poised above the terrestrial globe, within an immense radiance. His uplifted right arm blesses while his left displays the cross. All is gilded and the effect is transcendent, in keeping with late-18th-century theory on the Sublime.

In 1843, Thomas Baillairgé, François Baillairgé's son, drafted a twin-towered front of ashlar stone, centring on a triumphal arch, a Roman motif beloved of French Neoclassicism. The arch in banded stonework on a high base above the main entrance provides visual support for the whole upper story, which is capped by a pedimented frieze and a classical altar with a cross, masking the roof gable. The architect intended a matching south tower (replacing his grandfather's restoration work), both towers finishing with yet another story and cupola. Baillairgé's Gibbsian twin towers would have outshone the Anglican cathedral, but the north tower was not completed and the south one was not rebuilt.

Notre-Dame's dramatic urban position near the top of rue de la Fabrique facing the old marketplace was enhanced in 1857 by Charles Baillairgé's impressive cast-iron fence and gates. Commercial buildings were developed on either side late in the 19th century. The space in front of the cathedral was landscaped, and the city hall was built on the other side of the marketplace. In 1920–21 an interior renovation was undertaken, but fire again reduced Notre-Dame to nothing but damaged walls on December 22, 1922. Its reputation as Bishop Laval's church meant there was little question of rebuilding in a different form. The five distinct building campaigns over three centuries provide a moving record of New France's emergent national culture that combines elements of vernacular and high style in *un métissage canadien*, a Canadian mixture.

Sun. 25th — Christmas Day [1791]. I went with Madame Báby at 5 in the morning to the Cathedral Church, to see the illuminations of the altar, which to those who have not seen the highly-decorated Roman Catholic churches in Europe is worth seeing. The singing and chanting was solemn. I was wrapped up very much, and wore a kind of cloth lined with eiderdown, a very comfortable head-dress; but the cold was intense, for the Roman Catholics will not admit of fires in their churches, lest the pictures should be spoiled. I saw no fine pictures.

— Mrs. John Graves Simcoe

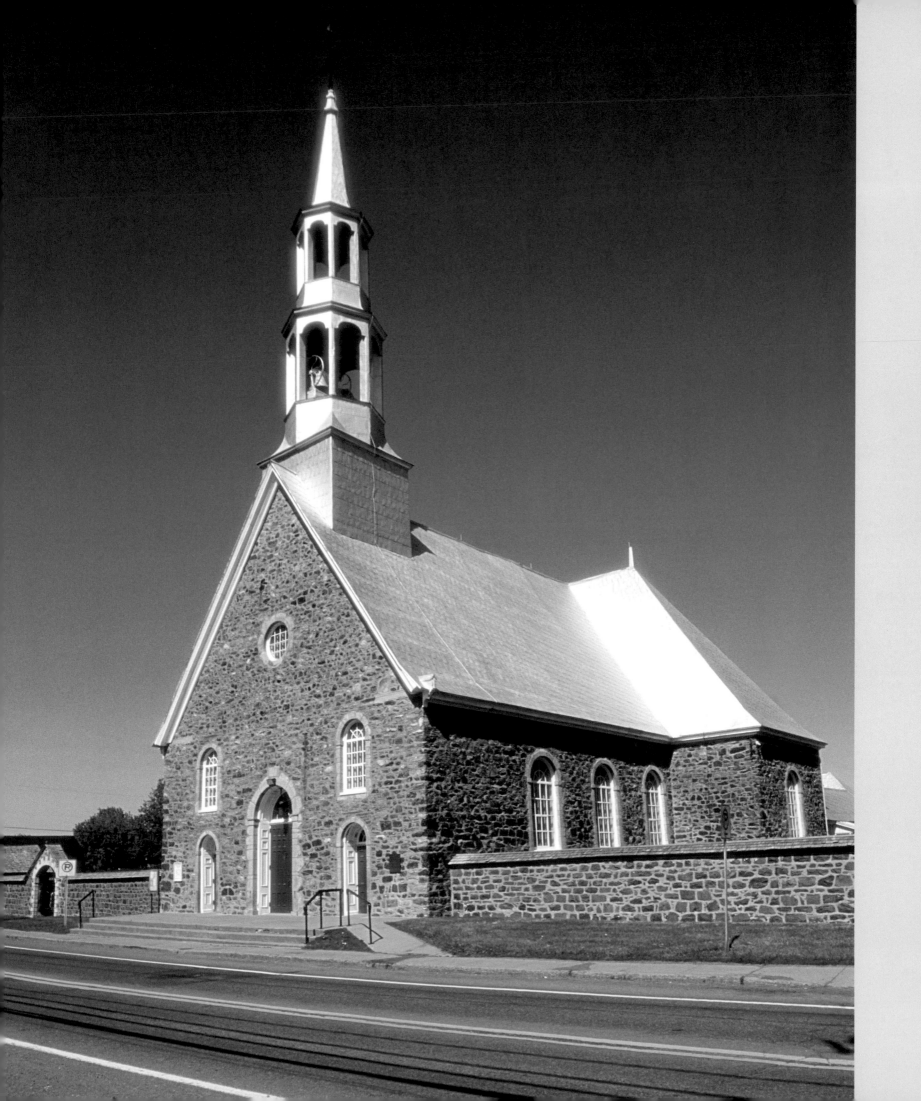

Les rivières sont des chemins qui marchent et qui portent où l'on veut aller.

— *Blaise Pascal, 1623–62*

Les rivières qui marchent

Saint-Mathias-sur-Richelieu, *near Chambly, Québec; Roman Catholic. Stone, 1784–88; alterations, 1805–18, René Beauvais and Paul Rollin, architects*

From the historic Chemin des Patriotes, Saint-Mathias-sur-Richelieu is flanked by an imposing stone cemetery wall with gates and a small building at each front corner. The wall and cemetery make it feel like a cathedral close, though the church is almost flush with the enclosing wall, giving it a strong urban presence.

THE RIVERS OF NEW FRANCE were crucial transportation and settlement corridors, especially the Chaudière and the Champlain, both linking the St. Lawrence with New England, one with Maine and the other with New York. Champlain explored the Richelieu River in 1608; forts were built — notably Fort Saint-Louis at Chambly (1665) — to protect the French colony from British invasion. The Chaudière was likewise a traditional route, followed by Benedict Arnold in his 1775–76 attack on Québec City. Both regions flourished in the 19th century because of the fertile farmland and developing industries.

The village of Saint-Mathias nestles below the Chambly rapids, where the river widens into a small lake. **Saint-Mathias-sur-Richelieu** has a complex history. Built in the 1780s, with interior work by Louis-Amable Quévillon (1749–1823) in 1794–96, it was fully renovated a generation later (1805–18): the choir was elongated, the *clocher* changed to a two-stage steeple, two flanking front entrances were added and a new sacristy was built with a later covered passageway (1834). These changes required rebuilding the vault and adding interior furnishings (1821–33). The parish instructed René Beauvais and Paul Rollin to copy various parts of neighbouring churches: the ceiling vault, retables, stalls, thrones, pulpit, churchwarden's seat, candlesticks, pews and confessionals were copied from five different churches. A strong cornice pulls choir, nave and transepts into a single space, and helps to

Sainte-Marguerite-de-Blairfindie, *L'Acadie, Saint-Jean-sur-Richelieu, Québec; Roman Catholic. Stone, 1800–01; Odelin and Mallioux, master masons; interior, 1805–25, Jean-Georges Finsterer, sculptor*

The church is a broad Latin cross. A handsome presbytery with a broad gallery stands to the west — connected to the church by a long covered passageway in matching stone — while an unenclosed cemetery surrounds the church.

FAR RIGHT **St. Stephen's**, *Chambly, Québec; Anglican. Stone, 1820; François Valade, contractor-carpenter; Louis Duchatel and François Morris, builders*

St. Stephen's utilizes French-Canadian forms: a Maillou plan, brown fieldstone set in coarse mortar, and details, such as the deeply moulded wooden cornice and the two-storied octagonal steeple of wood, with flaring octagonal spire and weathercock.

BELOW **Saint-François-d'Assise**, *Beauceville, Québec; Roman Catholic. Stone, 1857–60; architect unknown*

The Chaudière runs through Beauceville, right alongside Saint-François-d'Assise; the sacristy is immediately behind the church and the presbytery right behind that, on the left of the photograph.

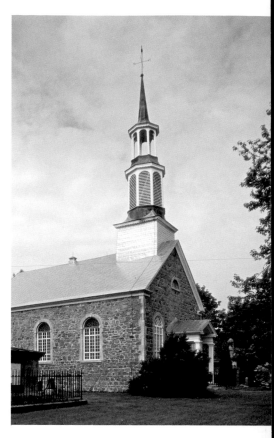

integrate the retable, with its opposing Solomonic or rope columns, into the whole scheme, though the result inside is somewhat fussy and not altogether consistent. The exterior, however, is a powerfully consistent presence on a generous site in a small town along an historic waterway.

Slightly later than Saint-Mathias, **Sainte-Marguerite-de-Blairfindie at l'Acadie**, now a suburb of Saint-Jean, demonstrates how the traditional church evolved. It is an enlargement of a Latin-cross plan, though with a narrower apse and small transepts. The large scale of the church (50 by 100 feet) is indicated by three doors and three windows in three tiers, around the niche with the patron saint's statue: Margaret was Malcolm of Scotland's queen in the 11th century. The church now sits in comparative isolation.

Jean-Georges Finsterer, a local sculptor, carried out the wooden vaulting and installed the high altar and tabernacle, retable and panelling. This work is similar to Quévillon's at Saint-Mathias, and the hexagonal pulpit (bought in 1804) is attributable to Quévillon: each panel (including the back panels) is centred on an emphatic piece of rock-and-shell ornament of Louis XV style. The masterful scrolling C- and S-shaped decoration that skips within the frieze around the interior is an animated late-blooming Baroque feature. Georges' son, Louis-Daniel Finsterer, was responsible for the side altars (1811–12). Faced with a rising tide of Anglicans and Presbyterians, Catholic churches such as Sainte-Marguerite were conscious assertions of *le patrimoine,* Québec's cultural heritage.

The Anglican presence is clearest at **St. Stephen's, Chambly**, a garrison church for soldiers at Fort Chambly, which is, ironically, Québécois in appearance. Though raised in 1820 by Church of England Loyalists, it shares little with churches in either England or New England, other than the windows, of a type common to churches in France, England and North America. Three departures from the local forms are: tall windows in the west front that match those in the side walls; the Palladian window (a favourite British-American motif) in the curving east end; and the open-gabled porch, like porches on New England houses. A vestibule, with stairs to the gallery, is also uncommon. The simply panelled pews retain their doors, while the raised pulpit is supported by elegant small columns. Is this a rare example in its day of accommodation or acculturation? The simpler answer is that the congregation hired a local contractor who built traditionally.

The Chaudière River, toward which Beaucéron villages are oriented, though not as placid as the Richelieu, functions in the same way as a local highway. Its churches have a strong regional identity, due to the limited period during which they were built, their sensitive use of various woods and an aesthetic that creates a sense of belonging. The village of Beauceville is typical in the way **Saint-François-d'Assise** and its presbytery face the river on the west bank at the end of the bridge. The centre of Saint-Joseph-de-Beauce is dominated by a complex of five church buildings, all facing the Chaudière. **Saint-Joseph-de-Beauce's** presbytery has identical facades facing the church and the river. The central section of the church's high narrow facade, by François-Xavier Berlinguet (1830–1916), projects and supports a square base for the bell tower and spire. The nave and choir, by Joseph-Ferdinand Peachy and sculpted by Louis and Francis Dion, form a single large space with a barrel-vaulted ceiling; the aisles are double height with coffered ceilings (repeated

Saint-Joseph-de-Beauce, *Saint-Joseph-de-Beauce, Québec; Roman Catholic. Stone, 1865–68; François-Xavier Berlinguet and Joseph-Ferdinand Peachy, architects; interior, Louis and Francis Dion*

Saint Joseph's octagonal pulpit is a masterly piece of detailing and construction, seeming to float ethereally above the congregation and barely attached to the column from which it hangs. Its dark wood, picked out extensively in gilt, coheres with the church's elaborate dark pews, showing the sensitive use of woods and the careful workmanship characteristic of the Beauce craftsmen.

at smaller scale in Saint-Maxime, Scott Junction, 1903–05). The decorative scheme is white, yellow and gold, enriched with a nicely detailed wood dado and richly carved pews and pulpit.

Saint-Elzéar (1849), by Thomas Baillairgé, lies several miles west of the river in a deep side valley, located on a small rise in the valley bottom. Léandre Parent, one of Baillairgé's students, was the sculptor for the interior; the high altar (1803–04) by Louis-Amable Quévillon was brought to Saint-Elzéar from Lévis, though its style contrasts with Baillairgé's interior. Several miles east of the Chaudière River is **Saint-Isidore**, located at the main intersection of the village. Jean-Baptiste Guillot's rather complex facade anticipates an interior that follows an earlier pattern by Thomas Baillairgé. The interior is a remarkable composition of carefully considered proportions, with three contrasting colours of dark woods in the rich Baroque pews. The pulpit, which continues the rich wood detailing, amplified by gold trim, is reached by a curving staircase that begins in the transept. The organ, choir and extra seating are accommodated in a large balcony with curved and panelled face, supported on slender cast-iron columns.

The building of **Saint-Georges, Saint-Georges-de-Beauce**, was delayed because parishioners disagreed over which side of the Chaudière it should be on. The church ended up on the west side, on a sloping site near the river. The vaguely Neoclassical facade is in three parts, with a large central spire, much smaller flanking spires, and a fourth still smaller spire over the crossing. The lofty interior (over 60 feet) is a harmonious composition, with towering nave and low side aisles in an eclectic combination of classicizing and medievalizing motifs, altogether surprising and delightful (see p. 1).

Saint-Isidore, *Saint-Isidore (Dorchester), Québec; Roman Catholic. Stone, 1853–60; Michel Patry and Jean-Baptiste Saint-Michel, architects*

Patry's facade is divided into three vertical sections with a Palladian window, a rose window and a triangular pediment in the central section. A square base supports the spire in two stages, with chamfered edges on the spire and upper section.

Some Beauce churches are noteworthy for their careful use of woods. Saint-Isidore has among the most beautifully juxtaposed varieties. The ornate dark pews contrast with an unusual blond wooden floor, where the diagonal pattern in the aisles — in the centre aisle a herringbone pattern — contrasts with the linear pattern under the pews.

Saint-Georges, *Saint-Georges-de-Beauce, Québec; Roman Catholic. Stone, 1900–02; David Ouellet, architect*

The ambitious size (2,200 persons) of Saint-Georges is explained by the hope that it would be elevated to serve as a cathedral, though that never occurred. Ouellet placed the church on a sloping site near the river, making the 222-foot central spire seem higher.

The interior seems almost as lofty as the spire; its height emphasized by the unified conception of the arcades that separate nave from aisles, rising up almost through the nave's full height. Its ornate decorative touches show how far Québec church design had progressed in 150 years from the more easily comprehended interiors of Île d'Orléans or the Chemin du Roy.

The Roman liturgy which [Bishop Ignace] Bourget introduced into his diocese matched his reverence for the papacy, his exacting sense of order, and the effusive piety which fitted well with ultramontane devotional celebrations. Thanks to him, the formality and sedateness of the services ... in Montreal, a true city of the north, gradually gave way to the Mediterranean warmth of Roman rites. As a result, new importance was accorded to gestures, to the public image, and to gatherings for magnificent ceremonies in immense churches.

— *Philippe Sylvain, 1982*

La ville aux cent clochers

MONTRÉAL, THE COMMERCIAL AND FINANCIAL CENTRE of the country until the late-20th century, was once the largest city in Canada. It was also "the city of a hundred church towers" (*la ville aux cent clochers*), and "the city of saints" (for its many streets with a saint's name). Montréal offered a secure operating base for many religious orders, each with its own institution and chapel; its religious buildings are mostly Roman Catholic and breathtakingly rich from generations of Catholics with a strong devotion to the Church.

Chapelle Notre-Dame-de-Bon-Secours suggests something of early forms, despite profound changes. Soon after arriving in 1653, Marguerite Bourgeoys of the Congrégation de Notre-Dame envisioned a chapel dedicated to Mary. Her small wooden building was replaced by Montréal's first stone chapel in 1673–78. Destroyed by fire in 1754, it was followed in 1771–73 by a larger building, just recognizable in the present church. It was aisleless, four bays long and apsidal, with a round-headed entrance, three windows to match, an oculus and an octagonal belfry.

Defensive fortifications, which surrounded the stone chapel, began to be demolished in 1805, providing space for a street and wharfage for tall ships. Thus Notre-Dame's apse addressed the river once again and sailors offered ship models, hung from the ceiling, to express gratitude for the Virgin's protection. Under Jackson John Richards, an itinerant Methodist minister who became a Roman Catholic

Notre-Dame de Montréal, *Montréal, Québec; Roman Catholic. Stone, 1823–29; James O'Donnell, architect; interior redecorated 1872–88, Victor Bourgeau, architect*
Late 19th-century Protestant churches displayed organ pipes decoratively; large Catholic churches commissioned expansive altarpieces. This extroverted example by Victor Bourgeau looks to northern European Gothic work. A eucharistic program (1872) devised by Notre-Dame's curé, B.-V. Rousselot, centres on the Crucifixion. The coronation of the Virgin appears above it, flanked by Old Testament prefigurations. French sculptor Henri Bouriché created the life-size figures.

Notre-Dame-de-Bon-Secours, *Montréal, Québec; Roman Catholic. Stone, 1771–73; altered by Henri-Maurice Perrault and Albert Mesnard, architects; interior, 1885–86, and enlargements, 1892–94, François-Xavier-Édouard Meloche, architect*

Notre-Dame-de-Bon-Secours is on the site of 17th-century predecessors. Re-cased and embellished in 1885–86, it was enlarged, then modified again in the 20th century (to reduce excessive loads over both ends of the church), before being renovated in the 1990s. A vista of 18th- and 19th-century buildings on rue Bonsecours frames its facade at the T-junction with rue Saint-Paul.

priest, serving here from 1815 to 1820, the chapel became "the cradle of the English-speaking Catholic community."

Jean-Claude Marsan frankly notes that Notre-Dame-de-Bon-Secours "suffered repeated alterations meant to embellish it, but which in fact were an insult to good taste." Montréal architects Perrault and Mesnard encased the old walls in 1885–86, adding a tower, corner turrets resembling Baroque-Revival spires and "other frills." Regrettably the early-19th-century Quévillon interior was transformed. The most surprising feature is Meloche's treatment of the enlarged east-end exterior, decked out in 1892–94 with a huge statue of *Our Lady, Star of the Sea* surrounded by angels (now much simplified). The Virgin raises her arms to the river to greet and protect all entering or leaving the harbour. The alterations, in period taste, reflect rising interest in Québec's cultural heritage, even if little authentic remains of the 18th-century church.

The enormous, brooding and glittering church of **Notre-Dame de Montréal** arose two short blocks away. Built in Montréal's *pierre grise*, a bluish-grey stone, it was roofed with imported English tin. It astonished citizens and visitors by sheer size alone. High, wide and handsome (136 feet across and 213 feet tall, on completion of the twin towers), the church loomed over Montréal's usual one- or two-story buildings. Unequalled for size in North America when built, it was second only to Niagara Falls as a destination for visitors. Its Gothic Revival style with pointed openings and battlemented profiles was unprecedented.

Old Montréal resembled a town in medieval France: long and narrow streets following the river were connected by closely spaced cross-streets, seldom truly parallel to one another. The Old Sulpician Seminary (1683–84) still occupies a large block on rue Notre-Dame, along a ridge 75 feet above the St. Lawrence. An earlier parish church stood in the middle of the street bounding one side of Place d'Armes. The new church faced Place d'Armes, next to the seminary, oriented more or less westerly.

Notre-Dame was the work of Irish émigré James O'Donnell (1774–1830). Born in County Wexford and apprenticed in Dublin, he settled in New York in 1812, but was persuaded to come to Montréal in 1823 to design his *chef-d'œuvre*. The church-wardens, ambitious for a magnificent church, wished to settle a point of honour in an ecclesiastical duel between the Sulpicians — long responsible for the city's parish church and masters of Montréal — and the Bishop of Québec. Franklin Toker notes that the Sulpicians (who assumed the parish from the Jesuits in 1657) became Montréal's seigneurs in 1663 and owed allegiance to the Superior General of the Sulpician Order in Paris, not the Bishop of Québec. Bishop Joseph-Octave Plessis appointed an auxiliary bishop for Montréal in 1821 and began a cathedral (old Saint-Jacques) west of the old city in 1823. It was intended to be the largest church in Canada with seating for 3,000. Notre-Dame, also undertaken in 1823, was to hold 8,000 or more of Montréal's Roman Catholics.

Notre-Dame rose quickly; the walls were completed by 1826. Highly articulated by Québecois standards, the church is geometric in conception, having a rectangular plan that encloses the paired towers (both unusual in Québec), faced with large blocks of cut limestone from nearby Mile-End quarries and characterized by repetitive detailing in Late Georgian tradition. Notre-Dame is a hall church with two rows of eight columns (46 feet high) connected by tie beams spanning the very wide

nave (67 feet) and aisles (each 27 feet). Builders hoisted the extensive system of deep galleries in double tiers into place. Gigantic trusses (hidden by the ceiling) concentrated the roof's weight on the columns. The interior structure was finished rapidly in 1827 and plastered, ready for whitewashing in 1828. In the race against Saint-Jacques, Notre-Dame was complete provisionally in 1829. Only half of each tower, the first two stages of five, was finished, owing to a shortage of funds; the remainder followed in 1841–43. It opened looking presentable but unfinished, somewhat different externally from today's church and very different internally.

Reactions to the initial interior varied according to the observers' origins, as Toker points out. In 1846, British author B.W.A. Sleigh approved with conventional piety "the solemn tone of the organ at Vespers, the choristers' chants, the candles burning on numerous altars, refulgent with gold and costly gems, the sombre and subdued light, reflected in a thousand prismatic colours from the stained windows [which] filled me with a religious awe." *La Revue Canadienne* complained in 1845: "You expect the interior … to be as somber, awesome and imposing as the idea of God who resides therein. Instead it is something hazy, dull, cold, unfinished; on the

Notre-Dame de Montréal, *Montréal, Québec; Roman Catholic. Stone, 1823–29; James O'Donnell, architect; interior redecorated 1872–88, Victor Bourgeau, architect*

O'Donnell visited quarries and the building site, then wrote that he "formed a few rough sketches in the Gothic style, as I considered it more suitable to your materials, workmen, climate, wants and means etc." The result is severe yet graceful, striking in skyline and soaring above the adjacent Seminary (1683–84). Baccerini's statues of St. Joseph, St. John the Baptist and the Virgin Mary (patrons of Canada, Québec and Montréal), ordered in 1864, adorn niches over the recessed triple porch.

Notre-Dame de Montréal, *interior*
Pierre Vignot (1858–1921) called Notre-Dame "the most colossal auditorium in Christendom." It was "marvellously resonant," according to Vignot, who gave a series of Lenten sermons here in 1905. "It is a delightful sensation, which I do not think one could experience elsewhere, to speak quietly with ten thousand souls." He also commented favourably on the church's sightlines, enhanced by a gently raking main floor and steeply stepped upper galleries.

Notre-Dame de Montréal, *interior*
A side altar in Notre-Dame is dedicated to Marguerite d'Youville, canonized in 1990 by John-Paul II. This historicizing academic altarpiece by M. Dubois is refreshingly explicit and intensely relevant. It shows Mère d'Youville, the founder of the Sisters of Charity (Grey Nuns), ministering compassionately in winter to those in need against the backdrop of the neighbouring Old Sulpician Seminary.

FACING PAGE **Chapelle du Sacré-Cœur, Notre-Dame de Montréal**, *Montréal, Québec; Roman Catholic. Wood, 1888–91; Henri-Maurice Perrault and Albert Mesnard, architects; restored and rebuilt, 1979–81, Jodoin, Lamarre, Pratt & Associates*

Sacred Heart Chapel, used for intimate celebrations and services, is an aisled, T-shaped masterpiece of eclecticism in wood. It extends crosswise behind the apse of Notre-Dame. The lower portion was restored after a fire in 1978, and a contrasting multiplanar ceiling has been installed that admits natural light. The theme of Charles Daudelin's contemporary retable, made of 32 cast-bronze panels, is earthly pilgrimage through life's difficulties.

ceiling a motley daubing of blues and greys, without poetry and without taste." In fact the windows were cheap and thinly painted glass. As a result, some French-Canadian writers objected to the nave's darkness and the east window's blinding light. Visitors from abroad were apt to find the light-and-dark contrast pleasing — reflecting Edmund Burke's view that the Sublime was stimulated by either dazzling luminosity or impenetrable gloom, and especially by "a quick transition" from one to the other. Henry David Thoreau found himself "instantly in an atmosphere which might be sacred to thought and religion, if one had any." He likened the whole to "a great cave in the midst of a city … where the still atmosphere and the sombre light disposed to serious and profitable thought."

In a parish covering 55 square miles and serving 80,000 parishioners in over a dozen branch churches, the Sulpicians were unable to finish the church, given demands on their resources for new churches in outlying areas, such as St. Patrick's and Notre-Dame-de-Grâce. Today's interior is the creation of James O'Donnell and Victor Bourgeau (1809–88). Bourgeau submitted a wooden model of the interior in January 1857, but it was only after the parish was subdivided in 1866 that Bourgeau's interior renovations (1872–79), startling and unlike anything ever seen in Québec, could proceed. They would soon be emulated throughout the province and beyond.

The main altarpiece and retable, 80 feet high, encompassed the whole apse; its white-pine figures, commissioned from the French sculptor Henri Bouriché of Angers, replaced the east window. The interior was coloured deep blue and azure, picked out in red and purple, with silver and gold leaf (the gold stars on the blue ceiling are a traditional Québecois feature). Bourgeau introduced decorative vaulting with melded ribs on the ceiling, as O'Donnell had intended. In fact the whole polychromatic scheme was based on F.J. Duban and J.B. Lassus' restoration of the Sainte-Chapelle in Paris (begun in 1837), complete with patterned ribs, ornate *colonnettes* and gilded capitals. The complex and sinuous pulpit, planned by Bourgeau in 1872 and sculpted by Louis-Philippe Hébert in 1883–87 (following figure designs by Bouriché), is a marvellous synthesis of Gothic and Baroque, much praised by contemporaries as "a little masterpiece of elegance and strength." The sensational results amounted to a vindication of historicism and eclecticism.

In 1869 Bourgeau addressed the light problem, which was compounded when Benjamin-Victor Rousselot insisted on closing the east window and installing the reredos in 1866. Bourgeau had worked with his father, a wheelwright, before becoming a joiner, carpenter, woodcarver, and then an architect. Had he reflected on Ezekiel's vision of wheels within wheels before he created four skylights in 1872–75? Shafts between the roof members connect to one strip window and three wheel windows in the nave ceiling. Apparently they were a limited success as a lighting solution.

Notre-Dame's mid-20th-century electric lighting contributes to the church's popular acclaim. Its effect is frankly theatrical, like O'Donnell's conception of the whole. The lighting engineers' approach is extravagant and gaudy, analogous to a 1920s Würlitzer jukebox, and unparalleled in Canada. Yet the church survives in remarkable condition, no doubt due to the unusual policy of visitors' admission fees. Notable events, such as Pierre Elliott Trudeau's stately funeral in 2000, suggest

St. Patrick's, *Montréal; Roman Catholic. Stone, 1843–47; Pierre-Louis Morin, architect, and Fr. Félix Martin, Jesuit mathematician*

St. Patrick's developed apace in the 1840s, along with the New Town, and the Irish church squared off against the dominant British with a show of mixed Irish and French architectural features, some Romanesque and some Gothic — *moyenâgeux* (medieval) covers both nicely. An especially acute gable and a conspicuous figure of the patron top the central porch, with deep roll mouldings above slender colonnettes.

that it is a national church. It was raised to the status of a minor basilica on Pope John Paul II's visit to Montréal in April 1982.

Montréal passed Québec City in size during the 1830s and the anglophone Irish — by 1841 there were 6,500 — who met in old Notre-Dame-de-Bon-Secours petitioned the Sulpicians in 1833 for a *petite église,* a daughter church. While Notre-Dame was a French-Canadian Gothic Revival church by an Irish-born designer, **St. Patrick's, Montreal**, expressed the aspirations of English-speaking Irish Roman Catholics in Québec in a design by two Frenchmen. The superior, Joseph Quiblier, wrote A. Welby Pugin, the great English advocate of revived Gothic principles, a touching letter in 1842 asking him to supply a design for "eight to ten thousand people with about half of these seated in pews. Our severe climate and the abundance of snow during the long winter period do not allow for exterior ornamentation…. Would you, Sir, be able to put forward a design for such a church and submit it to us without delay?" Pugin did not. The church that was built in 1843–47 would not have met his demanding standards, advanced in *True Principles of Pointed or Christian Architecture* (1841). Instead, a little-known French architect and a French Jesuit mathematician interested in architecture are credited: Pierre-Louis Morin and Father Félix Martin (1804–86).

St. Patrick's faces the St. Lawrence and the New Town from a large sloping site on Beaver Hall Hill. A boxy building, its most graceful exterior features are three entrances overlooking park-like grounds and a tall polygonal apse. Engaged in the front is a small tower between square buttresses ending abruptly in octagonal turrets above the roofline. Buttresses too slender to have much structural value parade around the church between tall lancet windows. A rose window floats in a blind-arched panel above the principal entrance. "Solid but naïve" in conception — Georges-Émile Giguère's assessment of Father Martin's Collège Sainte-Marie — seems apt.

The interior was influenced by Notre-Dame: a hall church, with lofty wooden arcades on compound piers leading directly into the apse and topped by ribbed vaults. However, St. Patrick's galleries do not extend down the length of the aisles, so its windows are visible to their full height. There are also long lancets in the choir and high above the altars cusped oculi supplement the lighting. Equally obvious are the tall appearance and slender proportions of its nave as against the immense width of Notre-Dame. St. Patrick's was decorated gradually in half a dozen campaigns, the most important being the installation of three altars in 1861 and a loving restoration (1987–93) under Monseigneur Russell Breen.

St. Patrick's, *interior*
The striking interior of St. Patrick's offers great height yet remarkable breadth. Its golden shell is bright with jewel-like colour in the windows and abundant intricate ornament. The compound piers are marbleized wood, the ceiling's vaults ribbed plaster. The polygonal apse is very tall, as are the three reredos spreading across the transepts and above the main altar. They are studded with a host of figures at various scales, as in some medieval work.

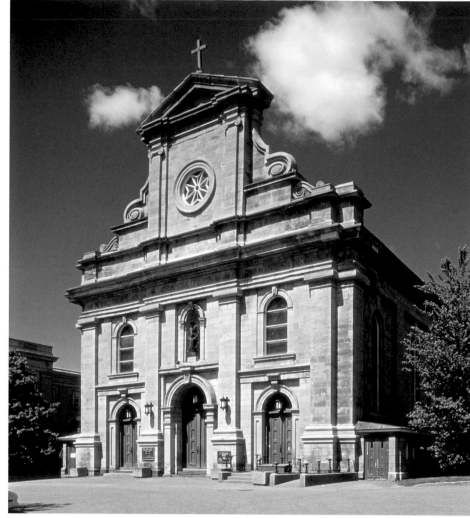

Notre-Dame-de-Grâce, *Montréal, Québec; Roman Catholic. Stone, 1851–53; John Ostell, architect; chapel and tower, 1927–28, J. Omer Marchand, architect; interior renovated, 1963, de Morin & Le Borgne, architects*

Notre-Dame-de-Grâce is an accomplished forerunner of changing taste: this Baroque Revival design draws on ancient Roman motifs favoured in Italian and French Baroque architecture but rarely reflected in 18th-century Québec (except in retables and tabernacles). In 1849, before working on Notre-Dame-de-Grâce, Ostell showed his versatility by preparing a Gothic competition design (as required) for St. James' Cathedral, Toronto, which was awarded second prize.

J.P. O'Shea's coordinated scheme of stained glass, adopting Renaissance or Baroque Revival style, adds clarity and unity to Notre-Dame-de-Grâce's reworked interior. Those in the aisles and transepts link interior design to exterior architecture by repeating pictorially the aedicule motif — a segmental pediment carried on Ionic columns — as in this Pentecost window. The Apostles gather around the enthroned Virgin as the dove of the Holy Spirit descends.

Even the seats are interesting, ending in tall buttresses with gablets and a prickly finial. They recall Pugin's biting comment: "*too much* is generally attempted … all the ordinary articles of furniture … are made not only expensive but very uneasy. We find diminutive flying buttresses about an armchair; everything is crocketed with angular projections, innumerable mitres, sharp ornaments, and turreted extremities."

Notre-Dame-de-Grâce is a smooth Baroque Revival design of 1851–53. A severe colossal Tuscan order, which alludes to ancient Roman temples, frames the facade and long flanks of this west-end church. The dove-grey ashlar wall advances and retreats, with doubled pilasters at the corners. Its centrepiece on the skyline is equally complicated, using a smaller Ionic order bracketed by consoles and capped firmly by a pediment. The composition recalls Chaussegros de Léry's Baroque Jesuit designs for both Notre-Dame de Québec (*see* p. 132) and Montréal's old parish church.

John Ostell (1813–92), London-born and English-trained, arrived in Montréal in 1834 and prospered immediately with work marked by "restraint, solidity of construction, and variety of style," as Jean-Claude Marsan points out. With anglophone and francophone clients, he was responsible for several major Montréal

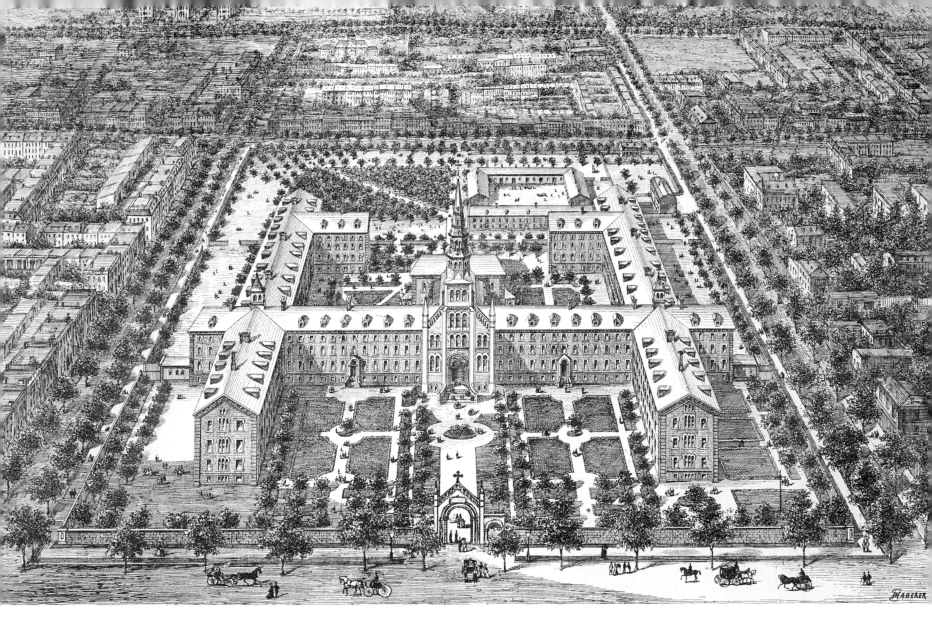

monuments, including the Custom Houses, Court House and McGill College's Arts Building. An Anglican who married into a prominent French-Canadian and Roman Catholic family, he was diocesan architect under Bishop Ignace Bourget and was also employed by the Sulpicians to design the old seminary's new wing.

Notre-Dame-de-Grâce's triple-doored facade and shallow-pitched roof hint again at a hall church. It was altered several times, notably in 1927–28, when J. Omer Marchand (1873–1936) added Chapelle Saint-Victor and a campanile sympathetic to Ostell's work, yet in the suave idiom of a graduate of Paris' École des Beaux-Arts. The reiterated giant order wraps the bell tower's corners while the new entrance incorporates an aedicule into the doorway's broken segmental pediment. The church interior, renovated in 1963, appears airy, for there are no galleries to interfere with the tall, round-headed windows.

The history of the **Maison mère des Sœurs Grises** (Motherhouse of the Grey Nuns) shows the enormous expansion of Québec's religious orders through the 18th and 19th centuries and their decline in the 20th. The Sisters of Charity (Sœurs de la Charité de Montréal), long known as Grey Nuns, outgrew their old convent at Pointe à Callières when membership and outreach increased in the 1850s and 60s in response, say Lauzon and Forget, "to a massive influx of destitute Irish immigrants

Maison mère des Sœurs Grises, *Montréal, Québec; Roman Catholic. Stone, 1869–71 (convent), 1874–78 (chapel); Victor Bourgeau and Alcibiade Leprohon, architects (restored 1995–96 by Desnoyers, Mercure & Associés, architects); bell tower, 1890, Perrault & Mesnard, architects*

This engraving is from the *Canadian Illustrated News* (December 4, 1875), which published an unusual bird's-eye view of "The General Hospital of the Grey Nuns, Montreal" as if drawn from a hot-air balloon anchored above the property's edge. It reported that between 1747 and 1875 "the hospital has cared for 1490 poor and infirm men, 3240 women, 1914 orphans, and 19,472 foundlings."

Chapelle Sœurs Grises, *bell tower*
The Motherhouse of the Grey Nuns is a huge, H-shaped landmark. It is focused on the chapel (1874–78), but the 1890 bell tower is almost the only part of the chapel visible looking toward the broad south front along boulevard René-Lévesque. At the end of an alley of trees, the large Romanesque Revival entry opens into the principal corridor and the chapel.

FACING PAGE **Soeurs Grises**, *interior*
The chapel is marked by a delicacy of tone: golden, marbleized columns with nearly matching colour in the capitals (even the slender cast-iron pair near the entrance) against white accented with yellow ochre. Equally heartening are the arching forms in the nave arcades, galleries and windows; the apse and its stalls; the altars, tabernacles and altarpieces; and the lacy wrought-iron grilles (ornamented with cast-iron sunflowers) high in the crossing.

in the late 1840s and to the human suffering brought about by industrialization and urbanization." In 1869–71, Victor Bourgeau and his partner, Alcibiade Leprohon, filled a whole city block with the new building; it has two open courts, a forecourt and a garden court, into which the chapel (1874–78) projects. The chapel is barely visible from the sides, but its Romanesque Revival tower, straddling the main corridor and chapel entrance, dominates the front and boulevard René-Lévesque. The tower's six arcaded stories and spire are based on late-11th- and early-12th-century churches in southern France.

By contrast, the rounded forms and delicate colouring of the interior are ingratiatingly feminine. Many altars — six almost surround the crossing — and multiple images in paint, sculpture and stained glass vie for attention. The central altar holds the remains of Québec-born Sainte Marguerite d'Youville (1701–71), founder of the Sisters of Charity (*see* p. 148), who was canonized in 1990. Three altars — white marble, round-arched, somewhat Byzantine in appearance — face us: the main altar (behind Sainte Marguerite's mahogany altar) is dedicated to the Holy Cross, the left to the Sacred Heart, the right to the Eternal Father. Two colourful altars (incorporating glass enamelled by the nuns) stand in the transepts and predate the chapel: one to Saint Joseph (1858), patron saint of Canada, and another to Our Lady of the Seven Sorrows (1857). This concentration on private devotion, characteristic of Roman Catholic places of worship, suits Bishop Bourget's time for, as Philippe Sylvain observes, he emphasized "such highly emotional devotions as those to the Seven Sorrows of Mary and to the Sacred Heart."

Demolition threatened the motherhouse in the 1970s, as did declining vocations. It was designated a heritage site in 1974 and the chapel was painstakingly restored in 1995–96, but soon the order agreed to sell the landmark to Concordia University, for preservation with its chapel. Nuns continue to live in the building; Concordia will occupy it between 2007 and 2022, gradually converting it into a fine arts complex.

Sainte-Brigide de Kildare was built following the partition of Notre-Dame's parish. A petition for another anglophone church began in 1850 and Monseigneur Bourget approved the parish in 1867. The builders, Quintal and Morin, chose Romanesque Revival (the great Irish national style) for the long-delayed church (1877–80), with an eclectic later spire (1885–86). Though round-arched, the spire uses varied geometric shapes (cubes, cylinders, cones) and historicizing enrichments. The aedicules garnishing the angles meld into gablets, suggesting a French Romanesque church in miniature, a tinsmith's confection characteristic of the late 19th century.

The curriculum of the École des beaux-arts in Paris focused rigorously on traditional planning and the articulation of functions before conceiving formal, generally monumental, solutions or choosing materials and detailing. No school was more conscious of earlier building traditions, nor any more highly regarded. It drew students from across Europe and abroad, including the gifted young Montrealer, J. Omer Marchand. He attended from 1893 to 1902, returned to Montréal late in 1902 and received the commission for the **Chapelle du Grand Séminaire de Montréal** not long after (1904–07). To accommodate growing numbers of seminarians, the new chapel filled the length and three-story height of one old wing of the seminary.

The approach from a plain anteroom is dramatic: an arched entrance is filled with wrought-iron gates rather than doors, each with a gilded cherub and the

Sainte-Brigide de Kildare, *Montréal, Québec; Roman Catholic. Tin-clad timber-framed spire, 1885–86; Quintal and Morin, builders (church, 1877–80; Poitras & Martin, architects)*

The spire of Sainte-Brigide de Kildare followed the church's construction by a few years, a common fundraising strategy. Quintal and Morin's tinned eye-catcher suggests French Romanesque and Byzantine overtones in a church that otherwise owes much to Irish Romanesque (appropriately for a church dedicated to Ireland's second patron saint). Such economy is more often encountered in rural rather than urban French-Canadian churches across Canada.

cipher AM *(Ave Maria)* surrounded by inscriptions, HAEC DOMUS DEI and ET PORTA COELI ("This is the House of God and the Gate of Heaven"). From a familiar metaphor, Marchand offered a hint of this house of the Lord through gates that are like a benediction. Mottled-green marble columns from Bordeaux, France, and capitals of fine white stone from Caen (which also clads the walls) support arches that carry the choir-and-organ loft. In the distance a much grander arch, on colossal columns of the same marble, frames the apse. Another arch, on colossal piers, embraces the organ loft while responding to the sanctuary arch.

Members of the congregation face each other in three blocks of stalls on either side, linked by patterns in the mosaic floor. A strong cornice connects exceedingly

tall windows, unifying other arching forms and emphasizing the space's great simplicity. A colourful open-timber roof inspired by the church of San Miniato al Monte in Florence offers glimpses of still greater height. Joseph Saint-Charles painted *The Presentation of the Virgin in the Temple at Jerusalem,* filling the half-dome of the raised apse and focusing the long perspective of the chapel: the child climbs the altar steps in the temple toward the High Priest, offering herself to the Lord, just as candidates for the priesthood do at ordination. The École des beaux-arts' search for *caractère* appropriate to the specific commission shows its legacy: grand simplicity, restrained richness, concentration and repose.

Chapelle du Grand Séminaire de Montréal,
Montréal, Québec; Roman Catholic. Stone, marble and wood, 1904–07; J. Omer Marchand, architect

Executed in 1904–07, the Grand Séminaire's chapel belongs to the same decade and grows from the same Beaux-Arts design philosophy as the Bank of Montreal headquarters by McKim, Mead & White of New York: overscaled, executed in the finest materials, exquisitely refined in detail and liberally funded.

J. CHARLAND
1962

We relied solely on the size and harmony of the volumes, the balance of the masses, the play of shade and light and the rhythm of the proportions to produce an interesting effect. Nothing was designed for purely ornamental purposes, but distinctly utilitarian elements were used to advantage.

— *Ernest Cormier, 1947*

Québec Modernism

Cathédrale Saint-Jean-Baptiste, *Nicolet, Québec; Roman Catholic. Concrete, 1961–62; Gérard Malouin, architect. Glass by Jean-Paul Charland & Éric de Therry.*
Part of the enormous window by Jean-Paul Charland, this scene shows John the Baptist, dressed simply in a green cloak, at the time of Jesus' baptism. Jesus is absent, but the Risen Jesus faces John from the rear of the sanctuary. The dove over John's head symbolizes the Holy Spirit, alluding to Matthew 3:17: "the heavens were opened and he saw the Spirit of God descending like a dove." The window was executed in the workshops of Max Ingrand in Paris.

MODERN CONCRETE TECHNOLOGY came earlier to Québec than to other parts of Canada. Late Roman and Byzantine structures exploited the architectural potential of concrete, but the technical expertise disappeared for more than a thousand years, only to re-emerge during the late 19th and early 20th centuries. The earliest example of concrete technology in Québec is Montréal's **Saint-Michael and Saint-Anthony**, designed in 1910 by Aristide Beaugrand-Champagne (*see* p.108). However, concrete was not commonly used until after World War II, when the International Style of Le Corbusier (1887–1965), Oscar Niemeyer (b. 1907) and others became influential. In the 1920s and 30s cautious concrete experiments took place in Montréal, where Ernest Cormier and Dom Paul Bellot (*see* p. 168) were leading figures. When Paul-Émile Borduas' "Refus global" called for alternatives to Québec's political, social and religious authoritarianism in 1948, the province was ripe for more artistic experimentation, attempted nowhere more vigorously than in the Saguenay–Lac-Saint-Jean area: by about 1960, writes Claude Bergeron, "the diocese of Chicoutimi had received both public and specialist attention for the novelty of its white churches with graceful lines that seemed the most audacious manifestations of modernism in Québec."

Ernest Cormier (1885–1980), whose work included the Supreme Court Building in Ottawa, bridged Art Deco and International styles. But his churches, though modern, seem modelled on ancient Roman basilicas, the result of his training at the École des Beaux-Arts in Paris. He first experimented with concrete churches in **Saint-Ambroise**. Its interior is marked by an unusual baldachin-like arrangement between sets of windows, which interrupts the aisles and creates important side chapels. This church coincided with the commission for the main buildings of the Université de Montréal (1924–67), which included a chapel. The chapel has now become part of the medical faculty, but its roof structure, though not accessible, is still intact. These early concrete experiments show best in the **Misión Católica Latinoaméricana Nuestra Señora de Guadalupe**, as Sainte-Marguerite-Marie is now named, at the north end of the Jacques Cartier Bridge, in an appropriately Latin-American style plaza. The façade's six Corinthian columns — a pair at each end with single columns between — create a strong arcaded entry. The motif of columns and arcade is repeated in the nave, with its clear-span flat ceiling, while the apse is emphasized by still larger Corinthian columns and pilasters, all of which blends Baroque, Neoclassical and Art Deco features (especially the windows). Rich details are everywhere evident: vividly veined marble dados, grey-and-white marble in the columns, and accents in red, gold and black mosaics in the chancel steps, pulpit and lectern. Latin-American side altars, carpets and traditional motifs now complement these.

The huge **Oratoire Saint-Joseph** by Dalbé Viau and Alphonse Venne was built on the north side of Mount Royal, beginning in 1924 after the crypt church was built in 1916. Its size reflected the impressive reputation of Brother André (Alfred Bessette; 1845–1937), a member of the Congregation of the Holy Cross. His small

Église Saint-Ambroise, *Montréal, Québec; Roman Catholic. Concrete and brick, 1923–28; Ernest Cormier, architect*

Cormier's earliest concrete design, with its high bell tower to one side, is almost self-consciously Byzantine in some of its details. The façade is focused on a baldachin-like entrance formed by two large Corinthian columns in marble. The roof of the baldachin is reflected in the pediment. The facade has a finely detailed brick pattern with regular soldier courses.

The interior repeats the motif in a most unusual way between paints of windows. In place of marble, the otherwise austere interior uses scagliola ("false marble").

chapel had become a pilgrimage centre, a precursor of Brother André's vision of an oratory dedicated to Saint Joseph. The Depression of the 1930s slowed the work. In 1937 Dom Paul Bellot (1876–1944) — who had visited Canada in 1934 (*see* pp. 168–71) to lecture on his combination of modernist architecture, Benedictine spirituality, modern aesthetics and innovative concrete technology — and Lucien Parent were invited to complete the oratory's dome.

Bellot's huge dome over the Latin-cross plan in the concrete and stone interior overawes pilgrims and visitors. Everything else in the interior pales into insignificance beside the utilitarian grandeur of the concrete. Most of the pilgrimage activity is confined to the lower levels, after a long stair, including wooden steps for pilgrims wishing to ascend on their knees up from the street level. The complex composition of crypt, terrace, facade and oratory almost matches the interior. It is grand — too grand for Brother André, who died the year Bellot began his work on the building — and unforgettably regal in its setting on the back of the mountain.

While the history of domes is two millennia long, 20th-century technological developments superseded older technologies. In one innovation, long spans could be bridged with relatively small beams by introducing compression into concrete through tensioned steel members, either before (prestressed) or after (post-tensioned) pouring the concrete. **Saint-Richard**, **Montréal**, by Maurice Robillard, makes economical and visually effective use of T-shaped precast and prestressed units, with

Misión Católica Latinoaméricana Nuestra Señora de Guadalupe, *Montréal, Québec; Roman Catholic. Concrete and brick, 1924; Ernest Cormier, architect*

Originally **Sainte-Marguerite-Marie,** Cormier's church now has the advantage of facing a spacious park created on recently cleared land. The plaza and fountains in front resonate with the Italianate façade, its six marble columns and three immense arches.

Inside, the huge Corinthian columns and arcade of the exterior are repeated along the nave walls, providing a large clear span and a flat ceiling, decorated in greens, white and gold.

Oratoire Saint-Joseph, *Montréal, Québec; Roman Catholic. Concrete and stone, 1924–67; Dalbé Viau and Alphonse Venne, architects; dome (1937), Dom Paul Bellot and Lucien Parent, architects*

In addition to the dome, Dom Paul Bellot added the enormous Corinthian colonnade across the north front of the oratory, somewhat similar to Cormier's colonnade at Sainte-Marguerite-Marie. It is one of Canada's most instantly recognizable facades. Both the entrances and the large semicircular window over the colonnade are deeply recessed. The oratory sits above and behind the crypt church (foreground) with the main access to the church from the plaza above the crypt or from the sides.

Looking along the nave to the altar, the main features of the design appear in simplified forms, stone walls and angular concrete arches. Bellot's distinctive polygonal members support the roof and dome over the crossing. The 16 windows in the drum filled with stained glass allow light to flood the church.

The concrete dome's main structural members are clearly exposed: four main columns (hung with banners), slightly arched main beams, a ring beam, the drum with its 16 windows and the dome itself. Dom Bellot's most visible work in Montréal underscores his imaginative aesthetic in the service of the Church.

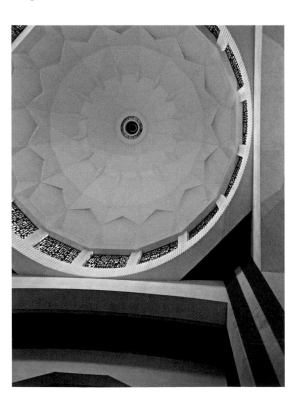

chunky uprights and thinner cross members, that are used horizontally for the roof and vertically for the exterior walls and the bell tower.

Cormier began experimenting with thin shells in 1928, first in airplane hangars in Montréal's east end. Using shells for churches was a natural extension, though not one either Cormier or Bellot took. **Première Église Évangélique Arménienne** (originally Saint-Gaétan) was designed by Louis-J. Lapierre. It uses thin-shell technology in the shape of hyperbolic paraboloids because of the shape's inherent strength. (The same form in wood was used the same year, 1966, in West Vancouver Baptist.) The shells', four low points rest on massive supports and four paraboloids vault upwards to create a large open span. The supports, help to articulate the separation between roof structure, grade and main floor.

It is surprising, however, that similar experiments occurred earlier in the Saguenay area, hardly the place to expect sophisticated innovations. **Saint-Marc, La Baie** (1955–56) is the earliest. Paul-Marie Côté emphasized the structure's folded concrete geometry externally by serrations along the ridge, while inside he contrasted the stark white shell with fieldstone walls in the chancel, transepts and entrance, along with a natural wood dado. A pastel green crown over a black granite altar echoes the green pews; the altar, pulled out from the wall, anticipates Vatican II's later liturgical reforms, in which the priest faces the congregation. On the west wall a small gallery is backlit by blue, yellow and clear glass rectangles. A freestanding bell tower rises high above the roof. Though Côté's church now seems slightly dated, its significance in Canada is as great as Marcel Breuer's chapel in Collegeville, Minnesota, from the same period.

Twenty miles away, the sides of **Saint-Raphaël, Jonquière**, are inclined, gently

ABOVE **Première Église Évangélique Arménienne**, *Montréal, Québec; Armenian Evangelical (originally Saint-Gaétan Roman Catholic). Concrete shell, 1966'–'67; Louis-J. Lapierre, architect*

Lapierre used four hyperbolic paraboloids separated by slots to span a large clear space that seems to float free of the ground, by virtue of four huge supports set deep in the ground at the midpoints of the four sides. While the perimeter lines of the shells are parallel to the streets, the axis of the church is on the diagonal, to take advantage of the tipped-up corners of the shells for the chancel and entrance.

Saint-Richard, *Montréal (Côte-Saint-Luc), Québec; Roman Catholic. Prestressed concrete, 1962–63; Maurice Robillard, architect*

Saint-Richard won the Prestressed Concrete Prize in 1963. The upper ends of the walls' precast units are slotted to take the roof members, while the bell tower soars above the entrance, using two spaced precast units to hang the bell. A finely modulated exterior results from the use of a very utilitarian building element.

Saint-Raphaël, *Jonquière, Québec; Roman Catholic. Concrete, 1959–60; Evans Saint-Gelais and Fernand Tremblay, architects*

Tremblay's lofty triangular concrete church won a 1961 Massey Medal for Architecture. The clear glass end wall emphasizes the subtle effects of the curved roof, and a tall freestanding bell tower to one side gives the church visibility throughout the town.

curved planes separated by a glass strip down the central axis. The chancel wall, too, is separated from the roof planes by pale-yellow glass strips and the glass entrance façade is broken only by a cantilevered porch roof. The building grows out of the ground, especially when snowdrifts fill the flatter lower sections of ribbed metal roofing. In conception it is related to Max Abramovitz's chapels at Brandeis University in Massachusetts.

The most uncompromising of the Saguenay churches is Léonce Desgagné and Côté's **Notre-Dame-de-Fatima, Jonquière**, with its conical form and glazed slots creating dynamic interior movement. The main entrance at the base of one slot has a broad projecting roof and spout reminiscent of Le Corbusier. Instead of the expected circular seating plan, six banks of pews are arranged almost parallel, reducing the form's dramatic potential. Two half-cones end in a glazed oculus, with one extending upward into a slender tapering spire that acts visually like a bell tower.

The soft curves, both in plan and section, of **Saint-Gérard-Majella, Saint-Jean-sur-Richelieu** echo some of the leading developments in post–World War II international architecture, especially Le Corbusier's chapel at Ronchamps in France's Vosges Mountains. Saint-Gérard-Majella (1726–55), a little-known Italian, was a Redemptorist lay brother, a gardener, porter, tailor, sacristan and health-care worker, called "the wonder-worker" because of his intercessory prayer. On his deathbed a note tacked to his door read: "Here the will of God is done, as God wills, and as long as God wills." This unassuming suburban church is a fitting tribute to an unassuming lay brother.

The warm brown brick gives the church an Arts and Crafts feel, though its curves are distinctly late 20th century. At the northwest corner a semicircular projection houses a now unused baptismal chapel. The exterior is puzzling; the main entrance at one corner is obvious enough, with recessed doors below a grey curtain wall. However, the composition of the curtain wall's material, which is repeated extensively on the north wall and high along the south wall, is not obvious.

The entrance to the nave is up interior steps from the front door, through a long narrow narthex that ends with the unused baptismal chapel. The nave's strong sense of enclosure and remarkably colourful light are a total surprise. A projecting balcony on the north side features cast-concrete Stations of the Cross — visually reminiscent of Georges Rouault's religious art — on its concrete rail. A quiet room for mothers and children on the left is balanced by the choir on the right. The generous curved chancel between is suffused with light from windows behind the choir, which also illuminate a magnificent stained-glass installation that screens the choir from the congregation. This off-centre element is balanced by a large cross suspended from the ceiling, located so that a subtle shadow of a strikingly emaciated and youthful figure of Jesus falls on the curved rear wall of the chancel.

Furnishings are simple. The form of the white altar is repeated in the simple plain white pulpit with varnished wooden reading stand. The baptismal font, which replaces the baptismal chapel, is varnished wood. The furniture's fabric repeats one of the fibreglass wall's colours. The carefully balanced asymmetrical elements create a dynamic harmony, combining movement and repose. By comparison with the larger and bolder cathedral church at Nicolet (*see* p. 174), which is strongly symmetrical, Saint-Gérard-Majella, from exactly the same period, is architecturally more satisfying: modest, reticent and communal.

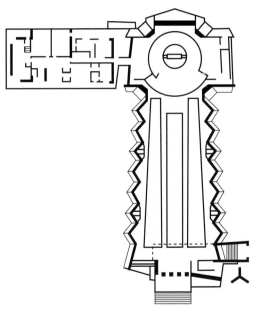

Saint-Marc, *La Baie, Québec; Roman Catholic. Folded concrete shell, 1955–56; Paul-Marie Côté, architect*

A traditional Latin-cross plan contrasts with the experimental triangular folded-concrete roof planes in Côté's design. The shell's structural strength is provided by the triangular folds. The generous site is planted with cedars and birches that soften the church's geometry and almost hide the recessed basement windows, which from the sides suggest the building is floating above the ground.

Notre-Dame-de-Fatima, *Jonquière, Québec; Roman Catholic. Concrete, 1962–63; Léonce Desgagné and Paul-Marie Côté, architects*

The two halves of the conical concrete form slip past each other, but are glazed so that light enters the two inclined slits, making this one of the most startling and unexpected sights in Canada. The brilliant white church has a strong sense of invitation as it soars to dazzling effect above the modest working-class neighbourhood.

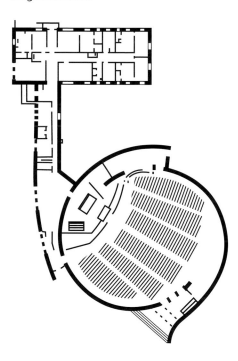

Saint-Gérard-Majella, *Saint-Jean-sur-Richelieu, Québec; Roman Catholic. Concrete and brick, 1961–62; Affleck, Desbarats, Dimakopoulos, Lebensold, Sise, architects*

Warm brown brick, laid in Flemish bond, is used for church, presbytery and tower. The tower supports four bells, whose mechanisms are exposed to view. Both front and rear walls move forward and upward in gentle curves, resulting in a composition that is eccentric but well balanced.

The logic of the building is unveiled only inside; a sense of enclosure comes from the sinuous asymmetrical curves of the roof, formed by concrete beams and precast concrete slabs, and from the plan's combined curves and straight lines. Fibreglass panels appear opaque and dull-grey on the exterior but are almost magically transformed into swaths of brilliant colour on the interior, especially on the north wall's floor-to-ceiling windows.

Idleness is the enemy of the soul; and therefore the brethren ought to be employed in manual labor at certain times, at others, in devout reading.

— *Rule of St. Benedict, ca 530*

Pray and Work

CHRISTIAN MONASTERIES BEGAN in the third century in Palestine and Egypt and spread quickly throughout the Mediterranean and beyond (*see* p. 376). Among the various rules for monastic life, the Rule of Saint Benedict (ca 480–547) was especially influential. It balanced worship, prayer and work. Today's Benedictine schedule is still woven around the medieval liturgical cycle, and Benedictine monasteries still follow Benedict's rule to welcome visitors. Two modern Canadian monasteries with dramatically different architectural styles follow the Benedictine rule: the **Abbaye de Saint-Benoît-du-Lac** in Québec and **Westminster Abbey, Mission**, British Columbia. Other communities in Canada also follow a monastic or quasi-monastic rule, not all of them Roman Catholic. The **Sisterhood of St. John the Divine, Thornhill,** Ontario is a cloistered group within the Anglican tradition, whose members have taken vows of poverty, chastity and obedience. By contrast, **L'Arche Dayspring, Richmond Hill,** Ontario is an ecumenical home for disabled adults, not cloistered in the traditional sense, but with roots that go back in large part to a monastic community of worker-priests at Taizé in Burgundy. All four include powerful modern churches with exquisite attention to detail, especially in their liturgically important features. All have exurban sites, three of which overlook water. All have a strong work ethic and a deep spiritual motivation.

Abbaye de Saint-Benoît-du-Lac was built by a group of French Benedictines who were deprived of their property in Normandy in 1901; they relocated to Belgium and then, in 1912, to the Eastern Townships. Their leader, Dom Paul Vannier, was drowned two years later with another monk when ice cut their boat apart. At the end of World War I, Benedictine authorities telegraphed: "Liquidate and come back." The community delayed, barely survived, then became autonomous in 1935 and ultimately prospered. They decided to build a major complex under the guidance of Dom Paul Bellot, who had visited Canada in 1934 (*see* pp. 159–62). He subsequently established a master plan, overseeing the first stage of building (1939–41).

Bellot's approach — harmony between the laws of geometry and of nature — was continued by Dom Claude Côté (1909–86) in the small Tour Saint-Benoît chapel (1947), guesthouse, *clocher* and church basement (1955–62). When Dan S.

Abbaye de Saint-Benoît-du-Lac, *near Austin, Québec; Roman Catholic. Earlier parts, brick and concrete, 1939–41; 1955–62, Dom Paul Bellot and Dom Claude Côté, architects; church, brick and steel, 1990–94, Dan S. Hanganu, architect*

The corridor from the entrance to the abbey church, by Dom Claude Côté, is a riot of coloured floor tiles and four colours of brick, with arches that repeat Bellot's characteristic polygonal arches, drawing the eye upward and forward.

Abbaye de Saint-Benoît-du-Lac, *exterior*
From the direction of the lake, the various parts of the composition rise above the rolling hills of the Eastern Townships. The flat gable on the right is part of Dan Hanganu's church, the octagonal tower in the centre is the roof of Dom Paul Bellot's chapter house, and the tall tower on the left marks the juncture between the guesthouse and the church. Although three architects were involved over more than half a century, the pieces form a harmonious whole.

OPPOSITE **Abbaye de Saint-Benoît-du-Lac**, *interior*
The nave walls in Hanganu's church show the careful detailing that every part of the building has been given: bronzed steel roof deck, bronzed steel columns, walls of brick, bands of stone and stainless steel light fixtures. Especially noteworthy is the way the walls step back as they rise. These reverse buttresses are then pierced with openings at the gallery level. The result is as aesthetically pleasing as it is spiritually calming.

Hanganu (b. 1939), a Montréal architect, won a competition to design the abbey church, he had to choose between imitating Bellot, which Côté had done, and introducing a new voice. He respected but did not imitate, by introducing a modern aesthetic and working with great restraint. Thus, the bright material colours — bricks, tiles and mortars (in zones of yellow, grey and red) that knit the patterned fabric together — in Côté's public corridor from the entrance to the church give way in Hanganu's aesthetic to an almost monochromatic palette.

Hanganu's church (consecrated 1994) is a rational structure that combines beige brick and stone bands with columns, beams and roof deck in bronzed steel. A blond organ case on the left, contrasting with the dark oak pews in the nave and chancel, pierces the whole height of the church flanked by banks of silvered pipes. The lively sense of repose assists calm, focused worship. There is almost no decoration: no gold, little colour and only two wooden sculptures — of the Virgin Mary and of Saint Benedict with Saint Scholastica, his sister.

Worship focuses on a plain raised altar — with a reading desk beside it and monks' stalls in front — framed by a series of planes: a large rectangular brick opening, a semi-transparent screen and the end wall with windows. The passage's brick walls and polygonal arches, which recollect Bellot's arches, have small rectangular windows

at the main floor level and large openings to the nave. The nave is defined by high steel columns, but the upper level is stepped back over the side passages, like reversed buttresses, and the nave's sense of spaciousness is increased by high slot windows.

If Saint-Benoît-du-Lac shows tight restraint in brick, steel and wood, **Westminster Abbey, Mission**, British Columbia, shows emotional expression in concrete and glass. In 1939 Mount Angel Abbey, Oregon, agreed to staff the Seminary of Christ the King in Ladner, BC. After a period in Burnaby, the seminary moved to Mission in 1953, when construction began on a new abbey, church and seminary. The abbey church designed by Asbjørn Gåthe (1921–94) is strongly European in feel. Its poured-in-place concrete frame evokes a late medieval church, with cruciform columns and repetitive ribbed vaults, whose intersections are often unsupported, drooping like lace from the roof. The large sanctuary appears uncluttered, despite the large concrete bas-relief Stations of the Cross using historical figures as their motifs.

Lutz Haufschild's glass appears to vibrate in the sunlight. Each window is dominantly but not exclusively one brilliant primary colour, blues mostly on the north, reds and oranges and yellows mostly on the south, earthy colours mostly on the west. Each part of the church has its own character and every interior vista

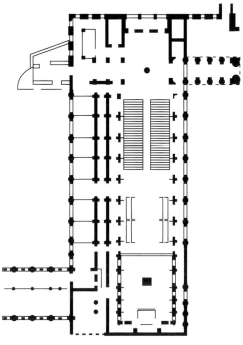

Westminster Abbey, *Mission, British Columbia; Roman Catholic. Concrete, 1953–82; Asbjørn Gåthe, architect*

The abbey church's exterior only dimly hints at the interior's riches. Like late medieval churches, it involved a remarkable collaboration between architect, engineer, glassmaker and sculptor. And like those churches, the total effect is not of competition but of cooperation. The plan is a Latin cross, with the altar under the crossing, roofed by a complex, baldachin-like structure surrounded by 12 large coloured-glass skylights.

is different. The general effect of the glass is not unlike the overall impact of the late medieval King's College Chapel, Cambridge (*see* p. 386), with huge windows filling the walls' upper registers. The exterior design — a concrete structure resting on low brick walls — seems rather prosaic in comparison.

The **Sisters of St. John the Divine** emphasize the life of prayer, their lives organized around three services of prayer each day. The group in Thornhill is best known for its involvement with St. John's Rehabilitation Hospital next door, a medical ministry that began almost with the founding of the order in 1884 by Hannah Grier Coome, who grew up in Carrying Place and Belleville and was married to an architect. Increasingly its activities focus on retreats and liturgical renewal, assisted by its new buildings with the convent chapel at the centre. There are two courtyards: public activities revolve around one, which includes an old wing, while the communal life of the sisters revolves around a second. Common areas between the two courtyards include the main entrance, the refectory and kitchen, and the chapel.

A remarkably successful feature of the chapel is the inclusion of a number of pieces from the order's earlier chapels. The entrance includes stained-glass windows from their 1892 Major Street chapel; off this a generous narthex has a limestone fireplace from an earlier building, and at the entrance to the chapel a limestone font is a gift from a Toronto church. Opposite the font, the limestone altar, designed for an earlier chapel in 1956 by Jacobine Jones (1897–1976), has symbols of the phoenix, the pelican and the eagle — three feminine images of God — in three panels. The high, curved ceiling of the chapel cups worshippers, as in the palm of a hand, and north light from the clerestory floods the intricately detailed acoustic cedar ceiling on the curved portion. A highlight of the simple but effective space is a new tracker organ that rises up to the highest part of the room. Under the high clerestory are 12 stained-glass windows, again from an earlier chapel, incorporated in a louvre-like arrangement. Behind the convent chapel is a Lady chapel that includes an oak altar and a stained-glass window, both from earlier chapels, while outside its main window is another Jacobine Jones sculpture, this one of Saint John.

The exterior of the whole complex, including the chapel, is unassuming. The buildings are a red-brown brick and the chapel is visible mainly by its windows. The entrance is tucked in behind the chapel, which from this side consists primarily of a soft grey lead roof that follows the curve of the chapel.

L'Arche Dayspring Chapel contrasts sharply with St. John's in siting, materials and approach. It is located beside a revitalized wetland with a nature walk around it. The chapel is the newest part of a complex that provides a residential home for disabled adults — and those who work with them — so that they can live in community with dignity. It is one of 190 homes worldwide associated with the work of Jean Vanier, the founder of L'Arche. Part of the inspiration for the homes is the worker-priest community at Taizé in France, an emphasis continued in the deep dedication of the workers in the L'Arche homes. This home was begun by Sue Mosteller, C.S.J. (Sisters of St. Joseph), and its first pastor was the well-known speaker and author Henri Nouwen.

Outside, the chapel is marked by a tall half-open bell tower, behind berms that provide some screening from busy Yonge Street. It has a broad aspect, as compared with the rather tight appearance of St. John's, with a generous deck along one face, and a deck at the end hanging over an ecologically significant pond, fed by a stream

St. John's Convent, *Thornhill, Ontario; Anglican. Brick, 2003–04; Montgomery & Sisam, architects*

The Anglican convent occupies a narrow site beside the separately administered convalescent hospital. Its interior reflects the cupped shape of the roof, a segmentally curved form providing fine acoustics. The movable furnishings (some brought from earlier chapels) focus on the altar by Jacobine Jones. The windows on the right face north to the street, providing gentle lighting and visual identification from outside.

BELOW **L'Arche Dayspring Chapel**, *Richmond Hill, Ontario; Ecumenical. Wood and stucco, 1997–99*

A tall freestanding bell tower marks L'Arche's Yonge Street entrance. The building is T-shaped: a long crossbar holds service areas and a shorter vertical stroke houses the chapel. The roofs of the two units create a butterfly shape, seen best from the other side of the pond. The lounge is flanked by decks that benefit from the quiet east-facing view. The wooden materials cohere nicely with the ecologically significant conservation area.

that is a tributary of the Rouge River. The building is T-shaped, with lounge, kitchen, entrances, bookstore, washrooms and offices in the long crossbar of the T, and chapel in the short leg.

The chapel is roughly square, with a central space appropriate for an intimate household group of 20 to 30 and surrounding flexible spaces to hold larger groups. The roof is a simply pitched shed roof; high windows along the east have louvres to screen out direct sunlight. The smaller Emmaus Chapel, which is for private devotions, has a fine window by Hans Rams; its ceiling is brought down to a more intimate scale by an open egg-crate grid. Both faces of the main door have images painted by members of the community and redone in larger compositions by Carolyn Whitney Brown. Massive Douglas fir columns create a sense of solidity, while plain furnishings, including some specially commissioned pieces, enhance the main chapel and the Emmaus Chapel.

These four communal churches are among Canada's most sparkling modern religious buildings. All utilize but adapt self-consciously traditional forms. None of the architects is a household name, but their creative work lifts the spirit and calms frayed Christian sensibilities, while making one optimistic about the continued relevance of monastic ideals in the 21st century.

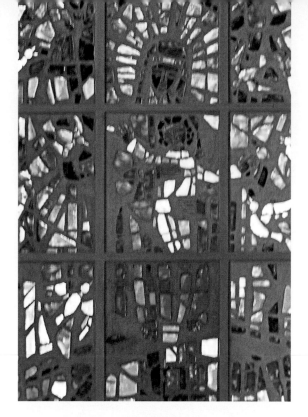

Église Saint-Gérard-Majella, *interior*
The glass screen wall uses almost medieval techniques to create a wonderfully evocative representation of the Virgin and child, in thick blue, yellow and orange glass, set in concrete. Like everything else in the church, it is part of a balanced asymmetrical composition.

Cathédrale Saint-Jean-Baptiste, *interior*
The huge window by Jean-Paul Charland of Nicolet features an immense image of John the Baptist. It was executed in the workshops of Max Ingrand in Paris almost entirely out of coloured pieces of glass, with a minimum amount of drawing on glass.

Glass Tapestries

MODERN CHURCHES, like medieval and early modern churches, have included colourful windows as a part of the design program, in many cases as essential or almost essential elements in the project. The windows constitute glowing tapestries of light within the interior, and sometimes from the exterior. The most successful designers have eschewed the use of 19th-century Victorian approaches to glass design, where much of the design is achieved by drawing directly on the glass, and have returned to medieval approaches, where the effects are dependent on the shape and colour of the glass and the way it is set. In some cases, the glass has been cast in concrete: **Saint-Gérard-Majella**, **Saint-Jean-sur-Richelieu** (*see* p. 164), is a fine example. The glass screen wall between the congregation and the choir is a wonderfully evocative representation of the Virgin Mary holding the baby Jesus, utilizing thick glass in blue, yellow and orange, set in concrete. Like everything else in the church, it is part of a balanced asymmetrical composition.

More frequently the glass is set in lead cames, H-shaped sections that hold the pieces in place. Joe Lobko's main chapel at **L'Arche**, **Richmond Hill**, Ontario, is lit both by direct and indirect lighting, in part by windows overlooking the pond. The smaller Emmaus Chapel — perhaps the chapel's name reflects that it holds only a few people — has a coloured glass window, glimpsed through a small opening behind the liturgical centre. *Sunrise*, designed by Hans Rams (b. 1974) of Germany, is a bright, narrow slash of coloured window along an exterior wall that ensures privacy while still admitting light from the outdoors.

Cathédrale Saint-Jean-Baptiste, **Nicolet**, is situated in a modest town adjacent to a rich agricultural area on the south side of the St. Lawrence River. It seems

designed to catch the attention of automobiles passing by, with a complicated white concrete paraboloid shell by Gérard Malouin of Nicolet (*see* p. 20). The attention of passers-by is captured by a massive screen of coloured glass (165 feet wide and 70 feet high), curved both in plan and in elevation, which gives the cathedral vitality and sparkle. The central motif of the entrance wall, facing another window of the exalted Jesus in the chancel (*see* pp. 109, 158), is an enormous image of John the Baptist by Jean-Paul Charland of Nicolet.

Dom Claude Côté's small chapel, Tour Benoît, at **Abbaye Saint-Benoît-du-Lac,** Québec, is constructed with the same boldly coloured brickwork and mortar of other early parts of the monastery. Its tiny nave, about the size of a processional chapel, includes striking glass work designed by Father Jean Rochon, O.S.B., and made in the workshop of José Osterrath in Cowanville, Québec. The window portrays St. Francis.

Montgomery & Sisam's **Convent for the Sisterhood of St. John the Divine, Thornhill**, Ontario, is lit mainly from high clerestory windows. At floor level, 12 windows by Brown, Brisley and Brown (executed by the Excelsior Glass Company) were installed from the Sisters' earlier Botham Road chapel (1956). Behind the chapel, on the right, is the window of the Lady Chapel, brought from their Major Street chapel, featuring in the top panel John taking Mary home after the Crucifixion.

ABOVE LEFT **L'Arche**, *interior*
Hans Rams (b. 1974) of Germany designed *Sunrise* for the Emmaus Chapel at L'Arche. The wide narrow window at eye-level, with its strong primary colours, makes the small adjacent chapel sing with vibrating light.

ABOVE **Tour Benoit, Saint-Benoit-du-Lac**, *interior*
The chapel windows were designed by Father Jean Rochon, O.S.B., and made in the workshop of José Osterrath in Cowanville, Québec. They portray the Benedictine family, this one of Saint Francis.

LEFT **St. John's convent**, *exterior*
The street elevation's carefully composed rectangles comprise a group of 12 windows by Brown, Brisley and Brown (from the Botham Road chapel). The Lady Chapel window on the right (from the Major Street chapel) shows John taking Mary home after Jesus' crucifixion. The clerestory windows permit an unobstructed view of the cupped ceiling.

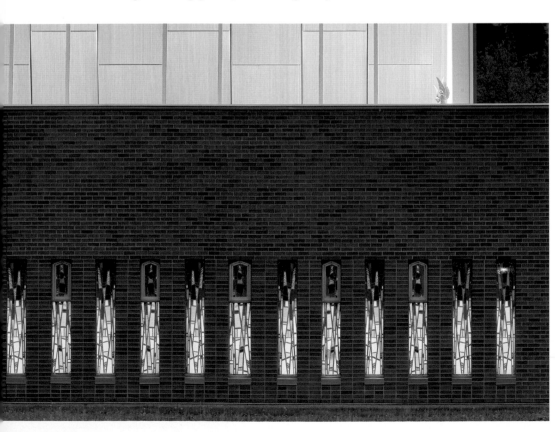

ONTARIO

Introduction

Loyalists to Modernists

We thank you for the sacrifice Of venturers of old,
Who dared to cross uncharted seas, Whose dreams made others bold:
For valiant souls and pioneers, For all who served their age,
And left for us who follow on A sacred heritage.

— *Voices United # 523 United Church*

New France

ONTARIO'S GEOGRAPHY is a mix of granite Shield, lakes, rivers and arable land. The St. Lawrence River is Ontario's connection with the sea through Québec, so the two regions have a symbiotic geographic relationship. Their central location and natural resources have decisively influenced their wealth and ultimately their role in confederation. The name "Ontario," taken from the old aboriginal name of the easternmost Great Lake, was applied to the province only in 1867. Until the end of the French régime, the region was the western part of New France, mainly useful as a way to get to rich fur country or to French settlements in Ohio, Michigan, the Mississippi basin and the Northwest.

Henry Hudson and his crew may have been the first Europeans to touch Ontario's northern shore on his fateful third voyage in 1610–11. But Samuel de Champlain and Étienne Brûlé were the first white men to explore central Ontario, travelling the Ottawa–French River route from New France in 1613 and 1615. Brûlé was probably the first to see Lakes Ontario and Huron. Later, René-Robert Cavelier de La Salle built the *Griffon* to sail the Great Lakes; he subsequently pressed westward to establish fur-trading posts and claim the Mississippi River basin for New France, eventually reaching the Gulf of Mexico in 1678. Other explorers and traders, such as Médard Chouart Des Groseilliers, Pierre-Esprit Radisson, Louis Jolliet,

Hay Bay Meetinghouse, *near Napanee; Methodist.*
Heavy timber frame, 1792 (enlarged 1835); builder
unknown

The oldest Methodist church in Canada, the building stands, almost miraculously, as a monument both to the innate design sense of pioneer builders and to the enthusiasm of early Methodism. Ironically, the monument to the founder of Methodism in Ontario, Barbara Heck (1734–1804), is in the Anglican cemetery of the Blue Church: "Barbara Heck put her brave soul against the rugged possibilities of the future, and, under God, brought into existence American and Canadian Methodism, and between these her memory will ever form a most hallowed link."

Louis Hennepin and — of great significance — the La Vérendrye family, were active through the late 17th and early 18th centuries.

Settlements around the Great Lakes were few: Sainte-Marie among the Hurons (1639–49, near Midland), Fort Frontenac (1673, now Kingston), Fort Niagara (1679), Fort Detroit (1701), Fort Michilimackinac (1715) and Fort Rouillé (1750–51, now Toronto). The arable areas between Lakes Ontario, Erie and Huron were occupied by France's allies among the Algonquian tribes, the Huron, Neutral and Petun. The Jesuit mission to the Indians was the first white settlement in what is now Ontario; they had arrived in New France in 1625 and were active in Huronia by 1634, though they were preceded there by a few Récollets (1615–29). The Sainte-Marie mission near Midland (*see* pp. 188–91) was then the largest settlement west of Québec.

During the Iroquois Wars, when the Iroquois martyred eight priests, the Jesuits burned Sainte-Marie, fleeing with the mission's Huron inhabitants to Christian Island in Georgian Bay in 1649. The fledgling white and Huron community abandoned their post there after one year of great hardship and the surviving Hurons

went to Québec City with their priests, settling north of the city at Wendake (Ancien Lorette). By 1653 much of southern Ontario was in Iroquois hands. However, carrying out raids on a wide front weakened the Confederacy and forced them to make peace with the French in 1701.

Loyalist Ontario

While New France gradually extended its influence in what became Ontario, the British were slow to show an interest in the region until the Treaty of Utrecht in 1713 granted them lands around Hudson Bay. During the Seven Years' War (1756-63) they occupied the Niagara frontier and gradually extended their control. Under the Treaty of Paris (1763) Britain gained control of the entire Great Lakes basin. The area served as an operational base for attacks on the Thirteen Colonies during the Revolutionary War, following which the Treaty of Paris (1783) settled the southern boundary of Canada along the midpoint of Lakes Ontario, Erie, Huron and

Blue Church, *near Prescott; Anglican. Frame, rebuilt 1845 (original building 1809); builder unknown*

Now primarily a cemetery chapel, this church has been called the Blue Church since its original construction for Loyalists in 1809. Though the present building is not original, it represents, on a slightly smaller scale, the character and colour of the original church in its rural setting a few yards from the St. Lawrence River.

ABOVE **St. Thomas'**, *Brooklin; Anglican. Timber and frame with board-and-batten siding, 1869–70, Gundry & Langley, architects*

Langley drafted this rare Ontario example of Rational Gothic in wood for a small rural Anglican congregation near Whitby. It is an asymmetrical and Picturesque design of board-and-batten, influenced by contemporary American building practice as well as ecclesiology, traditionally oriented, with a distinct chancel attached to its aisleless nave, and a small north porch. The windows are "pointed" with angular tracery and heads. Structural timbers on the west end carry the bellcote.

FACING PAGE **Our Lady of the Immaculate Conception**, *Guelph; Roman Catholic. Stone, 1876–88; Joseph Connolly, architect*

From the air, the vigour of Connolly's plan is obvious, though some of the details, such as the projecting ambulatory chapels around the apse, are apparent only in the church's shadow on the rather unfortunate sea of black asphalt. The sculptural quality of the exterior walls is shown by the deep shadow lines (*see also* p. 233). This depth of treatment contrasts with the smoothness of most of the interior surfaces.

Superior. Upper Canada was created in 1791, with the boundary between Upper and Lower Canada fixed at the Ottawa River.

Although the French had been in possession of what was to become Ontario for well over 100 years, there were few permanent settlers, perhaps 25 to 30 farms along the Detroit River by 1749. English settlements began in earnest with the arrival of the United Empire Loyalists, the first large wave, 7,000 to 8,000 strong, coming in 1783–84. They received Crown land to make up for the loss of their possessions in the original Thirteen Colonies. Subsequently "late Loyalists" came to Ontario more for the cheap land than to remain under the British Crown. The focus of Loyalist settlement was in the St. Lawrence–Lake Ontario townships, with the major concentration from Glengarry to Prince Edward County, as well as settlements from Niagara and the Grand River near Brantford to Windsor. Among the Loyalists were a substantial number of Indians — primarily Iroquois, who had been allies of the British and now settled along the Grand River — as well as free blacks, slaves who came with their masters and escaped slaves. The treatment accorded aboriginals and blacks by the newly dominant Loyalists over the next century and more was, in retrospect, shabby, disrespectful and prejudiced. Legal battles over land ended up in the Privy Council in Britain, which granted much of the First Nations' case but still "granted all rights of ownership to Ontario," holding that the First Nations' right to the land was only usufructuary, which prompted a land-claims lawyer to say, "Indians were used and fructed."

The Loyalists have left an indelible stamp on the culture and religion of southern Ontario. Its earliest churches are Loyalist, including the Anglican Chapel of the

Mohawks (1785; *see* p. 193), the Methodist Conger Meetinghouse (1809–11; *see* pp. 194–95) and Hay Bay Meetinghouse (1792). Other early churches include the Presbyterian St. Andrew's, Williamstown (1812–13; *see* pp. 195–96) and the Anglican Christ Church, Burritt's Rapids (1831–32; *see* p. 199). This small sample hints at Ontario's rich Loyalist architectural heritage: Methodist and Congregational meetinghouses, Presbyterian kirks and Anglican churches tempered by American Episcopalian traditions. Even the Sharon Temple (1825–31; *see* pp. 196–99), with its Quaker origins, shows the effects of Loyalist independence and spiritual traditions. In education, politics and religion, these settlers brought progressive ideas and institutions that shaped decisively the character of late 18th and early 19th century Ontario. The first lieutenant-governor, John Graves Simcoe (1752–1806), himself a British veteran of the Revolutionary War, had a deep commitment to the Crown and its control of the newly defined colony.

War of 1812 to World War I

By 1812, 80 percent of a population of about 100,000 was American in origin. When war broke out with the United States, most rallied to the British cause, though emotions were often mixed. British troops, with Canadian and native militia,

Dominion-Chalmers, *Ottawa; Presbyterian (now United). Brick, 1912–14; Alexander C. Hutchison, architect*

Hutchison combined elements found historically in churches of the Byzantine period or inspired by Byzantium: the central dome with light filtering through the windows in its drum, large round arches, small windows, squat octagonal and square towers and a strong use of light and shade. Off to one side of the bustling centre of Ottawa, Dominion-Chalmers has weathered the last century or so rather well.

successfully held most of the province against American attack, and the War of 1812 effectively convinced Canadians that they wanted to remain with the Crown, independent of the United States. Following the war, however, unrest in the province over governance grew with the strengthening of a fledgling Reform Movement, culminating in the abortive 1837 Rebellion that paralleled a similar rebellion in Lower Canada. A core problem was widespread hostility to the Anglican Church's entrenched rights, including the clergy reserves, lands set aside to support Anglican clergy. Disproportionate numbers of Presbyterians, Methodists and even peaceful souls such as David Willson's followers at Sharon Temple were involved in the unrest. One of those executed following the Rebellion was Samuel Lount, a member of the Children of Peace.

Methodism, which emphasized personal salvation and free choice, was the largest denomination in Ontario in the early 19th century, though members of the Anglican Church, which emphasized social and religious hierarchies, were better connected politically and exercised influence far beyond their numbers. Methodists, who had split off from the Established Church of England, arrived in Ontario from the United States after the Revolution, while Anglicans were already part of the establishment. Anglicans disdained Methodist "enthusiasm," but the Methodist clergy outnumbered the Anglican clergy two to one, or more, as they rode their circuits on horseback serving the common folk. In 1819 there were nine resident Anglican clergy, in 1820 there were 24 Methodist preachers and in 1817 there were seven Roman Catholic priests in Upper Canada.

The first 50 years of British settlement were crucial to Ontario's architectural character. Classical influences had focused on Renaissance models, but soon interest shifted back to the wellsprings of Renaissance architecture, to the Classical period itself. While Classical models dominated for a while, as in St. Andrew's, Niagara-on-the-Lake (*see* pp. 206–09), they gave way to the notion favoured by ecclesiologists in England that Gothic represented an ideal Christian architecture. The Gothic Revival swept all before it, not only in Ontario but elsewhere in Canada, beginning in the 1820s and continuing well into the 20th century (*see* pp. 240–55).

Ontario's population increased dramatically during the first half of the 19th century: between 1825 and 1842 it tripled to 450,000 and by 1851 it had doubled again, to 952,000. Most of the increase was through British immigration — 20 percent English, 20 percent Scottish and 60 percent Irish. As the population grew, more churches were built and old ones were replaced with new and larger structures. The influences of European and British thinking on church design can be seen in, for example, St. John the Baptist, Perth, and St. Joseph's, Douro (Irish Catholic); the Old Stone Church, Thorah, and Knox Church, Oro (Gaelic Scottish Presbyterian); St. Thomas', Shanty Bay, and St. Paul's, London (Church of England); West Dumfries Chapel, Paris, and Black Church, Oro (Methodist). What is remarkable about this church-building boom is how dominant Classical Revival was at first and Gothic Revival soon became.

One result of the 1837 Rebellions was the union of Upper Canada and Lower Canada into the United Province of Canada in 1841, intended to keep French Québec in a minority position. At first Canada West (Ontario) lagged behind Canada East (Québec) but by 1851 its population had surpassed Canada East's by about 60,000. Reformers were on the ascendant, and when they won the election of

Christ Church, *Burritts Rapids; Anglican. Frame, 1831–32; Arthur McClean, designer and builder*
Christ Church shows the gradual transition from Classical Revival to Gothic Revival in its mixture of styles and details. Its interior retains the gently curved gallery.

Christadelphian Church, *Toronto; Christadelphian.*
Brick, 1948–49; John B. Parkin Associates, architects

The Christadelphians' building in central Toronto
was one of the pioneering Modern buildings of the
city. It was an early project of John B. Parkin Associates,
a firm that became leading Modernist architects
following the International Style. The building won a
Massey Medal in architecture for 1950. John B. Parkin
and his brother Edmund were active Christadelphians,
which is a lay and non-Trinitarian movement that
emphasizes Bible study and the simplicity of the
worship and organization of the earliest days of the
church.

1847 they created the University of Toronto as a secular institution in 1849, in a
prelude to sweeping changes to higher education in the province. At the same time
they accepted Roman Catholic demands for church control of a separate school
system. When the LaFontaine-Baldwin government passed the Rebellion Losses
Bill, also in 1849, to compensate French Canadians and even some rebels, Tory
opponents claimed it was payment for disloyalty. In the mob action that followed,
the Parliament Buildings in Montréal were burned.

The rapid rise in Ontario's population meant a heavy strain on support mechanisms for new arrivals, especially those having trouble finding employment or
adjusting to conditions in the new land. When these difficulties were coupled with
occasional economic downswings, the need for soup kitchens and other social
services was sometimes pressing, especially in urban cores. Downtown missions
became common in the second half of the 19th century. Indeed, it is not too much
to claim that the churches' response to such needs, often based on liberal notions of
the social gospel, became the basis of Ontario's social welfare system. Recognizing
that the abuse of alcohol compounded the problems facing poverty-stricken families, the Women's Christian Temperance Union lobbied for prohibition, at the same
time as it lobbied for women's suffrage, the first organization to do so.

Church membership increased during the century's middle years; by 1872 ninety-
nine of every hundred Upper Canadians were affiliated with a church. The denominations themselves tended to be strongly Anglo-Saxon in their origins and character;
80 to 90 percent of the population was Anglican, Methodist, Catholic or Presbyterian.
If there was substantial church building during the first half of the 19th century, there
was truly massive construction during its second half. In 1800 the province's 20,000
inhabitants were served by a handful of churches. At the end of the century, 2.2 mil-
lion people called Ontario home and there were enough churches to accommodate

the entire population. In the 20 years leading up to 1871 alone, nearly 130 new churches were built each year. As Noll says, correctly:

The evolution of church architecture provided a graphic example of this confluence [between denominations]. Methodists who once had built inconspicuous halls that seemed to call people out of the world, now began to construct stately cathedrals that dominated the urban landscape. Anglicans who had once built churches resembling official government buildings now began to construct parish churches after models from an idealized rural England.

Post-World War I

The most decisive church-related event in Ontario following World War I was church union, which took effect in 1925, though it had been mooted much earlier. Methodists and Presbyterians, who had drawn apart in the mid-19th century, had submerged their differences by the end of the century. Discussions between the two had been underway since 1902 and a Basis for Union agreed upon in 1908. Anglicans were involved in early discussions but stayed out. Despite the deep interest of Presbyterians in union, about half did not join. In the end, church union involved Congregationalists, Methodists and Presbyterians, usually the less conservative ones. The impact of church union was huge, not merely organizationally — though that was substantial enough — but in terms of families, congregations and the social fabric of communities. However, the hope of a kind of "national church" was frustrated, in part by the actions of conservatives such as T.T. Shields (1873–1955) of Jarvis Street Baptist (*see* pp. 248–51), who withdrew from the Baptist Convention of Ontario and Quebec over theological differences with McMaster University, then a Baptist institution of higher education. While not many followed Shields out of the Baptist Convention, the tendency for conservative evangelicals to band together accelerated through the remainder of the 20th century, as witnessed by the founding of such organizations as the Evangelical Fellowship of Canada, the quickly growing strength of Pentecostals, and the development of evangelical schools, colleges and universities.

Sharp reductions in the numbers of persons attending church and the subsequent closings, mergers and new strategies advanced to meet this challenge (*see* pp. 274–85) are perhaps more pronounced in Ontario than elsewhere in Canada. The equilibrium has altered, so that the centres of strength are no longer in the large metropolitan churches, but in the rapidly growing suburbs and the megachurches found there. With the turn of the millennium these trends seem, if anything, to be accelerating, with tension building between conservative and more liberal churches, a development that resonates with the political tensions that accompany shifts in religious thinking.

The splurge of church building in the 1950s and 60s resulted in Modernism taking decisive hold of church architecture. This was a time of experimentation and innovation, but with the downturn in church attendance, the number of buildings decreased just at the time that architects were turning away from International styles of modernity and moving into a Post-Modern phase. The result is that relatively few churches built since the 1980s are good examples of Post-Modern and Deconstructionist architecture.

St. Catherine's Chapel, *Massey College, University of Toronto; ecumenical. Brick with wood interior, 1962–63; Ron Thom, architect, with interior by Tanya Moiseiwitsch (1963) and Brigitte Shim (2003)*

Ron Thom's strikingly coherent Massey College recreates an Oxford or Cambridge college. Like them, it has a chapel, though this is much smaller, shoe-horned into the basement by a corner stairwell. The chapel's interior is a masterpiece of wood vaults, with indirect lighting, the 40 or so seats focusing on an 18th century miniature Russian iconostasis (*see also* p. 27).

Sainte-Marie among the Hurons

THE ROUTINE TORTURE of enemies and the stoicism expected of those facing inevitable death were well known to the French. Champlain witnessed the terrible suffering inflicted upon a Huron by his Iroquois captors and terminated the ordeal by shooting the victim. In the 17th century Jesuit missionaries circled the globe; in 1626 there were 15,544 Jesuits, many of whom became martyrs in a number of locations. As they entered upon their mission at **Sainte-Marie-aux-pays-des-Hurons** near Midland, they knew of the dangers they faced.

In 1626 Jean de Brébeuf (1593–1649) founded a mission to the Huron, partners of the French in the fur trade, near Georgian Bay. He and his colleagues built a partially fortified mission post on the Wye River in 1639. In the public church, doors are on the sides, the altar at one end, and a huge stone fireplace stands at the midpoint of one wall. The details of the original building are not known, but the reconstruction carried out in 1964, which includes bark roofing, attempts to be faithful to the archaeological excavations, though some of the details are now disputed. In addition to the church intended for the Hurons, there was a Jesuit chapel in the European settlement.

While the Hurons were content to trade with the missionaries, living near or with them, and even considered converting to Christianity, the Iroquois (hereditary enemies of the Hurons) were determined to eradicate the "black robes." The **Martyrs' Shrine, Midland**, overlooking the site, memorializes the eight Canadian martyrs. The church's designer, Father John Filion, recognized his limitations: "I wanted a church both rustic and amateur and I am sure all the high class architects will agree that it is quite rustic and quite amateur."

ABOVE AND PAGES 190–91 **Sainte-Marie among the Hurons**, *Midland; Roman Catholic complex. Timber (various forms), reconstruction of 1639–49 complex; Charles Boivin and Jean Guiet, builders*

The Sainte-Marie mission post had a Jesuit-European area and a native settlement (shown here), with a wall between. The European area was more heavily fortified than the native area and included some stone walls and bastions. This church, which is about the size of a longhouse, served Huron worshippers. Another church, in the background, was for the Jesuits.

Sainte-Marie among the Hurons, *plaque*
This small lead plaque was found during the excavations in 1954 of the grave that had contained the remains of Fathers Jean de Brébeuf and Gabriel Lalement, both of whom were martyred in 1649: "P. Jean de Brébeuf bruslé par les Iroquois le 17 de mars l'an 1649" ("Father Jean de Brébeuf, burned by the Iroquois, 17 March in the year 1649").

France Bringing Faith to the Hurons of New France, *after 1666 (oil on canvas), anon., in the Ursuline Convent at Québec*

This work allegorizes French missions to aboriginals. The large oil painting, more than seven feet square, from about 1665–75, uses Anne of Austria (mother of Louis XIV) to personify France, standing before a French ship on a great river (the St. Lawrence). To the left, rude mission chapels of squared timber with a cross on the gable show construction methods similar to the Jesuit mission of Sainte-Marie-aux-pays-des-Hurons.

LEFT **Martyrs Shrine**, *Midland; Roman Catholic. Stone, 1925–26; Father John M. Filion, S.J., designer*

The church, built at about the same time as the Oratoire Saint-Joseph in Montréal and, like it, a national shrine, memorializes the eight Jesuits who were martyred between 1642 and 1649 while working among the Hurons.

Every establishment of Church and State that upholds the distinction of ranks and lessens the undue weight of the democratic influence, ought to be introduced.

— *John Graves Simcoe, 1793*

Unity of the Empire

HER MAJESTY'S CHAPEL OF THE MOHAWKS (St. Paul's), Brantford, is Ontario's oldest surviving church and one of two royal chapels in Canada. Dedicated by the Rev. John Stuart of Kingston in 1788, it replaced a chapel built for the Mohawks in 1712 at Fort Hunter, New York. When many of the Six Nations confederacy under Joseph Brant (1742–1807) remained loyal to the British Crown after the American Revolution, they were given 760,000 acres of Crown land along the Grand River. The Mohawks brought with them their Queen Anne communion silver, now divided between the Grand River and the Bay of Quinte groups. Joseph Brant and his son are buried beside the church in Brantford; there is also a memorial to the well-known poet Pauline Johnson.

The plain Georgian building originally had round-headed windows — which have since been Gothicized — and a tower with an octagonal drum and octagonal steeple, modified slightly from the original in its upper parts. The interior walls are wide pine boards with beading to make them look like more expensive narrow boards. But the most immediately symbolic features are the tablets of the Apostles' Creed, the Ten Commandments and the Lord's Prayer in Mohawk, brought from New York in 1784 along with the communion silver. The windows, designed by David Mitson of Dundas and made by M.C. Farrar Bell in England, were added in 1959–62 to tell visually the community's story from its early days.

As the Mohawk Chapel expresses Anglican convictions among Loyalists, the **White Chapel**, **Picton**, or Conger Meetinghouse as it is also known, expresses Methodist convictions. It resembles a New England meetinghouse of the 17th century. Rectangular form and narrow eaves give it a taut, constrained appearance. It may be that the need for the chapel arose from a camp meeting almost on the same

Sharon Temple, *Sharon; Children of Peace. Timber frame, 1825–31; David Willson, designer; Ebenezer and John Doan, builders*

Sharon Temple sits immaculately on its original site, now surrounded by mature trees and with additional 19th-century buildings that have been moved to the site: David Willson's study, Ebenezer Doan's house of 1819, and even Willson's round outhouse. The Temple is one of Canada's most unusual and, in many respects, most brilliantly designed buildings, showcasing the technological and cabinetry skills of its builders.

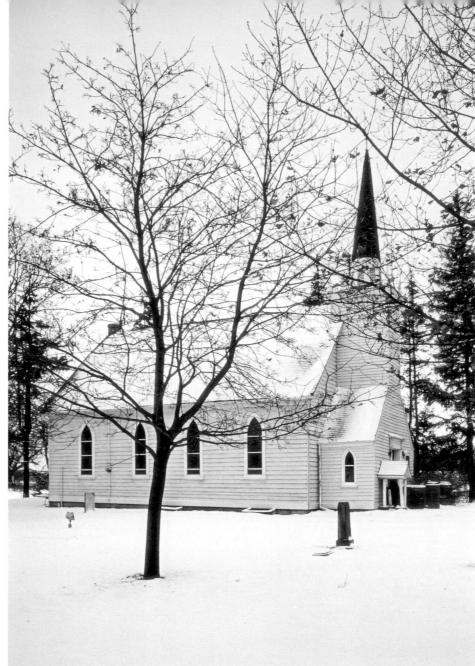

Chapel of the Mohawks, *Brantford; Anglican. Timber and frame, 1785; John Smith and John Wilson, builders*

ABOVE Much of the interior is original, including the interior panelling and ceiling. The chancel and windows have been redesigned.

ABOVE RIGHT The church once faced the Grand River, since the approach was by canoe; when a road was built in 1829, the tower was moved to face it. After the orientation was changed, the steeple was altered slightly and shed-like additions were placed on either side of the door, giving it a stolid appearance.

RIGHT The Apostles' Creed, the Ten Commandments and the Lord's Prayer have been in the church from the beginning. The tablets were brought from Queen Anne's Chapel in New York State and may derive from 1712. (For the Mohawk Bible, *see* p. 35.)

site, which began the great revival of 1805. The two levels of rectangular double-hung windows (12 over 8) effectively light the main floor and the balcony, as well as the double-decker pulpit. The pulpit is now somewhat lower than it was originally, judging from the new location of the sounding board above. In typical meetinghouse fashion, the door is on the (only slightly) longer wall, with the pulpit opposite and a carefully crafted U-shaped balcony above. The pews are simple three-board affairs. Though it ceased to be used regularly as early as 1823, the building is still in excellent condition.

From exactly the same period, but demonstrating the Scots' fondness for stone, **St. Andrew's, Williamstown**, exudes the more sophisticated style and higher social class of Presbyterians. This is the first Church of Scotland building in Upper Canada, founded by the Rev. John Bethune (1750–1815), a Loyalist and the first Presbyterian minister in the colony. It served settlers who had fought for the Crown in the American Revolution.

Williamstown is intimately associated with the Nor'westers; in fact, partners of the North West Company received special consideration in the allocation of pews here. David Thompson and Alexander Mackenzie, who donated its bell, are connected with the church. St. Andrew's reflects their ambitions and associated French influences. It was built by Québec masons in a lofty Neo-Georgian style, with round-headed Palladian windows of fine design and a very unusual semicircular gable truss in the front elevation. A mixture of meetinghouse and Established Church styles often characterizes Scottish kirks, and this is no exception: the pulpit was originally on one long wall, with a U-shaped balcony around it. Yet the door was always in its present location under the bell tower, with supports for the tower and steeple coming straight on through the balcony and nave. The original ceiling's design is unknown; possibly it was open to the trusses. The interior was completely altered in 1882, when the pulpit was moved opposite the door, the balcony was

White Chapel, *Picton; Methodist Episcopal (now United). Timber frame and clapboard, 1809–11; William Moore, builder*

Stephen Conger, a Loyalist from New Jersey, donated the site and may have contributed the materials for this handsomely utilitarian meetinghouse. Its severely geometric form, almost a cube with a near pyramidal roof, gives it a classic but tight appearance.

The preacher stands six steps above the congregation in the double-decker pulpit. Its panelled front and panelled door repeat in different proportions the panelled front of the U-shaped balcony.

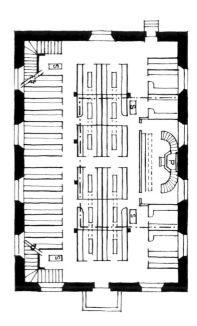

St. Andrew's, *Williamstown; Presbyterian (now United). Stone, 1812–13; François-Xavier Rochileaux, builder; John Anderson and John Kay, carpenters; steeple by Pierre Poitras*

St. Andrew's is the first Church of Scotland building in Upper Canada. Its exceptionally fine windows are strongly Palladian in style with small colonnettes, each with its own mini-capital, at the division points. The arches over the windows are carefully constructed of natural fieldstones, which have been selected to serve as voussoirs, the wedge-shaped pieces that make up the arch.

limited to the end under the tower, a domed ceiling was installed, a rose window replaced the central window above the pulpit's new location, and a porch was added. The resulting disjunction between exterior and interior shows changing tastes from the beginning to the end of the century.

The most remarkable religious building in Canada is **Sharon Temple, Sharon**. There is a purity of conception, design and execution — not to mention restoration — that puts all other religious buildings in the shade. Quakers came to Canada from the United States around 1801, constructing the Newmarket Meetinghouse on land donated by David Willson (1778–1866). But Willson and a small group soon broke away to form the Children of Peace, an egalitarian and millenarian community, similarly pacifist, whose centre was in Sharon (Hope, as it then was) in East Gwillimbury Township, near the lower end of Lake Simcoe.

The building intentionally expresses Willson's theology, much of which, like other 19th-century groups, drew undifferentiatedly on both Old and New Testaments. Like the first temple in Jerusalem, the Sharon Temple was intended to take seven years to build. A Willson hymn captures his general approach:

In peace I write this structure The Lord to gratify,
And raise to him an altar built for his name alone,
That when he comes descending he'll make with me his home.

We'll ring it round with columns, their number Twelve shall be,
To mind us of apostles that once the earth hath trod;
We'll try to follow after and build a throne to God.

We'll raise our semicircles and spring our arches high;
He is the executor that gives to me the plan,
He'll show the art to Woman that's bone of bone to man.

On Ararat we'll place it and Peace its name shall be,
A house of lasting blessing where grace is multiplied,
A rest for every nature and God is the inside.

Sharon Temple, *Sharon; Children of Peace. Timber frame, 1825–31; David Willson, designer; Ebenezer and John Doan, builders*
The totally unexpected interior of the building contrasts vividly with the utilitarian interiors found in contemporary Ontario religious buildings: carefully considered coves at the eaves, arched heads on the larger and smaller colonnades that support the roof and the upper cubes (the columns are named after the twelve Apostles and the four Gospels), but especially the curving stair, "Jacob's Ladder," that gives access to a balcony for the choir and musicians. The rigid double symmetry of the building is apparent from every direction. Dead centre in the building is the ark, a miniature building whose roof swoops to reflect the sweeping arcs above. On the far wall is one of Richard Coates' banners, "Plenty," illustrating Willson's visions. Moses holds an open book, God's revelation in the Law, and Christ, on the right, holds a sealed book, God's revelation still to come, while pointing to a dove, symbol of the Holy Spirit.

Sharon Temple, *exterior*

Annually, on the first Friday of September, the Temple is illuminated with candles in all the windows and in the lanterns at the corners of each stage of the building. The effect is magical. Even at dusk, the impeccable detailing and proportions of the building appear to good effect, and the amount of glass is breathtakingly obvious. Everything in the Temple is symbolically significant. David Willson's theology emphasized that the building must be four-square, with entrances from each direction, indicating people may come from anywhere. A modern drawing (right) of the timber frame shows accurately the economy, the integrity and the complexity of the construction.

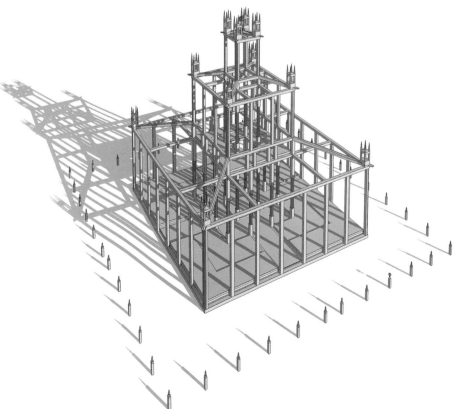

The structure is three graduated cubes, like a wedding cake; all four elevations are symmetrical and identical. The corners of the boxes are all picked out with small square lanterns with four pinnacles on each, the lanterns and pinnacles each made from a single massive timber. The windows are unusually large for a frame building erected in 1825 in rural Ontario and unusually numerous: the first stage has 24 windows, six to a side; the second has 12; the third has four. They differ slightly in size as the building rises. Tall doors are set in the middle of each elevation. A central space punctures all three levels with a balcony for the choir and musicians on the middle level, reached by a unique stair that curves vertically. The space is uncluttered, except for the columns that carry the upper stages. In the middle is an ark or tabernacle, itself a symbolic model of a building, within which is a square table holding a Bible. In 1990 a secret drawer was found in the ark holding an invaluable collection of material from David Willson.

In designing the Temple, Willson thought he was modelling it on the accounts of Israel's Tabernacle and the Jerusalem Temple, though the resemblances owe more to 19th-century musings on the Temple's form than to historic features of that structure. Like the Jerusalem Temple, Sharon Temple was used for special occasions, monthly meetings to raise money for charities, Christmas and an "illumination" event in September. An adjacent meetinghouse met regular worship needs.

The Children of Peace were marginally involved in the Rebellion of 1837 (one of its members was hanged for his part in it). The group played a role in the crucial elections of 1841, when Robert Baldwin (1804–58) ran both in this riding and in Hastings. He won both. His colleague in Lower Canada, Louis-Hippolyte LaFontaine (1807–64), however, did not get elected, so Baldwin resigned his seat in Hope (Sharon) and arranged for LaFontaine to run in a by-election there, with the strong support of David Willson. They visited the building together for the "illumination" in 1841, an event held on the first Friday of September since 1831 and still held today. With the Children of Peace all voting for him, over local objections to a French-speaking candidate, LaFontaine won and the two leaders of the Reform Movement sat in Parliament together, both with strong connections to Sharon and the Children of Peace.

The year Sharon Temple was finished, Christ Church, Burritts Rapids was built on an open site at an intersection of two rural roads, just north of the historic Loyalist village. Though superficially it looks Neo-Gothic (notice the crenellations and the pinnacles on the square tower), many of its details are Neo-Georgian: its low sloped roof, narrow eaves, returned cornice, oculus high in the gable end, quoins, and inside, most splendidly, its four turned Tuscan columns supporting the semi-elliptical balcony front. A generation later, the **Altona Meetinghouse** was constructed in Markham Township for the Mennonite community, a late-Loyalist group that had arrived from Pennsylvania in the early 1800s. The building is virtually as built, from its simple brick — almost classically proportioned — exterior with two doors facing the road to its plain interior with pine floors and pews and simple pulpit. Unlike some Mennonites in the Waterloo area, this group gradually adopted innovations from their neighbours.

Not all churches of this era were plain. Exuberantly Neoclassical in its exterior form and interior decoration, **St. George's Cathedral, Kingston**, derives from the work of the Rev. John Stuart, a Presbyterian turned Anglican, who conducted the

Sharon Temple, *exterior*
The ball suspended between the topmost lanterns represents the world and Christ's lordship of it.

ABOVE **Altona Church**, *Markham Township; Mennonite. Brick, 1852–53; William Feaster, builder*

The Mennonite Church at Altona is as it was built a century and a half ago. The low-pitched gabled roof and plain brick walls are Georgian in character, with excellent proportions in the window sashes, with twelve lights over eight, and panelled doors.

FACING PAGE **St. George's Cathedral**, *Kingston; Anglican. Stone, 1825–28; Thomas Rogers, architect; enlarged 1839–43; rebuilt 1899–1900 after fire; Joseph Power, architect*

St. George's interior has a sculptural Classical Revival quality; the crossing is its most ambitious feature. The dome over the crossing is carried on piers arranged in an octagonal pattern. The quality of detailing throughout is startlingly obvious: moulded plaster on the lower portions of the columns, relief work on the friezes, carefully correct capitals, panelled ceilings and marble floor.

first Church of England services in Upper Canada at Kingston. Stuart had gone to Fort Hunter, New York, as a missionary to the Mohawks under the Society for the Propagation of the Gospel (*see* pp. 32, 35, 193) in 1770. He came as a Loyalist to Upper Canada in 1781, later becoming a frequent visitor to the Chapel of the Mohawks and translated St. Mark's Gospel and the Book of Common Prayer into Mohawk. One of the founding members of St. George's congregation was Joseph Brant's sister, Molly Brant (1736–96), a powerful Six Nations matriarch who was the consort of Sir William Johnson. He was the superintendent of Indian affairs of British North America, before both came to Canada.

Originally a rectangular Classical basilica, St. George's became a cathedral in 1862. It was enlarged in 1891 to the design of Joseph Powers: the nave was doubled and a choir added, along with transepts and galleries and a large main dome. On New Year's morning 1899, fire destroyed everything but the walls. The church was immediately rebuilt, with Power again the architect — a long, narrow, Classically decorated church. It centres on a large, finely detailed dome at the crossing of the nave and transepts, carried on a complex system of vaults arranged octagonally. The nave, chancel and transepts have matching vaulted ceilings, creating a unified form whose interest is enhanced by the splendidly designed Classical mouldings: fluted piers, moulded plasterwork on the columns, vegetal motifs on the architraves and egg-and-dart trim. Below the marble floor under the dome is the tomb, the church's only burial, of Lord Sydenham (1799–1841), Governor-General of British North America, 1839–41, who by persuasion and constitution-making was responsible for linking Upper and Lower Canada.

The cathedral's exterior is smoothly dressed limestone in regular courses, with round-headed windows trimmed with projecting frames. The porch on the main façade has four massive Tuscan columns with a projecting pediment and gable, giving the street elevation *gravitas* and scale. But the most memorable features of Power's exterior are the main dome with its 16 windows and small cupola and the tower with bell-shaped cupola over the narthex.

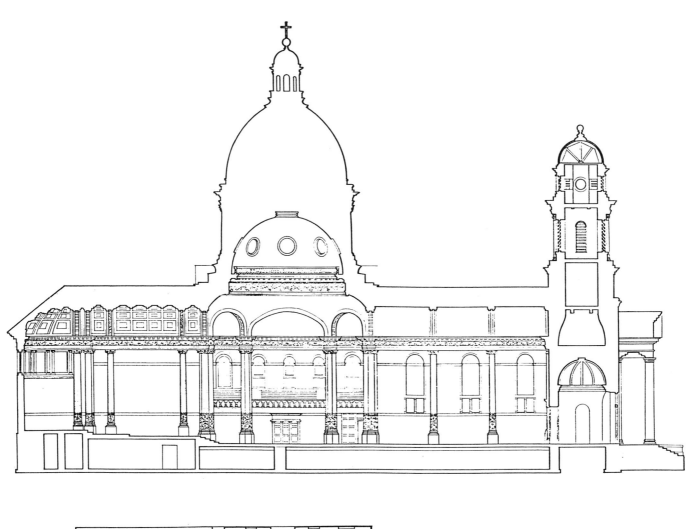

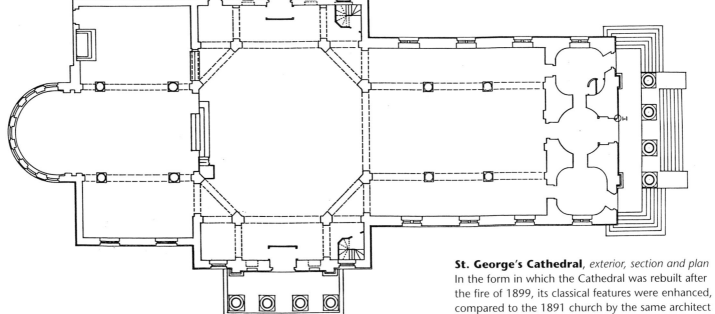

St. George's Cathedral, *exterior, section and plan*
In the form in which the Cathedral was rebuilt after
the fire of 1899, its classical features were enhanced,
compared to the 1891 church by the same architect
that burned. Joseph Powers' projecting porch is framed
with four massive Tuscan columns surmounted by a
boldly projecting pediment and topped with a cupola
that mimics in miniature the large dome over the
crossing. It might well be confused with the Kingston
City Hall, almost across the street.

Christian architecture is the name given to that peculiar style of building, commonly called Gothic, which ... derived its origin from the efforts of Christians ... to embody the principles and characteristics of their faith in the structures which they reared for the services of their religion. The name is used to distinguish it from Pagan Architecture ... the favourite style for civil and monumental architecture.

— William Hay, 1853

Niagara and Southwestern Ontario

St. Thomas, about six miles from Lake Erie, was founded by Thomas Talbot (1771–1853), an Anglo-Irish aristocrat and army officer. After serving on John Graves Simcoe's staff in 1792–94, he claimed an officer's grant of 5,000 acres in Upper Canada and began farming in 1801, apparently near the mouth of Kettle Creek. In the process of promoting settlement in the area, he acquired extraordinary tracts of land. Settlers constructed (**Old**) **St. Thomas Church**, a simple Georgian box, in 1822, in the village of St. Thomas (both presumably named for Talbot's patron saint). A stout wood-framed and clapboarded tower (dated 1824) was added with Talbot's help, topped with wooden battlements and a thin octagonal spire as tall as the tower itself. All the windows (including one above the doors' transom) and the paired belfry openings in the tower rise to pointed arches. The panes of glass in the lower window sashes are rectangular, but kite-shaped in the arched heads, where curved glazing bars crisscross one another, delicately interlacing.

The church's profile is what the Irish call "spike Gothick," but unmistakably Gothic for all its bluntness, and one of the earliest Gothic Revival churches in Canada. Perhaps Talbot suggested the style: his family's seat, Malahide Castle, County Dublin, is primitive Georgian Gothic, favoured by the Anglo-Irish to promote notions of ancient lineage and entitlement. Transepts and a chancel were

Old St. Thomas Church, *St. Thomas; Anglican. Brick, 1822; timber-framed and clapboard tower, 1824; builder unknown*

Originally a simple rectangle, this church stands on a triangular parcel of land where the town of St. Thomas originated. Backing up against the steep ravine of Kettle Creek, it faces north. The original building is predominantly salmon-pink to yellowish-buff brick (now stuccoed because of moisture problems). The transepts and chancel that make the church T-shaped are red-brick additions.

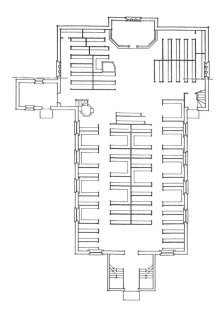

Old St. Thomas, *interior*
Bumpy transitions between successive portions give the church an ad hoc quality, but the interior is literally enlightening. The chancel window is stained glass (almost a necessity because it is south-facing) framed between ogee boards (to match the window), one for the Creed, the other for the Ten Commandments. All of the other windows are old clear glass. The effect is crystalline, even transcendent, especially for those tired of pedestrian stained glass.

added about 1850 in ruddy brick, each face centred on a graceful ogival window, a favourite among 18th-century "Rococo Gothick" designers.

St. Andrew's, Niagara-on-the-Lake, is the epitome of Anglo-American Neoclassicism in Canada. Antiquity's Greek Doric order with no base, symbolizing naked male strength, is wedded here to the decorous red-brick meetinghouse of New England. "Niagara," from *Oniaghara*, ("the mist that thunders"), was the name given not only to the cataract and the river but also to the first capital of Upper Canada. St. Andrew's is an unforgettable feature of the town. Its colossal order is not hackneyed and its context is memorable. With a carpet of lush grass under the red brick and white-painted wood, and a canopy of mature trees above, this is as gracious and serene a sight as any congregation might wish.

The original town plan of Niagara-on-the-Lake was a gridiron of four-acre blocks, further divided into one-acre lots. It called for a central four-acre block to be reserved as green space, a similar green in each quadrant, market squares in the middle of each side and hospitals or cemeteries in the corners. The four-acre blocks touching the central square were set aside for a church, school, courthouse and jail. More than 200 years later, St. Andrew's spacious grounds near the town's centre are heir to this Cartesian order.

The church, built in 1831, belatedly replacing one burnt in the War of 1812, is exceptional in Canada for its Greek Revival style. In 1753, when Roman antiquities were known in detail but ancient Greek monuments were virtually unknown — Greece under Turkish control was considered dangerous for travellers — Scottish architect and archaeologist James Stuart undertook to study Greek architecture. The first folio of Stuart's *Antiquities of Athens* (1762) contains small works but makes

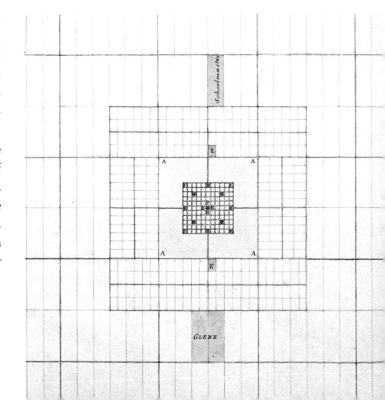

St. Andrew's, *Niagara-on-the-Lake, Ontario; Presbyterian. Brick and wood, 1831; James Cooper, designer; John Edward Clyde and Saxton Burr, carpenters and joiners*

St. Andrew's dignity and apparent monumentality arise from the ancient temple form and simple geometry of its grand porch as much as its unusually spacious four-acre site in the historic community's heart. James Cooper, who supplied the design for the church's principal elevation with this portico, was responsible for the York Market and Town Hall (Toronto) the same year.

"PLAN of a TOWN and TOWNSHIP" *(detail) for the Land Office Department, Canada, 1789, by Thomas Chamberlaine*

Niagara-on-the-Lake was planned in 1791 with generous road allowances (99 feet for principal streets, 66 feet for others), a military-minded gridiron like a Roman camp, except that the town centre grew up close to the fort and waterfront. Two years earlier Thomas Chamberlaine had drafted this little-known ideal plan to guide the development in Canada of new towns amply provided with amenities: large town lots, considerable green space, market squares handy to agriculture, hygienic locations for hospitals and cemeteries. Around this was a green belt, a series of "park lots" for country estates, and farmland. Four-acre blocks touching the central square of the same size (showing here as a Greek cross) were reserved for a church and public buildings. St. Andrew's benefits from this conception of colonial grandeur.

large claims for Greece's importance. The second folio (1789) illustrates more imposing monuments, including the Temple of Theseus (the Hephaisteion), which is doubtless the source of St. Andrew's majestically scaled, severely detailed Doric portico. British interest in Greek Revival may have been sparked by the British Museum's acquisition of the Elgin Marbles, while the Americans valued associations with ancient Greek democracy and had sympathy for modern Greece's struggle for independence.

Greek Revival structures are rare in Canada. The style required a knowledgeable designer, expensive publications, skilled workers and fine stone or marble (if masonry was used). The specifications for St. Andrew's refer to "Cooper's plan, the Grecian Doric." An elevation adapted from Stuart's *Antiquities of Athens*, to be executed in wood, is presumably by James Cooper, a member of the congregation. The steeple, on another piece of paper fastened above the first, is a design taken from Peter Nicholson's *Principles of Architecture* (1795) or *New Practical Builder*

St. Andrew's, *Niagara-on-the-Lake, Ontario; Presbyterian. Brick and wood, 1831; John Edward Clyde and Saxton Burr, carpenters and joiners*

Owing to very long windows (with triple-hung sashes), the absence of stained glass and the use of white paint virtually everywhere, the interior is wonderfully airy in spite of the deep gallery ranging around the three outer walls. Slender, unfluted Doric columns of Georgian style carry the gallery without blocking sightlines from the roomy box pews.

(1823–25). The brick body to which this steeple is attached is in the meetinghouse tradition and the Federal style (developed by Americans in the late 18th and early 19th century) as illustrated in the pattern book by Asher Benjamin, *American Builder's Companion* (1827). The unexpected result is most congenial.

The church's thunderous fluted columns are 5th-century B.C. Attic design of almost archaeological correctness, except that they are pine instead of marble; combined with an American Federal Style brick meetinghouse, the result is a temple-style building. The original steeple (three storeys with delicately proportioned columns and spire), felled by a tornado in 1854, was replaced with a shorter steeple and half as many columns designed by Toronto architect Kivas Tully.

Inside, the tub-shaped desk of the precentor stands in front of the pulpit, continuing an old Scottish tradition. Aided by a tuning fork, the precentor "lined out" the metrical version of the Psalms and the congregants sang them back to him. The practice arose when literacy was not widespread nor psalm books plentiful, and the organ was widely known as "the divil's own kist o'whustles." This tradition lingered to the end of the 19th century in western Ontario's Bruce Peninsula.

Windsor was once an outpost of the French empire. Louisiana's governor, Antoine Laumet (better known as Cadillac), founded Detroit in 1701. Father Armand de La Richardie established a Jesuit mission in 1728 and invited Huron and Wyandotte tribes, descendants of Christian converts in Huronia (*see* pp. 188–91), to live near a fort on the Detroit River's southeast shore. His successor, Father Pierre Poitier, built the first church of the Nôtre Dame de l'Assomption parish at la Pointe

St. Andrew's, *interior*
The semi-cylindrical black-walnut pulpit (1840), topped by a gilded dove, with double flights of winding stairs and a sounding board supported by Ionic columns, is a splendid piece of understatement by John Davidson. Mounted against the vestibule wall, it was originally accessed rather theatrically from the minister's study.

de Montréal opposite Detroit, in 1748–49. In 1765, about 60 French families living in the area petitioned for a separate parish; instead, "The Mission of Our Lady of the Assumption among the Hurons of Detroit" assumed care of both Huron and French parishioners in a second church, begun in 1767. Assumption is Ontario's oldest continuous parish.

Robert Elliott of Detroit designed **Our Lady of the Assumption** in 1834 for a still largely francophone congregation. Elliott, from County Tipperary, Ireland, emigrated to Québec in 1819, was an architect and builder in Rochester, New York, in 1827 and arrived in Detroit in 1834. The cornerstone was laid in 1842, the buff-brick shell completed in 1843 and the church opened in 1846. This is a major hall church in the first generation of Canadian Gothic and essentially Late Georgian in conception — like St. Patrick's in Montréal (*see* pp. 150–51) and St. Michael's in Toronto (*see* pp. 243–45) — with a tower remarkably like St. Patrick's. Assumption is a large, blunt work, with a strong profile rising above its well-treed and grassy grounds close to the river, but it seems justified and balanced. The church has been elevated to minor basilica status.

St. Paul's, London, built as an Anglican parish church, shows a busy architect plundering his own work. After a seven-year apprenticeship as a carpenter in England, William Thomas (1799–1860) became the partner of a carpenter-turned-architect, before architecture was a regulated profession. Apparently he was self-taught in design. Emigrating in mid-career after 14 years of English practice was unusual among architects. During 17 more years in British North America, he faced

Church of Our Lady of the Assumption, *Windsor; Roman Catholic. Brick, 1842–46; Robert Elliott, architect*

Even without a tower Assumption Church used to bulk large. It still does despite the overwhelming presence of the Ambassador International Bridge. The tower and sanctuary were added in 1874. Rosary Chapel, in pink brick, is a compatible addition from 1907–08.

A very decorative pulpit (1793), carved in Baroque style by François Frérot, survives from the third church (1781–85) and was installed in the nave of this, the fourth, in 1848 — a conspicuous reminder of the church's French-Canadian heritage.

similar challenges and dealt with them in the same way. It was usual from the late 18th century onward to view artists romantically, as geniuses making each work of art unique. Thomas, however, tended to repeat himself.

His most significant English church was St. Matthew's, Duddeston (1839–40), on the edge of Birmingham. An aisleless rectangle of red brick in mixed periods of Gothic with a projecting western tower, a short chancel and a U-shaped balcony, it resembles the better sort of English churches from the 1820s. This was Thomas' model for many of his Canadian churches. Bankruptcies and depression in the late 1830s led him to emigrate to the colonies. In mid-1843 he settled in Toronto. London was a small town, recently plotted and mainly wooden, when a major fire destroyed its Anglican church in February 1844. Thomas designed its replacement, which was completed early in 1846, unaffected by other fires that raged through large parts of London in October 1844 and April 1845. St. Paul's and St. Matthew's are very similar; both have insubstantial octagonal buttresses at the corners, thin angle buttresses on the tower and a silhouette that bristles with slender finials. Elevated to cathedral status in 1857, St. Paul's was extended in 1893–94, at which time galleries were taken down, while transepts and a new chancel were added along with other buildings (for the parish and diocese) snaking domino-like to either side.

West Dumfries Wesleyan Methodist Chapel (now **Paris Plains United**), north of Paris, knits together several vernacular styles with an unusual building technique that, with its nubbly texture, looks as if it is knitted of homespun wool. Built with volunteer labor, it is said to have been supervised by Levi Boughton and completed in 1845. Threatened with demolition in 1948, it was rescued by a band of volunteers.

The basic forms are Late Georgian, of golden-section proportions. The plan, end elevations, window openings, individual windowpanes and doorway all approximate a golden rectangle, whose sides are in the ratio of roughly 5:8. The roof is a simple shallow-pitched gable, with returned cornices; the entrance is centred, gracefully suggesting Classic Grecian temple form. But the building is not Greek Revival. The openings rise to pointed arches, hallmark of the Gothic Revival. Round-headed mouldings in the panelled doors are Italianate (together with seating and a communion rail), yet another mid-century convention.

The building utilizes a striking, labour-intensive construction in which small water-washed glacial stones ("cobblestones") in various shades of grey and beige are artfully laid up against a rubblework wall. Ovoid stones are laid end-on, some tipped diagonally rather than flat, in beds of mortar that have been "veed." The distinctive knobby texture alternates with the mortar's sharp V-profile. Contrasting smooth greige limestone quoins with chamfered edges, a favourite Georgian detail, bracket the facades emphatically. The combination of styles and building method is spoken of as a "vernacular"; when applied to construction it suggests locally familiar ways of working materials — something informal and indigenous, rarely self-conscious and in this case charming.

Just off the main street of Niagara-on-the-Lake stands **Free Kirk** (now **Grace United Church**), an attractive Romanesque Revival church built on Victoria Street in 1852. Its use of rust- and buff-coloured brick (the latter with a distinctly pink cast) was avant-garde for its time. John Ruskin's influential *Stones of Venice* had only begun to appear the year before and the second and third volumes, which have

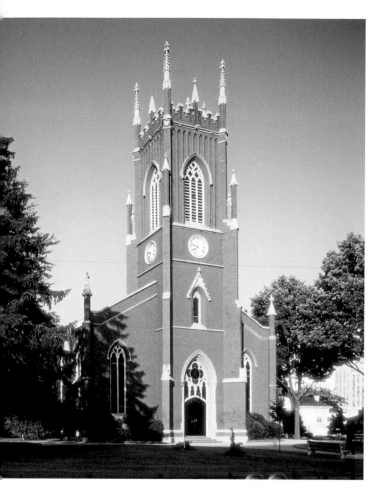

St. Paul's, *London; Anglican. Brick with stone trim, 1844–46; William Thomas, architect*

St. Paul's was designed in early Victorian Gothic — rather earnestly, with sufficient Picturesque variety (after medieval models). But it was economically executed in red brick and detailed so sparingly that the church seems lean, even gaunt. It became a cathedral in 1858 when the diocese of Huron was created.

The greatly extended interior, stripped of a gallery, is lushly Late Victorian in flavour, with its brass-railed, wood-covered marble font near the entrance, Staffordshire floor tiles throughout and Tiffany stained-glass windows (1897) at the new crossing. An initial feature pointing to Thomas' training as a carpenter is the quirky system of cusped wooden roof trusses, proudly exposed to view (as in his English churches), to carry the roof while ornamenting the nave.

much to say about the mixed use of colourful materials, did not appear until 1853. In the absence of distinctly Venetian details, however, a design such as this one was often identified as "Lombard," or simply Italianate.

The Free (Presbyterian) Kirk was built a decade after the Great Disruption of 1843, when Thomas Chalmers led many from the General Assembly of the Established Church of Scotland and founded the Free Church over a dispute as to who could nominate ministers to parishes. The Free Church movement had less significance in Canada, but it promoted development of new congregations and new churches by dividing Presbyterians between "Auld Kirk" and "Free Kirk."

By 1852 William Thomas had nearly a decade of experience as an architect in Canada. He had completed the handsome Niagara Courthouse and Jail nearby in 1846–47 and St. Paul's Anglican in London. In Toronto he had designed a half-dozen churches, including old Knox Presbyterian Church (1847–48). The choice of Romanesque, a "Christian" style, may have been a sly poke at St. Andrew's, the pagan temple the Auld Kirk occupied a few blocks away. The round-arched style also lent itself to brick, desirable because it is fire-resistant. After the breakaway

West Dumfries Chapel, *north of Paris; Wesleyan Methodist (now* **Paris Plains United***). Cobblestone masonry, 1845; Levi Boughton, supervisor*

More than a dozen cobblestone buildings are concentrated in the Paris area, including St. James' (Anglican) Church (1839) in Paris by Levi Boughton, a mason who had lived previously near Rochester, New York. Rochester is the centre of this unusual technique, which bears some resemblance to medieval flint walling in southeastern England.

congregation returned to St. Andrew's, the Free Kirk building was sold in 1875 to a Methodist congregation and is now Grace United.

William Thomas' design for **St. Andrew's** (now **St. Paul's Presbyterian**), **Hamilton**, was the most successful of his many churches, apparently stimulated in part by shameless sectarian competition. "How long do they intend," asked a letter to the press, "to lag behind their neighbours, and to suffer not only Roman Catholics and Episcopalians, but also the Free Church and United Presbyterians, and even Methodists to outstrip them in the laudable ambition of dedicating a handsome edifice to the worship of Almighty God?" The architect produced a design not unlike his own Knox Church in Toronto, already more complex than St. Paul's, London. St. Andrew's contours were more complicated than either, in detail consistently Decorated Gothic, and it was more heavily proportioned: it was as if Thomas had read John Ruskin's condemnation of "thin, unsubstantial English work" and looked at antiquarian publications illustrating medieval details, now available in quantity. In 1849 Thomas had lost the important competition for St. James' Cathedral in Toronto to Frederic Cumberland's bold and hearty design (*see* pp. 245– 48), but Cumberland would suffer the indignity of an uncompleted brick stump for two decades whereas Thomas could be proud of a project finished rapidly and completely. The impoverished congregants, on the other hand, were unable to bear either the cost or the controversy this caused. They split, but those who remained were forced to sell the building to the Park Street Baptists, who also found it unaffordable. After the Presbyterians were reconciled, they bought back the building and reoccupied it in 1874, when it was renamed St. Paul's.

The **Baptist Chapel** (now Walkerton Baptist), **Walkerton**, is a rare example of the sophisticated Arts and Crafts Movement. Arts and Crafts gained momentum toward the end of the 19th century and was still considered avant-garde at the beginning of the 20th. Baptists had just built a small chapel (1883) when they

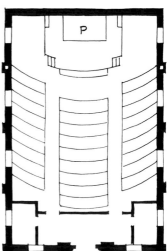

Free Kirk, *Niagara-on-the-Lake; Free Presbyterian (later Methodist, now* **Grace United***). Bichromatic brick, 1852; William Thomas, architect*

The red-brick church is buttressed in buff brick while the silhouette of the facade is enhanced by a corbel table with dainty arches echoing the large round-headed openings — all Italianate features. Setting the church back from the street and breaking up the wall surface, Thomas felicitously softened the church's impact on the residential street.

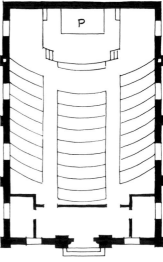

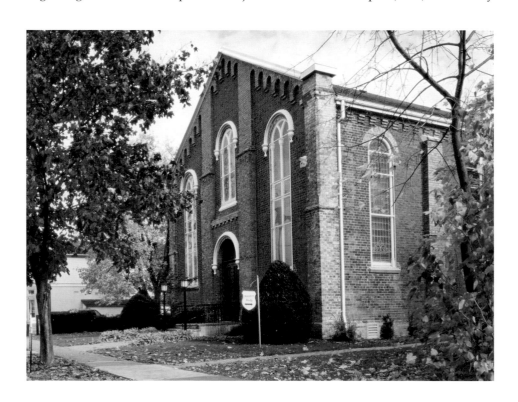

St. Paul's, *Hamilton; Presbyterian (originally St. Andrew's). Stone, 1854–57; William Thomas, architect*

William Thomas prepared a chromolithograph of his perspective drawing for this Presbyterian church in 1854, which unsurprisingly shows a more open setting than the hard urban reality now. A large budget encouraged rich treatment. It was executed wholly in stone, even to the spire — the only stone spire ever erected in Ontario — and it was finished with dispatch. The cost was ruinous.

The elaborate interior is richly carved in dark wood with robust arched and circular motifs, crowded together and endlessly cusped — not in the least "archaeological" in character and yet a motif that riffs on the decoration of the Doge's Palace in Venice (a highly improbable source for a Presbyterian kirk).

Carmel Presbyterian, *Hensall; Presbyterian (now Hensall United). Brick, 1886–87; George F. Durand, architect*

Bichromatic brickwork (polychromatic when black bricks, dipped in tar, added another colour) was dismissed as "streaky bacon style" by some, and apparently regarded as "Toronto style" elsewhere in Canada. It certainly enlivened what was otherwise a fairly conventional Gothic design — an improved version, it would seem, of the Wesleyan Methodist Church (1875) at Tara by Langley, Langley and Burke of Toronto.

approached Langley and Burke, probably knowing Edmund Burke was a committed Baptist himself. (He was the architect of Jarvis Street Baptist Church in Toronto; *see* pp. 249–53.) The 1883 building faces west; the 1889 building presents a handsome new frontage, with two new entrances, to the south. Burke's new nave and gallery effectively trebled seating (in stylish concentric seats), the old structure presumably serving as church hall and Sunday school. The baptistery takes the axial position of a communion table within a shallow chancel; the tank was situated within an arched recess, at the rear of the platform and raised to eye level, emphasizing the central position of adult baptism.

Generally the white-brick townscape of Hensall, north of London, is rather dour, but at **Hensall United** the delicate red-brick patterns of its surfaces are a joyful gift to the street. Throughout the second half of the 19th century, small local brickyards filled the building needs of rural communities due to the high cost of transporting brick. Abundant clay formed in lakes that covered western Ontario in the glacial period produced the yellowish buff brick that was the prevailing material throughout this region. Limited quantities of red brick were available from some brickyards. Here, however, it appears that white brick was stained red to outline delicately all the circular windows and those with arched heads and to band the building (through the buttresses and under the arches). This English technique — used with verve by William Butterfield (especially at All Saints', Margaret Street, in London, 1850–59) — was in vogue in the British Isles in the 1860s and 70s.

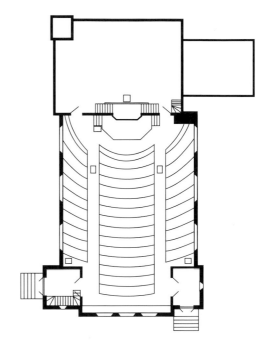

Carmel's architect, George F. Durand (1850–89), was a contractor's son (like many 19th–century architects) with a strong feeling for building materials. He headed a London-based architectural firm, long dominant in southwestern Ontario (1857–1914). Early in his career he was clerk of works for six years in the 1870s on the present New York State capitol at Albany. While the Hensall church was "on the boards" he designed the second-prize entry in the Toronto City Hall competition. He designed old Upper Canada College, Toronto, in 1888, but died before it was finished.

St. Mary's, near the Detroit River toward Windsor's east side, and Assumption in the west end (*see* p. 208) are the city's bookends. St. Mary's, one of the most beautiful places of worship on this continent, was designed in 1902 by American architects Cram, Goodhue and Ferguson. Without recognized architectural examinations or a self-regulating professional body, Canadian architects were likened to tradesmen; as American architects were more highly esteemed, Canadians lost out on important opportunities. The Ontario Association of Architects was created to prevent this from happening. The Ontario Parliament passed an Act in 1889 defining architects' professional activities, restricting the title "Registered Architect" to those recognized by the O.A.A. and licensing new members. Since 1931, practitioners from outside the province may be credited as "consultants" but not recognized as "architects."

St. Mary's origins are essentially American. Beginning in 1856, Hiram Walker of

Baptist Chapel, *Walkerton; Baptist. Stone and clapboard, 1883 and 1889; Edmund Burke of Langley and Burke, architect*

Arts and Crafts emphasized tradition, construction, handcraft, rational design, comfort, simple profiles, large planes, strong textures and saturated earthy hues (dry cocoa, dark chocolate, bottle green, wine, dry mustard). The new building is free-form rubble whose reddish cast is set off by bright orange-red brick trim in round-headed doorways and matching windows. Long roofs and the upper tower were originally red-stained fish-scale shingles. Small dormers in the main roof's long slope bring in some natural light and suggest cozy, domestic feelings.

Detroit bought riverfront land east of Windsor, constructing a grocery store, flour mills and distillery before settling there in 1859. A hotel, workers' housing and other investments followed. Although the "benevolent despot" returned to Detroit, Walkerville was developed under his supervision and was incorporated as a town in 1890. The posh suburb was annexed by Windsor in 1935.

After Walker died in 1899, the church was commissioned and endowed by his sons as a memorial to their mother, Mary, and their father. St. Mary's is a grey stone building of small size but stunning impact, sited brilliantly on a spacious block, like an island within the street pattern. This interrupts Walkerville's main street, Devonshire Road, which looks north to the river and south to the church's tower (centred on the axis). The church's asymmetrical wings spread wide: an office and parish house on one side, a rectory on the other. The complex is set well back from surrounding broad streets — beyond a handsome open forecourt facing St. Mary's Gate — and behind a low-walled kitchen court close to Niagara Street. A cemetery fills the east part of the block, with a substantial and refined lych-gate between the forecourt and the cemetery.

Cram, Goodhue and Ferguson (with offices in Boston and New York), though young, were already leading designers in "Modern Gothic" style when St. Mary's was commissioned in 1902 and built in 1903–04. Ralph Adams Cram had published *English Country Churches* (1898) and *Church Building* (1901). Twenty-two books and hundreds of articles would follow. He was the specialist in church design and history, Bertram Grosvenor Goodhue in detail and decorations and Frank Ferguson in structural design. St. Mary's is similar to two designs for "small churches" in *Church Building:* it is asymmetrical and entered through a powerful oblong tower, one with deep buttresses stepping up diagonally at the corners, the other with paired openings on the broader face in the belfry stage, a single opening on the narrower one.

In North America such work is referred to as Collegiate Gothic, a polished style inspired by Late Gothic, and is especially favoured at academic institutions. There is a strong whiff of vernacular in the substantial composition that sets the overall tone. Scholarly detail is subtly handled. The studious window tracery in the aisle wall here is typical: broad mouldings of S-shaped profile played off against small concave mouldings on one margin and a still smaller cylindrical moulding, for heightened contrast, on the other. The stonework is fastidious: the wall is hammer-dressed, with the outer portions of the tracery tooled in two directions with a comb-like chisel, resulting in a peculiar "sparrow-pecking" texture. The rest of the tracery is simply tooled in one direction. The result is both rough and elegant, like crushed velvet.

G.H. Edgell, Harvard's Dean of Architecture in the 1920s, commented: "A thousand associations make people feel that Gothic is the great church style." He admired such churches, for "they are built so well," and acknowledged their "assimilation of historic precedent," but lamely suggested "they cannot be said to be entirely unoriginal." Turning to the Cram firm's best work, such as St. Thomas' (1906–13) on Fifth Avenue, New York, he warmed considerably. Monumentality, originality and beauty, openness to many influences "but imitation of none" — in fact "deliberate deviation from historic form" — all earned his admiration, as did Goodhue's detailing, with its brilliant, rich and harmonious colour.

FACING PAGE **St. Mary's**, *Windsor; Anglican. Stone with half-timbering, 1903–04, Cram, Goodhue and Ferguson, architects, Albert Kahn associate architect*

Albert Kahn suggested Cram, Goodhue and Ferguson to the Walkers. He was associate architect on the project and Ernest Wilby, his chief designer, supervised its construction. The Walkers also commissioned Kahn (an important designer of industrial buildings) to produce other work, including Willistead Manor behind the church, which has become Windsor's art gallery.

ABOVE Architect and author Ralph Adams Cram thought England's little parish church "the most perfect type ever produced." The plan and certain features of a 1901 design by Cram from his *Substance of Gothic* seem to prefigure St. Mary's.

The architects and planners of the church complex designed a robust and handsome lych-gate to the left of the church. It leads from the church's forecourt, on herringbone paths fashioned with red-brick pavers, into the cemetery.

You have hunted us from every place as with a wand, you have swept away all our pleasant land, and like some giant foe you tell us "willing or unwilling, you must now go from amid these rocks and wastes, I want them now! I want them to make rich my white children, whilst you may shrink away to holes and caves like starving dogs to die."
— *Shingwaukonce [Ojibwa chief], 1849*

Spiritual Fusion

BELOW **St. Paul's**, *Wikwemikong, Manitowaning, Manitoulin; Anglican. Frame, 1849; builder unknown*
The oldest church in northern Ontario, St. Paul's is in the town, but still hints at its once isolated location overlooking the harbour in front of the lighthouse. The exterior is attractive if unremarkable; the upper stage of the tower and the spire make it visible from a distance.

BELOW RIGHT **St. Andrew's "Old Sheg,"** *Sheguiandah First Nations, Manitoulin; Anglican. Frame, 1886; builder unknown*
Abandoned for many years, this northern version of an English parish church has been lovingly restored. In the restoration there is a cautious fusion of Christian and First Nations spirituality.

MANITOULIN ISLAND became home to a number of native groups who were encouraged by the government to establish farms there in the 1830s. As those most active in colonial missions to indigenous peoples, Roman Catholic and Anglican missionaries were involved in the settlement.

The oldest church in northern Ontario is **St. Paul's, Wikwemikong, Manitowaning**, which survives much as it was built in 1849. A simple chancel is defined by a narrowing of the nave and a semicircular arch. Distinctive panelled walls are made from wide boards set in narrower frames, imitating deeply embossed masonry. A plain white clapboard church with a tall projecting tower and spire, it overpowers a neighbouring lighthouse. When this Anglican mission failed, it moved in 1864 a few miles north to **Sheguiandah First Nations** reserve. **St. Andrew's** ("Old Sheg") was badly vandalized over the years, but it has recently been renovated. The

church's traditional south porch with bell tower is balanced on the opposite corner by the vestry. Windows and doors are simplified Carpenter Gothic. The roof is framed by a scissor-truss, while the interior still has the original pews. A few miles west, a propane explosion in the old **Immaculate Conception** church at **M'Chigeeng First Nations** reserve resulted in a stunning rebuilding as a low tipi rising from earth berms, with half the building below grade. It is a rare example in a small church of a strictly centred altar, lit by a central skylight. The congregation encircles the altar on five carpeted platforms. A sense of intimate enclosure and peaceful prayer pervades the place. The form and the furnishings combine native expression and traditional piety: four carved evangelists support the altar, a baptismal font is carved from a tree bole and a large wooden bald eagle overlooks the liturgy. Lively modern stations of the cross by Leland Bell surround the space.

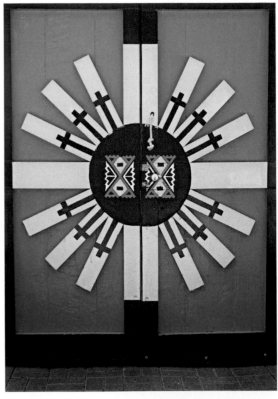

Immaculate Conception, *M'Chigeeng First Nations (formerly West Bay), Manitoulin; Roman Catholic. Timber, 1971–72; Fred May, architect*

The low tepee-like form of Immaculate Conception seems almost trite from the exterior, but that is a false impression. It is a thoughtful solution to the rebuilding of a church that was destroyed by fire. The door has a beautiful sunburst on the exterior and intricately carved panels on the inside, all linking native and Christian symbolism. The centred church plan of the interior also successfully merges native and Christian symbolism.

Canada is decidedly not the country we any of us thought it was....

I still think and hope that a livelihood may be made here, but this I

foresee — that Sturgeon Lake will be a very changed place in a few years.

— *John Langton, 1835*

Fringe of Settlement

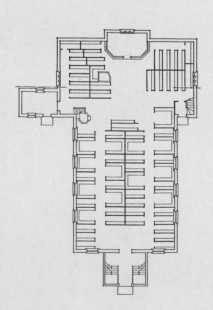

St. Thomas', *Shanty Bay; Anglican. Mud brick (cob), 1838–41; Colonel E.G. O'Brien, supervisor*

The Italianate design of this church is well suited to the mud-brick construction, which is hidden behind a heavy coat of stucco. Colonel O'Brien may have conceived the design; he also supervised the construction, donated the land and built the rectory nearby.

JUST NORTH OF BARRIE on the shore of Lake Simcoe, **St. Thomas'**, **Shanty Bay**, is one of the earliest churches in the area. The land was settled following the War of 1812. During the war, the United States had threatened to invade the colony from Georgian Bay. To encourage ex-soldiers to take up land nearer the bay, a road to Midland and Penetanguishene was cut through the bush from Shanty Bay, which had close ties with the governing authorities under Colonel E.G. O'Brien. In 1838–41 an Anglican church, perhaps designed by O'Brien himself, was built from "cob," an ancient material made of clay and straw. St. Thomas' derives much of its charm from the small windows, modest proportions and broad eaves characteristic of such construction methods. The design is Italianate, derived from Romanesque architecture, with round-headed openings and buttresses strengthening walls and tower.

The military road to Georgian Bay intersected the Barrie-Orillia road near Dalston, opening up **Oro Township** to settlers. **Knox** is midway to Orillia. Built by Gaelic-speaking settlers in a particularly gracious valley, it is surrounded by a large cemetery. The hip-roofed frame building is a typical meetinghouse, with wooden pews, an unadorned central pulpit and a cast-iron stove. Although it lacks the amenities of churches in more settled communities, Knox shows clearly the refined taste of its pioneer builders in its idyllic setting and the fine proportions of the Georgian windows and door.

A few miles nearer Barrie the **Black Methodist Episcopal Church, Oro Township**, served mainly free black settlers who had emigrated from the northern United States in 1817. By 1849 they had built an unadorned church with a gable roof from squared logs. The squared logs serve as the interior finish. It adopts a typical Methodist style, not unlike Knox's Presbyterian form, though the proportions are smaller and the details less handsome. Whereas Knox had a wooden plank floor, the Black Church's floor was originally beaten earth. There was little to distinguish

Knox Church, *Oro Township; Presbyterian. Frame, 1845; builder unknown*

Rural churches rarely retain the ambience they had when they were first built. Knox is one of the exceptions. Today the church is used for a service only once a year.

Black Church, *Oro Township; Methodist Episcopal (now United). Log with clapboard, 1849; builder unknown*

Both Knox Church and the Black Church — rather distinctively stained black, making the name seem logical — are from the same period, on the same road and only a few miles apart. But the contrast in the degree of finish within the same general meetinghouse style is considerable. The imitation log siding is from a mid-20th century renovation, while the interior retains most of its 19th-century character.

the pioneer liturgical arrangements of Methodists and Presbyterians. Both churches were surrounded by cemeteries, but the black pioneers' graves are almost entirely unmarked. Among the names of those memorialized on a common marker are Blackman, Handy and Washington. The settlement disappeared by the end of the 19th century, but the building recalls the black settlers who came to Ontario seeking freedom, dignity and independence, based on free land and equality with their neighbours.

Across Lake Simcoe is one of the province's forgotten architectural gems. Looking the part of an early settlers' church, **St. Andrew's ("Old Stone Church"), Thorah Township**, served Presbyterian settlers. They struggled to erect a church near Beaverton in the 1840s, providing the materials and the labour themselves. The stone walls were built of materials taken from the lake, the stones over the round-headed windows being carefully selected to form arches. The windows are masterpieces of skilful carpentry with 20-over-20 lights. Under the gabled roof, the interior with its U-shaped gallery focuses in a characteristically Presbyterian way on the raised pulpit (*see also* pp. 176–77). The pulpit is reached by twin curving stairs from within a railed communion area, furnished with bench and precentor's desk.

North and east of Lake Simcoe, extraordinarily scenic but uneconomic land was settled. This often dense bush is now thought of as "cottage country" — the Muskoka Lakes, the Kawartha Lakes and Georgian Bay — and is dotted with cottages built by summer residents from southern Ontario, New York, Ohio and Pennsylvania. The region has a blend of pioneer churches, town churches and

St. Andrew's ("Old Stone Church"), *Thorah (near Beaverton); Presbyterian (now United). Stone, 1840–53; John Morrison, builder*

The church sits in a large and well-filled cemetery dating from 1835 on land granted by the Crown, testifying to the size of this Gaelic Scots congregation on the east side of Lake Simcoe. It is simply Georgian vernacular, like many other Presbyterian churches of the period, and constructed in a mixture of limestone and granite. Built in a meetinghouse style, the door is in an end wall.

Madill Church, *near Huntsville; Wesleyan Methodist (now United). Squared log, 1872–73; builder unknown*

The Muskoka Road was extended to Huntsville in 1870, and settlers optimistically took up land along it, expecting it would be possible to farm it successfully. John Madill donated a corner of his allocation for a church, hence its name. The exposed squared-log building with half-dovetailed corners has a sound dry-stone foundation and vertical siding in the gable ends.

Christ Church, *Port Sydney; Anglican. Frame, 1873; builder unknown; rebuilt 2001–03, Hicks-Pettes, architects.*

This very fine frame church demonstrates the huge difference between the buildings for a recently arrived settler community of Methodists (above) and a longer established town community of Anglicans. The original church construction has been closely followed in the recent rebuilding, following a fire, within the constraints of the modern building code.

summer churches. North of the Muskoka Lakes the land is inhospitable, yet was also settled. Log buildings were still being built in the late 19th century. **Madill Church**, **Stephenson Township**, on the Old Muskoka Road to Huntsville, now west of Highway 11, was named after the settler who provided the site. A large, mostly unoccupied cemetery speaks of pioneer optimism. Built in 1872–73, the gabled building with a projecting entrance is in a good state of preservation, showing the essential soundness of squared-log construction. The interior's clapboarding, pews and hanging oil lamps add to its historic ambience. From the same year, only 5 miles away, is **Christ Church**, **Port Sydney**. This village church in traditional Gothic Revival style underscores differences between town and country and between Methodist and Anglican. The church serves the village year-round; however, its busiest times are in the summer when summer cottagers from Mary Lake and nearby camps fill it. It was burned down in an act of vandalism, but was rebuilt in 2001 as near to the original as possible. The only part to survive the fire was the lych-gate, now the repository of the melted bell.

The piety of the early 20th century prompted summer "settlers" to build their own churches. **St. Peter's-on-the-Rock, Stoney Lake**, is an informal white frame church perched on a low island in the most easterly of the Kawartha Lakes. Its dedication plays on Jesus' declaration, "You are Peter, and on this rock I will build my church," though the rock is almost too small to contain the church's footprint. Two brothers, A.W. and M.A. Mackenzie, both strong Anglicans, built it to welcome people of all denominations, who arrive by motorboat, canoe, rowboat and kayak

St. Peter's-on-the-Rock, *Stoney Lake; non-denominational/Anglican. Frame, 1912–15; Jim and John Cassidy, builders*

Cottagers' churches are different again from both rural and town churches. St. Peter's-on-the-Rock occupies a granite island at the juncture of Stoney Lake and Clear Lake. A cottage on another part of the island is for the use of the visiting clergy, two of whom come for one month each, for three summers in a row. Light and ventilation are controlled by shutters.

through Hell's Gate, a narrow channel that once was a stretch of fast water. Seemingly windowless, on summer Sundays large shutters hinged at the top open along the length of the nave and two small transepts, transforming the building into an accessible and inviting structure, with a truncated steeple at the end. The windows offer changing views of foliage, boats and sky — a far cry from images in stained-glass windows. The sound of hymn-singing, accompanied by an old pedal organ, floats out to boats on the Trent Canal. The interior's charming simplicity is enhanced by a nail sculpture by David Partridge and a natural granite font.

Exactly the same social conditions created **Union Church, Sturgeon Point**, a few miles west, near John Langton's original homestead. The building was a gift from Lady Flavelle (Clara Ellsworth), wife of Sir Joseph Flavelle, a wealthy meat packer, financier and philanthropist. She asked A. Frank Wickson to model it on a chapel in Athens, Georgia (by architect W.W. Thomas), which the couple had seen on a trip to Florida. Though the Flavelles were committed Methodists, just as the Mackenzies were committed Anglicans, Union is independent. It is not as dramatically sited as St. Peter's, but is structurally more interesting. The roof is a complex web of trusses and beams on an octagonal plan supported on a central column, all built in Georgia pine. Windows parade all around the building, protected under a gently curved umbrella roof with wide overhanging eaves surmounted by a small belfry.

In addition to its old churches, **Port Sydney** has a modern church — the **Port Sydney Bible Chapel**, which demonstrates careful attention to the needs of modern worshippers. Plymouth Brethren chapels were once almost aggressively unsophisticated, holding the view that chapels must be unlike denominational churches. This chapel shows how standards of design among Plymouth Brethren have merged with more traditional approaches. It combines a large, flexible worship space with Sunday school facilities on either side of a porte-cochère that suggests that even within a chapel in a small community the automobile is king.

Port Sydney Bible Chapel, *Port Sydney; Plymouth Brethren Assembly. Stone and frame, 2000, Roger Fennell, architect*

The Port Sydney Bible Chapel breaks from the highly simplified forms of buildings characteristic of most Bible Chapels, adapting to the need for multi-use spaces and easy automobile access. Its board-and-batten appearance and simplified gable trusses suit the Late Victorian ethos of much Port Sydney construction. Assemblies, derived from John Nelson Darby's movement of prayer and Bible study, especially concerned themselves with Biblical prophecy and the Second Coming of Christ.

Union Church, *Sturgeon Point; non-denominational. Frame, 1914–15; A. Frank Wickson, architect*

BELOW Union Church has a style that suggests it is a building carried out with enthusiasm and care. The wide overhangs, curving octagonal roof rising up to a belfry, double dormers and large windows all mark this as an elegant and refined structure.

LEFT The Georgia pine used to build the church gives the interior a warm yellowish cast. The octagonal roof is supported by a single central post, from which spring 16 inclined supports for the roof. Other rafters then follow the slope of the roof down to the walls, where major posts support the whole with the aid of trusses outside the line of the walls.

Come, bless the Lord, all you his servants,

Who minister night after night in the house of the Lord.

Lift up your hands towards the sanctuary and bless the Lord.

— Psalm 134: 1–2

Victorian Catholicism

Basilique-cathédrale Notre-Dame d'Ottawa,
*Ottawa, Roman Catholic. Stone, 1841–85; Antoine
Robillard, architect*

The Basilica's combination of gold trim, blue ceiling
and marbleized columns is mesmerizing in its effect,
calling for silence and worship. The interior contrasts
sharply with the exterior's convoluted construction history. Most dramatically, the altar rises high into the
apsidal vault.

THE PLAIN EXTERIOR of the **Basilique-cathédrale Notre-Dame d'Ottawa** does not
prepare one for the interior, where every part vies for attention. Under the deep
blue ceiling stands a sumptuously carved sanctuary (with patriarchs, prophets,
Apostles and evangelists, each one in his own niche with a crocketed pinnacle) and
a high altar that looks like a wedding cake whose icing has begun to melt. The
building took almost a half-century to complete and reflects the changing tastes of
the capital's citizens in the period before and after Confederation.

Construction began in 1841 to the Neoclassical design of Antoine Robillard, still
reflected in the front doors. When the Oblate Fathers assumed responsibility in
1844, they continued construction in the newly fashionable Gothic Revival style,
changing the nave's window heads from round to pointed. After it became a cathedral in 1848 twin towers (1859) and a choir (1862–64) were built. Under Bishop
Joseph-Thomas Duhamel, attention turned to the interior (1878–85), directed by
Canon Georges Bouillon, just as craftsmen who had worked on the Parliament
Buildings became available. The nave, without transepts, is separated from the
aisles by clustered columns, painted to look like marble, rising above the galleries
to a ribbed vault. The side galleries stop one bay short of the sanctuary to permit a
two-story space to hold large lateral altars, on the left to the Sacred Heart and on
the right to the Virgin Mary, in place of transepts. The main altar, by Philippe
Pariseau (who signed his work on the sanctuary stalls), Flavien Rochon, Philippe
Hébert and others, extends higher than the nave arcades and focuses on Christ in
Glory, with the Blessed Virgin and St. Joseph flanking him. Below the main figures,
low reliefs portray scenes such as the Nativity, the Transfiguration and the

Resurrection while the tabernacle door highlights a pelican feeding its young — a symbol of the Eucharist.

Begun only slightly later, **St. John the Baptist**, **Perth**, shows, in a small-town way, the same impulses as Catholicism stretched its muscles in the period between the union of the Canadas and Confederation. Father John McDonagh (1838–66), an inveterate church-builder from Ireland, built four churches while priest at Perth (Almonte, Perth, Ferguson Falls and Stanleyville). In Perth, he persuaded a Scottish Protestant to donate a 3-acre site for this Gothic Revival church, impressively stern on the exterior — the pinnacles over the buttresses are the only slightly playful elements — and equally impressive but more gracious on the interior. The 180-foot central tower and spire were planned from the outset, though it took almost 40 years to complete the broach spire; the high lancet windows go well with the scale of the steeple. The interior has been considerably modified, fundamentally by work in 1885 that completed the plasterwork on the clustered columns (originally they were 10-by-10 wooden columns) and the ribbed vault. Less satisfactory changes in the last half-century include a plywood screen to define the narthex and shortened front doors to permit a sloped floor. Among the many carefully preserved buildings of Perth, with one of the most handsome main streets in Ontario, St. John's tends to be ignored in its off-centre site; it does stand axially, however, at the end of a cross street that permits it to be seen as it was intended.

St. John the Baptist, *Perth; Roman Catholic. Stone, 1847–48; interior and tower 1885; designer unknown*

St. John the Baptist has a noble and dignified aspect, solid without being stodgy. The sidewalls are well proportioned with buttresses, topped with pinnacles, alternating with early Gothic Revival windows. The imposing front balances a very high projecting central tower and spire with two side towers, also projecting.

Much reworked in 1885, St. John's interior has benefited from a sensitively executed paint scheme in peach and pale green, which sets off the architectural elements to advantage. The space is grander than one would expect from the exterior, with clustered columns topped with capitals, from which ribbing springs to form the vault.

Our Lady of the Immaculate Conception, *Guelph;
Roman Catholic. Stone, 1876–88; Joseph Connolly,
architect*

The nave is flanked by high aisles, with clerestory
windows above the nave arcades. An unusual feature of
the interior is the series of seven chapels accessed from
an ambulatory around the apse, which project strikingly
on the exterior. The ribs of the vaulted ceiling are carefully articulated to convey a strong impression of the
design's indebtedness to medieval prototypes.

BELOW Looking like a French — or in some features,
English — medieval cathedral, Joseph Connolly's church
proclaims that Roman Catholics have arrived, even in a
heavily English and Scottish city such as Guelph. The six
statues above the central doors in the main facade are
the four evangelists plus Saints Peter and Paul; Our Lady
is at the peak of the gable (*see also* p. 183).

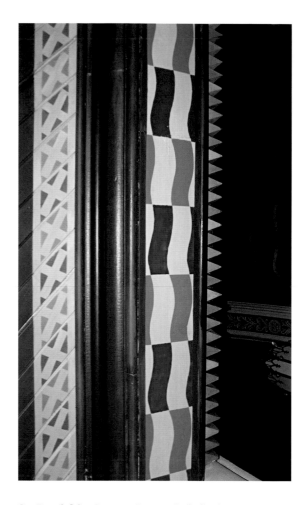

St. Patrick's, *Ottawa; Roman Catholic. Stone, 1866–73; Augustus Laver, architect, succeeded by King Arnoldi*

With a decorative scheme that almost matches the Basilica, but looking British rather than French, St. Patrick's interior includes a profusion of intricate stencil work: around windows, throughout the ceilings of the nave and aisles, and on the edges of woodwork. While extremely colourful, there is nothing garish about the decoration.

Our Lady of the Immaculate Conception, Guelph, occupies a stunning site that overlooks the downtown of this strongly British town, laid out by John Galt prior to settlement. He gave the site to Alexander Macdonell, Bishop of Kingston, to serve the Irish population. The "Church of Our Lady" looks straight down the main street from its hilltop, with pinnacled flanking towers providing a backdrop for the city's daily activity. It was designed by Joseph Connolly (1840–1904). His eclectic medievalist approach is clear in the exterior's articulation of elements: a high front with towers, wide projecting transepts, polygonal apse with seven projecting polygonal chapels, and pinnacles, crockets and spires galore. Though it is now surrounded entirely by asphalt — grass against the building would enhance it enormously — the alluring exterior makes one feel one must enter.

The interior is impressively high, with a plaster ribbed vault over the nave and high pointed arches over the columns, a blind arcade (a rare triforium in Canadian churches) above and clerestory windows above that. The nave windows are by A. Vermonet of Rheims, France, from the early 20th century. The seven windows behind and above the altar are by Mayer and Company, Munich: each window matches a New Testament scene with a theologically related scene from the Old Testament below it. An ambulatory behind the altar provides access to the seven chapels. Compared to the modulation of the exterior, the interior nave walls seem flat, deriving their effect from the paintings on them — the figures in the spandrels between the capitals are the eight Canadian Martyrs (*see* pp. 188–91) — rather than the architecture itself. Nevertheless, this is a brilliantly conceived project, beautifully implemented.

St. Patrick's, Ottawa, is the capital's first English-speaking Catholic church. It was designed by Augustus Laver (1834–98) of Laver and Stent, which was working on the Parliament Buildings at the same time. The design was altered as construction proceeded and was later completed by Fuller's pupil, King Arnoldi. Sir John A. Macdonald, the first prime minister of Canada, laid the cornerstone. Many of the early members were Irish, so shamrocks are ubiquitous in the building's decorative details. Like Ottawa's Basilica, St. Patrick's is colourfully decorated inside, though with a more restrained and balanced hand. Geometric stencilling appears everywhere, in the double-height nave with its clerestory windows, in the beamed and panelled roof and in the lower side aisles. The aisles have an alternating pattern of spandrels of three-leafed shamrocks and modified shamrocks, almost a triple yin-yang symbol. The semi-octagonal apse focuses on a large window above the high altar. The church's relatively plain exterior is dominated by a projecting central tower and spire.

It is a near miracle that the **Rideau Street Convent Chapel** (Convent of Our Lady of the Sacred Heart), **Ottawa,** has survived. Following the convent's demolition in 1972, the interior was re-erected in the National Gallery of Canada after strenuous public efforts to save it. Canada's only Late Gothic (Tudor) Revival wooden fan vault was designed by Georges Bouillon (1841–1932), the amateur diocesan architect-priest who was responsible for the interior of the Basilique-Cathédrale; his design was influenced by English stone fan vaults such as the one in King's College Chapel, Cambridge. The National Gallery maintained the interior's integrity by reproducing the original dimensions, windows, gallery, wainscotting and cast-iron columns, but without pews or the original *trompe l'oeil* vaults and

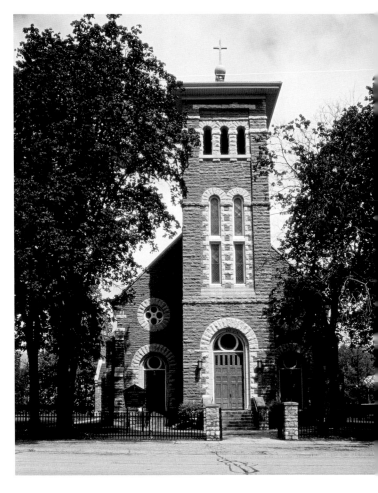

St. Joseph's, *Douro; Roman Catholic. Stone, 1893; John Belcher, architect*

Douro is a small village located on top of a drumlin in the Peterborough drumlin field. St. Joseph's rugged exterior walls in local stone, with contrasting window and door surrounds, advance almost to the main street, while the charming earlier rectory next door recedes. There is nothing in Douro to compete with St. Joseph's, which reminds the community of the success and prosperity the early Irish immigrants were able to achieve.

columns painted on the flat apse wall. The *Ottawa Daily Citizen* commented as construction was nearing completion in 1888: "The chapel may be said to be cozy, pretty, and elegant, and admirably adapted to the requirements of the lady students." Bouillon's basic design decision to have a central nave with side aisles of half the width made it necessary to have twice as many smaller vaults in the aisles, and thus twice as many columns as the nave required. This complex arrangement created a difficult challenge in the treatment of the nave arcade. The decorative scheme as it was just before demolition has been retained: cream, white, yellow and shades of blue, with stencilwork on the main walls.

Chapel, Rideau Street Convent (Convent of our Lady of the Sacred Heart), *Ottawa; Roman Catholic. Wood interior, 1887–88, re-erected in the National Gallery of Canada (1988); Georges Bouillon, architect*

The wooden fan vaulting in this chapel is unique. Like Connolly's Our Lady, this chapel is deeply indebted to medieval — here late medieval — models, all distinctively English. Carrying out a 19th-century replica of a stone vault in wood, especially in a design that had a nave and aisles, must have been an enormous architectural challenge. Bouillon pulled it off splendidly.

The contrast with **St. Joseph's**, **Douro**, could hardly be greater, an almost feminine delicacy in the chapel contrasting with the solidity and strength of this rural church. Much of Peterborough and the surrounding county were settled by Irish Roman Catholics. Peter Robinson (1785–1838), brother of John Beverly Robinson, who was a proud defender of Anglicanism and the Family Compact in Upper Canada, was involved in bringing 2,000 settlers from Cork in 1825. Douro has retained its strong Irish Catholic character ever since. St. Joseph's tall, square, rusticated stone tower and contrasting white stone window and door frames are a focal point of the community's main street.

> *He set me down in a plain that was full of bones…. They covered the plain…. He said to me, "O man, can these bones live?" I answered, "Only you, Lord God, know that."*
> — *Ezekiel 37:1–3*

Can These Bones Live?

BELOW LEFT **St. Mary Magdalene**, *Picton; Anglican (now a museum). Brick and stone, 1823–25; the Rev. William Macaulay, designer; 1864 (east end), 1867 (west end) by John William Hopkins, architect*

The church sits beside its rectory, both of which operate as a museum, with important insights into the role of Anglicans in the county. The stone additions at the other end contrast with the finer workmanship of the original building in buff and orange brick. In the foreground the Macaulay family plot has a prominent position.

BELOW RIGHT **Meetinghouse**, *Wellington; Quaker (now Wellington Community Museum). Brick, 1885; builder unknown*

The fact that the Quakers who built this meetinghouse identified themselves as Progressives may account for the building's Gothic Revival windows. This was the last of six Quaker meetinghouses in the county, an area that was one of their minor strongholds.

CHURCHES HAVE OFTEN BEEN REUSED after being decommissioned. Prince Edward County, a strongly Loyalist area, faced substantial church downsizing in the 1960s, especially among Methodist and Anglican churches, which were once so strong in the county. The Picton museum is housed in **St. Mary Magdalene**, **Picton**, built in 1823 by the first rector, William Macaulay (1794–1874), largely from his own funds; it was consecrated on a visit in 1831 by Jacob Mountain, Bishop of Quebec. Its warm beige and orange brick, with beautifully detailed windows filled with intersecting early Gothic Revival glazing bars, contrasts with stone additions (east end, 1864; west end, 1867) by John William Hopkins, evidently anticipating rebuilding the body of the church. Macaulay was again the main benefactor. When the building fell into disrepair and the area around it grew seedy, plans to build on another site were prepared (1904). The church continued to be used occasionally for anniversary services, but when parts of the roof collapsed it was sold to the township. Another museum, the Wellington Community Museum, occupies the **Quaker Meetinghouse**, **Wellington**. This rather uncharacteristic Quaker building was built in 1885 by a breakaway group after a schism in the Quaker community in 1881. It broke the Quaker mould by using Gothic details to mimic mainstream denominations,

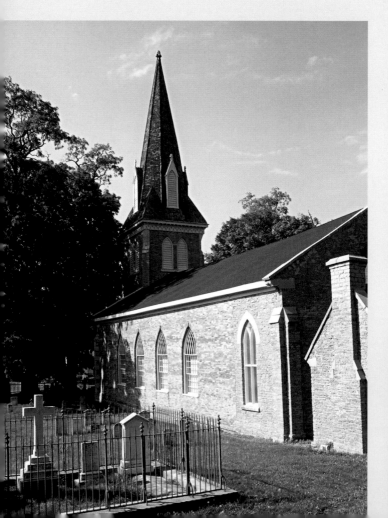

showing its "progressive" tendencies as compared to the "orthodox" Society of Friends. **Holy Trinity**, **Consecon**, a stone Gothic Revival church overlooking Lake Ontario, is now a library. Happily, both the exterior with its massive stone tower topped by a wooden "crown of thorns" and the interior were retained largely intact.

Bowerman's Church, Hallowell, was a Wesleyan Methodist meeting hall. It has a beautifully proportioned low-pitched roof and a fanlight in the gable, contrasting with Gothic details elsewhere in the building. The owners inserted two new floor levels to create additional living space; despite a 1999 fire, much is still original. The church is named after Mrs. Thomas Bowerman and was built on land donated by her husband. When he started a tavern, his wife went into the cellar with an axe and smashed the whisky barrels, which led to a revival in the county.

Mount Tabor Methodist, Milford (1865–67; later United), a brick church built almost single-handedly by Dr. Hautry Bredin, was decommissioned during its hundredth anniversary. The township bought it as a community hall. Since 1985 the church has been the home of the Marysburgh Mummers; theatre seats have been installed on the main floor, though the balcony pews are original. The west elevation of the building dominates Milford's lovely pond on the Black River, its high, narrow spire visible from all directions.

BELOW LEFT **Bowerman's Church**, *Hallowell; Wesleyan Methodist (then United, now private house). Stone, 1855; builder unknown*

This is the finest Methodist church in the county, with its Georgian proportions, low-pitched roof, returned cornices and fanlight in the gable. The Gothic windows show that the transition period from Classical Revival to Gothic Revival was a slow one.

BELOW RIGHT **Holy Trinity**, *Consecon; Anglican (now Consecon Public Library). Stone, 1847; builder unknown*

The best feature of this handsome stone church overlooking Lake Ontario is its heavy square tower that projects from the facade and is topped by an octagonal "crown of thorns."

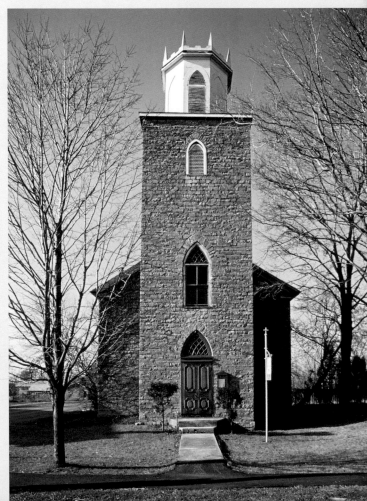

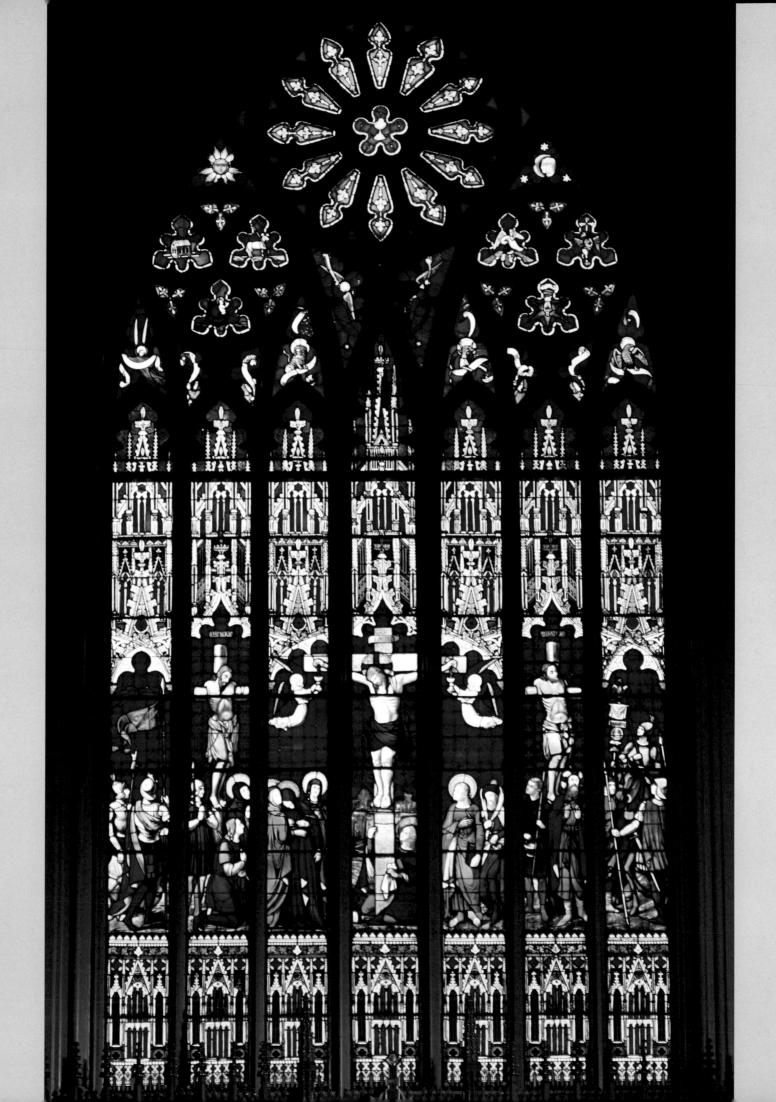

Toronto is a noble and promising city, — a young giant of the west, — a proud monument of British energy directed by the fostering care of Providence. And it may be imagined that it was with no little interest that I gazed upon its polished spires and brightly tinned roofs, glittering in the light of the morning sun, as the steamer rounded the point and swept up to the wharf.

— A.W.H. Rose, 1849

Victorian Toronto

St. Michael's Cathedral, *Toronto; Roman Catholic. Brick and stone with timber-framed interior, 1845–48; William Thomas, architect*

An astounding Crucifixion window, installed in 1858, is the focus of the cathedral's interior. It is an iconic tableau of intense color, by Étienne Thévenot from Clermont-Ferrand, a French pioneer of the medieval glass revival. Thévenot animated the very deep-blue sky with small blood-red squares of glass in the leading's regular grid, as recommended by Viollet-le-Duc, who restored cathedrals throughout France. The blue and red, falling into larger and smaller bands, are punctuated with plummy mauve and purple accents, enlivened by emerald, viridian and gold.

TORONTO'S RAPID GROWTH, from 224 inhabitants in 1799 to 15,336 in 1842 (when the earliest of "the Victorians" discussed here was built), was exceptional and matched belatedly by a multiplication of churches. Initially little York (as it was called from 1793 to 1834) had grown very slowly. The village's first church, known simply as "the Church at York," was not begun until 1805; then it was vandalized in 1813 and not repaired until 1818. Unprepossessing in appearance, it seems quite appropriate that it should have been described in a guidebook as "a meeting house for Episcopalians." The Anglicans went through three churches with rapidity. The first was replaced in 1833 and its Neoclassical successors burned down in 1839 and 1849. The great fire that destroyed the 1849 church led to the city's first building bylaw, which required buildings in the core to be built of brick or stone.

Sir Richard Bonnycastle, the English-born commander of the Royal Engineers, who lived in Kingston, once remarked on the "amazing diversity of sects in Upper Canada." This seemed to surprise him, although such diversity was also common in the Maritimes and to a lesser degree in Québec. In Toronto, surgeon and author W.H. Smith enumerated "twenty-one churches and chapels" by 1846, representing 13 or 14 denominations, including three sorts of Presbyterians (Church of Scotland, Presbyterian Church of Canada and United Secession Presbyterian, a wonderful oxymoron) and four of Methodists (British Wesleyan, Primitive

Little Trinity, *Toronto; Anglican. Brick, 1843–44; Henry Bowyer Lane, architect*

The tower and gable ends are castellated in perpendicular style, favoured in late Georgian churches (especially in Ireland). But Lane's detailing is mixed: early English lancets, simple decorated windows and great perpendicular subdivisions marshalled soldier-like into large and small lights. He caps the offset at windowsill level with stone, yet uses wood for door and window surrounds. Still, he understood the structural significance of buttresses: although slender, they are deep and strong.

After fire destroyed a later chancel (1889) in 1961 — replaced by offices — the church was simply refurbished, with the salvaged communion table under a new window, closer to the congregation and the 1850s pews.

Methodist, Canadian Wesleyan and one for "coloured people," presumably African Methodist).

Toronto's earliest surviving church building is **Little Trinity** (1843–44) on Parliament Street where King Street East follows the old shoreline near the Don River. James Worts built his windmill nearby in 1832 from which grew Gooderham & Worts distillery. There was no Protestant church in the area. Many families had been members of the United Church of England and Ireland and, as St. James' lies 10 blocks to the west, the Society for the Propagation of the Gospel contributed to a second Anglican church.

Trinity is an artful blend of two colours of brick: a sharp orange-red ("staring red brick," travel writer Anna Jameson called it on her visit to Toronto in 1836), on a thick base of so-called white brick (beige, mottled with pink) that rises to the window sills and weaves through the red brick as buttresses and a frieze. This is a very early Canadian use of coloured brick to make a decorative pattern that is based on construction and defines each structural bay. It is intuitive and owes nothing to John Ruskin's developing love of surface pattern unrelated to structure (expressed in the late 1840s and early 50s), through coloured brick, stone or marble. The accompanying Enoch Turner Schoolhouse of 1848 is from the days of sectarian schools and is equally colourful, as are the rectory (1853), the neighbourhood's story-and-a-half and two-story houses and commercial buildings.

Other denominations built in Toronto — Methodists (1818), Presbyterians (1820), Roman Catholics (1822–23), Baptists (1832) and Congregationalists (1834) — but none survives. Trinity is known anomalously as "Little" Trinity because the larger Church of the Holy Trinity (1846–47) came hard on its heels (beside today's Eaton Centre). Henry Bowyer Lane (1817–78) designed both, and a third Anglican church, St. George the Martyr (1844), all within five years. An itinerant colonial, born in Corfu (his father was in the British Army), he was educated in England, emigrated to Upper Canada in 1841 and settled in Toronto in 1843, before moving on to Australia in 1852, where he spent the rest of his life.

The architect William Thomas arrived in Toronto opportunely in 1843, when the Roman Catholic diocese of Kingston, covering all Upper Canada, had just been divided and the energetic Michael Power (1804–47) installed as its first bishop. There were 3,000 Roman Catholics in Toronto, more than one-quarter of the city's population. They were inadequately served by old St. Paul's Church (1823), on Queen Street East. Three other architects worked in the city (John Howard, Thomas Young and Henry Lane), but Thomas scooped all in 1844 with St. Paul's, London (*see* p. 209), his first church commission in Canada, and the princely Commercial Bank of the Midland District (whose facade is installed in and contrasts with Santiago de Calatrava's B.C.E. Galleria). The next year he also won the commission for **St. Michael's Cathedral** (and its bishop's palace of 1845–46).

St. Michael's is oriented traditionally on a once-splendid site, directly north of the green space that extended between Bond and Church streets, from Queen to Shuter. McGill Square set the church off like an English cathedral in its close; when Metropolitan Church bought and built on the square, St. Michael's grand scale was diminished. The cathedral is Decorated Gothic in brick, larger than St. Paul's, yet pinched in appearance. On the west front, slender colonnettes and niches decorate the buttresses. Roll mouldings enrich most window profiles while crocketed pinnacles

Little Trinity
The church's mural monuments are intact, including a pair to William and Harriet Gooderham that resemble Gibbsian Baroque designs, long out of fashion in the 1880s but suitably robust. William's monument calls the distiller and banker one of the founders and largest benefactors of Trinity. He was a churchwarden for 35 years.

sprout on the skyline. These bring texture to the smooth brick, but not at a distance. The tower, capped at first, was finished by Henry Langley in 1865–66, after Thomas' death, and is more intricate than Thomas intended. Dormers came later in a futile attempt to bring light to a solemn interior.

This was the largest church in the city, with a wide nave and tall aisles under a common roof. It has the sweep and openness that a timber frame offers. The framing in the arcade of a hall church continues into the roof structure, concealed behind the arcade's walls and above the ceiling, but helping to support the roof. Thomas did not introduce galleries, which would have interfered with the windows, but otherwise this scheme follows O'Donnell's economy at Notre-Dame in Montréal (*see* pp. 144–50.) The arcade's painted bands mimic large drums of stone; had the piers been stone, they would have been heavier and closer together. Bishop Power did not live to see the result. More than 90,000 Irish emigrants fleeing the famine landed at Quebec in 1847. Typhus spread among them and into communities welcoming them, and while calling on the sick in Toronto, Power contracted the disease and died.

St. Michael's Cathedral, *Toronto; Roman Catholic. Brick and stone with timber-framed interior, 1845–48; William Thomas, architect*

When built, the tower was incomplete and the spire missing, but St. Michael's Cathedral presented a breathtaking view at the end of the long green space of McGill Square for two decades. In a small city without another very large church it was most impressive. In 1870 the McGill family sold the square to Metropolitan Methodist's congregation for their new church (now Metropolitan United) and the view of St. Michael's vanished.

Power's successor after a long interregnum was Armand-François-Marie de Charbonnel (1802–91), a French aristocrat, who had already spent eight years in North America. Addressing the unfinished cathedral and its debt of more than £11,000, he sought donations and led the way himself. He hired decorators and got estimates in 1854–56 from artists in New York, Montréal, Toronto and France for a stained-glass window above the altar. Sweeping through seven lights, Étienne Thévenot's window is inescapable (doubtless by intention), bursting at once upon the gaze. Bishop de Charbonnel spent £400 of his own money for it and invited others to contribute further windows, though none lives up to the promise of the east window. The result is clamorous: uninspired later glass, some Austrian, much German (by Mayer of Munich), vies with painted wall and ceiling panels. Perhaps a bold approach is called for as the cathedral, looking tired outside and in, mounts an ambitious restoration campaign.

Frederic Cumberland (1820–81), a clever and ambitious young civil engineer with a London background, arrived in 1847 and quickly established himself as Toronto's leading architect. **St. James' Cathedral** was the feather in his cap. Tired of

St. Michael's Cathedral

William Thomas' interior is handsome. Widely spaced compound piers of wood, with slender colonnettes clustering round their core, make the church seem very open (although his signature roof trusses seem spidery).

William's talented youngest brother, John, was in charge of sculpture for the new Parliament Buildings at Westminster. The bishop at the cathedral's main entrance, along with other sculptural ornament, may have been influenced by examples of John's work, which William owned. It also suggests use of lavish publications of the 1820s by the English architect and antiquary Lewis Nockalls Cottingham.

government service at Admiralty dockyards in Chatham and Portsmouth, he had left the Old Country cheerfully, seeking opportunities and recognition in Canada. His brother-in-law Thomas Gibbs Ridout, the Bank of Upper Canada's cashier and the government's banker, smoothed his way socially and financially. Cumberland received significant commissions almost immediately, most near St. James': the registry office, county courthouse, post office, Mechanics' Institute and, farther afield, Osgoode Hall and University College.

When a devastating fire destroyed St. James' Cathedral, not yet a decade old, and three blocks of the city to the east on Easter Saturday, 1849, a competition was announced for a new church at least as large as the old, "in the Gothic style," of white brick and stone, "holding eighteen hundred persons," but "not to exceed Ten Thousand Pounds" (not counting a bell tower). Cumberland's design, drawn partly from his sketch of 13th-century Salisbury Cathedral and blended with other English precedents, won the competition but not the commission. The building committee, seduced by a non-competitor's larger and more expensive proposal, belatedly entered it into competition and nominated it for the commission! Ultimately the newly formed partnership of Cumberland and Ridout (T.G.'s engineer son, Thomas) *did* get the contract, to be executed in stages with an abbreviated tower (neither belfry nor spire) and temporarily shorn of porches and pinnacles. St. James' gradually evolved into something richer in detail and bolder in form.

Even then, Cumberland's ambitions were frustrated by the autocratic John Strachan (1778–1867), rector of all four churches on this site and first Anglican bishop of Toronto. One early project by Cumberland had been cathedral-like and liturgically oriented — as built it faces south — with aisled transepts as tall as the nave, flying buttresses arching over the aisles and a crossing tower. Bishop Strachan

FACING PAGE **St. James' Cathedral**, *Toronto; Anglican. Brick and stone, 1850–53; Frederic Cumberland, architect*
Cumberland intended St. James' to be truly neo-medieval, but Bishop Strachan reduced the height and depth of his transepts and removed their aisles. Even so, this transept (functionally a large porch) dwarfs its entrance. Like the whole building, it achieves prodigious effect by wide variations in proportion: from massive stonework at ground level, through the stepped but still substantial brick buttresses, tapering abruptly to slender pinnacles ornamented with thread-like colonnettes. Stone weatherings, to throw water off, are equally varied and ornamental.

Chapel of St. James-the-Less, *Toronto; Anglican. Stone with wooden porch, 1861; Cumberland and Storm, architects*
In 1833 the overcrowded burying ground at St. James' was a danger to public health. Toronto was not unique. Concerns voiced in London, Paris and elsewhere led to sanitary crusades for safe cemeteries. Ornamentally planted and filled with artistic monuments, cemeteries might be instructive, even recreational. With high mortality rates and the age-old notion of "a good death" as the gateway to salvation, a suitable funerary chapel seemed especially appropriate. The bold and masterful perspective in watercolour is characteristic of Storm's rendering style.

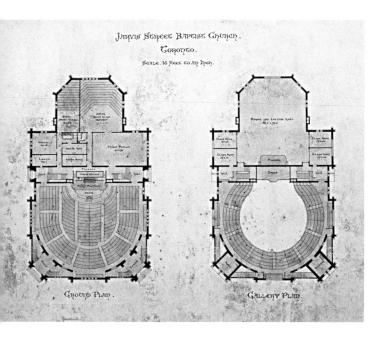

Jarvis Street Baptist, *Toronto; Baptist. Stone, 1874–75; Langley and Burke, architects*
    Langley and Burke's tall Gothic tower and spire dominate the southwest corner of Jarvis and Gerrard. The interior, including its skylight like a rose window, became a model for Methodist, Presbyterian and Congregational churches. A marble-fronted baptistery lies behind and above the pulpit.

rebuffed all such options forcefully, including stone construction, and insisted on long U-shaped galleries (removed in 1889–90) to satisfy pew-holders, on whose pew-rents much depended.

Still, architect and client could take pleasure in the resulting compromise after so much controversy: a nearly cathedral-like parish church and a true basilica, with beautiful arcades of stone carrying a functional clerestory to brighten the interior. The budget was so tight, however, that Cumberland waited two decades to see Henry Langley's completion of porches, tower and spire in 1873–74. These generally followed earlier suggestions by Cumberland's gifted partner, William G. Storm (1826–92), who is rarely given enough credit for his work on St. James' in the many thoughtful and artistic details.

In England in 1851, Cumberland visited his favourite medieval church and wrote

home: "I would give my ears to be asked to build a *small* Stone Church in Canada."
The **Chapel of St. James-the-Less** is Cumberland and Storm's ideal of the small
church. At the top of Parliament Street, well north of the city when built, it was both
a chapel of ease serving Anglicans distant from St. James' Cathedral and a cemetery
chapel. This new building type of the 19th century was a small church in which to
conduct the funeral service, surrounded in all directions by the burying ground.

The chapel was long planned but benefited from delays. The property is irregular,
a slightly uneven table of land backing onto the Don River ravine, and picturesquely
planned by the city's first architect, John Howard, in 1844. Cumberland and Storm
made the first drawings for the chapel in 1855. It was put to tender for contrac-
tors' bids in 1857 and 1859, but the cathedral had cost so much more than anticipated (almost £19,000 instead of £11,463) that there was no question of pressing

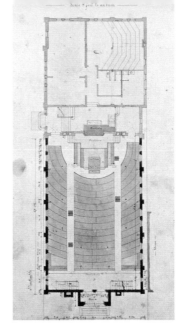

on immediately. Sales of cemetery plots, however, made a larger chapel possible in 1861, with funeral services held that year and regular Sunday services the following year.

Sited on a knoll to the left of the entrance drive, St. James-the-Less is asymmetrical, with a brawny little tower, splayed at first, then buttressed, capped by a tall spire. The west-facing double doors are approached by elongated shallow steps (with pall-bearers in mind). The porch is like a lych-gate, with built-in seating to either side, and deep enough to accommodate a long coffin. The simple small windows (nearly circular trefoils) lead to a gloomy interior, slightly relieved by the chancel's triple window. The chapel sits on a recessed mortuary vault (with double doors at the east end), a necessity before interments could take place in frozen ground. A trap with elevating mechanism in the chancel still allows a committal to be conducted within the chapel. This is a High Victorian masterpiece of great originality.

Jarvis Street Baptist is representative of rapid changes in Protestant church building from 1851 to 1881, when new construction outpaced expansion of the denominations themselves. According to William Westfall in *Two Worlds: The Protestant Culture of Nineteenth Century Ontario*, "Anglicans almost doubled their number of adherents while they trebled the number of their churches. The Presbyterians … and the Baptists grew a little more rapidly than the Anglicans, and they too trebled the number of their churches. The Methodists were even more prolific builders," as their churches increased five-fold. All major Protestant denominations erected stone churches on a public scale. However, after St. James' 1849 competition calling for Gothic submissions, Westfall writes, "revival of the Gothic and Romanesque was so extensive that these romantic forms defined (and perhaps continue to define) how a church should appear. The new medieval church, which occupied such a prominent place in almost every village and town, became the most powerful and enduring symbol of the Protestant culture of Ontario … Churches in Ontario began to look like one another, confirming visually the growing unity of Ontario Protestantism itself."

Baptists created a neo-medieval monument on Jarvis Street with an interior that was copied by Congregationalists, Methodists and Presbyterians. William McMaster, an Irish-born dry-goods merchant, politician and banker, and his American wife, Susan Moulton, were the driving forces behind the new church, supporting the project lavishly. Edmund Burke (1850–1919), clerk of session in the old Bond Street Baptist Church, was the architect. He was the son of a lumber merchant and builder and the nephew of Henry Langley, Ontario's most prolific church architect. At 14, Burke had been indentured to Langley; at 21 he was made partner.

A committee spent about two weeks in the United Sates looking for a model. They found it in the influential First Methodist Church (1866) of Akron, Ohio, and its recently built Sunday school (1870). The classrooms were on a radial plan with walls that could be opened to allow the minister to speak to all of the classes from a central point. In the most developed "Akron" churches, but not Akron itself, there were movable walls between the church and Sunday school as well, for joint functions or overflow audiences (*see* p. 391). The architects of Jarvis Street Baptist were credited with introducing "ecclesiastical amphitheatral construction" into Canada — churches with curved seating and horseshoe balconies carried on slender columns as in a theatre. This plan brought all close to the dais so that everyone might

Beverley Street Baptist, *Toronto; Baptist (now Toronto Chinese Baptist). Brick, 1886–87; Langley and Burke, architects*

FACING PAGE John Ross Robertson's *Landmarks of Toronto* (1904) gives rounded figures for the cost of this landmark across from the Art Gallery of Ontario: $2,000 for the lot (just large enough to hold Sunday school and church), $6,500 for the Sunday school and $12,500 for the church (seating 800), for a total of $21,000. A substantial (but not opulent) upper-middle-class house cost about $3,500 in the 1890s.

BELOW Robertson's *Landmarks* also notes the slenderness of the eight cast-iron columns supporting the balcony inside ("not more than four inches in diameter, so that there is no possible obstruction to the view"), the "ornamental iron work" fronting the gallery (as in many 1880s and 90s churches), the "folding opera chairs," described as "comfortable beyond expression" (still in place) and the "hospitable invitation, 'All seats are free.'"

see and hear the principal "actors": ministers, elders, choir, organist and organ (and, in Baptist churches, baptistery).

The church's square base carries a D-shaped, galleried auditorium with curving walls running behind a tower, asymmetrically placed at the southwest corner. Three large gables, each with a big traceried window, light the interior. Because the church would seat 1,300 in the pews and 2,000 with extra chairs, special attention was paid to circulation and egress. The auditorium backed against the Sunday school, an inverted T-shape to the east (now altered), also with gabled windows. There are entrances at each corner of the square, the easterly pair connected by a long hall serving both the "front" of the church and the Sunday school; the westerly pair (one in the tower, the other mirroring this) bracket a double porch in the middle of the west face. The double porch leads directly to the auditorium, the other four entries do so more-or-less but also lead to long runs of balcony stairs. The resulting active envelope and jagged profile might resemble a carousel if it were not such a solid structure, built with pinkish Queenston brownstone and beige Ohio stone dressings.

The interior uses walnut and chestnut, as well as neo-medieval columns of cast iron. In large churches and public buildings toward the century's end, architects

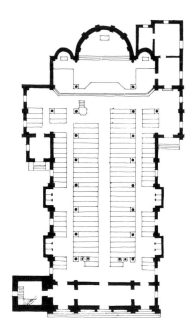

St. Paul's Basilica, *Toronto; Roman Catholic. Stone, 1887–89; Joseph Connolly, architect*

St. Paul's, Power Street, is like an early Christian basilica updated under Renaissance influence, a suave interpretation of Palladio's complex but harmonious church fronts, yet Victorian in its rich palette. The tower, consisting of four stacked cubes with flush bands of faint colour, is starkly geometric and almost monochromatic. Designed, like the church, by Joseph Connolly, the tower was executed in 1905 by Arthur W. Holmes, who had been Connolly's draftsman.

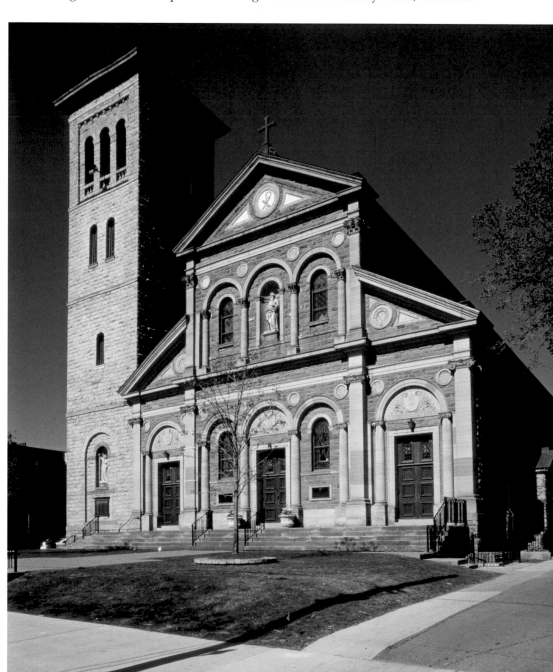

became conscious of the need for ventilation and Jarvis Street Baptist was equipped with ventilating shafts. The interior's nearly circular form contributed an unanticipated acoustic effect. In the words of an early visitor, "sweet strains of the organ float throughout the amphitheatre, and seem to linger" and then "to come back with power."

Beverley Street Baptist grew directly from Jarvis Street Baptist as a west-end mission church a decade later, with the same architects, Langley and Burke, and significant financial help from Jarvis Street's membership. Prudently, the Sunday school was built first (1880), and used for services until the project's other half could be carried out in 1886. The Toronto Chinese Baptist Church, its new owner, has restored it carefully.

In anticipation of the church, the Sunday school was built with two colours of brick skillfully laid, with corbelled eaves, some panelled brick and varied metal ornaments (remarkably intact) on gables and pinnacles. The two buildings, church and Sunday school, appear as one, in Picturesque asymmetry along Sullivan Street's long frontage. The yellow brick, more evident here than at Little Trinity but carefully balanced, brackets the red. Openings are simply round-headed. There is no sign of the artistic and powerful French Romanesque associated with Henry

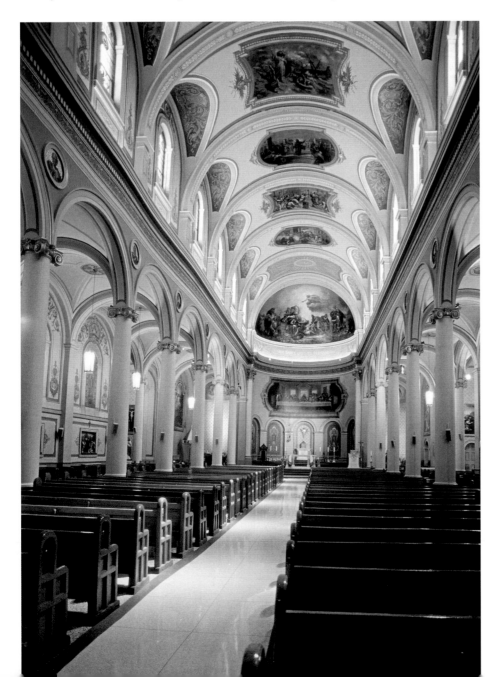

St. Paul's Basilica, *interior*
The interior is decorated around the life of St. Paul, beginning in the sanctuary ceiling with the conversion of Saul and continuing the length of the nave. The colouring in the church as a whole is sunny and apparently drawn from the stained glass: a pale apricot ground with bluish-green shades.

Elaborate architectural ornament above the arcades' frieze is mostly illusionist. The nave ceiling is a curved surface broken slightly by plain transverse bands arising from short piers. But all else is fictive: the sculptural-looking ornaments, the piers' and ribs' panelling, the elaborate cartouches that frame the painted panels in the ceiling. The life of St. Paul is oriented for viewing on entering the church, except for the first scenes, which only come into view on leaving it.

Church of St. Mary Magdalene, *Toronto; Anglican.*
Brick with stone trim, 1887–90, 1907–08, Frank Darling,
architect

Generous within, unpretentious without, this
simple red-brick building with grey-stone trim suits its
neighbourhood well. Roomy aisles and a tall nave —
lit by groups of round-arched windows with delicately
coloured glass — are embellished sparingly with
striking liturgical art.

Hobson Richardson of Boston, which began to appear in Montréal and Toronto in
1886, after his death. Instead, the general effect resembles north Italian work
described and illustrated in George Edmund Street's *Brick and Marble in the Middle
Ages* (1855; second edition, 1874). Burke's Romanesque was carried out in stock
brick, without using stone or marble or specially moulded bricks. The neighbourhood's red-and-yellow-brick houses with round-headed openings (like the church
office next door) suggest that builders were influenced by the Sunday school's
appearance to try something similar, if less vigorous.

The increasing use of colour in the Victorian period, in buildings as varied in
date and character as Little Trinity, Jarvis Street Baptist and Beverley Street Baptist,
is reflected in **St. Paul's, Power Street**, both outside and inside. One is hardly prepared for the serene Classicism of St. Paul's, however, after so much striving
Gothicism. The severe silhouette of the Romanesque tower contrasts with the rich
west-facing facade, which reveals the church's internal disposition: both nave and
aisles are defined by tall piers, Ionic below and Corinthian above, in the nave. Saint
Paul stands in a niche over the centre doors, flanked by round-headed windows on
both levels, linked harmoniously by arcades. The aisle doors are similarly framed.
The giant piers and the two-tiered arcade with smaller half-columns are in smoothly
dressed sandstone the colour of sponge toffee, standing proud of a rusticated
brownstone wall. The architect deftly filled the remaining empty spaces with
Venetian roundels, their eyes of either orange or bluish-green marble. All this *ital-
ianismo* reflects the Romanism — despite Toronto's anti-Catholicism in this period
— of its patron, Bishop Timothy O'Mahony.

Joseph Connolly (1840–1904) was trained in Dublin by J.J. McCarthy, whose
work was usually in a Gothic vein. Connolly arrived in Toronto in 1873, began Our
Lady of the Immaculate Conception at Guelph in 1876 (*see* pp. 233–35) and did a
great deal of work around Kingston, Hamilton and Guelph. McCarthy's Italianate
church at Thurles, County Tipperary, carried out while Connolly worked for him,
may have played a small role. There is an expansiveness to St. Paul's, clearly articulated in arcades under a barrel vault that ends in the half-dome of the apsidal chancel. The lucid mathematical precision of the planning is based on square bays in the
aisles, with bays twice as wide in the nave, and transepts with a cluster of four
squares. The church was elevated to the status of a minor basilica in 1999.

St. Mary Magdalene was begun in 1887–88 as an inexpensive church to be
upgraded later. By its completion in 1907–08, its most ambitious building plans had
gone unrealized. Theologically, liturgically and musically, however, it became a
leading Anglo-Catholic parish, celebrated for Dr. Healey Willan's long involvement.
The humble initial scheme began where High-Church thinking might dictate: in a
large polygonal chancel (squat initially, its temporarily roofed walls to be raised to
full height later), a vestry and a nave both low and small, producing a "camel-
backed church" on Ulster Street. The first two features can be traced in the present
building. The contractor, John Stroud, provided the font that is still in use, carved
by Benjamin Jones. The energetic curate behind this was Charles Darling, son of
Frank Darling, the former rector of Holy Trinity, Trinity Square. The architect was
his older brother, also named Frank (1850–1923). After training locally with Henry
Langley, he went to London and worked with Sir George Edmund Street and Sir
Arthur Blomfield, architects and writers of distinction.

About half the nave, on octagonal stone piers, was added in 1889–90 before the architect devised an eclectic fantasy in 1892. Two years later the chancel rose, with seven sanctuary windows and a tall, delicately detailed Romanesque chancel arch. When the nave reached Manning Avenue in 1907–08, the entrance stepped back through nooks, but an intended entrance figure of Mary Magdalene was the first elaboration of 1892 to disappear. On paper, Darling had embellished the facade: statues on tall, slender shafts approached Venetian splendor, set between vaguely Germanic octagonal towers, while a clergy house in Toronto Romanesque style was attached to the north, followed by a tall bell tower in an approximation of early French Gothic style. All this architectural art disappeared. To expand the sanctuary, however, and make room for liturgy, the chancel was stripped of furnishings except for William Rae's (*see* pp. 259, 272) great rood with Christ the King (1921), hanging from the ceiling, and a new altar (1963–64).

"St. Mary Mag" (as it is concisely, if irreverently, known) is more than "colourful vestments or clouds of incense," processions, "graceful and truly sacred music." For it "has developed a spirituality and style of worship that have given it a special place among Anglican churches in Canada." The present Anglican community comprehends that "Christ's re-united Church of the future will have some of that diversity."

St. Mary Magdalene Adding lustre to this deceptively plain place was Healey Willan's work (between 1921 and 1963) as arranger, conductor, choirmaster, organist and Canada's foremost composer of international renown. Father Henry Hiscocks' "instinct for Catholic worship, complemented by Willan's musical learning and genius, placed [the] parish on the cutting edge of liturgical change in the Canadian church" — so much so that it became "a power in the land."

Town planning is first and foremost a human issue: its problems are by no means exclusively technical and economic. It can never be carried on satisfactorily without a clear understanding of the contemporary conception of life.
— *Siegfried Giedion, 1954*

Church and City

St. Patrick's (now Our Lady of Mount Carmel), *Toronto; Roman Catholic, white brick with stone trim and timber-framed interior, 1870, Gundry & Langley, architects*

This accomplished view suggests the village-like character of St. Patrick's ward (bounded by University Avenue, Queen, Bathurst and Bloor streets) in its early years. The church served the Irish who emigrated in the 1840s and 1850s; Henry Langley (1836–1907) was Toronto-born but his parents were Irish. He and his partner Thomas Gundry were church specialists and began designing St. Patrick's in 1869. It appears between the presbytery and a parochial school, in afternoon sunlight against passing clouds. The artist was Langley's nephew, apprentice and later partner Edmund Burke, who possibly intended the sunburst as a symbol of rising fortunes among Toronto's Irish.

CHURCH BUILDINGS OFTEN STAND ALONE, occupying all available frontage, but they also have a responsibility to urban design. **Our Lady of Mount Carmel**, **Toronto**, had humble origins: a frame chapel (1861, burned 1864) served by a priest from the Roman Catholic cathedral. In 1867, Father Laurent promoted a complex in which the school would act as a chapel until the church was built (1870). Then land was purchased for the presbytery. All three were lined up on the west side of St. Patrick Street (north of Dundas Street West) until a Chinese Catholic Centre replaced the school; the presbytery was demolished in 2005 in what is now an intensely urban area. Similarly, compact developments for domestic, religious and educational use were erected by Anglicans until 1871, after which, property-based taxation provided for universal education and schools were no longer built by the church.

By the early 20th century everything had changed. Long, linear streets — avenues of some vision — replaced the short, narrow lanes, not the great boulevards of Baroque urbanism but commercially organized streets that followed the city's rapid expansion. **Holy Name**, **Toronto**, is carefully executed but plain over all: the south front alone is dramatic and sculptural, rising as a billboard of faith. Diocesan architect Arthur W. Holmes turned to James Gibbs' exceptional London church St. Mary-le-Strand (1714–17) for Baroque inspiration: a succession of alternately triangular and segmental pediments connect attached columns, cresting like waves as they frame Latin proclamations that translate as "HOLY, HOLY, HOLY" and "AT THE NAME OF JESUS EVERY KNEE SHALL BOW." **St. Pius X**, **Toronto**, reflects the notion of "keeping in keeping" with the streetscape, current in architectural practice in the late 20th century. Dedicated the year this pope was canonized, Pius X tucks a steel-framed basilica discreetly into a similarly constructed streetscape.

Holy Name, *Toronto; Roman Catholic. Stone, 1915; Arthur W. Holmes, architect*

Holy Name is in the 19th-century tradition of street architecture. Deliberately monumental, it is almost the only visual event in the two-story flatland of Danforth Avenue, east of the Don River. It sits on a rise of land, visible from a mile away in both directions, gladdening the heart of Riverdale.

St. Pius X, *Toronto; Roman Catholic. Brick, stone and steel, 1953–54; Venchiarutti and Venchiarutti, architects*

The north-facing front's abstracted planar forms correspond to the narthex, stairs and gallery. The church reaches the sidewalk and aligns with its neighbours, rising as much as they, except for the tall centre, reflecting the nave's height. Gated gaps offer firebreaks, while parking fills the rest of the property, hidden from Bloor Street. The sacristy, vestry and rectory are attached at the south end; altogether an urbane solution.

They took us where they worshipped their God [Haghia Sophia], and we did not know whether we were in heaven or upon earth, for there is not upon earth such sight or beauty. This much we do know, that there, God lives among men, and that beauty we can never forget.

— *Prince Volodymyr's emissary in Kiev*

Byzantium in Ontario

BYZANTINE CHURCHES are the earliest stylistically unified form of churches, recalled in the medieval period as the basis of Romanesque churches (*see* p. 378). Byzantine Revival churches were built from the late 19th century onward, especially in the Canadian West when immigrants from Eastern Europe took up free land and quickly established themselves (*see* pp. 290–93; 315–27). But when **St. Anne's**, **Toronto**, was built in this style in 1907–08, it must have seemed audacious, defying the prevailing upward-striving Gothic Revival taste of the time. Romanesque had been used for University College (1854–58), the Ontario Legislature (1899), other civic and educational structures and synagogues (*see* pp. 264–66), but only slowly for churches. While the building's shell is Romanesque Revival, the interior of St. Anne's is solidly Byzantine. For an Anglican church to be decorated exuberantly in an eastern iconographic and avant-garde fashion was daring. The form and decoration both have to do with the views of the rector, Canon Lawrence Skey, whose egalitarian vision prompted a competition, won by Ford Howland (1875–1948). Skey's anti-elitist views led him to select a team of painters and sculptors for the program of interior decoration who were not part of the establishment; William Rae, an architect, directed the group's work (*see* pp. 272–73). The interior was in serious jeopardy in the 1990s because of insufficient funds for restoration, but a grant from the Ontario government made a new slate roof possible, which has ensured no further damage will occur.

St. Anne's, *Toronto; Anglican. Brick, concrete and steel trusses, 1907–08; Langley and Howland, architects, with Burke and Horwood*

The clarity of Ford Howland's design is readily apparent: a large domed central space on a Greek-cross plan (all within a large rectangle), with the apse, nave, transepts and entrance all cohering within a major artistic program of embellishment by members of the Group of Seven. St. Anne's is one of the glories of Byzantine Revival style in Ontario, indeed in all Canada.

St. Anne's, *exterior*
The shell of St. Anne's is more Romanesque Revival
than purely Byzantine, but this combination is not
uncommon. The round-headed doors and six windows
forming an arcade above are balanced by the twin
flanking towers with octagonal belfries and cupolas.
The side entrances into the transepts widen the footprint to make a square, on which the pyramidal
roof rises up to the clearly expressed dome, with its
eight windows; their form is repeated in the main
windows of the nave on the ground floor.

The exterior of the church is more impressive from the rear. In buff brick, its
Romanesque doors and windows, flanking towers with cupolas, and central
octagonal dome make a strong but unexciting statement on the street. In plan, the
building is a large square with small extensions for the entrance, transepts and
chancel. The dome — with a large window in each of the eight segments — is carried on two large piers at the front and two large columns at the rear. These are
joined with arches, between which pendentives assist in carrying the dome, which
springs directly from the arches rather than sitting on a drum. Most surfaces are
decorated. St. Anne's glory is the chancel area and the dome, where much of the
work is by the Group of Seven. Some of the recent additions, such as the bronze
main doors with their bas-reliefs, work well with the form and decoration. Other
recent touches, such as the blue glass mosaics, are less successful. This is one of

Canada's true treasures, a powerful partnership of art and architecture, expressive of early 20th-century stylishness.

Built about the same time as St. Anne's, **Dominion-Chalmers**, **Ottawa**, faces the neighbourhood with rugged stone walls, squat towers and round-arched openings deriving from Romanesque influences (*see* p. 184). Inside, the design successfully evokes Byzantine centrally focused churches. A large domical vault rests on eight short barrel vaults around the periphery that in turn sit on eight colossal columns. On the axis of the narthex a platform at the front is backed by organ pipes and console, all fitting neatly under the vault opposite the entrance. The projecting platform now provides maximum flexibility for the many concerts held there, taking advantage of the church's lively acoustics. The radiating seating area slopes up to the perimeter walls and a gallery circles seven-eighths of the circumference, underscoring the centrality of the domed space. Natural light enters from two side walls, a window at the gallery's rear above the narthex and eight windows in the dome. The large and colourful capitals of the colossal columns hew to Byzantine models while the smaller perimeter columns have carefully designed Composite capitals.

Alexander C. Hutchison (1838–1922), who designed Dominion-Chalmers, was a prominent Montréal architect. His major and youthful work was Montréal's Hôtel de Ville (1872–78), done with Henri-Maurice Perrault (*see* p. 333) in the then popular Second Empire style. In the 1860s Hutchison had supervised the stonecutting for the Parliament Buildings after training as a stonecutter in his father's contracting business. (Hutchison was also responsible for Erskine and American Church, Montréal (1894), which has strong Richardsonian Romanesque features in two colours of stone.) Dominion-Chalmers' monotone exterior is dominated by a corner tower balanced by a lower octagonal tower. The four-stage tower sets a dignified tone with a single window — tall, thin and round-headed — in each face of the first stage, a triplet of windows in the second stage, a bell chamber with tall paired openings in the third stage, and a seven-part blind arcade in the fourth stage, below the square dome, recalling Second Empire detail. The main entrance is the fulcrum of the composition, with its arched porch and large round-headed window wheeling above it. The low octagonal lantern surmounting the roof hints at the Byzantine interior; its 24 windows, three on each face, provide light for the dome's eight interior openings.

Dominion-Chalmers' history mirrors the United Church's history. Its origins lie

Dominion-Chalmers, *Ottawa; Presbyterian (now United). Brick, 1912–14; Alexander C. Hutchison, architect*

Like St. Anne's, though more consistently so, the exterior of Dominion-Chalmers is Romanesque Revival. Inside there is neither the same quality of light nor of decoration as at St. Anne's. Yet there is a feeling of solidity — characteristic of a Presbyterian church perhaps — that serves the congregation well. Two of its most attractive features are the design of the balcony and the use of the corner spaces for stairs.

One of the capitals of the eight main massive two-story columns that support the dome shows the care Hutchison took with details to create a truly Byzantine effect inside. This capital is at the second-floor level, where a column arcade, visible on the right, frames the corner stairwell. The differentiated capitals work beautifully together and have been painted to reflect the riches of the Byzantine tradition.

Saints Cyril and Methodius, *St. Catharines;*
Ukrainian Catholic. Brick, 1944–46 (icons, 1965–72);
Father Philip Ruh, designer; Igor Suchaçev, artist

Saints Cyril and Methodius seems larger on the outside than it really is. Like Philip Ruh's other churches, it is thoroughly thought out and consistent, both inside and out. On the exterior a Byzantine-like brick band defines the floor level with dark brown, red and beige bricks, matched by two other bands at the roof level and an intermediate level, displaying crosses in the brick pattern.

in a Methodist Church begun in 1816; it merged with a second Methodist church in 1852. The resulting merged church was soon torn down and a larger replacement was named Dominion Methodist (1874–76), symbolizing Methodism's countrywide strength. Meanwhile, Bank Street Presbyterian, created in 1865, prospered so that by 1912 it could hire Hutchison to design anew for its growing congregation. It was renamed Chalmers Presbyterian when it moved to its new building. Then, following church union in 1925, it became Chalmers United. When Dominion United burned down in 1962, the two merged under the name Dominion-Chalmers.

The chunkiness and the detailing of Byzantine-inspired churches make them seem larger than they really are, as is the case with **Saints Cyril and Methodius, St. Catharines**. Ukrainians settled in Niagara later than in the West; it was not until the 1930s and following World War II that there were substantial numbers. Services were held from 1937; a church committee was struck in 1942, which bought a plot

of land alongside the Queen Elizabeth Way — the church is familiar to anyone travelling to Niagara Falls — and hired the well-known designer-priest Philip Ruh (1883–1962). Ruh designed a church similar to some of his other works (*see* pp. 318–21), especially the larger St. Josaphat in Edmonton. The plan is traditional: narthex, sanctuary (nave) and altar (chancel), with transepts making a Latin cross. Over the crossing is an octagonal dome on a drum, punctured with small windows.

It is a gem, unified inside and out, with the classic features of Byzantine and Romanesque Revival. The interior, painted by Igor Suchaçev (*see* p. 266) over a seven-year period, coheres well with Father Philip Ruh's architecture. The consistent decorative program centres on the Holy Doors in a three-stage iconostasis: the Annunciation is in the centre surrounded by the four evangelists; to the left is Mary, to the right Jesus. Icons on the sanctuary's left feature women (for example, the Samaritan woman and the young girl raised by Jesus) while the right features men. Facing each other are paired scenes: the Wedding Feast at Cana, for instance, faces

Saints Cyril and Methodius, *interior*
The iconostasis is a three-tier composition whose openings are modelled on Syrian arches. Above the Holy Door is a round icon with a seated Jesus displaying an open book. The ends of the iconostasis have Saints Cyril and Methodius on the right and Saints Olga and Volodymyr, rulers of Ukraine, on the left.

St. George's, *Toronto; Greek Orthodox (originally Holy Blossom Synagogue). Brick and sandstone, 1895–97; John Wilson Siddall, architect*

Converted in 1937 for use as the leading Greek Orthodox church in Toronto, St. George's corner cupolas and entrance have been altered and the mosaic of St. George added, but the bulk of the facade is as it was. The appropriateness of a Byzantine and Romanesque Revival structure for religious usage has allowed it to serve two quite different sets of needs.

FACING PAGE The interior's liveliness derives from the combination of the octagonal shell of the central part of the building with its dome and the octagonal balcony that mimics the exterior shape. In the adaptations for Greek Orthodox use most of the original elements have been retained — the lacy balcony front is especially noteworthy — but the richly decorative iconostasis and the frescoes by monks from Mount Athos have made the space a wonderful example of Greek piety and worship.

the Last Supper. Every square inch of the space is painted, yet it avoids garishness.

The exterior uses multicoloured but complementary brick in reds, beiges and browns to emphasize structural elements. The facade's central panel is beige brick, flanked by two round towers in red brick joined by a panel and by a pediment, also in red brick. Brickwork crosses carry around the building and unify it. The vaulted roof, covered in green copper, expresses on the outside the shape of the vaulted interior. The central dome and four cupolas, also in copper, have white exterior drums decorated with small blind arcades, a Romanesque motif.

Holy Trinity Russian Orthodox Outside of Russia, **Toronto**, and **St. George's Greek Orthodox**, **Toronto,** are downtown churches that share the fact that both occupy buildings originally designed as synagogues, from a period when considerable numbers of Jews lived in the city centre. St. George's acquired Holy Blossom Synagogue in 1937 (the oldest synagogue still standing in Toronto). Holy Trinity acquired Beth Jacob Synagogue, "the Great Synagogue," in 1966; it was designed in 1922 by Benjamin Brown, Toronto's first Jewish architect. In both buildings, the Romanesque Revival exterior and Byzantine interior reflected a preferred form for synagogues, sometimes, as in the case of Holy Blossom, with a Moorish twist, perhaps partly because they wanted to avoid Gothic Revival and partly because this new style was being used in civic buildings. In both, the facade is near the street line, with twin towers at the front corners — in Holy Trinity's case projecting. Both are brick, one red and one buff, with Romanesque detailing (more elaborate in the case of St. George's). The main space in each building is one floor above street level. Both are high cuboid buildings, focused on a central dome, and both have large balconies on three sides; in the case of St. George's the balcony is octagonal to reflect the dome above and the shape of the building shell (with a very fine cast-iron gallery front). Minor parts of Beth Jacob's decoration survive in the bands reflecting the structural members under the balcony.

Holy Trinity, *Toronto; Russian Orthodox Abroad (originally Beth Jacob Synagogue). Brick, 1922; Benjamin Brown, architect*

Holy Trinity's red-brick facade echoes the dominant character of its late-19th century residential neighbourhood. Its central dome, projecting square towers and cupolas make a strong statement of its Eastern Rite connections. The Russian émigré community arrived following World War II, quickly established a congregation and was soon able to purchase the building, which was originally a synagogue.

FACING PAGE **Holy Trinity**, *interior*

The iconostasis in Holy Trinity by Igor Suhaçev is a more elaborate version of one by the same artist for the iconostasis of Saints Cyril and Methodius in St. Catharines. Highly architectural in its overall conception, the iconography is set carefully into the architectural framework.

The entire interior of **St. George's** was painted in 1987 by Theophilos and Chrysostomos, two monks from Greece's Mount Athos where the rule of St. Pachomius is followed. "The chief scenes of the Pachomaioi frescoes are nearly all faithful reproductions of well-known masterpieces of Byzantine painting," writes Peter Jeffreys in his guide to the church. "The Pachomaioi frescoes, however, are more than mere copies: they are dynamic re-creations of masterworks of Byzantine art which possess a robust gracefulness and sublime elegance of their own. There is a transcendent beauty, a gentle sweetness and a deep pathos about their work, all of which enhance the monastic ethos of prayer and humility to which the Pachomaioi remain faithful as ascetic iconographers."

The curved iconostasis projects into the sanctuary, increasing the sense of a centrally planned space. It was designed by Karopoulos's local workshop in a dark walnut, with carved urns, grape clusters and acanthus leaves, all Classical motifs. The six large icons and the smaller festal icons are also the work of the Pachomaioi.

The interior of **Holy Trinity** is still being completed. A gilded iconostasis crosses the front between two of the four large Corinthian columns that carry the dome. Its impact is overpowering, with the three sets of doors and all the icons set within round-headed openings, seven in the first stage, 21 in the second stage and five in the third. The central place in the upper stage is occupied by Jesus, with holy book open. The major icons under the arches were done by Father Andrew, a monk from Holy Trinity Monastery near Utica, New York. The design of and iconographic work on the iconostasis was by Igor Suchaçev (*see* p. 263). Other parts of the decorative scheme are being done by Vladislav Fedorov and Alex Metcezev.

Radoslav Zuk, an internationally recognized architect and emeritus professor of architecture at McGill University, was the leading architects in the last half of the 20th century for Ukrainian churches (*see* pp. 368–69). He has designed (sometimes in association with or as consultant to other architectural firms) almost 10 in North America, seven of them in Canada. Zuk is a co-recipient of the Governor General's Medal for Architecture awarded by the Royal Architectural Institute of Canada, the highest architectural honour in Canada. In his churches, Zuk reinterprets Ukrainian traditions while retaining their essential elements, but he does so with deep indebtedness to the precision of Modernism's interest in mass, void and contrast. Zuk's most striking church in Ontario is **Holy Eucharist**, **Toronto**, looking west over the Don Valley Parkway and across the wooded valley to Toronto's downtown highrises. He took advantage of the long sight lines to create a distinctive silhouette, a tall domed tower to one side in front of a plain stone one-story facade, topped by a five-dome cluster that sits on a steeply pitched cross-shaped roof. The classically arranged components form a Modernist composition, whose plan is a large square structure that incorporates school rooms and rectory in the rear and a large meeting hall on the lower level. Inside, the church plan echoes the cruciform shape of the roof. The vibrant iconography, by Myron Levitsky, departs from the neo-Byzantine style that is more common in Ukrainian churches, though still depicting traditional subjects. Perhaps most remarkable of all in this brilliant interior is the resonance of the glass with the iconography, utilizing a similar palette of colours.

Thirty years after Zuk's pioneering design of Holy Eucharist, Robert Greenberg, emeritus professor of architecture at Ryerson University, designed **St. Elias**,

Holy Eucharist, *Toronto; Ukrainian Catholic. Brick, 1967; Radoslav Zuk, architect, interior by Myron Levitsky*

Holy Eucharist may have the most dramatic site for a religious building in Toronto. Seen from a distance its profile is strong, appropriate and unmistakable, as well as being clearly in the independent Modernist tradition. The steeply rising roof of Holy Eucharist is in a Greek cross form with slightly pinched arms. Between the roof and the one-story walls of the sanctuary is a continuous band of glass, while other bands of glass separate and define each of the planes of the roof. Five domes repeat the traditional motif of multiple domes, but here they are clustered together with small windows in their bases. Hanging like clouds from the ceiling, plain globes provide artificial light.

Brampton. It sits in a field just north of Highway 7 and west of Brampton, looking like a transplanted late-19th-century prairie church. Yet it is fully a late 20th-century church that uses traditional forms — modelled on Boyko-style churches in Ukraine, particularly St. George's in Drohobych — more literally than Zuk has done. The timber-frame and wood detailing is remarkable for its sensitivity. The wood exterior is mostly British Columbia cedar, with cedar shakes on the roof and five domes designed in a 17th-century Cossack style.

In the typical three-part plan, the narthex is modelled on the Court of Gentiles in the Jerusalem Temple, the nave replicates the Holy Place, and the sanctuary (altar) responds to the Holy of Holies. There is deep symbolism in a number of other elements in the design, and in the location of the various icons, characteristic of Eastern Rite churches. Here in St. Elias, the iconostasis has the usual three sets of

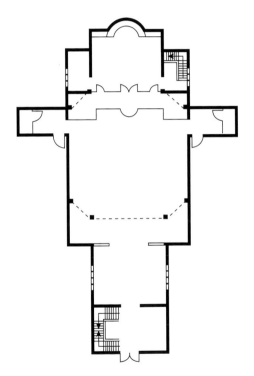

St. Elias, *Brampton; Ukrainian Catholic. Wood, 1994–95; Robert Greenberg, architect*

St. Elias, like Holy Eucharist, has a five-dome exterior. Despite being built nearly 20 years later, it is considerably more traditional in its approach. The Cossack-style domes are in their more usual places: a central dome and domes over narthex, altar and transepts or side altars. The all-wood construction is meticulously executed with carefully considered exterior details that read well, even from a distance.

The interior is determined equally by its traditional plan and its modern frame construction, with four tall 12-by-12 columns and a variety of horizontal beams and trusses, all bolted together with sympathetically designed steel gussets. The octagonal central dome is supported on an octagonal drum, carried in turn on a square formed by trusses and supported on the four columns. Its traditional centrepiece is Jesus Christ Pantocrator surrounded by eight angels.

doors; the central Holy Doors show Saint John Chrysostom and Saint Basil the Great, from whom much of the liturgy derives. Above this door is the icon of the Lord's Supper. To either side are Christ the teacher and Mary the Holy Godbearer. At the ends of the iconostasis are Saint Elias (Elijah) and Saint Nicholas of Myra.

Major icons appear on the central dome with its traditional centrepiece, Jesus Christ as Pantocrator ("ruler of all") surrounded by eight angels. Others are in large panels framed by the main structural members, integrating structure, detailing and decoration with a remarkable fusion of tradition and modernity. The services blend formality and informality; there are no pews — only a few benches around the walls — and children are fully engaged in the service as they wander around to participate or visit with their friends. It is a young congregation, blessed with beautiful voices, divided male and female with lilting antiphonal effect.

One quit the work with more regret than pleasure, for one felt that in the beautifying of this local gathering place — this home for the soul of a wide neighbourhod — rector, congregation and workman alike were serving a worthy ideal.
— J.E.H. MacDonald

Group of Seven in Church

St. Anne's, *Toronto; Anglican. Brick, concrete with steel trusses, 1907–08; Langley and Howland, architects, with Burke and Horwood; iconography by J.E.H. MacDonald, F.H. Varley, Franklin Carmichael and others (1923)*

The triangular pendentive on the left is by F.H. Varley, who painted himself into the "Nativity" as a shepherd, kneeling on the left. In the middle the rectangular panel is Frank Carmichael's "Adoration of the Magi." The Moses medallion under the main dome is also by Varley. On the right is "Jesus in the Temple" by Arthur Martin.

When Lawrence Skey, St. Anne's rector, held a competition for a new church in 1907, no one expected the building would become one of Canada's artistic treasures (*see* p. 259). The decision to build in Romanesque Revival style was unusual; the decision to embellish the interior with icons in a Byzantine manner was bold; the decision to hand the commission to unpopular artists, including three members of the Group of Seven, was almost laughable. The work was coordinated by William Rae, an architect, with J.E.H. MacDonald, F.H. Varley and Franklin Carmichael responsible for the painting, while Florence Wyle and Frances Loring sculpted four low-relief medallions. According to MacDonald, "The pictorial painting was separated from the flat and ornamental painting and it was done cooperatively but independently, all the associated artists working in their own studios, from small scale designs prepared by the decoration contractor, keeping their work in close harmony with the general design, using the same strength of colours throughout, and drawing on a common stock of materials for their supplies."

St. Anne's, of course, has no iconostasis, and this changes the relationship of the painting to the space. In St. Anne's there is an emphatic stress on the apsidal chancel with the sequence of five trapezoidal panels above the windows and two more above the organ pipes. Alongside these seven scenes illustrating events in the Gospels, the four major scenes on the triangular pendentives illustrate moments in Jesus' life (nativity, crucifixion, resurrection and ascension). They are unquestionably the highlight of the iconography, particularly "The Nativity" by Varley, with Varley himself painted into the scene as a shepherd on the left, kneeling, and "The Crucifixion" by MacDonald with its strongly Byzantine sensibility. Less frequently noticed are the medallions under the dome's windows — four portraits of major prophets (Moses, Isaiah, Jeremiah and Daniel) by Varley and four symbols of the Gospel writers (angel, lion, ox and eagle) by Loring and Wyle.

The whole iconographic suite is a remarkable indication of the artists' enthusiasm for their subjects; there is no trivializing of the images and no reductionism in the religious sentiments. Here tradition is wedded firmly to the artistic expression of the 1920s avant-garde.

J.E.H. MacDonald's "Crucifixion," seen here in a detail of one of the pendentives, is one of the most satisfying of the pieces of art, for it captures well not only the modern mood but the essence of Byzantine artistic style with its formality and somewhat mannered poses. The flat decoration on the arches adds significantly to the total impact, as does the carefully executed lettering in the texts.

Among the most satisfying but least noticed of the works of art are the medallions, four painted and four sculpted, just under the dome. The portraits of prophets are by Varley. His youthful "Daniel" is a fresh interpretation of that little-understood Old Testament figure.

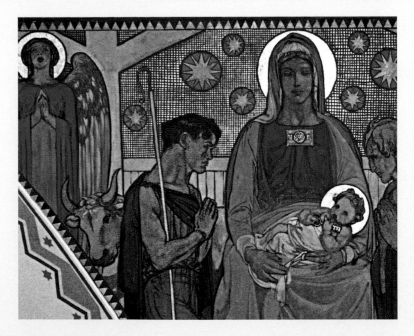

Varley's "Nativity," in a detail of another of the pendentives, shows well how the several artists were able to provide a unified body of narrative art by following similar conventions and using a common palette of colours. Mary is shown in her traditional blue, holding the Christ child, in the stable, effectively hinted at by the timber-frame construction behind. The most memorable feature of this is Varley himself, portrayed in a reverential pose, facing the child.

Frances Loring and Florence Wyle were two of Canada's most brilliant sculptors. For 50 years they shared studio space and a home in a church (originally Christ Church, Deer Park) that was moved to a new location in Moore Park. Their work is widely distributed across the country, much of it small in scale, like these four medallions representing the four gospel writers. Here the Gospel of Luke is represented traditionally as a winged ox.

Architecture should enliven, ennoble and inspire, and not gratify or glorify the banal. The doctrine of innovation for its own sake, founded on creative obsolescence, is a practice we have always resisted.
— *John C. Parkin*

Resisting Obsolescence

St. Peter's Estonian, *Toronto; Evangelical Lutheran. Brick and glulam, 1954–55; Michael Bach, architect*

Although St. Peter's is a fairly common A-frame style church, it is rescued from being humdrum by its careful detailing (note the standing seams in the copper roof that reflect the positions of the bents and the brickwork with slightly projecting bricks every third course). The warm red brick and human-scaled courtyard, by Ants Elken, make it an attractive oasis along busy Mount Pleasant Road.

AFTER WORLD WAR II Canada was blessed with substantial numbers of new citizens fleeing either from the ravages of that conflict or the fallout afterward, especially in Eastern Europe. Architects came with these immigrants. Eventually the groups began to build their own buildings and, as in the case of **St. Peter's Estonian Lutheran, Toronto,** hired one of their own, Michael Bach. Most of the congregation was forced to flee in small boats after the Russian takeover of Estonia. Bach said at the time, "No stereotyped style could reflect the forward-looking spirit of the congregation, whose struggle for freedom brought them to a new homeland from the political strife which was once their home. It was this freedom sought for, and this break from tradition on the part of the congregation, which led to the progressive design."

Straightforward in its conception, a blend of traditional sensibilities and modern aesthetics, the Californian-derived glulam A-frame was becoming a popular and inexpensive approach to modern design in the 1950s and 60s. The bents are in splayed pairs, whose ridge slopes down toward the east end as the plan narrows toward the chancel. The street edges of the inclined planes project, so that the roof forms a prow in green copper that seems to extend over the sidewalk. Two additions by Ants Elken, an Estonian graduate of Helsinki University, improved the facilities. He created a small courtyard and bell tower on the north that included a columbarium with walls containing niches for burials of urns; the columbarium, seen only from within the courtyard, is a brilliant solution to the ongoing identification of an

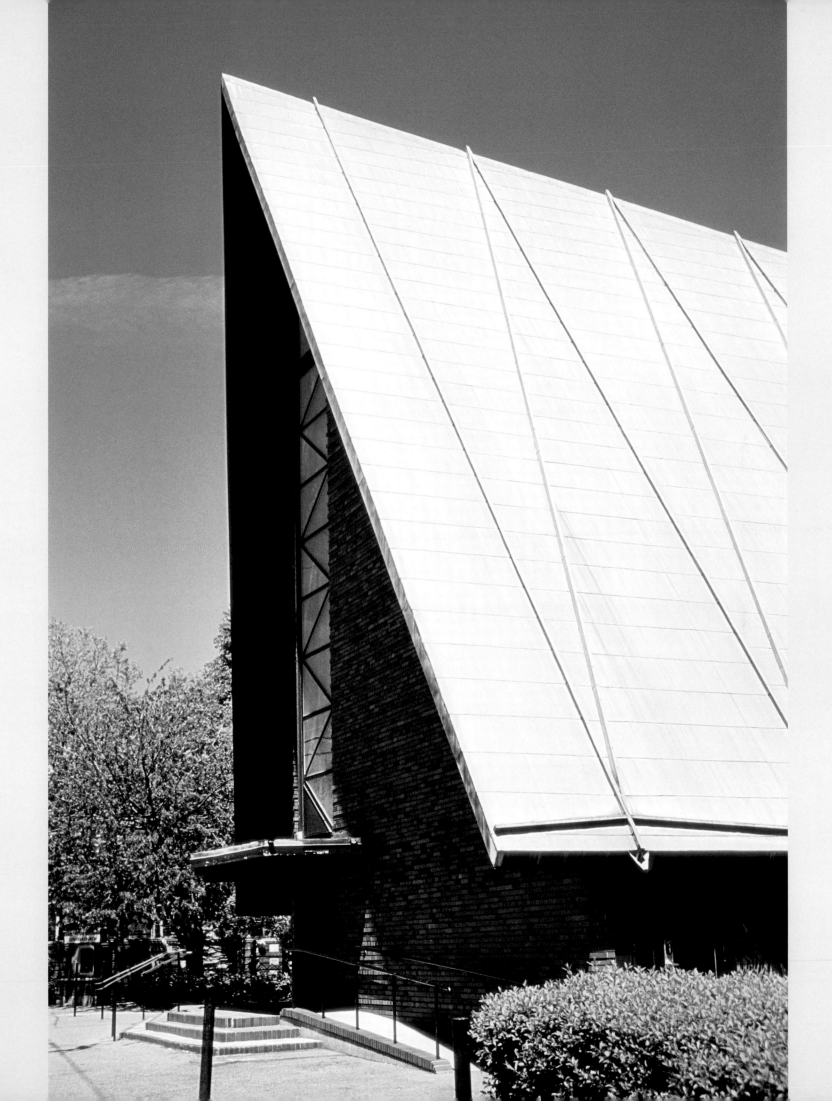

ethnic community. The courtyard covers a below-grade suite of rooms lit by a small ground-level skylight. Elken later removed the original window wall at the east end, added seven feet and closed it in with a triangular red-brick wall with light spilling vertically onto the chancel from a slot between the roof and the wall. The result inside is so consistent that it is difficult to identify the various stages: clean Modernist detailing, low stained-glass windows using earthy colours and a pervasive warmth hold it all together. Two émigré Estonian architects, both of whom taught at the University of Toronto, achieved one of the earliest and most successful of the new wave of Toronto churches.

Eberhard Zeidler, a young graduate of the Bauhaus, arrived in Canada and set up a practice in Peterborough in 1951. A few decades later, his firm was responsible for some of the most influential work being done by Canadian architects, both

St. Peter's Estonian, *stained glass and interior*
The glass sidewalls between the glulam bents are in a mixture of warm subdued colours and bold primaries. Elken's pyramidal skylight and, farther away, the columbarium can be seen dimly.

Though the interior has been altered by the removal of the glass end wall (replaced in a small addition, also by Elken, with a brick wall and continuous skylight that profiles the large cross), there is no sense of its having been modified. Both architects shared a common approach to detailing and the creation of a warm atmosphere.

locally and around the world. Among his early Peterborough-period works were a number of churches. **West Ellesmere United**, **Toronto**, demonstrates both the rapidly growing strength of Christian churches in the decades following World War II and the decline in their strength in the last decade or so; its ancillary facilities are now used by another church. Fifty years on, West Ellesmere's future may seem murky, but Zeidler's conception of the interior is crystal clear; two similarly curved side walls curve upward and inward, not quite meeting, so that a clerestory is created that allows a continuous band of indirect natural light to flood the nave from above. Zeidler's approach is more emotional — less hard-edged — than Bach's and Elken's work, coming from the same springs as the later work of Cardinal and Gaboury (*see* pp. 351–56).

Because of the continuing timidity of post-war Christianity's approach to

West Ellesmere, *Toronto; United. Brick and glulam, 1957, 1961; Eberhard Zeidler, architect*

The clarity of the conception reads well from the street, where the church is located in the midst of a residential subdivision, as was common in the 1950s. The 1961 educational and recreational facilities are attached at the rear of the 1957 structure, shown here. Near the door is a tall cross on a bell tower, just visible behind.

From both the outside and the inside, the form — and even the construction — of West Ellesmere is apparent: glulam arches with similar curves but rising to different heights cup the congregation. As well as a glazed clerestory, natural light also enters at the front and backlights the large cross, with simulated silver stars on the wall behind it.

Knox Fellowship Centre Chapel, *Toronto; Presbyterian. Brick, 1960–61; John B. Parkin Associates, architects*

The small chapel with its gracefully curved roof has a forceful presence across the street from the University of Toronto. Inside, the form is repeated in pairs of arches springing from the corners and in the glazed corner slots that shift to lights between the arches. The materials are plain: brick walls, wooden ceiling, and stained-glass bands. The Presbyterian Church in Canada's Latin motto is *nec tamen consumebatur* ("yet not consumed," referring to Moses' burning bush).

architectural design, even a major firm like John B. Parkin Associates wet its feet rather slowly (*see* **Christadelphian Church**, p. 186). The integrity of Parkin's Unity Church of Truth, Toronto, designed as a two-story concrete frame grid with solids and voids, on Eglinton Avenue, is now totally lost, but its conceptual clarity follows the dominant influence of John C. Parkin's insistent Modernism. Gradually even conservative clients had enough confidence to retain modernists like Parkin for new structures and additions. The **Fellowship Centre Chapel**, **Knox Presbyterian**, **Toronto,** was designed for one of Toronto's oldest congregations (founded 1820), which had moved to a new building by James Wilson Gray in 1909.

In the 1950s it acquired a separate recreational building across the street, which was later expropriated by the University of Toronto. A gymnasium, bowling alleys and meeting rooms had been used mainly for outreach to neighbourhood children and nearby university students. The replacement for these facilities sits beside the eclectic 1909 church, with a courtyard and square chapel facing the busy street. It was a major departure for Knox to build a "teahouse of the August moon," with swooping curved beams on the diagonals, slots in the outward-turning corners and purple brick walls. To establish its Presbyterian identity, a Celtic cross is silhouetted at night against the gymnasium's grey brick wall.

St. Mark's, *Don Mills; Presbyterian. Brick, 1961–63; John B. Parkin, architect; St. Mark's Court, 1988–90; Guido E. Laivke, architects*

In the early 1960s a new building was built alongside the old St. Mark's, separated by a courtyard and office areas; the original building became a Christian education wing. The new sanctuary, with hefty columns and beams reminiscent of the structure of late 18th and early 19th-century meetinghouses, aims for a linking of traditional ethos and a modern spirit of design.

As the church developed and as the community changed, the congregation's opportunities and roles changed. By the late 1980s the original A-frame building had been demolished and replaced with non-profit housing and underground parking. The second stage of the building had turned the main entrance to the rear, where it was accessed by automobile, and in the third stage this arrangement continued, with a small courtyard between church and housing (above).

St. Andrew's, *Toronto; United, previously Presbyterian and Methodist. Steel frame with brick, 1981–83; David Horn, architect*

St. Andrew's United faced difficult decisions as Bloor and Yonge became a second downtown crossroads. The congregation decided to stay in its historic location, but also decided to build an office tower, to subsume the church to the tower, to integrate parts of the old building into the new and to use the income from the new building to support its many ministries. The result is a successful experiment in urban church design, where the church entrance is well back from the street at the end of a fine courtyard.

Among the ways churches survive is the taking on of new roles that revivify them, going beyond the obvious strategy of merging adjacent churches of the same denomination. When a building becomes too large for a congregation, they often take in another, newer church to share the space. In one case an old 1950s church had a new church added beside it in the 1960s, but the congregation has returned to its earlier space, while a faster-growing church has taken over the newer and larger building.

Although it is common for churches of different denominations to share facilities, **The Cedars**, **Waterloo**, undertook a unique project: **Westminster United** teamed up with **Temple Shalom** Synagogue to build a symbolically important and functionally satisfying building, used jointly. Westminster is larger than Temple Shalom, so expressing the two spaces posed problems of equity. Architect Charles Simon solved the problem neatly by locating two separate spaces back to back, arranged in such a way that either can use the other's space. Since the holy days do not coincide and the major holidays are usually different, sharing space is effective and efficient.

Externally both communities are under the same roof — symbolically important — with each topped by a skylight that brings light onto each front wall. The two roof projections face each other — also symbolically appropriate — expressing a shared conviction of Christianity and Judaism's symbiotic relationship. It is a clearly thought out congregational program, carried out well by an architect whose mother was Christian and father was Jewish (*see* p. 27).

Some congregations have found opportunities to acquire funding for new projects that breathe new life into them. **St. Mark's Presbyterian**, **Don Mills**, built a modest A-frame church in the mid-1950s. By the early 1960s it needed a new church and included the old church as Christian education facilities. A quarter-century later, the original building was replaced with non-profit housing, controversially but successfully mixing units for the disabled, subsidized housing and rentals at full market value (*see* p. 279).

In the urban core the pressures are more intense than in the suburbs, especially when land values skyrocketed in the late 20th century. After World War II **St. Andrew's Presbyterian**, **Toronto** (1875–76), found itself in a decaying neighbourhood, creating pressure to abandon its location and move to the suburbs. The church, designed by William G. Storm (1826–92) in a Romanesque Revival style with a

FACING PAGE **St. Andrew's**, *Toronto; Presbyterian. Stone, 1875–76; William G. Storm, architect; Centre, 1987–90, Paul Northgrave, architect*

St. Andrew's Presbyterian made the decision in 1969 to remain in its historic facilities. Seen here with Roy Thomson Hall in the foreground, the new condominium structure sits atop a new social centre behind Roy Thomson Hall. The sale of air rights was a crucial tool in the project's viability, making possible denser land use than was otherwise possible.

LEFT **Church of the Redeemer**, *Toronto; Anglican. Stone, 1878–79; Smith and Gemmell, architects*

Occupying the important intersection of Bloor Street West and Avenue Road, diagonally across from the Royal Ontario Museum, the Church of the Redeemer has been substantially transformed by selling its air rights in 1980 and permitting the large Renaissance Centre to build beside and behind it. Though the church is dwarfed by its neighbours, its charming Gothic Revival style permits it to hold its own visually.

Scots accent, stood at the corner of King and Simcoe Streets. It was one of the most influential Presbyterian churches, central in the maintenance of Presbyterianism after church union, along with Knox (*see* p. 278). In 1969 it decided to stay, and the area is now full of excitement, thanks to David and "Honest Ed" Mirvish's theatres; the CN Tower (1976); the Eaton Centre (1978); Roy Thomson Hall (1982); the Rogers Centre (1996); and various restaurants and commercial towers.

At the time, a Toronto zoning bylaw permitted the selling of air rights, transferring unused coverage of one lot to the owners of an adjacent lot. St. Andrews struck a deal with the Sun Life Company, bringing the congregation a jointly developed condominium on church property and cash. The church remains intact, the manse provides offices and a new social centre adds three floors of program space, including a parking garage, with condominiums above. The result is an invigorated congregation, improved facilities and a new sense of its mission, while continuing its leadership in liturgical renewal, theological concern and vigorous social action. A similar development took place in the **Church of the Redeemer, Toronto** (1879, Smith and Gemmell), at Bloor and Avenue Road. The church sold some property along with its air rights but remains vigorously present in its historic building diagonally across from Daniel Libeskind's addition to the Royal Ontario Museum.

St. Andrew's United, **Toronto**, is another United Church produced by mergers, in this case five. Its strategic Bloor Street location brought intense commercial pressures when Bloor and Yonge became Toronto's second city centre. The congregation realized that changing times called for changed ministries, so various alternatives were considered, most presupposing a continuing presence. Ultimately St. Andrew's demolished its 1923 Gothic Revival building (originally Presbyterian) in favour of a new office tower, receiving in return a new church at the rear of the project with an identifiable separate entrance at the end of an attractive courtyard and ongoing income to support the church's mission.

When the **Salvation Army Scarborough Citadel, Toronto,** developed a complex scheme for housing, church and community facilities, it was important to give appropriate recognition to the parts. Though the church is outweighed by the slab apartment building, each reads distinctly, especially by differentiation in colour: the housing is mainly a neutral grey and the church is yellow. The housing is geared to residents' income, serving single mothers, students and families with low incomes. It won a *Canadian Architect* magazine conceptual award in 1993. The architect, John van Nostrand, designed the church to be a two-story block on a busy corner; it slips under the 12-story slab, projecting both to north and south beyond the slab's facades. Its facilities include a gymnasium, educational areas and community spaces. The entrances for the housing and the church are separate, but they are visually related and both are easily accessed by car, as the suburbs seem to demand. Inside, the church has a lean, crisp ambience, using a limited palette of materials (blond wood, glass, steel). A small balcony can be closed off with sliding barn-type doors.

On the Lawrence Avenue side are two stained-glass windows, a long horizontal slot and a vertical, door-shaped window with symbols and symbolic colours, speaking to Salvation Army traditions. A platform with ample room for a brass band fills the front, in front of which is a wide kneeling bench, the "mercy seat" or "penitent form," for those wanting to pray, make a commitment or rededicate themselves. The whole complex is no-nonsense and sure of itself, like the Salvation Army.

Scarborough Citadel, *Toronto; Salvation Army. Concrete, brick and tile, 1992–94; John van Nostrand, architect*

The Salvation Army Citadel is outweighed by the large attached social housing project, co-financed by the Ontario Ministry of Housing; visually, however, through the effective use of colour, each has its own value. The housing complex is a neutral grey-blue while the church uses different materials (brick and tile) in a sharply contrasting yellow. North and south faces are differentiated: housing units on the north are wider to permit more glass; south units are narrower but deeper, and the south face incorporates additional colour.

FACING PAGE The interior, seen here looking to the rear, is crisply detailed. A simple pulpit sits at the drop from the platform to the main floor, and spreading across in front is a long kneeling bench for those who wish to pray. A balcony at the rear can be opened up by sliding two wide doors apart on barn-type hardware. Facing Lawrence Avenue is a long slot of coloured glass, and, not seen, another window with Salvation Army symbols.

WEST AND NORTH

Introduction

Fur Post to Pacific Rim

Although it was the movement of settlers from or through what is now Ontario and Quebec that turned the fur preserve into a farm belt, the West was never a child of the East. Because of their founding connection with the Hudson's Bay Company, what have become Canada's four western provinces are quite distinct in origin from Quebec or Ontario.

— *Peter C. Newman, 1987*

Origins to First Contacts

THE WEST AND THE NORTH fit together both in physical geography and in human settlement. It is commonly believed that humans first occupied the Americas about 12,000 B.C., after crossing the Bering Strait into Alaska, the Yukon and British Columbia. They gradually moved south and east through Arctic and sub-Arctic regions. When other parts of Canada were covered by ice and glacial lakes, indigenous groups were living in the North and West. Long before European settlement there were extensive inter-tribal contacts, with trade in silver, obsidian, copper, amber, iron, shells and silica, creating trade routes later followed by European explorers.

European exploration began from the east, but soon included visits by sea to the West Coast. However, neither those coming from the east nor those coming from the Pacific understood the geographic implications of what they saw. Maps of the mid-18th century left much of western Canada blank, filled with an enormous "western sea" or covered with writing to hide an embarrassing uncertainty. Coastal exploration by the Spaniard Juan Francisco Bodega y Quadra and Captain James Cook, as well as further land-based exploration, finally produced workable maps of the West by the 1780s. It was the North West Company that took advantage of the new knowledge, especially Alexander Mackenzie, David Thompson and Simon Fraser (*see* pp. 195–96).

Furs, mines and missions

The founding of the Hudson's Bay Company in 1670 and the exploration that resulted was based on furs. The HBC's concession from the Crown on all land draining into Hudson Bay (Rupert's Land) impeded settlement, as did the founding a hundred years later of the Montréal-based coalition, the North West Company. The intense rivalry of these two economic giants meant speedier exploitation and mapping of the West and the Northwest. Trading posts were developed, but farms and settlements were not welcomed.

Lord Selkirk founded the Red River settlement, or Assiniboia, for destitute Scottish crofters in 1811–12. A few years earlier the first white woman to move to the West, Marie-Anne Lagimodière (grandmother of Louis Riel), had arrived in St. Boniface. Hand in glove with fledgling agrarian settlements went the spread of Christianity. This took two main forms: giving solace to European settlers and converting the First Nations. Roman Catholics and Anglicans were the most active denominations, with Methodists and Presbyterians as junior players. Although Anglicans were active widely, especially near the coast, the most intensive efforts were undertaken by the Oblates of Mary Immaculate (*see* pp. 300, 306–08, 315), who were invited to Canada from France in 1841 and moved into the Northwest in 1845. The Catholic Church became established in the West largely due to the order's work in British Columbia. Their first mission was in Kelowna.

Settlement was sporadic. On Vancouver's Island, as it was then known, arable

Father Pandosy's Mission, *Kelowna, British Columbia; Roman Catholic. Squared log, half-dovetailed, 1859–60; Charles Pandosy, designer and builder*

Father Pandosy established the first Oblate mission in the province's interior at Kelowna; from here the Oblates carried out extensive missionary work through the valleys of southern B.C. His small church and outbuildings have been preserved along with other pioneer buildings.

areas around the southeastern coastline were slow to be cleared. The British government had granted the island to the HBC in 1849 and it was under the authority of company official James Douglas (1803–77). He served as governor of the island from 1851 to 1863 and of the mainland colony of British Columbia from 1858 to 1864. The two colonies were merged under the name of the mainland colony in 1866, with the capital at Victoria.

Gold was discovered on the Fraser River and in the Cariboo in 1858 and later in the Yukon in 1898. As early finds petered out, disappointed miners moved on, only to experience more disappointment. Gold was not the only mineral to draw attention; silver, copper and coal were also important, sometimes found in the same areas. During the gold rush and before the Cariboo Trail was built, manageable routes were needed to the gold fields. One route — though it required a large number of transfers from boat to land to land to boat — went through Skookumchuck, between Chilliwack and Hope on the Lillooet River, which flows into Harrison Lake. The Oblates encouraged local native groups to build the third church on the site, **Church of the Holy Cross**, **Skatin (Skookumchuck)**, which is remarkable for its European appearance. Everything is articulately hand-carved: a dove hanging from the ceiling, crosses, pews and altar rail, all consistent with, but more elaborate than, the flamboyant exterior. Its most unusual architectural feature is the combination of central pointed arch over the brilliantly carved main altar plus two half-arches over the two side altars, all strongly three-dimensional.

The creation of the North-West Mounted Police (later renamed the Royal Canadian Mounted Police) in 1873 influenced radically the peaceful development of the Canadian West. Unlike the American West, there was not a single shooting death in a bar in the Yukon during the gold-rush period.

Major settlements before the late 19th century were few and far between: New Westminster, Victoria, Vancouver, Fort Edmonton, Saskatoon, Regina and Winnipeg. Most took second place to or originated as HBC trading posts. By 1870, however, the West and the Northwest were mapped and could be traversed by road as well as river. Minerals were being found, lumbering was important and cattle were being herded on the grasslands. On the other hand, buffalo herds were becoming depleted and native peoples were being confined to small "treaty" areas and their children sent to residential schools.

Territories and Provinces

The population of the Northwest was a vibrant mix: First Nations, with whom treaties regarding rights and land had been made, Métis with mixed ancestry, who were essential to the effective functioning of the region, and a few whites, most of whom were Catholic. Lord Selkirk's Red River colony had added the first European farmers and settlers to the region.

For a decade and a half the government had failed to address the long-standing grievances of the French-speaking Métis over rights and representation, land claims and access to bilingual courts. In 1869 the federal government, ignoring historic Métis claims and ardent objections, sent survey crews to Red River to prepare the way for settlers from Eastern Canada, Europe and the United States. After a Métis group led by Louis Riel captured Upper Fort Garry, Riel was elected president of a

St. Saviour's, *Barkerville, British Columbia; Anglican. Frame with board and batten, 1869–70 (restored 1958); Rev. James M. Reynard, designer*

Barkerville was a booming gold-mining town at the end of the Cariboo Road, a place of dreams for both the miners and the hangers-on that gold attracted. This handsome small church, finely detailed in its way, evokes the frontier conditions that pervaded all such mining towns and is mute testimony to the church's influential role in the community.

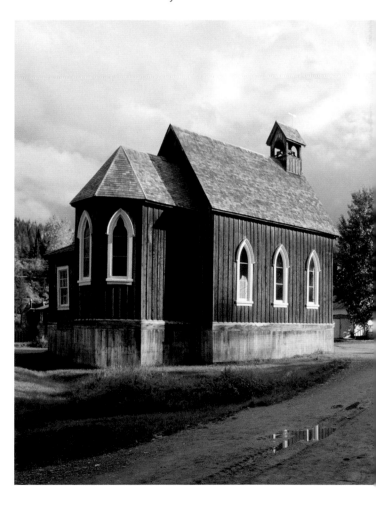

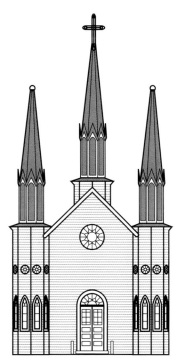

Church of the Holy Cross, *Skatin (Skookumchuck), British Columbia; Roman Catholic. Frame, 1895–1906; builder unknown*

According to local lore, the church was built following the designs on postcards of Chartres Cathedral and the Church of Saint-Denis in France. This truly exceptional church is accessible only with the greatest difficulty along logging roads and hydro rights-of-way. The church has been measured and drawn by University of British Columbia architectural students.

provisional government and developed a "bill of rights" as a basis to bargain with Canada. The Manitoba Act (1870) admitted a very small Manitoba to Confederation, making Riel Manitoba's founder.

Change came to the West rapidly after the completion of the Canadian Pacific Railway in 1885. Land issues continued to influence events. Métis who had migrated from Manitoba to the south branch of the Saskatchewan River again faced land-claim problems. Surveyors used American models to lay out square townships, which clashed with traditional Québécois and Métis long-lot patterns of settlement. Gabriel Dumont, the Métis leader in Batoche (*see* pp. 313–15), brought Riel back from Montana in 1884 to help the Métis negotiate with Ottawa once more. Riel gained the support of the non-native population by advocating the setting aside of more land for homesteading as well as free title to land. However, when he suggested occupying Fort Carlton, an HBC post, to force the government to meet Métis demands, the non-native residents withdrew their support. Unlike the Red River insurrection, this one was swiftly put down by troops sent by train from central Canada. The North-West Rebellion collapsed after a major defeat at Batoche. Dumont fled to the United States. Riel surrendered, was tried for treason and executed November 16, 1885. The government still failed to recognize the grievances and resolve them justly.

Even after the railway enabled settlers to move to the West, settlement was slow. Deliberate efforts were made by the federal government to attract more settlers from Europe (*see* pp. 310–29), including the granting of free land. Mennonites arrived in 1874; Icelanders in 1877 (some of whom created a Republic of New Iceland); Mormons in 1887 to evade anti-polygamy laws in the U.S.; Ukrainians in 1891; Doukhobors in 1899; Hutterites in 1918. During this period of settlement, the provinces of Alberta and Saskatchewan were created in 1905 and Manitoba gained additional territory in 1881 and 1912.

These new communities built, and to some extent continue to build, in their own traditions; all have contributed significantly to the architectural and the religious character of the West. It is the forms and decorative arts brought with them from Eastern Europe — domes, icons and bell towers — that have shaped how the church architecture of the West is perceived in the rest of the country. The reality is, however, that the range of architectural expression among these communities is greater than often thought and, among Mennonites, Doukhobors and Hutterites, plainer than the highly visible Ukrainian churches might suggest.

At the same time as immigrant groups were building their own places of worship, Roman Catholic, Anglican, Methodist and Presbyterian missions continued their work. Given the distances between western towns, the remoteness of some settlements, the mountain barriers and the sparse population, it is not surprising that much of the West was strongly in favour of church union in the early 20th century, with discussions and actions — in the form of union churches — beginning early in the century. The maintenance of long-standing denominational distinctions must have seemed less important than a strong and active Christian presence, and the hope of forming a national church.

Church architecture in the West covered a wide range of styles and forms of expression. Several types of wood-frame churches are found throughout the West and the North, drawing on the settlers' European traditions or missionary practice. Something as simple as timber construction might be quite varied: squared logs with half-dovetailed corners, round logs with saddle-and-notch corners, or *pièce-sur-pièce* (called Red River construction in Manitoba). Relatively little stone building was done in the early days. The first stone structures were built in the Red River settlement, and gradually stone construction developed throughout the West. But to this day, wood is often the material of choice, especially in British Columbia. Brick was rare in the 19th century; though it became more common during the 20th century, it never acquired the role in the West that it did in Ontario.

The North

As Europeans engaged on a relentless program of exploration and exploitation, the North became romanticized with the notion of the Northwest Passage. The region loomed as a vast empty space of boreal forest, muskeg, snow and ice, difficult to penetrate and more difficult to inhabit. To most people living in other parts of the country, the North remains a frontier region. Hugh Keenleyside comments, "In Canada the frontier has persisted longest in the North. Here indeed is a true frontier and one that will never be conquered…. [H]ere will be a permanent source of energy from which Canada will draw strength in the never-ending fight to guard and maintain the personal and human rights of her people…. The frontier is a bastion of freedom, and the North is a permanent frontier."

The North West Company operated in the North from about 1800 onwards, building Fort Good Hope (*see* p. 337) in 1805. The challenges were immense. The trip from Montréal to Fort Good Hope took two years each way. William Morrison points out that "the average time from the day a copper kettle left the company's warehouse in London until the beaver pelt that paid for it arrived was an astonishing seven years. The feat was analogous to trading with Mars." While the fur trade changed the social and economic portrait of the North, the arrival of missionaries altered its spiritual character. Led by Anglicans and Roman Catholics, missionaries influenced all regions: the Anglicans were particularly influential in the Yukon and eastern Arctic and the Roman Catholics in the Mackenzie Valley.

The North has been slow to achieve self-government. The final stage was the creation of Nunavut from the eastern part of the Northwest Territories and most of the Arctic islands in 1999, with the Yukon and the remainder of the Northwest Territories remaining more or less as they had been. The challenges, to include the North as a whole in the prosperity of the rest of the country, remain.

Toward the Pacific Rim

Two seemingly indisputable facts now dominate Canada's West and North. The first is Alberta's remarkable growth and resulting assertiveness, based on oil, natural gas and the continued migration of people to the province, hoping to share in its wealth. The second is that the West Coast looks increasingly to countries around the Pacific Rim — China, Japan, South Korea, India, Australia and New Zealand — for exports, imports, immigrants, political contacts and cultural influences. These changes are reshaping Canada's sense of itself, as European influence diminishes and Pacific Rim influences from the West Coast gradually filter through to the rest of the country, in the process changing some religious traditions.

St. Nicholas' (also known as **Kennell Church**), Lumsden Rural Municipality, near Craven, Saskatchewan; Anglican. Wood, 1900; rebuilt 1910

Picturesquely sited on the Qu'Appelle River's south bank, St. Nicholas' is a landmark visible from roads in the valley and on the hillcrest above it. In 1910, with funds from English friends, the community undertook building, dragging lumber by sleigh 15 miles from Craven, but the site proved too remote. It was "taken apart board by board" and reassembled farther to the east in the summer of 1910.

Architectural traditions have merged in recent years, with modernism, for example, influencing the ways in which local traditions are expressed, whether First Nations or Ukrainian (*see* pp. 318–19, 336). Conversely, indigenous traditions have influenced the way modern architectural concepts are expressed (*see* pp. 350–51, 366–67). While these indigenous influences have been felt and incorporated in religious buildings in other parts of the country, they have been strongest in the West and the North. In the West, architects such as Douglas Cardinal and Étienne Gaboury have carved out huge reputations and won major projects, including international competitions. In some older churches, indigenous art (paintings, sculpture, glass) has been incorporated into traditional buildings. Perhaps no church has done this more sympathetically than St. Andrew's Roman Catholic Cathedral in Victoria (*see* p. 332). In the North, the decoration of a number of buildings has been influenced by indigenous art forms, though in some cases the decoration has been undertaken by European missionaries (*see* pp. 336–338) who were sensitive to those traditions. Finally, in a few cases architects have undertaken to build in forms that recall traditional First Nations' forms (*see* p. 350).

Churches have been open to this fusion of artistic efforts, more open in their own ways than governments, banks and universities. The West has more enthusiastically embraced Modernism and cultural diversity than the rest of the country has. In other parts of Canada, these trends — especially the embrace of Modernism — has tended to be a function of large urban areas. By contrast, some of the most startlingly modern buildings in the West are in small towns or in rural areas (*see* p. 356). This means, regrettably, that some of the best examples are not well known in the rest of the country.

Church of the Blessed Virgin Mary, *Saint Julien, Saskatchewan; Ukrainian Catholic. Frame, 1926–27; Vasyl' Zadorozny, Ivan Feschuk, Ivan Tuchak and Pylyp Shwaykivsky, carpenters, interior by Tymko Yakimchuk*

Shrubs, thickets and woods dot this checkerboard landscape where prairie giants — railside grain elevators and roadside Ukrainian churches — are kings and queens. A log church was built at St. Julien in 1903.

TOP LEFT **Avonmore**, *Edmonton, Alberta; United. Brick and wood, 1988–90*

Avonmore experiments with low brick side walls and high-pitched roofs, with glass between the two roof planes. The roofs sit on the modified square plan in a diagonal fashion, creating a strong sense of movement and careful balance. The overall approach borrows from but is substantially different than the A-frame.

LEFT **St. Anselm's**, *Vancouver, British Columbia; Anglican. Stone and wood, 1952–53; Douglas C. Simpson, architect*

Located on the University of British Columbia campus, St. Anselm's is one of the earliest mainstream churches to break with conventional church design. Its A-frame became the prototype for a generation of church buildings, though not all those that followed in the next quarter-century combined stone, wood and natural setting as wisely as St. Anselm's.

This is a vast extent of country here. The H.B. Co. have Posts from this to Hudson Bay and from Labrador to the Pacific Ocean, and in all this region of thousands of square miles but two missionaries are to be found — church ministers — and one or two R. Cath. Priests. ... We had in our congregation last Sunday an Indian cannibal. ... He however declared his intention to strive to serve the Great Spirit.

— Reverend James Evans, 1838

Pre-Confederation Northwest

Cathédrale de Saint-Boniface, St. Boniface, Manitoba; Roman Catholic. *Stone, with timber belfries and tin-clad spires, 1839; builder unknown*

William H. E. Napier's water-colour (1857), "St. Boniface Cathedral, Red River Settlement" shows the third church built on this site in what is now part of metropolitan Winnipeg.

THE TWO EARLIEST SURVIVING CHURCHES in Manitoba stand close to the junction of the Red and Assiniboine Rivers: the oldest wooden church in Western Canada, old **St. James', Winnipeg** (1853); and the earliest stone church, which has given its name to the site known as **St. Andrew's-on-the-Red**, **Lockport** (1845–49). Each was near a Hudson's Bay Company post. St. James' was close to Upper Fort Garry, where downtown Winnipeg stands today, and St. Andrew's was close to Lower Fort Garry, north of the city a few miles downstream. Each is a rectangular block about three times as long as it is wide, both under low-pitched roofs without chancels but with lancet windows in the aisleless naves. Both are plain Georgian structures, and originally each was distinguished by a plain tower, about three times as tall as it was wide.

Many of the HBC fur traders were Scots, probably Church of Scotland or Free Kirk in background, but early churches in the Red River Colony were either Anglican or Roman Catholic, perhaps because they were the most active denominations in setting up missions in the west and because the London-based company's key personnel were mostly adherents of the Church of England. Although Anglican parishes had been established in the East by the early 1800s, there were none west of Lake

ABOVE **St. Andrew's-on-the-Red**, *Lockport, Manitoba; Anglican. Stone, 1844–49 (1889); William Cockran designer*

William Cockran (1798–1865) of the Church Missionary Society employed Duncan McRae (1813–98) to build the church situated near an important set of rapids on the Red River, in a simplified Gothic Revival style. Though one end looks severe, the tower gives its entrance portion a distinctive profile.

The interior's elegant pew ends are matched by the capping of the dado. The kneelers are its most distinctive feature: it may be the only church in Canada to enjoy buffalo-hide coverings.

Huron. The great church of Saint-Boniface was a direct outgrowth of the Métis mission begun in 1818, which ministered to the francophone community. The Society for the Propagation of the Gospel, as it had in other parts of the country, sent a missionary to Rupert's Land. On his arrival, William Henry Taylor (1820–73), an English schoolmaster from Newfoundland, was ordained priest in St. Andrew's Church, in December 1850. He soon developed a good congregation and a regular Sunday School. In 1853, the HBC donated a site just west of the Red River, high above the Assiniboine River — a location chosen after the devastating flood in 1852 — where he built St. James'.

The earnest simplicity of the Gothic Revival detailing in these two churches — St. James' windows with a central mullion and St. Andrew's similarly detailed panelling in the pulpit — resembles scores of rural Late Georgian churches constructed throughout Britain in the 1820s and 30s. St. Andrew's basic design and the simple beauty of its dappled native limestone are echoed in other examples of several denominations. However, none can claim anything like as effective a silhouette as the broached spire and belfry — each triple-arched face looking as though it had been cut out of white card — that crown St. Andrew's. The pews in St. Andrew's have kneelers covered with buffalo hide, reflecting the church's locale and period.

The building technique used by the builders of St. James' is consistent with its

Old St. James', *Winnipeg, Manitoba; Anglican. Timber, pièce-sur-pièce, 1853; builder unknown*

The oldest surviving wooden church in western Canada, old St. James' is located above the flood plain of the Assiniboine River just west of the Red River. Its clapboard exterior treatment covers its most interesting feature, the Red River — or *pièce-sur-pièce* — construction, a typical Québécois and Métis form of construction, which suggests its builders' origins.

The construction details are clear on the inside, where the plaster has been removed. The beams supporting its flat ceiling are tied to the vertical wall supports by knees, reminiscent of the knees used in shipbuilding.

Father Lacombe's Chapel, *St. Albert, Alberta; Roman Catholic. Timber, pièce-sur-pièce, 1861; Father Albert Lacombe, designer and builder*

Father Lacombe's Chapel, overlooking the Sturgeon River, is now back in almost its original location; it has been moved several times. In line with frontier Roman Catholic piety, the interior centres on a simple altar preceded by an altar rail that seems rather insubstantial. Father Lacombe lived in a loft, which has now been removed, over one end.

FACING PAGE **McDougall Mission**, *Morley, Alberta; Methodist. Frame, 1862; Rev. George McDougall, designer and builder*

McDougall's gravestone records "The deceased was for 16 years chairman of the Wesleyan missions in the North-West. He lost his way on the prairie about 40 miles east of this place on January 24, 1876. His body was found on the 5th of the following month ...."

The plain building's details combine rustic construction with a desire to make an impact, seen especially in the tower's broader base and louvred openings under a modest cap and small spire.

locale. Red River construction is derived from old French *pièce-sur-pièce* work. It features widely spaced vertical squared timbers on a sill, into which horizontal timbers are mortised and tenoned, a strikingly different method from Scandinavian saddle-and-notch log construction. This structural system is masked by clapboarding at St. James' to protect it from the weather, though the timber is visible inside because the plaster was stripped away in 1967. This technique evokes early medieval European traditions in wood, which were drawn on by other settlers later in the century (*see* p 312).

Another example of *pièce-sur-pièce* construction is **Father Albert Lacombe's Chapel**, **St. Albert**, just beyond Fort Edmonton and now a suburb of Edmonton. It sits above the Sturgeon River, giving easy access to the North Saskatchewan River, the main east–west canoe route used by fur traders. Father Lacombe (1827–1916), the Oblate priest who built this, the oldest known standing structure in Alberta, in the style he brought with him from Québec, was called "noble soul" by the Cree and "the man with a good heart" by the Blackfoot. The *pièce-sur-pièce* technique is visible on both exterior and interior. The building is plain and gable-roofed, with a rectangular window or door in each bay of the structure. The interior's simplicity matches the exterior; it is focused on a small altar against the east wall that is separated from the nave of

the church by the simplest of altar rails, matched in its spareness by the pews, with only one rail for back support.

Father Lacombe lived and worked in Alberta for over 60 years, moving to Pincher Creek in southern Alberta in 1885, where he occupied a somewhat similar "hermitage" and founded **St. Michael's, Pincher Creek.** When Crowfoot, with other native chiefs, visited Ottawa in September 1885 after remaining neutral in the Riel Rebellion, he said of Father Lacombe: "This man is … one of our people. When we weep, he is sad with us; when we are filled with joy, he rejoices with us. We love him because he is our brother."

Methodists vied with Roman Catholics for predominance, especially in Alberta. Perhaps the greatest Methodist missionary family in the West was the McDougalls — George and John, a father-and-son team, and their wives. George McDougall, chairman of the Wesleyan Missions in the Northwest for 16 years, established the **Methodist Mission** at **Morley**, Alberta (*see* pp. 286 – 87) in 1862. He died after losing his way east of Morley in the middle of winter; his body was found two weeks later and buried at Morley, looking out to the Rockies. A monument pays an unusual tribute to the Stoney Indians. "They rendered to Caesar the things that were Caesar's and unto God the things that were God's." George's son John continued his work and their combined efforts covered 77 years.

The moment the bells ring for church, every one issues from his house, and they walk up to church in two long lines: there is no waiting for a second bell; none of the thousand and one excuses which we find for staying away from church in England; no one prefers cooking his sunday dinner to going to God's House, no one remains at home because he has no clothes good enough to go to church in; none are too young or too old.

— Edmund Hope Verney, 1863

Vancouver's Island and British Columbia

BRITISH COLUMBIA JOINED CONFEDERATION in 1871. A few churches predate that event, modest but thoughtful Church of England frame buildings, built from a huge endowment of £25,000 given by Angela, Baroness Burdett-Coutts, to support an Anglican mission in the region.

St. Stephen's, Saanich, though Anglican, stands on a site given by a Presbyterian. The redwood lumber came from California, since there were no sawmills in the area in 1862. Its exterior has been modified somewhat over the years, with decorative (but not functional) buttresses and a vestry (both added in 1930) as well as a lych-gate (1963). The church retains the exposed timber frame and clapboard infill shown in old photos. The interior is clad in warm-hued V-joint boarding applied vertically, with a confusing combination of scissor-trusses and steel rod cross-ties. A somewhat grander version with a similar roof is St. Paul's (Anglican), Esquimalt, British Columbia, from 1866, sometimes known as the Naval and Garrison Church or Admiralty Church.

No church conveys as accurate an impression of the conditions of early days on Vancouver Island as **St. Peter's, Duncan (Quamichan)**, designed by Edward Mallandain in 1874. It is a simplified St. Paul's, with rectangular chancel, no transepts, trefoil windows, a south entry porch and an unusual semi-octagonal

St. Peter's, *Duncan (Quamichan), British Columbia; Anglican. Timber-frame and wood, 1874–76; Edward Mallandain, architect*

St. Peter's shares many features with the much better known St. Paul's, Esquimalt, though the effect is startlingly different — like the town mouse and the country mouse — partly because of St. Peter's rural location and its dark brown stain. The west end of the church has an unusual semi-octagon to make space for the font located under the small steeple.

BELOW LEFT **St. Stephen's**, *Saanich, British Columbia; Anglican. Timber-frame and wood, 1862; John Wright and George Sanders, architects*

St. Stephen's is British Columbia's oldest church that is continuously in use and still on its original site. Its location, surrounded by the fields that attracted early settlers to this area, is masked by a dense grove of trees in the historic cemetery, the two beside the door having been planted the year the church was built.

BELOW RIGHT **St. Peter's**, *Duncan, interior*
St. Peter's deep chancel is typically Anglican in design, placing the altar or table just out from the wall; nearer the congregation the pulpit on the left balances a lectern on the right. The panelling is herringbone-patterned in the upper register and vertical in the lower, while the windows suggest two different periods, the ones in the sidewalls being earlier.

FACING PAGE **St. Ann's**, *Duncan (Quamichan), British Columbia; Roman Catholic. Frame, 1903; builder unknown*

St. Ann's began in an 1859 building, though the present one is from 1903. It still sits grandly, for its size and materials, in its original location. The steeply sloped steeple on top of the projecting square tower above the entrance and the two oculi give the church a strong Québec feel. This is not accidental; the earliest bishop and missionaries came from Québec.

west end (added in 1893) with a small square belfry. The dark-stained clapboarded church sits discreetly on a small hill carpeted with flowers in the spring, surrounded by huge fir trees and a historic cemetery.

Roman Catholics founded a diocese that included Oregon, British Columbia and Alaska as early as 1847, with Modeste Demers (1809–71) as Bishop. Roman Catholic missionaries began working in the **Duncan (Quamichan)** area with First Nations peoples, and **St. Ann's** was built in 1859, though the present church — the fourth St. Ann's — dates from 1903. Its main door effectively utilizes First Nations' symbolism and imagery.

The gold rush of 1858 altered British Columbia decisively, helping to move the centre of activity to the mainland, opening up new transportation routes and creating settlements that soon replaced the HBC posts, as happened at **Yale**, where the **Church of St. John the Divine** recalls the civilizing influences of Christianity. Yale's location at the head of navigation, where the Fraser Canyon narrows into an impassible barrier, caused it briefly to be the largest city west of Chicago and north of San Francisco, with 17 saloons and 23 hotels. Its population then is difficult to estimate and sometimes much exaggerated, but it was swollen briefly by the decline in California's gold fields. In a three-month period in 1858, 23,000 left San Francisco by sea and another 8,000 by land, bound for Yale and the Fraser River.

The Anglican church in the centre of the boomtown announced its presence with a small belfry above the entrance to a clapboard building on an exposed timber frame. The roof has scissor-trusses (now stiffened with tie rods) and plain V-joint siding. Its original chalice and patten, some original glass and exceptionally fine

St. John the Divine, *Yale, British Columbia; Anglican. Timber-frame and wood, 1863; builder unknown*

The church stands in the centre of what was once a boom town, above the rushing waters of the Fraser. Thousands of hopeful prospectors came through Yale on their way to the mines of the Fraser and the Cariboo gold rushes. The timber frame is expressed visually on the exterior, while the small decorated porch and belfry above it add interest to a common style and set it apart from Yale's other buildings.

linens, hangings and vestments from its early days are on display in the church and adjacent museum. Many of the linens were produced in Yale's All Hallows School, British Columbia's earliest private school for girls (begun 1884), where both settler and First Nations girls were taught needlework. When the transcontinental railroad was being pushed through in the 1880s, Yale was an important centre for construction activity.

The Cariboo Road that took miners upriver in search of new gold deposits began at Yale and ended at the famous **Barkerville**, the real and metaphorical end of the road. As a boom town it exceeded Yale at its height. At the end of the main street, as if the town focused on it, is **St. Saviour's Church** (1869–70) built, to a design by the Rev. James M. Reynard (*see* p. 291). The *Cariboo Sentinel* reported during construction: "The new church now building promises to be an elegant structure. … The style is 'Early English' in which architectural effect is attained by due proportion of parts, bold and simple forms, rather than by elaborate ornament. … We congratulate the friends of the Anglican Church on possessing a church so appropriate to their worship. Certainly those who wish to pray, as their forefathers prayed, may do so here, in a church which in form, if not in material, will remind them of the village churches of the 'fatherland.' "

The *Sentinel* got it exactly right. St. Saviour's looks for all the world like a stone church of the Middle Ages. The church's narrow nave is masked on the front elevation by an appendage that makes it look bulkier than it really is. But it is well lit inside by three lancet windows on the left, two flanking the door and three more in the semi-octagonal chancel. Real flair was expressed in the roof over the door, whose curve mimics the curve of the pointed windows, the bell tower and the arch to the chancel. The board-and-batten exterior is repeated on the interior, even on the ceiling.

The Oblates of Mary Immaculate from Oregon were extremely active in British Columbia's interior, where pride of place goes to Father Charles Pandosy (1824–91), who arrived in the Okanagan Valley in 1859. **Father Pandosy's Mission**, **Kelowna**, (*see* p. 290) was the first European settlement in the valley and a key centre for further work. Oblates from Kelowna founded **St. Anne's**, **Upper Similkameen Reserve**, near **Hedley**. The small log church (later clapboarded), with priest's quarters above, was built in the 1860s. When gold brought prosperity to the area, a new church was built between the original building and the cemetery.

East of Hedley, near the American border, is **Greenwood**, a coal-mining town whose **Church of the Sacred Heart** is a particularly fine example of Oblate work. A heart-warming story of mid-20th century social action took place in the town. A

St. Anne's, *Upper Similkameen (Chuchuwayha), Hedley, British Columbia; Roman Catholic.* *Clapboard on log, 1860s; frame, 1914 (restored 1992); builder unknown*

The juxtaposition of the original small log church and the later clapboarded church higher up the hill, in the context of a native reserve (Upper Similkameen) beside a small mining town, shows two stages of Oblate missionary work half a century apart. In the earlier building (whose date cannot be established with certainty), the priest lived in a loft above the church, as Father Pandosy did in Kelowna and Father Lacombe in St. Albert.

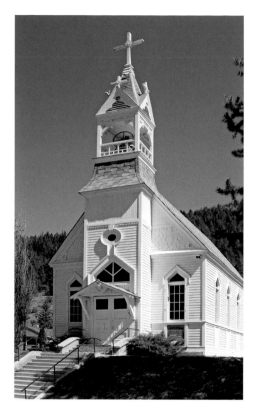 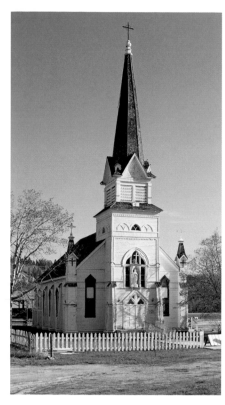

LEFT **Church of the Sacred Heart**, *Greenwood, British Columbia; Roman Catholic. Frame, 1898; builder unknown*

The Oblate church in Greenwood from the same period has a different character from St. Eugene's mission, but it shares with it good taste, a sense of place and carefully executed details. It, too, is in clapboard; while it lacks St. Eugene's buttresses it has a prominent drip moulding just below the windows to give it a more horizontal character.

RIGHT **St. Eugene's**, *near Cranbrook, British Columbia; Roman Catholic. Frame, 1897; builder unknown*

This white clapboard church has small lancet windows with arched tops under straight-edged trim and a more intricate pointed window above the door, with the Virgin occupying the central panel. It is finished with a number of carefully thought-out details: buttresses that narrow as they rise, shaped shingles in the gables, several string courses, an unusual broach spire decorated with cast-iron finials and two small spires on the front corners. After building the church, the Oblates opened a residential industrial school a short distance away in 1912.

FACING PAGE **St. Peter's** (*"Stolen Church"*), *Windermere, British Columbia; Anglican. Frame, 1887; builder unknown*

This church was literally stolen from its original location in Donald, B.C., when a parishioner and his wife decided not to move with other residents to Revelstoke and arranged surreptitiously for St. Peter's to be relocated to their preferred location. Efforts to take it back were unsuccessful.

group of 1,200 Japanese-Canadians, mostly Roman Catholics, were interned in Greenwood in 1942. At war's end, when the Canadian government planned to deport them to Japan despite many being Canadian-born, Greenwood residents placed an advertisement in the *Vancouver Province* (March 20, 1945) requesting that the Japanese-Canadians not be deported because they were such good citizens. Fifty or so years later, the film *Snow Falling on Cedars* (1999), which depicts Japanese-Americans in the U.S. Pacific Northwest, was filmed in Greenwood and many of the descendants of the original Japanese-Canadian residents were extras in the film. An equally fine Oblate church is **St. Eugene's Mission** (1897), just north of Cranbrook, British Columbia, where an imposing residential school (1911) and its grounds have been turned into a golf course and casino. "The standard of finish and the quality of workmanship at St. Eugene remain unexcelled … varied clapboard panels are contained within pine wood trim … a beautifully constructed tabernacle punctuates the sanctuary," writes Barry Downs in *Sacred Places*. In Alberta, the second Pincher Creek Church (recently demolished) was virtually identical to the St. Eugene's Mission church, which suggests that the Oblates used stock plans that crossed provincial boundaries.

There is a strange story concerning **St. Peter's, Windermere**, an Anglican church originally built in Donald, British Columbia. When the railway divisional point was moved to Revelstoke, the CPR agreed to move Donald's buildings there, and the church, along with other buildings, was dismantled in 1900 prior to moving it. Rufus Kimpton and his wife decided to move to Windermere instead. They were so attached to the church that they had it carted away by barge and wagon and re-erected in Windermere. Whether it was stolen property (as some suggest) or not, the church was reconsecrated in 1905.

At first in small and then in larger groups from Central and Southeastern Europe, came people strange in costume and in speech; and holding close by one another, as if in terror of the perils and the loneliness of the unknown land, they segregated into colonies tight knit by ties of blood and common tongue.

— *Ralph Connor, 1909*

Prairie Settlement

SOME OF CANADA'S most significant religious groups came to farm the empty West. Often deriving from the left wing of the 16th-century Reformation, they have made a distinctive mark on the country — especially the West — not least because many had an unbending commitment to pacifism. Moravian Brethren arrived in the 1770s in Labrador (*see* pp. 56–61) and in 1894–95 in Alberta at Bruderheim ("home of the brethren"). The small number of Mennonites who came to Upper Canada in the 1780s, following the American War of Independence, were much exceeded by those who came to southern Manitoba in the 1870s, attracted by land and exemption from military service. The Mennonites originated in two distinct areas in Europe: Switzerland and South Germany, and Holland and North Germany, the latter including large numbers from Poland, Russia and Ukraine. Among the various groups, some hold conservatively to their inherited traditions — the Amish and Old Order Mennonites — and some adapt to the surrounding culture and embrace a degree of innovation.

Frelsis, *Grund, Manitoba; Lutheran. Frame, 1889 (belfry 1896); Byring Hallgrimsson and Arni Sveinson, builders*
The Frelsis ("Freedom") Lutheran church was built by Icelanders who settled at Gimli in 1875 and then moved to better land at Grund in 1881. The church shows the builders' reliance, even in rural locations, on typical late 19th-century Gothic Revival details and their independence in applying those details, seen best in the handling of the tower's base and its steeple.

Old Colony Worship House, *Chortitz, now in Steinbach, Manitoba; Mennonite. Square timber, 1881; builder unknown*

On the back wall, opposite the entrance, is a railed area with a long bench for elders and the lectern. Other seating is in two blocks, for females (right) and males (left). Hat racks for the men (white-painted boards with nails) thread through the structure. The Chortitz meetinghouse was built to store offerings in kind, like European tithe barns, and the space is interrupted by posts and struts bracing the joists overhead for grain storage.

The meeting room fills four-fifths of the building. The fifth bay, across the right end of the building, houses two small rooms, each accessed from the large meeting room: one for the elders (with its own door to the exterior), the other a retiring room for women and for nursing children. The hatch in the end wall's attic portion (under the window) gives access the loft.

Between 1874 and 1881, about 7,000 Mennonites came to Manitoba from southern Russia. These German-speaking settlers had been drawn by Catherine the Great to nearly empty Crimean lands in the 18th century. When Czar Alexander II terminated their exemption from military service, the Canadian government guaranteed such an exemption, promised religious freedom and granted large blocks of land for settlement. By an amendment to the Dominion Lands Act, Mennonites would also be permitted to settle in villages instead of each family being required to live on its own homestead. The Mennonites then recreated the compact *Strassendorf* pattern they had followed in Russia, frequently a single street extending about half a mile along a creek bed, lined by housebarns (joined houses and barns).

Mennonite meetinghouses, like meetinghouses in other religious traditions, are typically simple, domestically scaled buildings, usually in the centre of the village. The **Old Colony Worship House** (1881) from Chortitz, south of Winkler, moved to the Mennonite Heritage Village at Steinbach, Manitoba, in 1967, exemplifies the fact that these are "plain folk," a people called apart. Their appearance is simple, their manner straightforward, their dealings upright — all characteristics of their place of worship. Unlike the houses that stand on narrow strips of land with their gable end to the street, the meetinghouse presents a long flank to the principal street, behind a line of trees (which unites and defines the community visually from end to end). It is rectangular, except for a later vestibule, with long horizontal lines of white-painted cove siding, typical of the late 19th century and the first half of the 20th. The windows are large but evenly and widely spaced.

The meetinghouse is a strapping construction of squared timber, contributed by community members and painstakingly assembled. Each piece of material is fitted to the next by a long tongue projecting vertically from the end and lodged in a matching recess, then securely fastened by a round pin driven horizontally into a hole from one side to the other. The timbers are also secured below and above by larger, vertical pins at regular intervals. A matching groove is cut into the upper and lower surfaces and fitted with a spline to prevent drafts. This well-defined, purist and sturdy image suggests the strength of Mennonite religious beliefs and their social order, which have caused these people to be uprooted many times over the centuries and led them to migrate—from the Netherlands to Russia, the American colonies, Canada and South America.

The graceful wooden **Frelsis** church at **Grund**, in south-central Manitoba, is Manitoba's oldest surviving Icelandic Lutheran church, far from Lake Winnipeg, where New Iceland was established in 1875. Icelanders set out from Gimli in March 1881 and travelled nearly two hundred miles over snow and ice for 16 days to reach this site. Sigurdur Christopherson and Kristjan Jonsson had chosen Grund ("grassy plain" in Icelandic) in 1880 as their new home; by 1883 it had 17 Icelandic families. Christopherson continued recruiting settlers from New Iceland, Iceland itself and Ontario; 700 Icelanders lived in the district by 1890, maintaining their tradition of evening Bible-reading and family prayers.

More than 99 percent of Icelanders claim affiliation with the Lutheran church, and Icelandic churches in Manitoba are typically Lutheran. Frelsis ("Freedom") Church was organized on January 1, 1884, and its construction completed in 1889 by volunteers under the direction of two carpenters, Byring Hallgrimsson and Arni Sveinson. It sits on a knoll in an attractive landscape of undulating land dotted with

sloughs, with a wooded area to the north offering a windbreak.

A projecting tower, lancet windows, an open belfry and the spire's curving "candle-snuffer" profile resemble Gothic Revival churches of Atlantic and Central Canada, but unfamiliar elements seem vaguely Baltic: the wider tower portion with windows flanking the door, arching trim echoing the lancets and the "cross-stitching" decoration at the top of the tower. A diminutive rose window and doors with arching panels add to the building's refined appearance. The vestibule's curved silhouette prepares us for a ceiling of pressed metal curving over the church's interior. This Victorian technology hides the roof trusses in a way that English Gothicists would have found unacceptable. Lutheran churches are typically Catholic in liturgy but Protestant in emphasizing Scripture; at Grund the altar is within a railed enclosure, surmounted by an elaborate Gothic niche, while the pulpit is to one side outside the railing.

Manitoba's Red River Rebellion (1869–70) resulted in a considerable influx of French-speaking Catholic Métis and English-speaking Protestant Métis into Saskatchewan, concerned for the survival of their culture. In 1871 Métis and

Frelsis, *Grund, Manitoba; Lutheran. Frame, 1889 (belfry 1896); Byring Hallgrimsson and Arni Sveinson, builders*
The nave is entered under a low gallery, which produces a cozy effect, but because the pressed-metal ceiling is segmental in profile most of the space is rather taller than expected. The intricately detailed Gothic altarpiece features a gesturing white-robed figure of Christ whose crucifixion wounds are visible. Taken together, the character of this light-coloured interior is focused, bordering on the austere, yet pleasing.

Saint-Antoine-de-Padoue, *Batoche, Saskatchewan; Roman Catholic. Pièce-sur-pièce (Red River construction) with siding, 1883–84 (tower, 1888); Ludger Gareau, builder*

Built for the Oblate Mission, this church stands at the centre of Battle of Batoche National Historic Site. The interior of the church had not been completed before the battle and only a few rows of seats were in place, close to the east end. The open nave area was used as a makeshift hospital during the battle. Although the church was closed in the 1970s and the furnishings dispersed, an astonishing number have been recovered for the extensive restoration.

French-Canadians started Batoche on a grand plateau within the sweeping embrace of the South Saskatchewan River.

The Oblates, who arrived at **Batoche** in 1881, constructed the rectory and **Church of Saint-Antoine-de-Padoue** in 1883–84. The builder was Québécois carpenter Ludger Gareau (1855–1954), who moved west via St. Paul, Minnesota, in 1878. He then travelled up the Saskatchewan Valley with the Métis. Using *pièce-sur-pièce* technique for both buildings, he clad them with boards milled in Prince Albert. In this and the pointed "Gothic" windows he may have been influenced by Winnipeg's Red River churches (*see* pp. 296–300). The large rectory, which would also serve as convent, hospital and school, advanced quickly, its upper floor serving the congregation until the church was ready. There were few flourishes in the church, whose interior is simple but tasteful: a segmental boarded ceiling, as blue as the sky, above a dentilled ivory-coloured crown moulding; sculptures of Saint Anthony of Padua, the Virgin and the Sacred Heart against the end wall; framed lithographs as altarpieces and stations of the cross; and a choir gallery with fretted pendant trim resembling an ornamented awning. A Chicago harmonium of 1892, purchased in Winnipeg, supplied music in the gallery, and a cast-iron stove supplied heat.

The just-completed rectory and church became the focus of the Battle of Batoche, May 9–12, 1885. About 900 government troops — well armed with rifles, two cannons and a murderous Gatling gun borrowed from the U.S. — faced fewer than 300 ill-equipped Métis and aboriginals, many of whom were in rifle pits around the church (which is pocked by bullets). On today's tranquil, nearly empty site it is hard to imagine the battle that raged and took at least 25 lives. Far in front of the church is a common grave where nine Métis casualties are buried. Years later, Gabriel Dumont was buried under a monumental boulder, at the very edge of the Saskatchewan's steep bank.

DISTINCTIVE ONION-DOMED CHURCHES are found in all provinces, but nowhere as frequently as in the prairie provinces. The form's origin is the Byzantine Christianity of Syria, Turkey and Greece (*see* pp. 380–81) — developed and modified over 1,500 years throughout southeastern Europe, southern Russia, the Balkans and the Caucasus — often on a Greek-cross plan, with an open central dome and an iconostasis, or screen of images, separating the sanctuary from the nave.

Waves of Ukrainian immigrants came to Canada beginning late in the 19th century. Unlike Reformation-rooted Christians such as Moravians, Mennonites and Icelanders, however, Eastern Rite Christians were connected with the Greek Orthodox Patriarch in Constantinople, with the Russian Orthodox Patriarch in St. Petersburg or with the Pope in Rome. A few Ukrainians may have arrived with Mennonites in the 1870s, but the largest number, about 170,000, came between 1891 and 1914 in response to farming opportunities. Others arrived after World War I, after World War II and in the 1970s and 80s. Their earliest settlement was east of Emerson, Manitoba (1896), followed by Star, Alberta (1897), northeast of Edmonton in Lamont County. The county is known as the "church capital of North America"; of its 47 churches almost three-fourths are Eastern Rite. In some cases, such as Father Achille Delaere, a Fleming from Belgium and a Redemptorist, Roman Catholic priests adopted the Ukrainian Rite and language.

> *Icons are in colours what the Scriptures are in words: witnesses to the Incarnation, the fact that God has come among us as a person whom we can see, touch and hear, to offer us the new life and begin the new creation.*
>
> — *Seventh Ecumenical Council in Nicaea, 787*

Their earliest church is old **St. Michael's**, **Gardenton**, begun in 1897, the year after Ukrainians arrived in southeastern Manitoba. Bringing with them a rich history of log construction, they chose the nearly vacant bush country on the American border east of Emerson because it was wooded — not with oak, familiar to them, but with poplar, spruce and tamarack. The church recalled traditional forms, more closely then than it does now, for it was built originally of squared logs and thatched. The logs were cut and brought to the site in the winter of 1897–98 and the church was finished in May 1899. In 1901 the log walls were covered with coved siding for protection, while hipped roofs replaced the thatch.

In 1915 the original design was altered. The nave was transformed with a

Old St. Michael's, *Gardenton, Manitoba; Ukrainian Orthodox. Log and thatch, 1897–99; siding and shingle roof, 1901; Wasyl Kekot, builder*

RIGHT AND FACING PAGE Old St. Michael's represents a direct cultural transfer from Ukraine to the Canadian prairie. Several types of design were transmitted from the homeland but this, in Bukovinian and Galician tradition, is probably the most common. However, the three windows with pointed arches (strikingly like those in the Red River churches) may well have been added when St. Michael's was altered.

Although full of pattern and colour, the humility of St. Michael's interior is striking. Orthodox churches are adorned with icons, traditionally conceived and richly executed. St. Michael's are inexpensive chromolithographs (common in early Eastern churches) and reminders of the financial sacrifice involved in most church-building enterprises.

ABOVE Processions are an important part of both regular and special Ukrainian services. This banner features Saint Michael the Archangel.

ABOVE AND FACING PAGE **Church of the Nativity of the Blessed Virgin Mary**, *Dobrowody, Saskatchewan; Ukrainian Catholic. Frame with tin-clad dome, 1911–12; F. Nowakowski, builder*

Between a tight rectangular narthex and a more generous polygonal apse, St. Mary's broad nave rises confidently, through squinches, into a lozenge-shaped drum, then swells into the large and lazy curves of an octagonal onion dome, finishing in the contrasting profile of a spiky, crenellated cupola.

Inside, humble little St. Mary's is remarkably otherworldly. Above a marbleized dado and ivory walls, the sanctuary rises into a half-dome and the nave into a full dome, both cerulean blue studded with stars, transforming this fragile wooden shrine into a mirage of distant Byzantine Ravenna's stone and marble, glass and gold mosaics. The walls are decorated, edged with traditional Ukrainian patterns, possibly based on textile designs.

workmanlike octagonal drum and dome topped by an onion-shaped cupola in sheet metal, with smaller hexagonal cupolas over the sanctuary and narthex. In spite of their squat simplicity, many of the earliest Eastern churches share design principles seen here. The three well-articulated elements are arranged hierarchically east to west: the west-facing narthex, followed by the wider cube of the nave, then contracting into the restricted space of the sanctuary, toward the east.

The natural lighting of the interior from five small windows was augmented by two, smaller still, in the drum over the crossing. In their soft glow, the nave focuses on an iconostasis depicting the saints, Old and New Testament histories and later traditions. At the centre of this low wall is the Beautiful Gate (or Royal Doors) used only by clergy to access the dim holy of holies and its altar. The deacons' doors to either side (sometimes called Angel Doors for their images of archangels Michael and Gabriel) are for servers. An example of the small scale here is the narthex ceiling (which is segmental, echoing the opening into the nave): a tall person can easily reach up and touch it. By the same token, this scale enhances the contrast with the width and height of the domed nave. The congregation outgrew the church, built a larger one in 1934 and now uses old St. Michael's, which is an historic site, only part-time.

Dobro Wody, meaning "good water," must have seemed auspicious in 1904, when settlers arrived in **Dobrowody, Saskatchewan**, from a village of the same name in western Ukraine. The **Church of the Nativity of the Blessed Virgin Mary** was finished in 1912 and served 40 families. By 1941 there were 30, rising to 130 by 1961 and falling to just 10 families by 1975. This corresponds with growth, drought and economic depression pre–World War II, renewed growth after the war, and rural depopulation owing to mechanization and opportunities for employment elsewhere during the 1970s.

The church is secluded in trees behind a cemetery on an unmarked side road north and east of Rama. Beside the cemetery a broad drive leads to the parish hall, on open ground; the church, nearly ringed by tall spruce in a grove of poplars, stands next to it. After a century's vicissitudes, the church appears surprisingly unchanged (except for white and grey vinyl replacing yellow-painted wooden siding with brown trim). It appears dramatically, as if levitating within its now shaft-like site. Inside, the narthex, constrained by a tiny gallery, gives way to a nave so wide and tall by comparison that it seems positively large. The iconostasis is also very open in character: the sanctuary is fully visible, adding its depth to the church's length. St. Mary's was decorated by Paul Zabolotny in 1936.

Many Manitobans may agree with a Winnipegger who praised the **Church of the Immaculate Conception of the Virgin Mary, Cook's Creek**, Manitoba: *"That's my idea of a church!"* Father Philip Ruh (1883–1962), who was born near the Franco-German border, trained with the Netherlands Oblates, studied Ukrainian for two years, was received into the Eastern Rite and immigrated to Canada in 1913, a missionary to Ukrainians in Alberta. Based on limited architectural studies in seminary, Father Ruh designed several dozen churches in the prairie provinces. One of his first contributions, in 1915, was altering little St. Onuphrius, Smoky Lake, Alberta (just 39 by 23 feet and not quite 30 feet high); it was moved to Canada Hall in the Canadian Museum of Civilization, Gatineau, Québec, reopened in 1996 and reconsecrated — a working church again. At Mountain Road, Manitoba,

Ruh undertook to build the largest wooden church in western Canada, St. Mary's (1924–25), planned on a Greek cross with a large dome at the centre (destroyed by fire in 1966).

When he was transferred to Cook's Creek in 1930, Ruh immediately began another large church boasting five domes — four clustered diagonally around the highest dome over the crossing — and nine decorative cupolas, one at each end of the church's cross-shaped plan in addition to those on the domes. Opening in 1940, it was finished in 1952. The complexity of its varying silhouettes, recalling Kiev's churches, makes it seem even larger than its 98 by 131 feet. In Ukrainian tradition, standing capacity (before seating) was 1,000. Modern building technology is combined

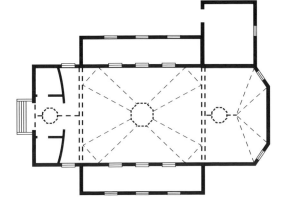

Church of the Immaculate Conception of the Virgin Mary, *Cook's Creek, Manitoba; Ukrainian Catholic. Reinforced concrete and concrete block, 1930–52; Father Philip Ruh, designer*

This "prairie cathedral" is extraordinary for its contemporary building technology despite more-or-less traditional appearance and its design by a parish priest rather than an architect. Father Philip Ruh built many churches on the prairies, in various materials, each with volunteer labour under the direction of a "master carpenter" he trained to complete the work.

The emphatically vertical interior (an urban Ukrainian tradition), bounded everywhere by marbleizing, is a honeycomb of tight, domed spaces carried on starkly modern reinforced-concrete columns. Some consider the result Baroque Revival — stripped down — yet it almost seems Post-Modern, decades before Post-Modernism, in its smooth, geometric and multihued forms.

with vernacular elements: stuccoed concrete block and reinforced concrete arches rise on a reinforced concrete slab, with some steel framing, all colourfully painted — unlike the sophisticated polychromatic masonry of Ruh's otherwise similar Saints Cyril and Methodius (1944–46) in St. Catharines, Ontario (see pp. 262–64).

The **Ukrainian Cultural Heritage Village**, **Mundare**, Alberta, occupying a beautiful prairie site that replicates conditions a century ago, preserves three restored churches. The oldest is **St. Nicholas Russo-Greek Orthodox Church**, from Kiew, with a gable-roofed nave and narrower and lower extensions for the narthex and semi-octagonal sanctuary. Over the nave the roof changes to a domed octagon. The interior has a wooden panelled dado with wallpaper above (the best the parishioners could do). The iconostasis is a solid wall with three doors to the sanctuary. More elaborate decoration appears in **St. Nicholas Ukrainian Greek Catholic Church** at Buczacz. The two are formally similar: plain gabled three-part buildings, though the Buczacz church has three domes. Over the double door is an oculus. The splayed form of the bell tower is enclosed with a door and windows at ground level and louvres at the bell level. The finer interior is marked by barrel vaults in both the nave and chancel. But its tour de force is the noted church-painter Peter Lipinski's decorative touches: the floral frieze is particularly handsome, contrasting with the banding of the walls, corner mouldings, dado and starred ceiling. A third church in the village, **St. Vladimir's Ukrainian Greek Orthodox Church**, from **Vegreville**, is more ambitious structurally: the dome's octagonal drum floats above the crossing of nave and transepts, not directly over any walls. Pendentives in the drum's inner corners (to change shape from a square to an octagon) are decorated with heads of angels, painted, like the rest of the interior, by Vadym Dobrolige.

St. Nicholas', *Kiew (now in Ukrainian Cultural Village, Mundare, Alberta); Russo-Greek Orthodox. Clapboarded log, 1908 (restored to 1925–30); builder unknown*

ABOVE The church has been moved to a new site in the Ukrainian Village east of Edmonton, located on a low rise with bell tower to one side and processional cross on the other. The simple geometric forms are effectively juxtaposed: three gabled cubes in the church, a gabled cube on a trapezoidal form in the bell tower and the linear cross.

LEFT An unfinished wooden floor contrasts with varnished V-joint panelling in the dado, which contrasts with the wallpaper on the upper walls. The main room fills the gabled form of the structure, so that the iconostasis — a frame wall with the traditional three doors — also fills the gable. The inexpensive icons occupy their customary positions: the Holy Mother to the left with the Son to the right of the (central) Holy Doors, here curtained, and the Last Supper above it; the last two are not visible in this photograph. The altar is decorated simply with a brass patten and brass candleholders.

St. Nicholas Church, *Buczacz (now in Ukrainian Cultural Village, Mundare, Alberta); Ukrainian Greek Catholic. Frame, 1912 (restored to 1928; Yarema Yanishewski, builder*

The interior of the Buczacz church is quite carefully considered, with vaulted (and starred) ceilings and wall decorations thoughtfully painted by Peter Lipinski in 1917, including decorative bands at the ceiling and dado. The iconostasis is a frame half-height wall with three sets of doorways, one of which is visible on the left. The round-headed windows suggest this congregation is better able to provide a more sophisticated setting for worship. The flags are used in processions.

FACING PAGE **St. Vladimir's**, *Vegreville (now in Ukrainian Cultural Village, Mundare, Alberta); Ukrainian Greek Orthodox. Frame, 1934; interior by Vadym Dobrolige; builder unknown*

This building illustrates how the circumstances of Ukrainians improved in a quarter-century: the plan is better articulated, with transepts, and with a large open dome over the crossing, supported on pendentives. The interior decoration — which includes a scene of Ukraine's baptism in 988 led by Saint Vladimir and Princess Olga — is carried out with delicacy and sureness of touch.

Toil and Peaceful Life
The Welfare of the Whole World
Is Not Worth the Life of a Single Child.

— *Precepts inscribed (in Russian and English) at the front of the meeting room*
in the Doukhobor Community Home, Veregin, Saskatchewan

AN ELABORATE AND BEAUTIFUL HOUSE seems an unlikely shrine, but the **Doukhobor Community Home**, **Veregin**, Saskatchewan, might be to them what St. Peter's is to Roman Catholics. It combines two building types: a hall where people gather for worship or a meal and accommodations for their leader.

Doukhobors, more correctly the Union of Spiritual Communities of Christ, arrived in Canada in 1898 with promises of free land and exemption from military service from Clifford Sifton. They left their Russian homeland, after protesting militarism and violence, with the help of Leo Tolstoy, who donated the proceeds from his novel *Resurrection*, and North American Quakers. More than 7,000 Doukhobors emigrated through Batum on the Black Sea to three enormous tracts, totalling nearly 750,000 acres, in today's Saskatchewan. They established 61 villages based on individual homesteads combined so that they could live communally in two rows of houses on either side of a street. They set up flour mills, blacksmith shops and a brick factory and began selling grain.

The term *Doukho-borets* ("spirit-wrestler") was applied to them in 1785 by a Russian Orthodox archbishop who thought they wrestled against the Holy Spirit (and the Church) because they rejected the Church's reverence for icons, the priesthood, sacraments and even the Bible. They maintained that the spirit of God dwells within each believer, and relied on orally transmitted teachings and their own psalms and hymns. They adopted "spirit-wrestler" as their self-designation, but understood it to mean wrestling with and for the Spirit. Czarist authorities regarded them suspiciously: they were beaten, imprisoned, resettled or exiled.

Peter Vasil'evich Verigin (1859–1924) inherited the Doukhobor leadership in 1886 and was exiled immediately to Siberia. From exile, he called on his followers to refuse military service, return to communal life and abstain from alcohol, tobacco

RIGHT **Verigin's Tomb**
The inscription on Doukhobor leader Peter "Lordly" Verigin's tomb says, "Here flowed once in Doukhobor tears a coffin with body of a leader strong. With mournful prayer of spiritual wrestlers into the bowels of earth grievously lowered..." The site is outside Cranbrook, near a suspension bridge built by Doukhobors over the river.

FACING PAGE **Doukhobor Community Home**, *Veregin, Saskatchewan; Doukhobor. Frame, 1917–18; builder unknown*
The Community Home combines a meeting hall for religious purposes on the lower floor with the leader's dwelling above it, in a Prairie landmark of simple plan but remarkable elegance.

and meat. In 1895 he directed military conscripts to burn their weapons, demonstrating their rejection of violence. On June 29 (Verigin's birthday and the feast of Saint Peter and Saint Paul) thousands of Doukhobors obeyed; thereafter Doukhobors celebrated "Peter's Day" as Peace Day. Released in 1902, Verigin joined his followers in Canada and founded the village of Veregin. But in 1905 the federal government disavowed collective ownership, required individual registration of homesteads and an oath of allegiance, and opened noncompliant Doukhobors' reserves to the public. Verigin led 6,000 of his followers to southern British Columbia in 1907, where their sawmills, brick making, preserving and canning helped them prosper.

"Toil and peaceful life" was Verigin's resounding motto. His two-story Community Home (replacing an octagonal building of 1908, which burned down in 1916) houses leadership and administration on the second floor, linked visually to the plain meeting room below by a two-tiered veranda surrounding the square building. The posts support decorative railings and pierced ornamental metalwork. An external staircase, angling around the southwest corner, links the floors but separates the spaces. The result is unlike all but the most ostentatious Victorian examples of Canadian "gingerbread" in fretted and turned woodwork. "Besedka," a *dacha* in Georgia that belonged to Peter Verigin's mentor, Luker'ia Kalmykova (the first and only woman leader of the Doukhobors), was also a white-painted frame building surrounded by ornamental verandas, but it was tiny, unlike the grand Community Home in Veregin.

Sunday morning worship is held in the frugal meeting room, with its painted floor and dado, varnished wood ceiling (from which four bare light bulbs dangle on cords) and pleasing benches on S-shaped supports. Little suggests religious purposes except Russian and English precepts on the walls and bread, salt and water

Doukhobor Community Home
The house has an ornamental balustrade (above), enriched by staggered connecting pieces (a motif traceable to 18th-century chinoiserie, such as Chippendale's "Chinese" fretwork). This meandering, rectilinear design is repeated at the top of each bay, above a contrasting, curvilinear pattern of arcuated, intricately pierced tin panels, producing a fringe, in effect, on both levels.

The interior (right) has no cross, iconostasis, images or symbols of any kind, font, lectern, pulpit or communion table. At any gathering, however, bread, salt and water — symbols of goodwill — sit on a table.

— the only symbols recognized by Doukhobors. All sit facing the table: women on one side, men on the other. Singing a cappella is an important part of Doukhobor life. Women and girls stand to sing in one group to the left, men and boys to the right (as in Orthodox churches).

Peter "Godly" (commonly "Lordly") Verigin was killed in an unexplained 1924 train explosion at Farron, between Brilliant and Grand Forks, two major concentrations of Doukhobor settlement. His plain but carefully landscaped tomb is outside Cranbrook, above the junction of the Kootenay and Columbia Rivers. Doukhobors acquired a negative reputation in the 1940s and 50s when a small breakaway group, the "Sons of Freedom," burned several schools in British Columbia and staged nude protest marches over educational issues.

After the United States entered World War I, hostile American reactions to **Hutterite** pacifism prompted them to move from North Dakota to Canada in 1918. They established 10 colonies in southern Alberta that year, 14 more in the next four years and another 23 by the end of the 1930s, new groups splitting off when a colony grew larger than 100 persons. Jakob Hutter (burned at the stake in 1536) had founded a communal Christian group in Moravia and the Tyrol that imitated the sharing of goods in the earliest Christian community in Jerusalem. The colonies remain strongly communitarian, holding goods in common, speaking Tyrolian German and retaining old-fashioned dress.

They practise agriculture with state-of-the-art equipment and, though communal, each family has its own house in the **Pincher Creek Colony**, Alberta. The colony was established in 1927 and is relatively liberal. Its church is a frame building with a semi-hipped roof and windows down both sidewalls. Men sit on the left — their pews have a rail at shin height to hold their hats — and women on the right; children sit at the front and seniors at the back. Two ministers, the financial officer, field boss, other trustees and the German teacher, who keeps an eye on the children, sit across the front. Services are in High German, though most families speak Low German; everyone speaks English, learned at school.

Pincher Creek Colony, *Pincher Creek, Alberta; Hutterite. Frame, 1945, builder unknown*

Hutterite colonies include a cluster of houses with communal dining room, laundry, kitchen and church, surrounded by farm buildings, and beyond that the agricultural fields. The church is the plainest possible; in Pincher Creek it is covered with insulbrick. Seen from its windows, the individual family houses in a tightly woven pattern show the importance of intimate village life.

Bell Towers of the Eastern Rite

Immaculate Conception of the Virgin Mary, *Cook's Creek, Manitoba; Ukrainian Catholic. Reinforced concrete, 1930–52; Father Philip Ruh, designer*
While Father Ruh was deeply involved in construction of the "Prairie Cathedral" (and other buildings with which he was associated), he depended heavily on foremen — Michael Yanchesky and Victor Garbet here — assisted by volunteer labour. The double-tiered tower topped by a cupola, modelled on the domes of the church (*see* pp. 318–20), holds three bells in the upper story with large arcades.

Easter is a feast of joy and gladness that unites the entire community in common celebration. For three days the community celebrates to the sound of bells and to the singing of spring songs — vesnianky. Easter begins with the Easter matins and high liturgy, during which the pasky (traditional Easter breads) and pysanky and krashanky (decorated or coloured Easter eggs) are blessed in the church. Butter, lard, cheese, roast suckling pigs, sausage, smoked meat, and little napkins containing poppy seeds, millet, salt, pepper, and horseradish are also blessed.

— Z. Kuzelia and P. Odarchenko

CANADA'S UKRAINIAN POPULATION originated in forest-covered mountainous regions with a history of log construction, and their earliest houses and churches in Manitoba were of round or squared log. A separate sturdy bell tower was generally constructed, raising the bell enough to be heard clearly but not so much that it threatened the belfry's collapse. This almost universal attachment to bells and belfries is especially suitable in a church that depends entirely upon the unaccompanied voice in its liturgy.

At the Ukrainian Catholic **Church of the Assumption of the Mother of God, Ashville**, Manitoba, the belfry is of dovetailed squared log. The bells are suspended from a stout framework of timber in the octagonal upper story (with dainty round-headed openings), while the square lower story gives support and stability. **St. Elias', Sirko**, Manitoba, was built for its Ukrainian Greek Orthodox congregation from notched round logs in 1906 but covered with cove siding early on to protect the logs, while roofing boards and shingles replaced the original thatch. The belfry is constructed of strong and heavy tamarack, simpler in style and detail, with a play of closed and open forms and a sawtooth pattern ornamenting the first row of shingles.

With sawmills and comparatively light "balloon-frame" construction, both church and bell tower began to look almost weightless, as at the Ukrainian Catholic church of **Saints Vladimir and Olha, Valley River**, Manitoba. Both church and bell tower are clad in cove siding. Finally, in the Ukrainian Catholic **Church of the Immaculate Conception, Cook's Creek**, Manitoba, modern building technologies led to a tall domed bell tower of reinforced concrete; the result hovers between Baroque and Post-Modern architecture.

TOP LEFT **Assumption of the Mother of God**, *Ashville, Manitoba; Ukrainian Catholic. Frame, 1906, bell tower, dovetailed squared timber, ca 1912; builder unknown*

The Assumption of the Mother of God, one of the oldest Ukrainian churches in Manitoba, stands a little over four miles north of Ashville. Regular services were discontinued in the 1980s and an annual service was held on the patronal festival until the church closed recently. Its early and interesting belfry, built to house a large bell purchased in 1912, is surrounded by young poplars and looks more perilous year by year.

CENTRE LEFT **Saints Vladimir and Olha**, *Valley River, Manitoba; Ukrainian Catholic. Frame, 1924; Anthony Yaworsky, foreman, and volunteer labour*

The double-cube bell tower with deep eaves around the lower story is traditional in profile, but instead of round log or squared timber the material is modern mill-sawn lumber (two inches thick when rough). The paired openings in the belfry refer to familiar Ukrainian forms and relate specifically to the round-headed windows of the nearby church, which is dedicated to the patron saints of Ukraine. This belfry houses one bell.

BELOW **St. Elias'**, *Sirko, Manitoba; Ukrainian Orthodox. Church: notched round log, 1909–10; clad in cove siding later; bell tower: dovetailed squared timber; Manoly Khalaturnyk, designer*

Tamarack was favoured for bell towers because of its enormous strength, and a small grove of mature trees — now of unusual size, one foot in diameter at chest height — stands nearby (to the left). The bell tower is surrounded by the cemetery with its distinctive Ukrainian grave-markers. A much larger church (1950) standing directly to the west replaced old St. Elias', which was restored In the 1980s.

We are still far from having attained perfection in the construction of our Churches. ... The good that has been wrought by the revival of a purer taste in Architecture, and a recurrence to better principles, is but the harbinger of the good yet to be achieved.

— *Raphael and J. Arthur Brandon, 1849*

Late Victorian Gothic Revival

THE HOPE EXPRESSED ABOVE was achieved in a plethora of Gothic Revival churches, *de rigueur* in church design for almost a century. **Christ Church Cathedral, Vancouver**, British Columbia in its present setting seems an unusually modest Anglican cathedral from the outside — perhaps consistent with the original intention to be more protestant and evangelical than the earlier Anglo-Catholic St. James' (*see* p. 342). Although this 1894 cathedral by C.O. Wickenden is overshadowed today by bulky office towers and the Hotel Vancouver, it retains the character of a large English parish church. The interior is larger than the exterior suggests. The narthex, reached through a side porch, is partially covered by a large new tracker organ in a starkly modern idiom. By contrast, the church beyond the narthex appears dark and confusing, but once eyes adjust to the light, the logic of the wooden columns, arches and exposed roof members becomes clear, even exciting. As the sidewalls are low, the narrow lancet windows are small but interesting. While the redesign of the chancel and the replacement of many of the original pews may be questionable, the aim to marry the old forms with modern design concepts is entirely laudable.

A congregational study in 1971 recommended demolishing the cathedral and incorporating a replacement within a high-rise complex by Arthur Erickson. The congregation approved the plan, but vigorous opposition and the designation of

Christ Church Cathedral, *Vancouver, British Columbia; Anglican. Stone, 1894–95 (expanded and renovated 1909, 1930, 1998, 2004); C.O. Wickenden, architect*

The dark interior exudes feelings of warmth, piety and community closeness, much of it owed to the almost parish-church ambience Wickenden created. His intricately detailed timber columns, trusses and tie beams, which only barely separate aisles from nave, focus on the chancel.

Christer Church Cathedral, *chancel*
The chancel has been redesigned in line with recent liturgical thinking, moving the altar onto a new platform that thrusts out toward the congregation, to create a stronger sense of kneeling around a table for the Lord's Supper. The lectern in the foreground balances the pulpit on the other side, while the choir stalls remain in their traditional location.

The beautifully executed gardens and courtyards behind the church's chancel and on a higher level to the left set the cathedral off as in a modern re-creation of a cathedral close. Water, plants and trees attract lunch-hour visitors to enjoy these oases of shelter in the midst of Vancouver's urban busyness.

the building as a provincial heritage site staved off destruction. The cathedral is now set off brilliantly by landscaped areas on three sides of its sloping site, so that it is one of the most handsomely situated churches in Canada, with lush green gardens on several levels, enclosed sitting spaces, pergolas, waterfalls and flowering trees, all within sight of the mountains across the inlet.

St. Andrew's Cathedral, Victoria, British Columbia, is one of the best examples of Picturesque Gothic in western Canada. The Roman Catholic cathedral was built in 1890–92 as the centre of the oldest diocese west of Toronto, part of the Archdiocese of Oregon, and its bounds included all British Columbia, the Yukon and Alaska, an area comparable to western Europe. The building nearly duplicates the parish church in Vaudreuil, Québec, by the same Montréal architects, Henri-Maurice Perrault (1857–1909) and Albert Mesnard (1847–1909). Its urban impact depends on its lofty double-tower facade, and its High Victorian character is emphasized by its asymmetrical spire (a replacement about 1900 after a storm toppled the original). The exterior materials include granite and brick with gilded roof trim and crosses.

The Latin-cross plan features a wide colonnaded nave with narrow side aisles and wide transepts. The plaster ribbed vault mimics medieval ribbed vaults in stone. The columns forming the nave's double arcade are cast iron covered with

St. Andrew's Cathedral, *Victoria, British Columbia; Roman Catholic. Brick, 1890-92; Henri-Maurice Perrault and Albert Mesnard, architects (restored 1987 by Bawlf, Cooper & Associates)*

The picturesque exterior of the Roman Catholic cathedral in Victoria is partly due to its carefully chosen materials, especially the red brick with the numerous contrasting stone string courses and window heads, and partly to the way it balances contrasting elements, such as the tall spire on the left and the stumpy tower on the right.

The interior's columns, arcades and ribbed vault are successful aspects of the church's design; the interior is enhanced by an appropriately decorative paint scheme. Its most memorable feature is the sanctuary, where two bentwood boxes (by Charles Elliott) support the altar and two large candleholders flank it, all beautifully executed First Nations carvings.

St. Andrew's Cathedral
Behind the choir gallery three small quatre-
foil windows are by Tim Paul, another First
Nations artist.

plaster, topped with unusually wide capitals. The double arcade — the upper one a blind arcade — in turn has high clerestory windows above it, the whole design handled in a sure-footed way. The space's attractive impact owes almost as much to the colour scheme as to the architecture: the primary palette blends green, gold and white, highlighted by blue, pink, dark orange and black in the panelled chancel, arches and blind arcades. The fine stained glass includes some Arts and Crafts windows. Interior changes following Vatican II embraced First Nations art: behind the first gallery three small quatrefoil windows by Tim Paul use West Coast imagery of the raven and the moon. Two West Coast bentwood boxes by Charles Elliott that serve as altar supports are of special interest. They are designed so that each of the eight faces (which include Jonah, Pentecost, Raven Woman and the Eucharist) can be turned to face the congregation when liturgically appropriate.

In a province famous for its rural places of worship, **St. Paul's United, Boissevain,** Manitoba, is an urban landmark but not an inner-city church. It was built in 1893, when the town was small but growing quickly, a decade after Methodists arrived. Not large in size (about 54 feet square externally) with the rough rubble-stone walls of the Selkirk limestone typical of many Manitoban churches, St. Paul's rises unencumbered in an open setting. It stands especially tall because it is built above a high basement, used for the lecture room and classrooms. The entrance is through the corner of the building, a form associated with banks and churches in the 1870s, 80s and 90s. The entrance tower, belfry and steeple and the high gables on all four sides combine to produce an attractively Picturesque silhouette.

The corner entrance addresses the intersecting residential and commercial streets, as well as anticipating the diagonally arranged interior. This amphi-theatral plan, which contributes to an appearance of greater size, was a new development associated with the Akron plan that first appeared in Canada at Toronto's Jarvis Street Baptist Church (*see* pp. 248–49, 251–53). The curved seating at St. Paul's sweeps a full quarter-circle like a large fan. Four passages take the congregation to their seats: two narrow ones set against the walls and two wider ones from the entrance toward the core of the church. Methodists favoured such a plan because the circular pews emphasize the common litur-gical focus. The communion table, font, pulpit, organ and choir are gathered together in the dark-panelled corner directly opposite the entrance. Generous light comes from large windows in the east, north and west walls, filling the central space.

The architects, Edward Lowery and Son, based in Winnipeg, had already designed a similar church in the Twin Cities of Minneapolis–St. Paul. They developed their ideas further with the Boissevain church, and while it was under construction an important variant was published in a Presbyterian pub-lication, *Designs for Village, Town and City Churches* (1893), with a perspective sketch of the exterior and a floor plan. This version showed a purer form of an Akron plan, with a Sunday school east of the church and doors between the two spaces that could be opened to unite the spaces (*see* pp. 390–91).

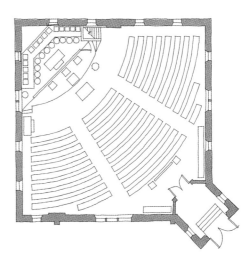

St. Paul's, *Boissevain, Manitoba; originally Methodist (now St. Paul's United). Brick, 1893; Edward Lowery & Son, architects*

Boissevain was surveyed in 1881 and Methodists began organizing a circuit in 1882. In 1886 they held their first service in a harness shop, and met thereafter in a railway coach standing at the station on Sundays. In 1887 they built a small church on Johnson, a fine residential street on the eastern edge of town, opposite the South Railway Street elevator. The "Stone Church" followed in 1893, with a corner entrance.

The entrance set up the kite-shaped plan of the interior with its wedges of seating. Such plans were favoured by Methodists as offering a "direct and unobstructed view of choir and pulpit from all parts of the auditorium"— an intimate experience shared by the whole congregation in curved seats arranged wheel-like around a liturgical hub.

The North

THOSE WHO BUILT THE EARLY CHURCHES in the North tended to come from inland, not from the Arctic. Roman Catholics and Anglicans were again in the lead. Several of these seemingly plain churches have outstanding artistic elaboration in the interiors, with careful integration of painting, carving and architecture.

Among the early and distinctive churches in northern Saskatchewan was Holy Trinity, Stanley Mission, Saskatchewan, designed and built by the first Anglican pastor from the Church Missionary Society to the area, Robert Hunt, in 1854–60. He imported stained glass from England for it. The church sits at a bend on the north bank of the Churchill River, backed by the forest, and is the only remaining building of the mission. A new spire was put in place by helicopter in 1988. At about the same latitude, on another of the great North West Company routes, is St. Charles' Mission, Dunvegan, Alberta, on the Peace River. An Oblate missionary post, it was built in 1883-84 by Fathers Émile Grouard (1840–1931) and Auguste Husson; the latter is credited with carpentry skills and the former with the stencilled interior paintings. The construction is of squared logs with half-dovetailed corners. The

St. Jude's Cathedral, *Iqaluit, Nunavut; Anglican. Glulam, 1970–72; Ron Thom, architect*

Ron Thom is known for his clearly articulated modern buildings that in some cases make references back to historic precedent. In the case of the Iqaluit Cathedral, the reference is clearly to an igloo — an indigenous design that suits perfectly the northern climate and landscape — as Thom's perspective drawing deliberately emphasizes. The church was destroyed by an arsonist in late 2005.

painting over the altar is especially unusual, painted by Grouard on a tanned and blemish-free moose hide. Another log church, equally unassuming, is **Christ Church ("Log Cathedral"), Whitehorse**, Yukon. Like St. Charles' Mission, Christ Church makes no pretense to be anything but a simple log church, though it was distinguished by being the only log-built cathedral in the world until it was replaced by a new cathedral in 1960. The Log Cathedral is now home to **St. Simon's**, a First Nations congregation.

Fort Good Hope, Northwest Territories, on the east bank of the Mackenzie River just below the Arctic Circle, was established by the North West Company in 1805. Our Lady of Good Hope Church was built and decorated by the Oblate priest Father Émile Petitot (1838–1917), an ethnologist, linguist and geographer; the carving was done by Father Jean Séguin. All the surfaces of the remarkable interior are lavishly decorated with intricately carved woodwork and painted panels of biblical scenes, much of it carried out with homemade paint made of natural dyes and fish oil. Father Petitot said he was inspired by Chartres Cathedral, as he aimed "not only

Christ Church ("Log Cathedral"), *Whitehorse, Yukon; Anglican. Log, 1900; Rev. R.J. Bowen, builder*

The railroad from Skagway, Alaska, had just been built when the Rev. R. J. Bowen and his wife arrived in Whitehorse in 1900, following service elsewhere in the Klondike before the 1898 gold rush began. Bowen brought his box of carpentry tools with him. In a few months he had the small church in a condition that it could be used, and by the next year the rectory was built.

Our Lady of Victory, *Inuvik, Northwest Territories; Roman Catholic. Wood blocks, with bronze roofing, 1958–60; Brother Maurice Larocque, designer*

The "Igloo Church" has become an icon of modern churches in the Arctic, mimicking the shape of an Inuit igloo but also looking uncannily like a Byzantine church. The building was designed by a lay missionary and built by local labour, using both recycled local materials and wood brought 1400 km by boat. Special care was taken to prevent the perma-frost from thawing and unsettling the building's foundations.

to glorify the church but to inspire awe and wonder in the local population," setting a precedent for mission churches in the Mackenzie District.

More recently, at **Kugaaruk** (formerly Pelly Bay), Nunavut, a stone church was erected in 1941 by Roman Catholic priests, Fathers Pierre Henri and Franz van de Velde. Though now replaced by a more functional building, **St. Peter's** stands as a charming, and rare, example of stone construction in the North. Anglicans opened **St. John's** in 1953 at **Kingnait** (formerly Cape Dorset), Nunavut, just before Cape Dorset was recognized nationally and internationally for the quality of its art, both sculpture and print material. Indeed, James Houston, who promoted Inuit sculpture, arrived at Cape Dorset the same year the church was built.

A major Anglican church, **St. Jude's Cathedral**, was built at **Iqaluit**, Nunavut, by Ron Thom (1923–86). Tragically, it was burned by an arsonist in 2005. Like other northern churches, it was extensively decorated with Inuit work, including a soapstone baptismal font, a cross of narwhal tusks, wall hangings and woven baskets. The cathedral served both as the parish church and as the seat of the bishop of the diocese of the Arctic, the largest Anglican diocese in the world. Its form, though obviously inspired by the traditional form of an igloo, was much more successful than Our Lady of Victory, Inuvik, Northwest Territories.

St. Peter, *Kugaaruk (Pelly Bay), Nunavut; Roman Catholic. Stone, 1941; Fathers Pierre Henri and Franz van de Velde, builders*

This stone church, rare in northern Canada, has been replaced recently, but the stone building stands as a tribute to the enterprising spirit of the early Oblate missionaries. The stone is local, the mortar made of clay and seal blubber. While the body of the church is very plain, the tower and spire are unusual: the stone tower is almost as wide as the church and the spire combines closed and open stages.

St. John's, *Kingnait (Cape Dorset); Anglican. Frame, 1953; builder unknown*

Cape Dorset, on Baffin Island, was the site of a Hudson's Bay Company post in the early 20th century. By mid-century the Inuit had built this Anglican church, and in 1996 the Inuit rector of the parish was elected bishop of the diocese of the Arctic, the first Inuk to be so honoured.

Our guiding principle was that design is neither an intellectual nor a material affair, but simply an integral part of the stuff of life, necessary for everyone in a civilized society.

— *Walter Gropius*

Modernist Stirrings

Temple of the Church of Jesus Christ of the Latter Day Saints, *Cardston, Alberta; Mormon. Granite, 1913–23, Hyrum C. Pope and Harold W. Burton, architects*

The Cardston Temple of the Church of Jesus Christ of the Latter Day Saints is built mostly in white granite. The geometry of the building is complex; there is a central cube with extensions on all four sides to create a cruciform shape, and diagonal extensions at the corners, with all the elements being different heights. While the windows are generally narrow vertical slots, the building's main faces combine horizontal and vertical elements with Aztec-derived motifs.

CANADA DID NOT QUICKLY EMBRACE full-blown Modernism, but there were unexpected anticipations. One of Canada's most surprising buildings is the **Cardston Temple of the Church of Jesus Christ of Latter Day Saints** in southwestern Alberta. Mormons from Utah came to Alberta in the 1880s. Cardston was the first location selected for a temple outside the United States. The architects from Salt Lake City were Hyrum C. Pope and Harold W. Burton, two enthusiastic young followers of Frank Lloyd Wright, who won a church-wide competition and went on to design other Mormon buildings in a similar style. Their innovative structure in Wright's idiom is hardly indebted at all to typical church structures and, rather daringly, they included Aztec and Mayan overtones in the decorative touches. The church sits on a generous site on a low rise, a little to one side of the main intersection of Cardston. The first view of it shocks. The building looks like a Roman mausoleum faced with British Columbia white granite. On its large site it looks smaller than it really is.

Mormons distinguish between temple and church, following ancient Jewish differentiation between the temple in Jerusalem and the many synagogues found widely throughout the Mediterranean. Thus, certain Mormon functions take place solely in temples, including baptism, endowment, sealing and second endowment. Those entering Latter Day Saint temples wear white dresses and suits, like Jewish priests and Levites, to symbolize leaving the world behind.

A bas-relief sculpture behind a fountain and pool portrays Jesus at the well of Samaria; once outdoors, it is now enclosed just inside the main doors. Wright's design principles are evident in the public areas: clean use of modern materials,

Temple of the Church of Jesus Christ of Latter-Day Saints
The small detail shows the careful articulation of the planes and volumes, together with the pyramidal roof capping the whole complex and the decorative elements.

BELOW Indebtedness to Frank Lloyd Wright is quite obvious. The Temple is entered from a landscaped courtyard that leads into a semi-public entrance, and from there to private areas. The entrance courtyard has been modified by enclosing within the narthex a fountain and pool that were originally outside. The courtyard effects a restful transition into the inner parts of the building.

contrasting ceiling heights and floor levels, carefully designed approaches, strong sense of enclosure, water features, surface decoration and contrasting woods. Exterior walls extend into and embrace the landscape, enclosing service areas; a landscaped entrance courtyard makes an effective transition between the drives and sidewalks and the entrance lobby. Strong intersecting horizontal and vertical lines and graduated masses build up to the main focus of the structure — the central temple block — with surface decoration recalling Wright's Imperial Hotel in Tokyo. The building is a stunning foretaste of Canada's slow turn to Modernism. It is altogether unforgettable.

Several years later, Christian Scientists in British Columbia built **First Church, Victoria**, on a constrained site at one end of a long narrow park. The dome is pierced with a large central oculus — like Rome's Pantheon — and round-headed windows puncture the dome's drum. The plan advantageously separates various functions, with an assembly room on the ground floor and an uncluttered worship space one floor up. Inside, the church has a circular plan, surrounded by simple Tuscan columns that carry a Classical entablature and the drum. The pulpit is backed by a low-relief arch and by paired columns, and the organ pipes by smaller arches. The church handsomely and sensibly adapts a Classical model in Modern materials, on a novel plan that works well on its sloping urban site.

St. James', Vancouver, is a daring and important design. The architects were London-based Adrian Gilbert Scott (1882–1963) with Canadian architectural firm Sharp and Thompson; Scott was subsequently responsible for the rebuilding of London's Houses of Parliament after World War II. St. James' is a centrally organized

First Church, Victoria, *British Columbia; Christian Science. Brick, stone and concrete, 1919–20; George Foote Dunham, architect*

Taking advantage of the visual opportunity on a sloping site, the architect of First Church put the main hall one floor up under a large dome, behind a massive two-story-high Ionic portico that carries around the corners to Ionic pilasters on the sidewalls. The Classical details found on the exterior carry through into the interior, where the pulpit occupies an area between pairs of columns, at the focus of the sloped circular floor. Windows in the drum under the exterior dome add a sense of weightlessness to the rational and well-considered layout.

but complex space, high and cubic with an octagonal tower and pyramidal roof above, in a Byzantine form but with connections to Art Deco. The nave is a modified square, flanked on all four sides by barrel-vaulted extensions to make it cruciform, but with the corners cut off to reflect the octagonal tower. This ancient style of central plan, however, is not functionally centralized, since the seating is arranged axially, directed to a chancel that focuses on the altar against the chancel wall — reflecting the church's Anglo-Catholic theology, which is more conservative than much post–Vatican II Roman Catholicism. Some details are particularly well thought out: decorative details that provide lively shadows are cast in place at three separate eave lines; the hanging lights in the nave recall the exterior details around the eaves; the delicate cresting on the sounding boards over pulpit and lectern are consistent with the details at the ceiling level; and the small baptismal chapel to the right of the entrance is a masterpiece of careful detailing. The conception, the construction details, the methods and the exterior design make this building another important anticipation of Modernism in Canada.

If St. James' anticipates Modernism, 20 years later **St. Mary's Cathedral, Calgary**, half-heartedly embraces it while harking back to late — very late — Gothic Revival. Maxwell Bates (1906–80) was a significant modern painter who qualified as an architect through practising with his father and a cousin in England. Since art

St. James', *Vancouver, British Columbia; Anglican. Concrete, 1935–37; Adrian Gilbert Scott with Sharp and Thompson, architects*

This church's exposed monolithic poured-in-place concrete was a daring departure from the norm. It fits snugly on its site by locating a narthex along one angle of the octagon at the street corner, with a triple portal surrounded by receding frames that give strong shadow lines.

While the concrete construction is as apparent on the inside as on the outside — it is two separated concrete structures — its severity is softened by the wooden ceiling, the wooden reredos, the wooden canopies over the pulpit and the reading desk. Indeed, the laciness of the edges of the ceiling and the canopies give the space an almost insubstantial quality.

was his major interest, he did not practise architecture for long, but during the 1950s he designed several churches. Three were built, two survive. St. Mary's is south of the Elbow River facing Rouleauville Square, its tall central tower being the neighbourhood's main focus. The brick detailing recalls the influential Scandinavian designs of Eliel Saarinen in the 1930s and 40s (Cranbrook Educational Community outside Detroit is best known). Inside, a number of alterations to its original appearance have made the church something of a conundrum. The most important change is that the nave's ceiling, originally flat inverted pyramidal acoustical panels that gave the interior a clearly Modern feel — though an approach modelled on much earlier Roman basilicas — has been changed to a mock Gothic pointed arch ceiling, making it seem more prosaically Gothic Revival than it was. Framing the chancel is a massive concrete coffered double arch, which in turn frames a round arched window in the rear of the chancel, highlighting an attractive stained-glass Resurrection window. The nave is flooded with light from large, high clerestory windows, coloured glass being reserved for small windows at the rear of the two transepts and one clerestory window on each side over the transepts. Though his second church, St. Martin's (Anglican), was sold in 1999 and demolished, the third of Maxwell Bates' churches, a small Roman Catholic parish church, St. Anne's Korean , Calgary (1957) survives.

Cathedral of the Immaculate Conception of the Blessed Virgin Mary, *Calgary, Alberta; Roman Catholic. Brick, 1954–57; Maxwell Bates, architect*

Bates' tower projects from and rises high above a square facade, centred on a Romanesque-style door. Long slits in the brickwork emphasize the tower's verticality; an open brick crown finishes off the composition. St. Mary's character reflects the early modernism of Eliel Saarinen, the Finnish architect who emigrated to the United States.

A Resurrection window — designed by Bernard Gruenke and manufactured in 1988 by the Conrad Schmitt Studios, New Berlin, Wisconsin— acts as the focus of the nave.

All architecture is shelter, all great architecture is the design of space
that contains, cuddles, exalts or stimulates persons in that space.
— Philip Johnson

Western Modernism

WHILE THE STIRRINGS OF CANADIAN MODERNISM were felt early in Alberta and British Columbia, full-fledged Modernist architecture began to appear in the 1950s with churches such as St. Anselm's on the University of British Columbia campus, a fieldstone-walled A-frame (*see* p. 295). Mature Modernist churches were built in the 1960s, and none is more characteristic of new approaches to church design than the **Unitarian Church**, **Vancouver**, designed by Wolfgang Gerson (1916–91) on a corner lot. The worship space, a series of rectangles, has a pure, uncomplicated integrity, approached best from the courtyard and the folded glass pergola that precedes the entrance. The windows are long rectangular slots whose effect is strongest inside, where they provide a penetrating connection with the outdoors, allowing the landscape to calm the worshipper. The ceiling is handled in the same fashion, with a long central skylight over the main aisle and another at right angles to it over the platform, so that the space is literally flooded with natural light. Artificial illumination comes from numerous bulbs in open square frames floating down the two sides of the nave, with a larger open rectangle over the platform. On either side of the platform, two enormous wall hangings in natural colours add to the warmth of the interior. While severely modern in its appearace, the church is a delightfully sympathetic example of one kind of Modern architecture — opening up to the outside, soothing, spatially sophisticated, with inexpensive but attractively chosen materials and carefully considered details.

West Vancouver Baptist was designed by Arthur Mudry on several of the same principles as the Unitarian Church of Vancouver but is totally different in impact. The latter is rational and reserved, while the former is emotional and exuberant. Both have a campus-type organization, made possible by the favourable B.C. climate,

West Vancouver Baptist, *West Vancouver, British Columbia; Baptist. Wood and glass, 1966–67; Arthur Mudry, architect*

The inescapable feature of this church is the interior's relation to the outside, through large sections of glass in the walls and gables. The roof comprises four hyperbolic paraboloids separated by strips of glass in the form of a cross, as they rise up to a high peak over the nave.

Vancouver Unitarian Church, *Vancouver, British Columbia; Unitarian. Brick and steel, 1964; Wolfgang Gerson, architect*

Vancouver Unitarian Church revolves around a partly glass-roofed courtyard scheme of three separate buildings: church, offices and education building. Forty years on it seems fresh and creative, the courtyard filled with flowers, the trees and shrubs looking at home, and the building weathering to fit into its environment. The rational interior features flat roofs, rectangular spaces and long vertical slot windows, some of which have coloured glass panels, connecting the space with the outside.

where glass-roofed courtyards join small units. Both invite nature inside and both use expanses of glass, including within the roof structure. West Vancouver Baptist's roof is dramatic: four tilted hyperbolic paraboloids sit on massive stone piers at the corners (*see* p. 163 for the same form on piers at the midpoints). Lower rectangular spaces — narthex, extension to the seating, and chancel — surround the square main space. Consistent with Baptist theology, a prominent baptismal tank occupies one end of the chancel's platform, with a brightly coloured stained-glass window directing attention to this important rite of entry. The church fits beautifully into its almost overgrown treed surroundings. Its sense of shelter "cuddles" worshippers and encourages them to go out to their daily lives reinvigorated.

Whereas these two representative examples of West Coast Modernism underscore the connection between nature and interior space, **St. Mary's**, **Red Deer**, Alberta, an icon of Canadian modern architecture from the same period, takes a totally different point of departure, enclosing the congregation with a sinuous series of opaque brick walls. The original conception has been regrettably compromised by later additions unsympathetic to its original purity. Douglas Cardinal, the innovative Métis architect, now barely acknowledges the building. The discerning visitor, however, can see the brilliance of the original concept behind the alterations and the kitschy decorations. The altar is lit by a skylight that bores down through

West Vancouver Baptist

The four hyperbolic paraboloids of West Vancouver Baptist are read differently on the exterior, where the curved forms are clearer than on the interior. Three of the four walls and all four gable ends are glass, so that the surrounding lush vegetation can be seen not only from inside, but right through the structure from the outside, making it seem almost impermanent.

St. Mary's, Red Deer, *Alberta; Roman Catholic. Brick and suspended concrete shell, 1965–68; Douglas Cardinal, architect*

PREVIOUS PAGE The interior is an almost entirely enclosed space that wraps around the faithful and shelters them, with two piercing lights from above the main and the side altar.

ABOVE St. Mary's is remarkable for its swooping roof reminiscent of the pilgrimage chapel at Ronchamp, France, by Le Corbusier, a turning point in European architecture. The sensuous curves both in plan and section are a precursor to other works by Cardinal — the Canadian Museum of Civilization in Gatineau, Québec, and the National Museum of the American Indian in Washington, D.C. These photographs were taken before the additions that compromised its integrity.

the roof to point at the liturgical centre. The seating arches around the chancel, following the curves. Cardinal's European and First Nations' ancestry shines through clearly in his buildings: "I must not let technology destroy myself and everything around me. I must reorient my whole existence. I believe that the life force in each of us which binds us together as a species is a stronger force than our individual egos. When I come to the Lodge I become in tune with myself and all being. I feel totally at one with nature and all life around me. The sky becomes bluer and the trees seem to whisper to me, the sun seems to penetrate my very being, every breath of air gives me new life. I feel totally alive. My soul runs with the deer and flies like a bird and I feel reborn." This statement of his personal philosophy is the most appropriate comment on St. Mary's.

There is something kindred in the design philosophy and swirling form of **Église Précieux-Sang**, **St. Boniface**, Manitoba (a community with Métis roots). "Precious Blood," designed by Étienne Gaboury (b. 1930), sits comfortably on a large grassy site (shared with an angular pre-existing rectory of white brick) at the intersection of residential streets. Low walls relate to small neighbouring houses,

while the monumental roof seems scaled to the area's mature trees. The principal material is glazed ruddy-brown brick, supplemented outside by matching tile like that in modern silos. The wall winds continuously (except at the main entrance) in a plan resembling the letter Q. Curving projections house a secondary entry and a series of confessionals near it; angular projections house sacristies and washrooms. The roof is a ridged and twisted cone — resembling nothing so much as a mangled screw of gigantic proportion — spiralling as it rises. The red-cedar shakes covering it manage many changes of plane with apparent flexibility, bending over rafters here, involuting between confessionals there.

The exterior and interior of great buildings are usually reflexive, the outer aspect arising partially from the inner disposition of functional elements, and the core developing further ideas the periphery seems to posit. The circulation winds clockwise from the main entrance of Précieux-Sang into the near darkness of the circular nave; the only natural light is from a single skylight hidden at the roof's highest point. Individual but fixed low-backed seats are arranged as in a Greek theatre, gently raked around a dais with a stupendous block of Tyndall limestone

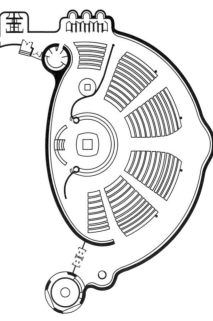

for the altar, which seems to levitate in defiance of gravity. To exit through the main doors is exhilarating, a passage counterclockwise from darkness into light, under the cascading red, white and blue light of stained glass in the coiling roof above the main entry. This rigorously focused but inviting church, somewhat compromised now by indifferent pieces of sculpture, breathes the refreshing air of the second Vatican Council.

Gaboury, a native Franco-Manitoban, devoted his University of Manitoba thesis to church design in 1958. He had learned much from his devout, poetically inclined mother. A year spent in France, studying at Paris' École des beaux-arts and visiting sites, was a revelation: "My epiphany occurred during a visit to the … chapel at Ronchamp, designed by Le Corbusier. This tiny chapel was devoid of any reference point, measure or scale … as if the very rules of architectural composition had been tossed aside. Yet this minuscule chapel was every bit as powerful as the cathedral at Chartres! Even more than its unusual, immeasurable form, the true wonder of Ronchamp was the extraordinary quality of space and light, … of space created by light. Le Corbusier gives us the key … when he states that architecture is the quest for 'indescribable space.'"

Returning to Canada in 1959, Gaboury established himself quickly as a distinguished designer. In his first decade of practice he undertook at least eight parish churches, largely for francophone communities. Précieux-Sang — the most important — evolved slowly (design studies having begun in 1961) into a work of genius.

Clifford Wiens (b. 1926) has been called "Saskatchewan's most respected architect." His most unconventional work is **Lady of the Lake Chapel**, near **Silton**, Saskatchewan, in the Qu'Appelle Valley. A Roman Catholic seasonal chapel, this little-known masterpiece of 1969 is well hidden, nearly invisible in fact, tucked into a bowl-shaped hill. From the verge of the road along the hillside's rim, its weathered shingles are lost among the trees. The roof barely breaks the line of the distant horizon — Last Mountain Lake and the encircling hills.

Thickets grow round the square chapel, contributing to a metaphor of discovery, loss and return. Stepping-stones descend the hill, skirting and then leading away from the structure. When the path circles back, it arrives unexpectedly at a substantial concrete pier supporting (at eye level) a massive glulam beam carrying the roof. The large beam crosses the dirt-floored chapel to another concrete pier, also outside. A second beam criss-crosses midway, meeting the first at a central steel junction (supported from the peak by a tension rod). This pyramid of timber has no walls: the chapel is open at the corners as well as on all sides. It reminds us of the late-18th-century fascination with the primitive, with simple forms, with sensory experience and intense emotions, yet it is as original as any of the 20th century's most avant-garde architecture.

The present **Cathédrale de Saint-Boniface** (1970–72) is the Coventry Cathedral of Canada: in both cases ruins were incorporated into the replacement. Étienne Gaboury rebuilt Saint-Boniface following Basil Spence's strategy at Coventry (1956–62). Both architects stabilized the ruins to create an enclosed commemorative precinct, for historical context and powerful counterpoint.

Before the mid-19th century, the number of clergy was inadequate to serve the population in any but the most densely settled areas, let alone to evangelize thinly populated regions. At St. Boniface, Manitoba (*see* p. 297), at the forks of the Red

Précieux-Sang, *St. Boniface, Manitoba; Roman Catholic. Brick and tile with glue-laminated beams, 1967–68; Étienne Gaboury, architect, with Denis L. Lussier*

FACING PAGE Précieux-Sang (Precious Blood) is "a temple to the transcendence of matter, ascension towards light, exaltation of spirit, a quest for the infinite." The architect furnished his own dramatic design for this stained-glass window of saturated colour: between divergent folds of the helical roof over the main entrance, it calls up a recurrent biblical metaphor of taking refuge in the shadow of the wings of the Lord.

FOLLOWING PAGE Précieux-Sang is a highly unconventional tour de force. It bursts with energy. The spiralling roof is supported by a pinwheel of 25 immense glulam beams (each 9 by 72 inches and 100 feet long). A simple altar is the unequivocal focus of this powerful 85-foot-high space.

Lady of the Lake Chapel, *Silton, Saskatchewan; Roman Catholic. Concrete, wood and steel, 1969; Clifford Wiens, architect*

RIGHT The Lady of the Lake Chapel stands above Saskatchewan Beach, a summer community (now becoming year-round) on Last Mountain Lake (seen in the distance). Viewed from the shore-access road, the peak of this seasonal chapel breaks the horizon.

FACING PAGE (ABOVE) Backless seating frames the glacial-erratic boulder that serves as an altar, features that contribute to the under-statement and naturalism of the structure. Looked at from below, the dark roof is a hollow pyramid, a primary geometric shape, remarkably pure, just visible in the reflected light.

FACING PAGE (BELOW) A discreet cross appears in the steel junction where four beams, which form a cross larger than the chapel itself, meet at the centre of the space.

and Assiniboine Rivers, the French, Scots and Métis felt abandoned. In 1818, Miles Macdonell, the Hudson's Bay Company governor, called for missionaries to help pacify the settlement after conflict arose between HBC and North West Company fur traders. Bishop Plessis of **Québec** sent Father Joseph-Norbert Provencher and two companions to establish a Roman Catholic mission. Lord Selkirk granted it 20 square miles opposite the HBC fort and the Selkirk settlement. Father Provencher was named auxiliary bishop for the entire Northwest in 1820. The energetic Alexandre-Antonin Taché arrived in 1845; he became Provencher's coadjutor, superior of the Oblates of Mary Immaculate and in 1853 bishop, while still in his twenties.

The third church at St. Boniface (1839) was a fortress-like stone cathedral (*see* p. 297). It burned down in 1860 and was replaced by a fourth church. Around these churches grew the francophone settlement of St. Boniface, now within metropolitan Winnipeg. Jean-Omer Marchand of Montréal, recently returned from the École des beaux-arts, Paris (*see* pp. 154, 156–57), designed the long and imposing fifth **Cathédrale de Saint-Boniface** (1906–07), which was executed in the finest Tyndall limestone. Marchand differentiated and integrated the complex elements in Beaux-Arts fashion: to carry the belfries, for instance, he used corner buttresses to define twin towers traditionally, then attached attenuated columns to these unconventionally. Wooden belfries, terminating in very Parisian tall domes, topped the towers.

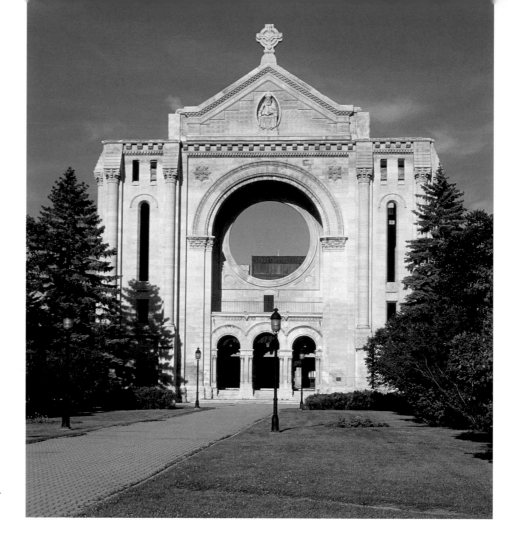

RIGHT **Cathédrale de Saint-Boniface**, *St. Boniface, Manitoba; Roman Catholic. Tyndall limestone, 1906–07 (burned 1968); Jean-Omer Marchand, architect*

In his Cathédrale de Saint-Boniface, Marchand joined three magnificent portals and grouped them with a deep-set circular window under a soaring arch, all detailed in understated Romanesque Revival style. A magisterial, larger-than-life bishop and missionary (patron of the city and church) is featured in the gable. Almost all the west facade survived a 1968 fire that destroyed the interior and large portions of the aisle walls.

FACING PAGE **Cathédrale de Saint-Boniface**, *Ruins of limestone (1906–07), reutilized, with glass-and-steel additions, 1970–72; Étienne J. Gaboury, architect*

One major key to the success of the present cathedral is the old, apparently windowless apse. Paradoxically, Gaboury used it to flood the sanctuary with light from an unseen source, in Baroque fashion. Fronting the uppermost cupped space, above the nave roof, is a plane of west-facing glass. Nothing detracts the eye from its gradually changing radiance, through the day and the seasons, cascading onto the altar. In the courtyard of Cathédrale de Saint-Boniface, short columns of brown-black Cor-Ten steel age gracefully, evoking stone predecessors and the western half of the old church. Beyond is the glass-walled narthex of the new church. While the stone storm porch offers a contrast, its random ashlar masonry matches the inner surface of the old walls. The narthex's shed roof of steel bends, rising seamlessly into the purist shape of the nave's pyramidal roof.

This strikingly vertical design dominated an exceedingly deep lawn (created by the demolition of the fourth church), extending to the river road. In 1968 fire devastated this cathedral, but the west end survived with the exception of the timber-framed belfries.

Gaboury's rebuilding (1970–72) was more radical than Spence's solution at Coventry because it set a low, square building of steel and glass under a short pyramidal roof within the eastern portion of the ruined nave, against the old apsidal sanctuary. He transformed the old nave's western section into a court open to the sky, recalling the atrium of an Early Christian basilica, such as Sant'Ambrogio in Milan (*see* p. 381). The result builds slowly and dramatically. At a distance, the old facade and its flanking conifers resemble a flat stage-set between curtains. Then, through the empty circular window, new elements appear tantalizingly and a steel truss is visible: replacing belfries, it carries bells behind the giant arch and above the great window. Marchand's crisp details and beautiful Tyndall limestone still register, but the entrance becomes truly theatrical when viewed diagonally.

The courtyard is an enclosure of broken walls with restricted lateral views yet, as in ancient sacred space, vaulted by the sky. Gaboury's pyramidal geometry maintains the court's openness, lifts the spirit and permits a glimpse of the east end's remains. An inviting glass-walled narthex steps forward under a shed roof and reaches laterally (beyond the old nave walls) to shepherd the flock toward the fold. Its compact interior is spacious, inviting and surprisingly bright. Gaboury's column-free nave, a little less than a square, is arranged transversely and is slightly wider than Marchand's cathedral — a major change from the profound axiality of

St. Nicholas', *Winnipeg, Manitoba; Ukrainian Catholic.*
Concrete, 1964–66; Green Blankstein Russell, architects

St. Nicholas' respect for context is typical of the best work of the 1960s: conspicuous on its corner lot, the church recedes across a slightly elevated forecourt, without overwhelming Bannerman Avenue. An administrative wing, chapel and monastery (on the left side of this inverted L-shaped complex) step toward the sidewalk, in line and in scale with neighbouring houses. The open bell tower, a ladder-like concrete structure near the intersection, was added in 1968.

Greek-cross plans of five squares are traditional in western Ukraine's stone churches in the Ternopil' district. St. Nicholas' related plan is executed in High Modernism's untraditional forms and technology: tall barrel vaults — accented by rainbows of stained glass — spring from low walls in its very short arms while an enormous reinforced-concrete dome covers the nave (in the crossing), a moving auditorium for 825 souls.

the former long, thin nave and flanking aisles — while its roof ridge is almost as high as the old walls. Gaboury retained the apse and installed semicircular seating in the nave, with the altar almost at the geometric focus of both. The organ console is nearly central, in the front row of seats beside the nave alley, and the choir joins the congregation at the front. The auditorium is informal and domestic, encouraging a sense of community and giving priority to the sacraments. Like other Gaboury churches, an important cycle of stained glass is included: transparent and stained glass was installed in Saint-Boniface's side walls, superimposing the Passion on the surrounding landscape in partly abstract, partly expressionist idiom. Gaboury won the commission for the stained glass in competition in 1984, a dozen years after the cathedral's completion.

From the threshold to the moving band of light high in the apse, Marchand and Gaboury's Saint-Boniface is rich in highlight and shadow, reminding us that imagery of light and darkness recurs in scripture and devotional literature. Saint Ambrose (d. 397), for example, speaks of "Splendour and glory of the Father, the light out of which light comes … dawn of the day's brightness. … May the day go joyously in the morning of purity, in the high noon of faith and without nightfall upon the spirit." St. Bernard of Clairvaux (1090–1153) comments, "The approach is not by a physical progression, but by flashes of succeeding light, and these are not corporal but spiritual. … The soul must seek light by following the light."

Eastern-rite churches in the West have also experimented successfully with modern adaptations of traditional forms. **St. Nicholas', Winnipeg**, blends ethnic vernacular with other historicism to express contemporary architectural and liturgical ideals. It draws on classicizing conventions, two centuries ago, with large vaulted spaces in "paper architecture," so called because it was impossible to achieve until the improvement of concrete technology early in the 20th century.

Sherwood Park Alliance, *Edmonton, Alberta; (Christian and Missionary) Alliance. Brick and steel, 1979–81 (with later additions); Kim Lau, architect*
This church on Edmonton's fringe shows the size, complexity and visibility characteristic of many modern suburban churches. The semicircular building on the right contains the sanctuary; the school and gymnasiums are on the left; and common administrative areas are in the middle. Its auditorium, which seats about 1,700 persons, is entirely without windows, giving the impression of a theatre inside.

Ukrainians began settling in northern Winnipeg in 1895 and built a small church in 1899–1900. Their third St. Nicholas' documents progress through the generations in contrast with early Manitoban Ukrainian churches, a transition from Old World subsistence farming to affluent Winnipeg's commercial, financial and professional world. Alex Nitchuk, a parishioner, and Bernard Brown shared the project for one of Winnipeg's leading firms, Green Blankstein Russell.

St. Nicholas' reinforced concrete faced with Manitoba Tyndall limestone is structurally ambitious. While the exterior also bubbles with large fibreglass orbs over the four corners, echoing small traditional wood-and-tin *bani*, concrete vaults rise around the dome. The underlying geometric basis echoes Étienne Boullée's metropolitan cathedral (projected 1781) and Claude-Nicolas Ledoux's 1804 church plans for his ideal town, Chaux. Avant-garde International Style building of the 1950s and 60s, like Toronto City Hall, influenced concrete-shell technology.

Internally, equally smooth arched forms of Modernist purism develop from the tabernacle (a small-scale replica of the church) through the baldachin (a fibreglass canopy modelled on a sail vault), and the barrel vault of the sanctuary, to the all-embracing dome. Instead of an iconostasis, a few icons on pedestals contribute an unaccustomed openness, while the sanctuary is lifted up and the altar drawn forward in a treatment paralleling the widespread influence of Vatican II. This is a place of worship that expresses its tradition, its place and its time.

Holy Family Parish, *Medicine Hat, Alberta; Roman Catholic. Brick and stucco with steel frame, 2004–05; Michael Boreskie, with Sahuri, Hutchinson, Brzezinski, architects*

There is a sense of amplitude and generosity in the large church built for Holy Family Parish. Inside, this is enhanced by an inviting narthex, and especially by the inclusion of a number of sculptures—including the 14 Stations of the Cross—by Timothy Schmalz.

Church design, especially in growing suburban evangelical churches, has changed in a generation. **Sherwood Park Alliance, Edmonton**, is a typical example of the momentum toward size, complexity, visibility and windowless auditoriums. The Christian and Missionary Alliance in its early days had a kind of revival flair, deriving from A. B. Simpson (1843–1919), an influential maritime Presbyterian. That zeal is retained in this prominent church in Edmonton's affluent Sherwood Park. The church exudes self-confidence within its traditional missionary role. Looking at first glance a little like a shopping centre at a major intersection, when considered more carefully the building is both coherent and complex: church facilities, a secondary school with two large gymnasiums, a primary school (a new one will soon be built) and — providing needed social services across the intersection — a warehouse for skateboarders, mountain bikers and computer nuts. The elements in the main building are unified by repetitive use of circular towers and a restrained palette of materials: brick-red tile walls, green metal siding, and white superstructures. This megachurch's auditorium originally held 2200, it now holds fewer as a result of redesign, and is a windowless half-circle amphitheatre in plan. The theatre approach is carried through in its atrium or narthex, an important multifunctional space with a large glass skylight, typical of many new churches where the atrium or narthex becomes a major activity centre. Inside, the amphitheatre focuses on a rugged cross sitting on the stage, about the right size for a Roman crucifixion, making an unusual symbolic attempt to reproduce how crosses were fashioned and located. At **Holy Family Church**, **Medicine Hat**, Alberta, a large Roman Catholic church followed a more limited version of the same approach, with a similar large narthex and amphitheatre, with a better use of windows and skylights and an exceptional use of sculpture.

Sts. Peter and Paul, *Mundare, Alberta; Ukrainian Catholic. Brick, 1968–69; Eugene Olekshy, architect*
While the interior of the Mundare church has the distinctive feel of a Ukrainian church, the exterior departs from traditional forms. It retains the freestanding bell tower, though the form is unusual: tall, open, with the bell hung low and an open dome. The church, too, is untraditional, with octagonal low brick sidewalls supporting a low roof around the perimeter; the central section of the roof is higher, capped by another open dome with eight legs.

St. Stephen Protomartyr, *Calgary, Alberta; Ukrainian Catholic. Brick, 1978-82; Radoslav Zuk, with McMillan Long, architects*

Radoslav Zuk of Montreal won the Governor General's Medal for Architecture in 1986 for this modern appropriation of traditional Byzantine design. The church was listed in the Royal Architectural Institute of Canada's selection of the top 500 architectural projects in Canada during the 20th century, a rare honour in the last quarter-century for churches, which now seem ignored in competitions.

FACING PAGE Zuk's daring interpretation of the typical Byzantine-inspired dome can be understood easily in this photograph, which shows how he cut the dome into four sections, all huddling together but at different elevations.

A smaller rural church, **Sts. Peter and Paul**, **Mundare**, Alberta, replaced a church of 1910 that now sits beside the new church. The monastery of the Basilian Fathers, a Ukrainian Catholic missionary order that has worked in Alberta since 1902, and a museum that displays the history of Ukrainian settlement in the area are adjacent. The church by Eugene Olekshy reconceives traditional Ukrainian forms: outside, a central dome, more implied than stated, and a tall open bell tower in brick, repeating the form of the church's open dome; inside, an octagonal plan with almost circular seating and a dark, enclosed space, with frescoes and stained-glass windows to complement an ornate imported chandelier and the icon of the Mother of God of Pochaiv.

St. Stephen Protomartyr, Calgary, by Radoslav Zuk, is a self-assured, vigorous late 20th-century building that faces its residential neighbourhood with warm brown brick both outside and inside. Cedar shakes on the roof, cedar ceilings inside and cedar siding harmonize with copper roofing on the towers. The anticipated dome is unexpectedly sliced into four quarter-domes reaching upwards on towers of different heights, a kind of spiral to heaven. The interior space that soars up into the tower "recalls the traditional canopy over the altar. The choir is on a mezzanine … clearly visible to the nave."

Ukrainians illustrate how communities that once introduced the traditions of their homeland later adapt to the culture and the aesthetic of their adoptive country, without giving up their original architectural forms. A century after their humble efforts to repeat what they knew at home, they had developed a sure touch with forms and styles still authentically their own, but utilizing new materials and methods of construction.

CHANGES

So, after all, we did gather up his [Polycarp's] bones — more precious to us than jewels, and finer than pure gold — and we laid them to rest in a spot suitable for the purpose. There we shall assemble, as occasion allows, with glad rejoicings; and with the Lord's permission we shall celebrate the birthday of his martyrdom.

— The Martyrdom of Polycarp (died ca 155)

Changes

THE CHURCHES DESCRIBED AND ILLUSTRATED in the previous chapters are Christian churches. They express in built form communal belief in God and devotion to Jesus. Christianity maintains Judaism's convictions about God, Scripture and ethical behaviour; but by the late-second century Christianity and Judaism had effectively parted company. Sharing of structures may have happened in the very early period, though we have no evidence of this. In one case (*see* pp. 26–27) we note a modern building designed for use jointly by both Christians and Jews; in a couple of other cases Jewish synagogues were adapted for Christian use (*see* pp. 264– 66). Certainly Christians and Jews built in parallel fashion for a period, but as the church departed more and more from the synagogue — facing new organizational, practical and aesthetic questions — Christians drew ever more heavily on Roman forms and building techniques. By the end of the reign of Constantine (ca 285–337), with its endorsement of Christianity, churches had become so grand and sumptuous they would hardly have been recognizable to earlier generations.

Origins

Houses

The first meetings of believers were in houses, according to the New Testament: "Aquila and Priscilla and the church that meets in their house" (1 Corinthians 16:19); "the house of Titius Justus, next to the synagogue" (Acts 18:7). Archaeology suggests the earliest remains of a house-church are at **Dura Europos**, a Roman garrison town on the Euphrates River in Syria, where a church, a synagogue and cults such as Mithraism all adapted existing houses to their religious needs. Christians often depended on wealthy believers to host meetings and meals, and

PREVIOUS PAGE **Monastery**, *Khirbet Qumran, West Bank; Jewish. Stone and mud brick, 200–100 B.C. (destroyed A.D. 69); builders unknown*

The buildings at Qumran show how religious groups lived 2000 years ago when they withdrew from society. This Jewish monastic group may have been a model for Christian monasteries when they developed in the third century A.D. Like later Christians, the Qumran "monks" spent their days in worship, study, copying of scrolls and interpretation of Scripture. The buildings (on the left of the image) are silhouetted against the Dead Sea; on the other shore is Jordan.

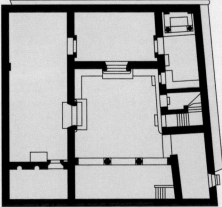

House-Church, *Dura Europos, Syria; Christian. Stone and mud brick, built ca A.D. 230, adapted as a church ca 240; builder unknown*

The earliest known remains of a church are at Dura Europos, on the Euphrates River. An early Christian group converted a house, built against the city wall, into a church. The courtyard in the foreground led to a suite of rooms, perhaps the women's quarters, which were adapted for worship. The room on the right held a baptistery embellished with frescoes that are now in the possession of Yale University.

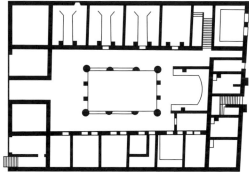

Housebuilders' association, *Ostia, Italy. Brick with marble, early second century A.D.; builder unknown*

This small association building displays typical features: a central courtyard with a series of dining rooms on either side, a few ancillary spaces and a discreet entrance from the street, along whose frontage there were shops for rent. A second floor might have apartments, either for the association's officers or for rental purposes.

FACING PAGE **Basilica**, *Trier, Germany; Protestant. Brick, ca 310 A.D.; Constantine the Great, patron*

Now used as a Protestant church, the majestic basilica was built as Constantine's throne room and was decorated sumptuously with gold, marble and mosaics. Though a basilica, it lacks the columns, aisles and galleries of most basilicas. It demonstrates clearly how churches were closely modelled on imperial prototypes, making a strong political statement about their status and function from the fourth century on.

eventually perhaps to donate the house to the group. The Dura house was built about 230, extensively modified ten years later for Christian use and destroyed with the rest of the city in 256. Other Christians met in upper-class urban houses with fine dining rooms, in village houses (the "house of Peter" in Capernaum), in small apartments in multi-story buildings (Rome's "titulus churches"), in shops (Corinth) or outdoors.

Associations

Roman society was held together by associations, including trade unions, ethnic groups, religious and funerary clubs and philosophical clubs. Some associations, such as the **Housebuilders' Association, Ostia**, had purpose-built structures; others used a patron's house. Excavations carried out in Ostia disclosed the meeting places of 59 associations, ranging from one or two rooms to complexes with courtyards, gardens, dining rooms and rental properties. Ephesus had 60 association buildings, attested in inscriptions that often note the group's purposes and rules. One inscription describes members' donations of columns, areas of mosaic floor, bricks, roof tiles and money. Church meeting places were indistinguishable from associations, filling the same communal functions, including burials and meals and worship.

Basilicas

When Jews built monumental buildings in the first century B.C., they sometimes utilized simplified basilicas, with nave, aisles, apse and clerestory. Basilican synagogues were common by the second and third centuries A.D. When Christians began to build monumentally in the third century they followed the synagogue design. Archaeologists have discovered a purpose-built basilican church from about 290 at Aqaba, Jordan. Constantine and his mother, Helena, built glorious structures in the 320s and 330s at Bethlehem, Jerusalem, Rome and Trier, which led

to a frenzy of copycat basilica building. Monumental basilicas swept simpler structures off the ecclesiastical map.

Memorials

The only challenge to the basilica's dominance was the octagonal or round memorial (*martyrium*). Its form focused on a special place within the structure. In contrast to the basilica's horizontal axis, memorials emphasized the vertical link between God and the cave, miracle site, grave or martyr's shrine on which the church was built. Memorials were usually domed to underscore their centralized focus. Initially the octagon was preferred, as in Capernaum's church, built to memorialize the place of one of Jesus' healings.

Memorials and basilicas were sometimes linked. When Constantine built the **Church of the Nativity in Bethlehem** (339), he linked an octagon to shelter the cave of Jesus' birth with a basilica to shelter pilgrims. He also covered two Jerusalem sites recalling Jesus' death with the Church of the Holy Sepulchre: a circular memorial covered Jesus' tomb; a few yards away exposed rocks marked the site of Golgotha; and a basilica held the throngs of pilgrims. Often memorial spaces had imaginative roofs or domes, first found in southern Syria (**Bostra Cathedral**) resulting eventually in stunning Byzantine churches. Islamic buildings, including Jerusalem's Dome of the Rock, later used this form.

Monasteries

Two kinds of Christian monasteries developed in the late third century in Egypt and Palestine. Coenobitic ("communal" from *koinos*) monasteries served close-knit communities; they were usually walled, with a large basilica, refectory, workrooms and library. Eremitic ("desert" from *erêmos*) monasteries fostered solitary contemplation in a cave or hut for six days, then on Sunday all members of the community came together at the mother house to eat and worship. The *laura* (cluster of cells and mother house) resembled a mother hen with chicks.

The model for these Christian monasteries is uncertain, but two examples suggest Judaism as the source. **Qumran** (*see* pp. 368–69), home of the Dead Sea Scrolls, was a coenobitic and largely male Jewish monastery with refectory, meeting rooms, kitchen, workrooms, stable and ritual bathing pools. The **Therapeutae**, by contrast, were an

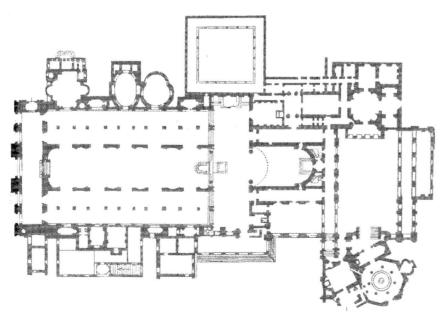

FACING PAGE **Church of the Holy Nativity**, *Bethlehem, West Bank; Christian. Stone, after 529; Justinian (built on surviving remains of Constantine's church of 339)*

The great Constantinian church does not survive intact, though some parts of the present building are from the fourth century. Constantine's octagon over the cave has been replaced with a central apse and two side apses. The function of the structure derives from the growing importance of pilgrims who wished to visit sites associated with Jesus' life, here a cave below the chancel floor.

ABOVE **St. John Lateran** (**San Giovanni in Laterano**), *Rome, Italy; Christian. Brick, 314–18; Constantine the Great, patron*

St. John Lateran, to one side of central Rome, shows another Constantinian approach to the combining of linear basilica — the earliest Christian basilica in Rome and also the cathedral for the city of Rome — and octagon. The octagon is the baptistery (315–24), turned into a major element in the composition by virtue of its location in the streetscape (lower right on plan).

eremitic — and mixed male and female — group located near Alexandria. Philo describes their buildings in the first century, though no remains have survived.

There was more than one theological imperative for church design. The fundamental point was to build a "house for the congregation" (*domus ecclesiae*) like an association, rather than a "house for the god" (*domus dei*) like a Roman temple. The early church's need for group cohesion was expressed through provision for baptism, worship, study, social service and outreach. The ways early church architecture met these needs persist today.

Byzantine

Constantine

The Byzantine period begins with Constantine, who ruled from 306 to 337. He rehabilitated Rome's exhausted and fractured society, first by tolerating Christianity in 313, then in 324 by establishing an eastern capital at Byzantium (renamed Constantinople, now Istanbul) and finally by calling a council at Nicaea in 325 to reach consensus on doctrinal issues. His architects linked state power and

Monastery of St. Simeon Stylites, *Qalaat Samaan, Syria; Christian. Stone, 476–92; builders unknown*

Behind the massive facade of St. Simeon in northern Syria are four basilicas radiating from a central octagon that housed the remains of the pillar on which Saint Simeon Stylites ("column sitter") lived for 38 years. Saint Simeon was the best-known person of his day and the monastery was an immensely popular pilgrimage centre for Christians looking for meaning in a disintegrating world. The basilicas could function together — in which case an apse at one end served as the liturgical centre — or separately.

Cathedral of Sts. Sergius, Bacchus and Leontius,
*Bostra (now Bosra), Syria; Syrian Christian. Stone,
488–512; builder unknown*

The first experiments in centrally planned
churches were carried out in Syria, utilizing late-Roman
techniques of roofing large spaces and adopting
Roman canons of taste in dynamic spatial relationships.
Bostra Cathedral's form is a large circular space within
a square whose corners are occupied with niches
within niches. An apse, flanking apsidal chapels and
two service areas occupy the front wall.

LEFT Concentric with the circle, on plan, a quatrefoil
inner structure revolves around four L-shaped piers —
supporting the dome — and columns. The dome, as
shown in the section (below), was probably a conical
wooden structure, though some reconstructions show
it as a concrete dome. The archaeological evidence is
inconclusive.

St. Catherine's Monastery, *Mount Sinai, Egypt;*
Greek Orthodox. Basalt, 548–65; Stephen of Aila

St. Catherine's, one of the most important
monasteries in the history of Christianity and famous
for its manuscript library, is in a desolate valley below
Mount Sinai, where Moses received the Law from God.
The rugged reddish mountains around it create an
awe-inspiring setting for the events of the Exodus.
Many monasteries were walled, like St. Catherine's,
giving the impression of a fortress.

ecclesiastical goals through form, volume, size, decoration and detail of the buildings they designed. Emphasizing the analogies between political and church power,
they built massive structures and vaulted huge spaces in ever larger basilicas, especially in the Latin west, and increasingly creative centralized spaces in the east.

St. John Lateran (**San Giovanni in Laterano**), the earliest Constantinian basilica
in Rome (314–18), included a basilica and an octagonal baptistery, whereas old St.
Peter's in Rome (Basilica di San Pietro in Vaticano) was still a typically Roman basilica. In a new design departure, St. Peter's (begun in 320) had mini-naves at right
angles to the main nave, forming transepts that focused on the altar. **Santa
Costanza**, the burial place of Constantine's daughter Constantia, also blended the
old with the new: the form is a classic circular mausoleum but the interior has 12
pairs of granite columns with massive imposts that carry the brick arcade and
drum, with windows to light the central space (*see* p. 386).

Meanwhile, the dramatic possibilities of centrally focused buildings were being
explored in the east. At the rural Syrian site, **Qalaat Samaan**, where Saint Simeon
Stylites (died 459) lived on a pillar (Greek, *stylos*), a central octagon — roofed with

a wooden pyramidal covering — linked four basilicas in the form of a huge cross. The Church of the Prophets, Apostles and Martyrs (464) in Gerasa (Jerash) also experimented with a cross-shaped and colonnaded form and a pyramidal roof at the crossing. The most influential eastern experiment, however, was **Bostra** (Bosra) **Cathedral** (completed 512), where a large circle (118 feet in diameter) was inserted into a square, amplified with three apses. The playful central space was carried on piers and columns, arranged in a quatrefoil form, and its restlessness was emphasized by niches filling the square's corners.

The late fifth and early sixth century was also a formative period for Christian monasteries. Mar Saba (begun 483), the most influential, is also one of the few still functioning in the Judean wilderness. Mar Saba combines both eremitic and coenobitic traditions, with individual cells and caves across from the mother house. Justinian's **St. Catherine Monastery, Mount Sinai** (548–65) — walled, self-contained, centred on its basilican church and still functioning — is in the coenobitic tradition. The church's west facade is marked distinctively with flanking towers.

From the late sixth century, surprisingly, there were monasteries on Ireland's

Gallarus Oratory, *Dingle Peninsula, Ireland; Christian. Dry stone, 9th century or earlier; builder unknown*

Beehive houses (from the sixth century) and church buildings, such as here, were built of thin courses of corbelled stones in a mortar-free construction, providing a dry and warm interior. Ireland had Christian monasteries from the fifth century onward, drawn from Western Europe but in turn nurturing the cultural and theological roots of western European civilization during the Dark Ages, when the influences moved in the other direction.

Haghia Sophia, *Istanbul, Turkey; Byzantine Christian (then mosque, now museum). Stone, brick and concrete, 532–37; Anthemius of Tralles and Isidorus of Miletus, architects for Justinian*

The Haghia Sophia's interior is shocking in its volume, complexity and movement. No building has been more influential in the history of architecture for the way it merges a domed and centred space with a linear spatial development through a series of diminishing volumes along an axis.

The exterior seems a massive blob of concrete, brick and stone, hardly expressive of its glorious interior, though its dome indicates the size and height of this brilliant experiment. Part of its attraction is its setting in Istanbul, at one side of the central open space, near the Topkapi and overlooking the Bosphorus.

Dingle Peninsula and Skellig Islands. They were small clusters of beehive houses or cells with a small church, such as the later **Gallarus Oratory**, built in the same style. The beehive structures were built of meticulously laid up dry-stone walls with no mortar. Each course of stone was laid sloping down and out, so water could not be driven in by wind and rain. Missionaries began arriving in Ireland in the late fourth century from France, and monasteries began soon after. The beehive form probably came from the Mediterranean, since the same form is found in southern Italy and north central Syria, among other places.

Justinian

Justinian (ruled 527–65) imitated Constantine's ambitious artistic and architectural programs. In addition to rebuilding Constantine's **Church of the Holy Nativity, Bethlehem**, he was responsible for the **Haghia Sophia, Istanbul** (Santa Sophia; 532–37 and 558–63), the most influential church structure of the last 1500 years. Haghia Sophia's huge cubical volume was surmounted by a massive dome more than 104 feet in diameter, flanked by two semi-domes, stabilized by six low rectangles around the edges, and further complicated by niches. The design geniuses of its overpowering spatial effects — Anthemius of Tralles, Isidore of Miletus, and Justinian himself — juxtaposed verticality (the dome's height was almost 185 feet) and directionality (the sequence of narthex, semi-domes, central square and apse). Natural light enters from windows in the drum under the main dome, two semi-circular tympana, semi-domes, apse and niches. The plain exterior deliberately contrasts with the sculptured interior featuring richly decorated walls (gold, glass mosaics and frescoes), floors (mosaics and marble *opus sectile*), furnishings (ivory, marble and silver plate), lamps (bronze and silver), sculpture, glass and illuminated manuscripts, all set off by a scintillating use of natural light. This mature Byzantine building is the prototype of subsequent efforts to unite the architectural, sculptural and decorative arts in one building.

Haghia Sophia was the high point of incorporating icons in architecture. In the following century an iconoclastic controversy rocked the Eastern Church, when some church fathers argued that icons should be rejected on the grounds of Old Testament prohibitions against images and the superstitions attached to them. In 730 icons were prohibited; they were reinstated in 787 by the Council of Nicaea (which also condemned inconoclasts), forbidden again in 815 and reinstated in 843. Since then the Eastern Church has consistently approved their use.

Medieval

Despite the architectural importance of imaginative experiments in centralized plans, the rectangular basilica remained dominant in both East and West. The explanation is simple: basilicas were easy to build and "provided the maximum effect for the minimum effort," as Cyril Mango says. When Europe's intellectual and spiritual life emerged from the Dark Ages, after controversies, religious changes, invasions and decline, the West was influenced afresh by Roman and Byzantine forms. This influence originated in Sicily and northern Italy, beginning about the ninth century. By 1100 Crusaders brought back first-hand knowledge of the Holy Land; they encouraged pilgrimages, fostered cults of relics and encouraged monasticism. But much had been lost. Architecturally the imaginative concrete technology developed in the Roman and Byzantine periods had disappeared. New construction techniques, particularly ribbed stone vaults, were invented but concrete did not reappear until the 19th century (*see* pp. 159–67).

Romanesque

Romanesque architecture's formal continuity with Byzantium can be seen in **Sant' Ambrogio, Milan**, a brick basilica of the 11th and 12th centuries preceded by an atrium, like St. Peter's in Rome seven centuries earlier. The facade and the flanking towers are fresh, but the nave arcade and the octagonal crossing tower with its vault echo Roman practice. Its plan — a continuous narthex and nave, aisles half the width of the nave bays, and three apses — borrows heavily from Roman basilicas. Pisa Cathedral (1063–1118) also has a simple basilican plan with transepts and a tim-ber-framed trussed roof. But the scheme's complexity is remarkable, with a separate

Sant'Ambrogio (St. Ambrose), *Milan, Italy; Roman Catholic. Brick, 9th–11th centuries; builder unknown*
The 9th century campanile predates the rest of the early Romanesque building; the plan is traditional, with an atrium in front of a basilica. The main facade has an unusual double arcade in red brick that follows the slope of the gable and is integrated into the atrium's colonnade. The church itself is a late Roman basilica, with later interior elements by Donato Bramante.

baptistery (1153), campanile (the leaning tower, 1174) and flanking loggia of the Campo Santo (1278), all ornamentally encrusted.

Germany's Aachen Cathedral, an octagonal domed basilica (790–800) began as Charlemagne's chapel and tomb. It was developed as a cathedral for royal coronations and, from 1349, became an important pilgrimage site. It was expanded in the 14th and 15th centuries with the addition of a choir hall and chapels in the then fashionable Gothic style. In France, Saint-Sernin in Toulouse (1080–1120) is an almost purely Romanesque pilgrimage church built on an expanded Latin-cross plan with five aisles; the nave's double side aisles are followed by single aisles around transepts and apse, permitting pilgrims a continuous path around the church interior. The nave's groined barrel vault changes at the crossing into an octagonal ribbed vault that springs from massive arches. Radiating chapels and a clerestory roof point toward later Gothic developments.

Durham Cathedral in northern England (1093–1130) shows the distinctive marks of English Romanesque: more elaborate ribbed groin vaults, elongated nave and double towers on the western elevation flanking a large rose window. The three-story nave arcade has alternating round and composite columns supporting the vault, gallery and clerestory windows. Ely Cathedral's awesomely long Romanesque nave (1100–1189) is trumped by its most unusual element, the Gothic replacement of the original Romanesque tower over the crossing — an octagonal stone lantern with a brilliantly framed timber roof whose windows flood the crossing with light. Some Romanesque churches borrowed from the Crusaders' experiences in the Holy Land, such as Cambridge's small Church of the Holy Sepulchre ("The Round Church," 1130), intentionally mimicking Jerusalem's Church of the Holy Sepulchre, which had recently been retaken by the Crusaders (1099).

Wells Cathedral, *Wells, England; Anglican (previously Roman Catholic). Stone, begun 1180 (west facade, 1209–50); Adam Lock, master mason*

The west facade of Wells Cathedral, designed with 500 niches for sculptured stone figures of saints and great persons, was intended as a backdrop for ecclesiastical processions. This extensive program of decoration was probably not completed but about 300 statues survive; originally they were colourfully painted and highlighted with gold leaf.

The unique scissors truss in the interior was an emergency addition about a century later, when a tall spire over the crossing of nave and transepts was attempted. Its construction de-stabilized the structure, with the result that structural necessity helped create one of the most unusual Gothic interiors.

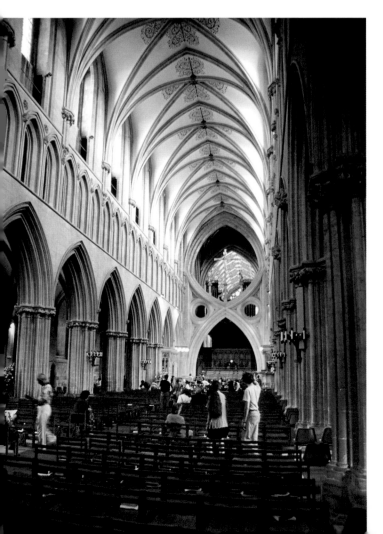

Gothic

As Christian Norberg-Schulz puts it, "Romanesque architecture … fulfils the promise of the early Christian churches, and prepares for the vision of heaven offered by the Gothic cathedral." The well-known characteristics of Gothic architecture (12th to 15th centuries) — complex vaulting, soaring heights, dramatic lighting, exuberant decoration — were rooted in Romanesque experiments. Stone construction was creatively developed to span large spaces and to open up large windows in the walls to permit natural light to enter. **Wells Cathedral** (1209–50) was the first English cathedral built entirely in the Gothic manner. Its animated west front is 150 feet wide and 100 feet high, with almost 300 of the original 500 larger

Milan Cathedral, *Milan, Italy; Roman Catholic. Stone, 1387 onward; Simone da Orsegnigo (and many others), master mason*

The late Gothic facade of Milan Cathedral is unlike any other in the vitality of its four-story elevation and the organization of its ornate decoration. It was very slow to be completed, and though a large number of master masons were involved in the work, it has retained a remarkably unified design. A walk on the roof permits one to look down on the city through a forest of pinnacles.

than life-size statues remaining. The unique interior has mid-14th century scissor arches to shore up the crossing, whose vaulting anticipates the mature fan vaulting of King's College Chapel. Salisbury Cathedral (1220–58) is a model of order in its beautifully preserved Cathedral Close. Its spire, at 404 feet (completed 1330), is the tallest medieval structure in the world. A three-aisled nave and four square-ended transepts lead on a seemingly never-ending path through a dramatic choir and the square-ended Trinity Chapel ... and beyond.

Notre Dame de Paris (1163–1285) was completed as Paris took centre stage in European politics and commerce. Its five-aisled plan sweeps around a full-width apse, incorporating transepts as a minor element within the nave. As the nave arcade rises it steps inward with a gallery on the second level and a magnificent clerestory on the third level, all supported by daring flying buttresses that allowed huge windows to be placed in the wall.

More memorable, however, than the individual features of such Gothic buildings is the presence of the cathedral in the urban plan, dominating the rest of the town or city. In Italy the Duomo (Siena Cathedral, begun 1226) sits unforgettably on a broad platform hovering over the city. A grand reconstruction project, begun in 1321 but never completed, was to have incorporated the Duomo as the transepts of the Duomo Nuovo, but the project was abandoned and the high Gothic west front (1284–1310) was an addition. The best known late Gothic structure, however, is **Milan Cathedral** (1387 to 19th century), with its lacy marble-over-brick exterior, enormous size, window tracery and forest of pinnacles. In England, **King's College Chapel**, **Cambridge**, begun by Henry VI and finished by Henry VII and Henry VIII, plays the same role. Exhibiting a powerful purity of design, the high rectangular space (290 by 40 feet) is roofed by elegant fan vaulting, with about two-thirds of its exterior walls glazed with late-medieval stained glass, virtually all of which has survived. Surprisingly, the chapel remains almost as it was built. Some alterations are complex: the crucifix on the rood screen, for example, was removed by Edward VI, restored by Mary, altered by Elizabeth, elaborated by Archbishop Laud, and removed once again by Oliver Cromwell. Though Cromwell destroyed many decorative windows elsewhere, the windows of King's survived.

Reformation and Baroque

King's College Chapel marks the effective end of Gothic architecture. Beginning about 1400, humanism triggered an enthusiasm for things classical. But that classicism was linked with interests in exploration, science, individuality and secularism. Humanism bridged the gap between medieval and modern approaches, between supernaturalism and naturalism. This "renaissance" initiated debates about faith and reason that were accelerated by the invention of the printing press which disseminated religious, political and secular texts, including classical literature, in the original language and in translation. The Renaissance's questioning of traditional authority contributed to the 16th-century Protestant Reformation and the 17th-century Catholic Counter-Reformation that followed. Both influenced religious thinking, ecclesiastical organizations and church building, eventually leading to the dynamism of 18th-century Baroque architecture. This was precisely the period

FACING PAGE **King's College Chapel**, *Cambridge, England; Anglican (previously Roman Catholic). Stone, 1446–1515; Reginald Ely, master mason*
The form of King's has, for a late Gothic building, an almost modern feel. Its almost purely rectangular plan has small cells down both sides and a nearly rectangular cross-section. There are no columns obtruding in the space; the only division is the organ screen (1533–36) in about the middle of the structure, dividing nave from choir, between which there is no difference except for the stalls.

BELOW King's exterior is almost as simplified as its plan and section. The dominant impression is its verticality, especially of its immense windows filling almost completely every inch between its soaring buttresses, which are each topped with a tall pinnacle. The four corners of the building are each marked by another very much larger pinnacle, almost a tower.

when Canada's earliest churches were built, and thus it is these movements that were most influential in the period of first settlement.

Renaissance

The cultural rebirth known as the Renaissance began in Italy, where Roman civilization and architecture were part of the ancient fabric. When Brunelleschi designed Florence's Church of San Spirito (1434-82) and the octagonal dome of Florence Cathedral (1436), he signalled a classical approach to spatial integrity and the beginning of a new architectural epoch. Bramante's design for a new **St. Peter's Basilica in Rome** (ca 1506), subsequently modified by Michelangelo and Giacomo della Porta, includes a dome 138 feet in diameter and 390 feet above the floor, supported on 60-foot-square piers. Built of brick and stone, it is many times the weight of the similar-sized Pantheon in Rome, which is made of concrete (11,000 tons versus 3,000 tons). In the next generation, Andrea Palladio's influential villa designs set a pattern for broader architectural movements in the English-speaking world, where the facade corresponded to the interior details.

Reformation

Renaissance scholarly humanism triggered a religious reform based on reading and interpreting Scripture in the original Hebrew and Greek, largely free of traditional church interpretations. This Reformation, rooted in Bohemia, Switzerland, Germany, Holland and England in the 15th and early 16th centuries, took many forms, ranging from pietist movements such as the Moravian Brethren, left-wing movements such as Mennonites and Hutterites, Lutherans, Presbyterians and Reformed churches. Anglicans viewed themselves as somewhere between Roman Catholics and Reformers. The earliest architectural expressions of Reformation principles are found in modifications to old structures, which give new meanings to old elements, such as the relocation of altar, pulpit and baptismal font; the removal of barriers between clergy and people; the elimination of images and relics of saints; the reduction in the medieval sense of mystery and the implementation of new liturgies. For example, the small Gothic parish church of St. Edward, King and Martyr, in Cambridge was conservatively altered, as Will Dowsing's diary reports: "1643, January 1. Edward's parish, we diged up the steps, and brake down 40 pictures, and took of 10 superstitious inscriptions."

Counter-Reformation and Baroque

The Roman Catholic Church replied to the Reformation with progressive reforms and reactionary responses. The Society of Jesus (Jesuits), founded by Ignatius Loyola in the 1530s and recognized officially a decade later, aimed for strict obedience to the Church and the Pope and was influential in New France's development. Other orders also called for religious renewal, among them the Ursulines, who were particularly important among Québec's women and children (*see* pp. 124–27). The Council of Trent (1545–47, 1551–52, 1562–63) advanced the program of renewal, urging faith, grace and sacraments; rebuking corruption of the clergy; encouraging pastoral care and urging missionary work.

Though the Counter-Reformation's architectural expression in Baroque design (ca 1600–1750) is sometimes dismissed, the style has excitement, movement, colour,

FACING PAGE **Piranesi etchings**
TOP **Veduta interna della Basilica di S[an]. Pietro in Vaticano**, *interior view of St. Peter's in the Vatican*
BOTTOM **Veduta interna del Sepolcro di S[anta]. Costanza**, *interior view of the tomb of St. Costantia [Rome]*
A prolific master of drawing, Giambattista Piranesi (1720–78) produced a series of etched views of Rome in the 1740s, concentrating on both ruins and still-standing buildings. His drawings were marked by a high degree of accuracy, while exploiting their dramatic potential and romanticizing some of their features. His view of the interior of St. Peter's, Rome (top) highlights the baldachin of 1624–33 by Gianlorenzo Bernini. He exaggerates the building's length, but gives a wonderfully complex impression of the nave arcades' scale and the barrel vault. The etching of the interior of **Santa Costanza** (lower), exaggerates the height slightly by reducing the size of the figures. Nevertheless, he captures the architectural essence of the memorial to Constantine's daughter, with its central dome of about 70 feet diameter, its paired Corinthian columns and its dramatic use of light.

BELOW **St. Paul's Cathedral**, *London, England; Anglican. Stone, 1673–74; Christopher Wren, architect*
Wren produced a number of schemes for St. Paul's, including the first one, illustrated here, "the great model," not built, that emphasizes the degree to which he was influenced by Baroque sensibilities. Its large central dome, which centres a bilaterally symmetrical plan, is supported on eight great hollowed-out piers, with four subsidiary domes on the diagonals, linked with mathematical precision through the centres of the piers (*see* plan below). His Baroque approach is equally evident in the external form.

James Gibbs, *Book of Architecture*, 1728
James Gibbs' *Book of Architecture* was deeply influential for a long period after its initial publication in 1728. Among the most copied aspects of his work were his studies for towers and steeples, theoretical designs that were never built, but adaptable to the timber construction and carpentry skills of settlers in British North America who were looking for church designs to remind them of their homeland.

drama and its own integrity. After Carlo Maderno extended **St. Peter's** nave and designed the facade (1606–12), Bernini completed its huge baldachino (1624–33) and built the colonnades around the square (begun 1656). There is an imaginative sense of movement, both inside and out, in the surfaces and volumes, and an awe-inspiring use of space that contributes to the Vatican's iconic status in church architecture.

While Baroque never took firm root in England, it deeply influenced Christopher Wren (1632–1723), an astronomer, mathematician and self-taught architect who met Bernini on a trip to Paris in 1665. The next year the Great Fire savaged London and its churches — 87 of them were destroyed or damaged in a few days. Wren proposed a New Plan for London to Charles II with "a Baroque system of piazzas and radiating streets." His plan was not adopted, but he did get a commission to rebuild **St. Paul's Cathedral,** one of the churches that had perished in the fire, and 51 other churches, mostly eclectic in character. His first scheme for St. Paul's, "the great model," was a domed centralized space with four ancillary domes on the diagonals, which shows the Baroque influences. Apparently the clergy did not find this design sufficiently cathedral-like and it was rejected. His next effort, which was built, combined a long basilica with a domical crossing, the effect of which, both externally and internally, is overpowering.

James Gibbs (1682–1754) was a Scot training to be a Catholic priest in Rome when he began to study painting and then architecture. In 1709 he went to London, where he designed St. Mary-le-Strand in 1714 and in 1722–26 the enormously influential St. Martin-in-the-Fields. That ongoing influence was mediated through his folio publication *Book of Architecture* in 1728, and the *Rules for Drawing the Several Parts of Architecture*, a kind of manual for builders, in 1732. During the early part of his London period, Christopher Wren was his mentor and primary influence. Gibbs' theoretical drawings, such as his towers and steeples, served as models for designers, especially in the colonies, and in a number of cases a direct influence can be traced.

The New World

By the early 17th century, church architectural norms were well entrenched in the countries from which Canada's people came. Design ideas came with the colonists to both New France and British North America. Roman Catholicism's powerful movement of reform and renewal was deeply influential in New France, while the Protestant Reformation was similarly dominant in British North America. The Reformation, of course, took a number of radically different forms, so the shape of Protestant Christianity was convoluted: Puritans, Presbyterians, Congregationalists, Baptists, Quakers, Mennonites, Moravian Brethren and many other groups. And the Church of England, in its peculiarly accommodating way, became a model for Anglican (or in the United States, Episcopal) churches that ranged from Low-Church Evangelical Anglicans to High-Church Anglo-Catholics.

Had settlement of North America occurred at another time, Canada's churches would look very different. Originating in the early 17th century and flowering in the 18th, Canada's earliest villages, towns and cities reflect developments and divisions in Britain and France. Soon it absorbed influences from the newly independent United States of America, from mid-19th-century famine-ravaged Ireland, from late 19th-century Ukrainian or Russian steppes, and from each successive wave of immigrants. From whatever source, immigrants brought convictions and tastes and ideals formed elsewhere — and diverse architectures. Inevitably these influences were reshaped by Canada's politics, society, geography, culture, conflicts and neighbours, including First Nations peoples. Its church architecture absorbed, while transforming, the forms, religious values, liturgical practices and aesthetic tastes of those home countries.

The fundamental shapes of congregational spaces developed in the Roman period and the utilization of basic Roman forms is still common, though the variety possible within those forms is immense. Nevertheless, two recent developments in church architecture are found mainly, if not only, in North America: Akron plan churches and megachurches.

The Sunday School movement, from which the Akron Plan derived, had its origins in Robert Raikes (1736–1811), who thought children working in factories and mines would benefit — like society itself — from being given basic and religious education on Sundays. The first school opened in 1780. By the time Raikes died there may

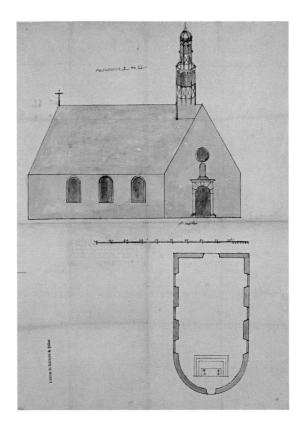

"Plan d'Eglise," *Jean Maillou, ca 1715*
Maillou's unsophisticated drawing from the early 18th century shows his plan for a stone church. The so-called Maillou plan is the simplest and easiest to build of the three main types of Québec churches: in plan, a rectangle with a semicircular apse of the same width, and in section, one-story walls with a triangular roof structure.

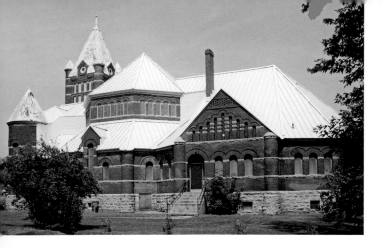

ABOVE AND RIGHT **St. Paul's**, *Winchester, Ontario; Presbyterian. Brick, 1895; G.F. Stalker, architect*

Winchester's Romanesque Revival exterior expresses both the octagonal nave in the centre and the semi-octagonal education facilities on the right. Fully developed Akron plans like this include large doors — in this example dropping into the floor and rising into the ceiling — to permit the Sunday School area to become part of the church. This is a rare example, where the sliding doors between the nave and the education areas are at the rear of the church. The sloping floor of the nave's octagonal space holds pews that circle around the pulpit, behind which is the front entrance.

BELOW **Holy Family**, *Medicine Hat, Alberta; Roman Catholic. Brick and stucco with steel frame, 2003–04; Michael Borskie with Sahuri, Hutchinson and Brzezinski, architects*

Holy Family is one of the new breed of churches that rely on everyone coming by car. It looks more like a large evangelical Protestant church than a Roman Catholic parish church, with its large narthex, amphitheatrical seating and provision for musical instruments. A ladder-like steeple is centrally located over a large skylight, the fulcrum of the nave. The colourful exterior contrasts buff brick and white panelled walls with an earthy-brown steel roof over the nave and sky-blue roofs over adjunct areas.

have been a half-million children attending such schools. While the movement spread to Europe, it was only partially successful. But it became very important in North America, especially among Protestants, where facilities for Sunday Schools were often included in church buildings. The Akron plan was designed around an open rotunda with classrooms splayed around it, opening into the rotunda, with sliding doors or shutters between. One of the rationales for this plan was the so-called Uniform Lesson system, in which all parts of the Sunday School worked from a similar lesson for the day. A developed form of the Akron plan creatively combined the Sunday School with the church nave by having an opening between these two main spaces. Usually Akron-style Sunday Schools were linked with an Akron-style centralized plan for the nave, usually with a semi-circular balcony. The term Akron plan has come to mean semi-circular amphitheatrical seating in the nave.

St. Paul's, **Winchester**, **Ontario**, by G.F. Stalker (1841–95), is an exceptional example of an Akron design. The exterior is Byzantine inspired, with an octagonal nave thrusting through the roof plan. Behind the nave is the Sunday School, expressed externally by a half-octagon; inside, segmentally arranged classrooms open around a central meeting area. What makes the Winchester plan unusual are the well-preserved counterbalanced sliding doors that disappear into the ceiling and the floor. This arrangement permits the nave and the Sunday School to form a single space. Of course, this required some rearrangement of the nave, since the flexible plan works only if the Sunday School is behind the last row of seats in the

nave, rather than behind the pulpit. As a result, the narthex and main entrance are behind the pulpit, and entry to the nave is on either side of the pulpit.

The second recent development in church design builds indirectly on Akron plan buildings. Most megachurches adopt an amphitheatrical layout, primarily in order to seat large crowds within a short distance of the preacher. Usually located in the suburbs, these churches are built where land values are lower, so that large parking lots can be accommodated, recognizing that most people now arrive at church by automobile. Megachurches are often large windowless spaces, but they usually include a large atrium or narthex, along with other social and multifunctional spaces, so that the life of the church is found as much in ancillary spaces as in the nave. The most striking feature of this trend is that megachurches can be found in very large urban metropolises, in medium-sized cities and even in rural areas. So successful are they that one major denomination has developed a scheme to close 21 churches and build one megachurch in their place.

Holy Family, Medicine Hat, Alberta, was created when three smaller parishes — Christ the King, St. Mary's and St. Joseph (Shuler) — merged and moved to a new location on one edge of the city. A major contribution to the cost of the new building came from the sale of the three old properties. Its brick-over-steel structure, with no interior columns, is intended to demonstrate a sense of unity and equality within the congregation. The building is distinguished by restraint and the effective use of light, including a large central skylight. Incorporated in the design are a number of sculptures by Timothy Schmalz; selecting all the work from a single

Trinity, *Oro, Ontario; Presbyterian. Bichromatic brick with steel frame, 2002–03; David McCauley, architect*
Trinity Presbyterian's exterior deliberately returns to 19th-century precedents with its bichromatic brickwork and pointed openings. Its thoroughly modern interior, however, is totally new: no pulpit, font, lectern or organ, only electric keyboards, guitars and drums. Like larger megachurches, its other facilities include an open narthex, coffee area and gymnasium.

Emmanuel, *Barrie, Ontario; Fellowship Baptist. Brick and glass with steel frame, 2004–05; Ted Handy, architect*

TOP Emmanuel is nestled in a grove of pines and birches, about 10 miles south of Barrie. Its porte-cochère leads through a glass entrance wall, beyond which is a monumentally long, high narthex, not the expected worship space. Its functional design builds on the contrast between an exposed steel structure and warm wooden roof decks. It pays a modest debt to predecessors with its glass and steel tower.

RIGHT The design's starting point is the generous narthex, running from front to back. Another long circulation space bisects it, forming a cross in a plan that is the church's organizing principle — architecturally, functionally and theologically. Four major blocks of space rotate around the central point: administration, worship, youth and education. The exposed steel frame includes bridges that give access to second-floor facilities and mechanical services. Tall glazed doors between the narthex and the sanctuary provide light in the essentially closed worship area, illuminated from high slots between the roof and walls.

artist was also intended to emphasize cohesiveness. **Sherwood Park Alliance**, **Edmonton**, Alberta (*see* pp. 363, 365), creates a similar though grander impression; its larger size is partly the result of including a Christian primary and secondary school — along with the requisite gymnasia and labs — with the church facilities. It shares essential features of megachurches, a large site housing complex facilities and an inward-turning worship space.

Barrie, Ontario, is a booming city 60 miles north of Toronto, near enough to function as a bedroom suburb but retaining a connection to the surrounding farms and rural communities that are in constant danger of being swamped by the rapid growth of the city. A number of large churches have been built in the countryside north, west and south of Barrie. Between Barrie and Orillia three small historic Presbyterian congregations — St. Andrew's Oro Station, Central Church Oro and Guthrie — struggled to survive in rural conditions, with a total Sunday attendance of about 50 persons in 1995. The three congregations united as **Trinity Presbyterian, Oro**, under a dynamic young evangelical minister. Initially they met in a school but the congregation began to attract substantial new members and within a short time a new church had been built. The congregation continued to grow so that even in its new expanded facilities two services were needed, and plans were soon underway for a large new addition. The building successfully wraps large and lofty spaces with plain materials, resulting in a flexible building that retains visual connections with its rural location. A strong sense of community is enhanced by its large narthex and coffee area.

Conclusion

The story of Canadian churches continues. Admittedly, there is pessimism about the future of Christianity but there is also reason to hope. In rural areas churches play important roles as key community organizations. In city cores churches have found new roles to ensure they continue to provide significant social services. In suburban areas churches are in transition, with the greatest growth occurring in the large evangelical amphitheatres.

Four trends should be noted. First, long-standing architectural traditions seem in jeopardy, as architects experiment with new forms. Change is necessary for a vibrant architecture, but many architects seem ignorant of historical precedent, resulting in buildings that are often trivial and insubstantial, with a showy theatricality that is unhelpful in expressing faith and encouraging worship. Among the truly significant fresh departures in the last generation are work by two western architects, Cardinal and Gaboury (*see* pp. 350–57, 359–62), both deeply engaged with Roman Catholic tradition.

Second, churches will continue to disappear, some due to accident and some to deliberate destruction. Several churches selected for inclusion in this book suffered fires (by arson, by lightning or by inadvertence) while we were writing; two others had recently been rebuilt after disastrous fires. Yet fire is not the main challenge facing churches. Structural decay, reductions in attendance, economic pressures, denominational priorities and a flight to the suburbs will result in more closures. New groups will rescue some churches through purchase and reuse, but others will disappear, with the loss of many superb buildings. A case in point is **St. Stephen-in-the-Fields,**

Emmanuel *interior*
FOLLOWING PAGE Two large three-dimensional steel trusses and a network of smaller trusses support a steel roof deck, providing a clear-span space for 850 persons. The V-shaped trusses have catwalks that connect with steel platforms to provide easy access to audio-visual and electrical facilities, with which the worship space is amply provided. The sanctuary's platform is flexible, with a simple lectern replacing a fixed pulpit. To one side, the baptismal tank is partly screened by low glass panels. Flexible seating that can be reconfigured in a number of arrangements drops down gradually on descending platforms.

St. Stephen-in-the-Fields, *Toronto, Ontario; Anglican. Bichromatic brick, 1857–58 (rebuilt after a fire in 1865); Thomas Fuller, architect*

St. Stephen was rebuilt by Gundry and Langley with alterations and additions, so only the general outlines of Thomas Fuller's building survive. Though it is no longer in the fields, it preserves some sense of its generous setting. The area around Kensington Market has seen persistent demographic changes over the years, but the neighbourhood conveys the mood of Toronto toward the end of the 19th century. St. Stephen has been an influential mother church to others, including St. Mary Magdalene, St. Anne's, and St. Thomas', all west and north of it.

ABOVE LEFT A chromo-lithograph by Fuller himself from about the same viewpoint shows Fuller's original vision of the building. The west front is almost the same. On both side elevations, however, a new aisle has been added that has a series of gables that permit much larger windows than would otherwise be possible in such low side walls, giving it a more picturesque outline. Dormer windows over the nave also aimed to lighten a dark space. These additions and alterations were part of Gundry and Langley's rebuilding, completed in 1866. The camelback chancel is Eden Smith's replacement of 1890.

Toronto, struggling under the burden of a huge debt. The building is a distinguished one by Thomas Fuller (1823–98), architect for the first Parliament Buildings in Ottawa (1859) and subsequently Dominion Chief Architect, supervising the design of more than 140 buildings.

Third, Canada's demographic makeup is changing dramatically enough that it appears that visible minority groups are coming to take centre stage, especially in suburban metropolitan areas, such as Malvern in Toronto, Ahuntsic in Montréal or Langley in Vancouver. When the demographic changes are combined with the surging popularity of evangelical and charismatic churches it is clear that Canadian Christianity will look different in the next generation. Other kinds of minorities will influence the future, too. In Toronto the **Metropolitan Community Church**, originally known as the gay church, then the gay rights church and then the equal marriage church, now thinks of itself as the diversity church (*see* p. 26). The building was once a Methodist Church, serving the then new suburb of Riverdale. The architects designed the building with Akron-style facilities that stand almost as built yet the building serves a wholly new type of community from the one originally envisaged. Two services in the morning, with strong singing and theologically sophisticated sermons, attract more than a thousand persons, the largest of the Metropolitan Community Churches among 250 churches worldwide. The Christianity of the future will see still more diversity and more adaptive reuse of old buildings.

Fourth, the balance between small rural churches, large urban churches and growing suburban churches is now changing, but in a different way from the 1950s and 60s. The point is clearly seen in **Emmanuel Baptist, Barrie**, whose roots go back to 1927, then to a 1950s church with a growing daughter church begun in 1992. By the early 2000s the parent church had decided to move from its original location to a new location south of Barrie along a highway where several other new churches were being constructed at the same time. Emmanuel built in what is almost a protypical idiom, with a very large narthex shaped like a cross, where a major part of the life of the church occurs. The narthex — with light entering through high slots — looks out in four directions to treed areas around. In the arms of the cross are the worship centre, the administration areas that include a library, the educational facilities and the youth facilities that include a gymnasium. Like the narthex, the worship space is multi-functional — it can be used, for example, for dinner theatre — designed on a series of descending platforms, all focused on a large, high platform at the front. Deep steel trusses span the column-free auditorium that holds about 850. Despite its size, two services are needed on Sunday to hold the crowds.

The trend to larger and fewer churches along the edges of built-up urban areas portends a major shift in the way Christianity is developing. On the one hand, these churches are a reflection of the way society has developed: more mobile, less neighbourhood centred, regionally organized rather than locally, emphasizing competition and growth. The congregations in such areas are drawn from wide catchment areas: no one walks and the church mounts a large range of programs to meet congregational needs. On the other hand, megachurches also directly influence the way the people in their congregations look at the surrounding culture: the church is the main — sometimes the only — place where there is a sense of community, a place for Christian groups for youths and acceptable entertainment.

While we foresee tensions between those who embrace traditional ways of thinking and those who seek to adapt Christianity to a new set of conditions, and while we anticipate loss of many worthy church buildings, we also expect that some of these same historic structures will find new and very diverse congregations and new adaptive uses. Whether readers belong to traditional denominations or new communities, whether their buildings are recent or old, whether they are descendants of the original residents of Canada or newly arrived, they need to consider afresh their heritage, their traditions and the realities of their faith as expressed in built form.

> *The very principle of religious architecture has its origins in the notion*
> *that where we are critically determines what we are able to believe in.*
> *To defenders of religious architecture, however convinced we are at*
> *an intellectual level of our commitments to a creed, we will remain*
> *reliably devoted to it only when it is continually affirmed by our*
> *buildings. In danger of being corrupted by our passions and led away*
> *by the commerce and chatter of our societies, we require places where*
> *the values outside of us encourage and enforce the aspirations within*
> *us. We may be nearer or farther away from God on account of what is*
> *represented on the walls or ceilings. We need panels of gold and lapis,*
> *windows of coloured glass and gardens of immaculately raked gravel*
> *in order to stay true to the sincerest parts of ourselves.*
> *— Alain de Botton, 2006*

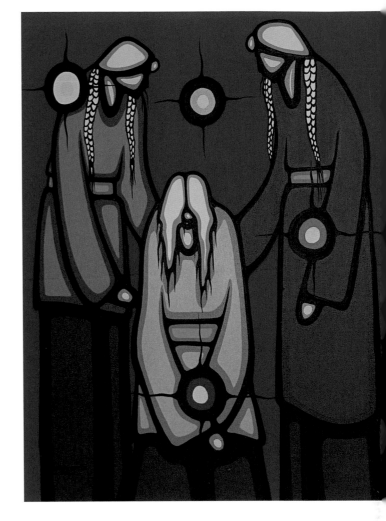

"Suffering and Growth," *Leland Bell, acrylic on canvas, 1983;* Omond Memorial United, *North Bay, Ontario*

This painting by Leland Bell, or Bebaminojmat (b. 1953 on Manitoulin Island), expresses the artist's personal outlook and spirituality. His art, he says, comes from his relationship with the Creator. He uses circles and colours symbolically: yellow for the East; red for the South, the place of all young life; Black for the West, the place of life; and white for the North, the place of healing. Leland Bell's work includes the Stations of the Cross in the M'chigeeng First Nations Church (*see* p. 221).

NOTES AND SOURCES

ABBREVIATIONS
USED FOR WORKS FREQUENTLY CITED:

BSSAC
Bulletin of the Society for the Study of Architecture in Canada

Baskerville, *Ontario*
Baskerville, Peter A. *Ontario: Image, Identity and Power.* Don Mills ON: Oxford University Press, 2002.

Bergeron, *Architecture des églises*
Bergeron, Claude. *L'architecture des églises du Québec, 1940 –1985.* Québec: Presses de l'université Laval, 1987.

DCB
Dictionary of Canadian Biography. 15 vols. to date. Toronto: University of Toronto Press, 1966–2005. *Dictionary of Canadian Biography Online:* www.biograph.ca/EN

Downs, *Sacred Places*
Downs, Barry. *Sacred Places: British Columbia's Early Churches.* Vancouver: Douglas & McIntyre, 1980.

Duffus, *Thy Dwellings*
Duffus, Allen F., et al. *Thy Dwellings Fair: Churches of Nova Scotia, 1750–1830.* Hantsport NS: Lancelot Press, 1982.

EB
Encyclopaedia Britannica. 15th ed. Chicago: Encyclopaedia Britannica, 1977.

Finley, *On Earth*
Finley, Gregg. *On Earth as it is in Heaven: Gothic Revival Churches of Victorian New Brunswick.* Fredericton: Goose Lane Editions, 1995.

Gibbs, *Book of Architecture*
Gibbs, James. *A Book of Architecture: Containing Designs of Buildings and Ornaments.* London, 1728. Reprint. New York: Benjamin Blom, 1968.

HAC
Historical Atlas of Canada. 3 vols. Toronto: University of Toronto Press, 1987–93.
Volume 1. *From the Beginning to 1800.* Ed. R. Cole Harris.
Volume 2. *The Land Transformed 1800–1891.* Ed. R. Louis Gentilcore.
Volume 3. Addressing *the Twentieth Century 1891–1961.* Eds. Donald Kerr and Deryck W. Holdsworth.

Hayes, *Historical Atlas*
Hayes, Derek. *Historical Atlas of Canada: Canada's History Illustrated with Original Maps.* Vancouver: Douglas & McIntyre, 2002.

JCAH
Journal of Canadian Art History.

JSSAC
Journal of the Society for the Study of Architecture in Canada.

Kalman, *History of Canadian Architecture*
Kalman, Harold. *A History of Canadian Architecture.* 2 volumes. Don Mills ON: Oxford University Press, 1994. [Contains endnotes with detailed references.]

MacRae and Adamson, *Hallowed Walls*
MacRae, Marion, and Anthony Adamson. *Hallowed Walls: Church Architecture of Upper Canada.* Toronto: Clarke, Irwin, 1975.

Noll, *History*
Noll, Mark A. *A History of Christianity in the United States and Canada.* Grand Rapids MI: Eerdmans, 1992.

Noppen, *Les églises du Québec*
Noppen, Luc. *Les églises du Québec (1600–1850).* Québec: Éditeur officiel du Québec; Montréal, FIDES, 1977.

Robertson, *Landmarks of Toronto* 4
Robertson, John Ross. *Landmarks of Toronto: A Collection of Historical Sketches of the Old Town of York from 1792 until 1837 and of Toronto from 1834 to 1904.* Vol. 4. Toronto: J. Ross Robertson, 1904. [The fourth of six "series" of *Robertson's Landmarks* contains nearly all his essays on Toronto churches.]

Simmins, *Documents*
Simmins, Geoffrey, comp. and ed. *Documents in Canadian Architecture.* Peterborough ON: Broadview Press, 1992.

TCE
The Canadian Encyclopedia. 1985. 2d ed. Edmonton: Hurtig, 1988. 4 vols. *The Canadian Encyclopedia* Online: www.histori.ca/default.do?page=.index or www.thecanadianencyclopedia.com/index.cfm ?PgNm=HomePage&Params=A1

Thompson, *Prairie West*
Thompson, John Herd. *Forging the Prairie West.* Illustrated History of Canada. Toronto: Oxford University Press, 1998.

Traquair, *Old Architecture*
Traquair, Ramsay. *The Old Architecture of Quebec.* Toronto: Macmillan, 1947.

Tuck, *Gothic Dreams* **(1978)**
Tuck, Robert C. *Gothic Dreams: The Life and Times of a Canadian Architect, William Critchlow Harris (1854–1913).* Toronto: Dundurn Press, 1978.

Tuck, *Gothic Dreams* **(1995)**
Tuck, Robert C. *Rêves gothiques, l'architecture de William Critchlow Harris, 1854–1913/ Gothic Dreams: The Architecture of William Critchlow Harris (1854–1913)* Charlottetown: Confederation Centre Art Gallery and Museum, 1995.

White, *Cambridge Movement*
White, James F. *The Cambridge Movement: The Ecclesiologist and the Gothic Revival.* Cambridge: Cambridge University Press, 1962.

Wills, *Ancient English Ecclesiastical Architecture*
Wills, Frank. *Ancient English Ecclesiastical Architecture and Its Principles, Applied to the Wants of the Church at the Present Day.* New-York: Stanford and Swords, 1850.

Churches

12 *Architecture has its political use*
    Christopher Wren, "Of Architecture," quoted in: Stephen Wren, *Parentalia; or, Memoirs of the family of the Wrens*, 1750, reprint (Boston: Gregg Press, 1965).

15 *Architecture for churches is a matter of*
    Donald J. Bruggink and Carl H. Droppers, *Christ and Architecture: Building Presbyterian and Reformed Churches* (Grand Rapids: Eerdmans, 1965) 1.

Atlantic

19 *Style*
    For styles in Canada, see Shannon Ricketts, Leslie Maitland and Jacqueline Hucker, *A Guide to Canadian Styles* (Peterborough: Broadview, 2004).

30 *By God's will … sailing southward*
    Legend on the controversial "Vinland Map"; Hayes, *Historical Atlas* 10.

31 *The community abounded*
    Marc Lescarbot, *History of New France*, ed. W.L. Grant (Toronto: Champlain Society, 1911) 225, quoted in: Kalman, *History of Canadian Architecture* 20.

33 *Nova Scarcity*
    W. Stewart Wallace, *United Empire Loyalists* (Toronto: Glasgow, Brook, 1914) 62.

    ensure that a sufficient Mainteynance
    Henry Paget Thompson, *Into All Lands: The History of the Society* (London: Society for the Promoting Christian Knowledge, 1951) 17.

    violent temper and scandalous life
    Michael Godfrey, "John Jackson," *DCB* 2. 293–94.

    population numbers
    HAC 1, 50.

34 *St. James' Chapel, Long Reach*
    Finley, *On Earth* 74 –77.

35 *request for religious instruction*
    Milton W. Hamilton, "Theyanoguin," *DCB* 3. 622–24.

    19th-century religious character
    HAC 2, pl. 52; *HAC* 3, pl. 34.

36 *A Book of Architecture*
    For example, St. Paul's, Halifax, was said to be "exactly the model of Marybone Chapel," London, illustrated in Gibbs, *Book of Architecture* pls. 24–25.

    Essay on the General History of Manners
    See Peter Collins, *Changing Ideals in Modern Architecture 1750–1950*, 1965, 2d ed. (Montreal: McGill-Queen's University Press, 1998) 31–34.

37 *reality, the absolute necessity*
    Ecclesiological Society, *A Few Words to Church Builders*, 3d ed. (Cambridge, 1844) 29, quoted in: White, *Cambridge Movement* 98.

38 *All Saints', McKeens Corner … wooden*
    For Edward Medley's dependence on R.C. Carpenter's prototype, see George L. Hersey, *High Victorian Gothic: A Study in Associationism* (Baltimore: The John's Hopkins University Press, 1972) 83–92. All Saints' and four other churches by Medley are discussed in Douglas Scott Richardson, "Hyperborean Gothic; or, Wilderness Ecclesiology and the Wood Churches of Edward Medley," *Architectura* II, no.1 (1972) 48–74. Finley, *On Earth* 136, identifies two more.

39 *How grateful to a Christian*
    John Medley, *Elementary Remarks on Church Architecture* (Exeter: P.A. Hannaford, 1841) 38.

40 *United Church of Canada voting*
    HAC 3, pl. 34.

    All Saints', Clifton Royal
    Tuck, *Gothic Dreams* (1978) 64–65, 72.

42 *O Lord! We would not advise*
    Attributed to the Puritan Thomas Prince (1687–1758) on the taking of Louisbourg in 1746. Quoted in: William Wood, *The Great Fortress: A Chronicle of Louisbourg 1720–1760* (Toronto: Glasgow, Brook, 1915) 84.

    promising "sainthood"
    Website of the Constitution Society: www.constitution.org/jw/acm_2-m.txt.

    very gentle ascent
    Letters of Cornwallis to the Duke of Bedford, July 23 and 24, 1749, Record Group 1, vols. 35, 40, Public Archives of Nova Scotia.

44 *exactly the model*
    Rev. William Tutty, letter of March 17, 1750, quoted in Duffus, *Dwellings* 48.

46 *a Bostonian Wren building*
    J. Philip McAleer, *A Pictorial History of St. Paul's Anglican Church, Halifax, Nova Scotia* (Technical University of Nova Scotia: Resource Centre Publications, 1993) 69, 76–77.

    The communion table … upholstered in blue
    Report of a talk by Mr. Peter Lynch, *The Halifax Evening Mail* 13.77 (1 April 1892).

    the bell
    Duffus, *Thy Dwellings* 60–63.

48 *a frame that came from Boston*
    Duffus, *Dwellings* 55.

50 *sawn boards came from New England*
    Duffus, *Dwellings* 66–70.

56 *Many of the People of the Church*
    Act of George II, November 10, 1747: www.mun.ca/rels/morav/act.html

    festive simplicity
    The expression is Hans Rollmann's (personal communication); we are indebted to him for supplying much information, pictures, and a critique of the text in this section. See his website: www.mun.ca/rels/morav/.

59 *The Saviour's blood and righteousness*
    Hymnal and Liturgies of the Moravian Church (Chicago: Moravian Church in America, 1969) no. 327.

60 *O for a thousand tongues to sing*
    Hymnal and Liturgies of the Moravian Church (Chicago: Moravian Church in America, 1969) no. 216.

    The new church is neat and friendly
    Report of the visitation of the mission in Labrador by Br. L.T. Reichel, 1876 (from: periodical accounts, 30/314 (1877) 145–56, translated from the German in *Missions-Blatt der Bruedergemeine*); quoted http: www.mun.ca/rels/morav/texts/reichel2.html.

63 *What is here presented*
    "Introduction," Gibbs, *Book of Architecture* i.

    about Ninety Houses up
    William Pagan, *The Papers of Col. Edward Winslow, Loyalist*, comp. Rev. William O. Raymond (Saint John NB, 1901) 201, quoted in: William Nathaniel Banks, "Castine, Maine, [and] St. Andrews, New Brunswick, Canada," *The Magazine Antiques* 118: 1 (July 1980) 111.

    took the leading part
    W.S. NacNutt, *The Atlantic Provinces: the Emergence of Colonial Society, 1712–1857* (Toronto: McClelland and Stewart, 1965) 155.

    the frame work erected … more forcible than
    Melville N. Cockburn, *A History of Greenock Church, St. Andrews, New Brunswick, from 1821 to 1906* (n.p. St. Andrews NB, 1906) 4–7.

    Steeples are indeed of a Gothic Extraction
    Gibbs, *Book of Architecture* viii.

67 *the pulpit alone*
    Scott sent a West Indian trader to Honduras "specially for that purpose": Cockburn, *A History of Greenock Church* 6.

    One often sees the phrase
    John R. Hume, *Scotland's Best Churches* (Edinburgh: Edinburgh University Press, 2005) vii.

    House of Worship to be called
    Brenda and Lloyd Parsons, *Moncton's Civic Treasure: The Free Meeting House, A National Historic Site* (Moncton NB: Betsons Publishing, 1997) especially 14.

    perhaps the work of Shepherd Johnson Frost
    Althea Douglas, "Shepherd Johnson Frost: A Forgotten Architect," *BSSAC* 15:3 (September 1990) 60–67.

67 *Lloyd Johnson or Johnston*
     Johnson's obituary in *New Brunswick
     Courier* (Saint John, NB, December 24,
     1842) says he was born in Leitrim,
     Ireland; see also *Morning News* (Saint
     John, NB, December 26, 1842).

    rough masonry … purely Gothic
     Advertisement in the *Courier* (Saint
     John NB, September 20, 1823),
     progress and completion (*Courier,* July
     16,1825), in: Archibald Lang Fleming,
     *A Book of Remembrance, or the History of
     St. John's Church, Saint John, New
     Brunswick* (Saint John NB: Corporation
     of the Church, 1925) 17–19.

68 *John Cunningham*
     Gary K. Hughes, *Music of the Eye:
     Architectural Drawings of Canada's First
     City,1822–1914* (Saint John NB: New
     Brunswick Museum and Royal
     Architectural Institute of Canada,
     1991) 1–3.

    Joshua Mauger … assisted more than 200
     Donald F. Chard, "Joshua Mauger,"
     DCB 4. 525–29.

    Seth Noble
     J.M. Bumsted, "Seth Noble," *DCB* 5.
     627–28.

    Noble began to stir up his flock – a ludicrous
     James Hannay, "The Maugerville
     Settlement, 1763–1824," *Collections of
     the New Brunswick Historical Society* 1
     (Saint John, NB, 1894) 68–76.

69 *diminutive rendition*
     Finley, *On Earth* 29.

    The resolute plainness
     Stuart Smith, "Architecture in New
     Brunswick: An Historical Survey,"
     Canadian Antiques Collector 10: 3
     (May/June 1975) 37, speaking of the
     Moses Pickard house, Keswick (rather
     than the meetinghouse) and of
     Maugerville in general.

71 *We have no history but that which we make*
     [John Medley], *"Other Little Ships" (A
     Sermon Preached … in the cathedral
     Church of S. Peter, Exeter …)* (London:
     Society for the Propagation of the
     Gospel in Foreign Parts, [1878]) 8.

    the first pure cathedral
     "Annual General Meeting of the
     Exeter Diocesan Architectural Society,"
     Ecclesiologist 7 (June 1847) 242.

    both of meaning and beauty… venerable
     "Suggestions for Co-operation with
     the Objects of the Society",
     Ecclesiologist 1 (November 1841) 18.

    close or mechanical imitation
     "A Hint on Modern Church
     Architecture," *Ecclesiologist* 1 (June
     1842) 135.

72 *betwixt an English Cathedral*
     "Fredericton Cathedral," *Courier*, Saint
     John NB, June 28, 1845.

    the finest specimen
     Wills, *Ancient English Ecclesiastical
     Architecture* 33, 35.

    roses encircling tulips
     Simon Jenkins, *England's Thousand Best
     Churches* (London: Penguin Books,
     2000) 473.

    the same shell which contained
     "Mr. [A.J.B. Beresford] Hope's Essay
     on the Present State of Ecclesiological
     Science in England," *Ecclesiologist* 7
     (March 1847) 87.

73 *the richest style*
     John Medley, *Elementary Remarks on
     Church Architecture* (Exeter: P.A.
     Hannaford, 1841) 34.

74 *as though it had stood*
     "Exeter Diocesan Architectural
     Society," *Ecclesiologist* 13 (August
     1852) 295.

    the frightful expense
     "Colonial Church Architecture,"
     Ecclesiologist 8 (June 1848) 362.

    ring with music
     Malcolm Ross, "John Medley," *DCB*
     12. 713–17, here 714.

    the impossibility of procuring
     Wills, *Ancient English Ecclesiastical
     Architecture* 109.

    symbolic teaching … so that the very
     Medley, *Elementary Remarks* 33.

    Ancient English Ecclesiastical Architecture
     Frank Wills, *Ancient English
     Ecclesiastical Architecture and Its
     Principles, Applied to the Wants of the
     Church at the Present Day* (New-York:
     Stanford and Swords, 1850).

    Ecclesiologists were driven by a hunger for
     Chris Brooks, *The Gothic Revival*
     (London: Phaidon Press, 1999) 254.

    symbolizes some doctrine
     Wills, *Ancient English Ecclesiastical
     Architecture* 46.

75 *material fabrick symbolizes*
     *The Symbolism of Churches and Church
     Ornaments: A Translation of the First
     Book of the Rationale Divinorum
     Officiorum, Written by William
     Durandus, sometime Bishop of Mende,*
     with an introductory essay, notes and
     illustrations, by John Mason Neale
     and Benjamin Webb, 1843, reprint
     (New York: AMS Press, 1973) xxvi.

    arrived with trivial injury
     "The Cathedral, Fredericton, New
     Brunswick, North America," *Illustrated
     London News* 14 (April 28, 1849) 276.

    An air chamber
     The New-York Ecclesiologist 3
     (November 1851) 190 (note).

    dark and most insidious design
     Loyalist, July 23, 1846, quoted in:
     Finley, *On Earth* 88.

76 *slavish literal copying*
     Wills, *Ancient English Ecclesiastical
     Architecture* 91.

    The progress of ecclesiological gothic
     Chris Brooks, *The Gothic Revival*
     (London: Phaidon Press, 1999) 254.

    not to create a splendid picture
     John Medley, *Elementary Remarks on
     Church Architecture* (Exeter: P.A.
     Hannaford, 1841) 34.

    an era of Gothic church building
     Ross, "John Medley," *DCB* 12. 714.

    exact imitation of real ancient designs
     "A Hint on Modern Church
     Architecture," *Ecclesiologist* 1 (June
     1842) 133–135.

    When buildings are derived
     A. Welby Pugin, *The Present State of
     Ecclesiastical Architecture in England*
     (London, 1843) 108.

78 *Snow and rain with us always comes*
     William Grey, "The ecclesiology of
     Newfoundland," *Ecclesiologist* 11
     (1853), 156–61, here 161.

    Most Holy Trinity … mariner rowdyism
     W. Gordon Handcock, *Soe Longe as
     There Comes Noe Women: Origins of
     English Settlement in Newfoundland* (St.
     John's NL: Breakwater, 1989), quoted
     in: Margaret McBurney and Mary
     Byers, *True Newfoundlanders: Early
     Homes and Families of Newfoundland
     and Labrador* (Toronto: Boston Mills
     Press, 1997) 45–46.

    contingent upon seats
     www.heritage.nf.ca/society/rhs/
     rs_listing/134.html.

    He came to St. John's
     Fabian O'Dea, "Patrick Kough," *DCB*
     9. 435–36.

80 *the intention was certainly better*
     "S. John's Cathedral, Newfoundland,"
     Ecclesiologist 8 (April 1848) 275.

    Greatness of dimension
     Edmund Burke, *A Philosophical Enquiry
     into the Origin of our Ideas of the Sublime
     and the Beautiful* 2d ed. (London, 1759)
     72.

    Man's relative insignificance
     James Stevens Curl, *A Dictionary of
     Architecture* (Oxford: Oxford
     University Press, 1999) 648.

81 *two aesthetics: … beautiful [and] great*
     Burke, *A Philosophical Enquiry into …
     the Sublime and the Beautiful* 124.

    it is at once the most conspicuous
     "The R.C. Cathedral, St. John's, N.F.,"
     Canadian Illustrated News 3 (April 15,
     1871) 227.

    a plain wooden building
     Paul O'Neill, *The Oldest City: The Story
     of St. John's, Newfoundland* (Portugal
     Cove-St. Philip's NL: Boulder
     Publications, 2003) 22–24, 543, 546.

    a wretched building
     Raymond J. Lahey, "The Building of a
     Cathedral, 1838–1855," in J.F. Wallis et
     al. eds., *The Basilica-Cathedral of St.*

John Baptist, St. John's, Newfoundland, 1855–1980. (St. John's, 1980) 27.

81 *they had seen the success … years of vexation*
Raymond J. Lahey, "Michael Anthony Fleming," *DCB* 7. 292–96; Lahey, "The Building of a Cathedral" 27–28.

of the most perishable material
Quoted in: M.F. Howley, *Ecclesiastical History of Newfoundland* (Boston, 1888); rpt. (Belleville ON: Mika Publishing, 1979) 337–38.

the Irish finally had arrived
John Edward FitzGerald, "Building the Cathedral," www.heritage.nf.ca/society/building_cathedral.html.

Ole Jörgen Schmidt
Hans Rollmann, "Schmidt's cathedral," St. John's *Telegram* (Sunday, September 18, 2005) A10, and Dr. Rollmann's outline for an essay, "Ole Jörgen Schmidt (1793–1848): Architect of St. John's Roman Catholic Basilica," for a book on the Basilica (following a 150th-anniversary symposium in 2005), edited by John Edward FitzGerald.

most extensive cathedral
The model was "exact and complete inside and out": Lahey, "The Building of a Cathedral" 28.

82 *entire and unqualified satisfaction*
Quoted in: O'Neill, *The Oldest City* 557.

massiveness and strength
J.A. Picton, "A Few Observations on the Anglo-Norman Style of Architecture, and Its Applicability to Ecclesiastical Edifices," *Architectural Magazine* 1 (1834) 289–90.

contemporary Rundbogenstil
Michael J. Lewis, "Rundbogenstil," *Dictionary of Art* 27 (New York: Grove, 1996) 334–36.

North Italian work, which Thomas Hope illustrated
Thomas Hope, *An Historical Essay on Architecture,* 2 vols. (London, 1835) 1: 209.

83 *swift "hauls" of materials*
Lahey, "The Building of a Cathedral" 28–30, 32–36.

a cathedral church in miniature
The crowd estimate from "Laying of the Foundation-stone of the Catholic Cathedral," *The Newfoundlander*, May 20, 1841, and Fleming's description of the model are quoted in: Howley, *Ecclesiastical History of Newfoundland* 357–60.

Purcell prepared the triple windows
Vindicator, St. John's (April 23, 1842), paraphrased in: Lahey, "The Building of a Cathedral" 33.

as cheap in the long run
Lahey, "The Building of a Cathedral" 32–35.

preached an eloquent sermon
Patriot, St. John's (January12, 1850) quoted in: Lahey, "The Building of a Cathedral," 36.

most influential Irish immigrant
John Edward FitzGerald, "Bishop Fleming and the Roman Catholic Church": www.heritage.nf.ca/society/fleming_church.html.

a wooden shed
"S. John's Cathedral, Newfoundland," *Ecclesiologist* 8 (April 1848) 274.

84 *a most impracticable climate … more study*
"S. John's Cathedral, Newfoundland," *Ecclesiologist* 8 (April 1848) 277.

all ornament should consist
A. Welby Pugin, *The True Principles of Pointed or Christian Architecture* (London: John Weale, 1841).

85 *one crying in the wilderness … and with fire.*
Matthew 3:1-12.

86 *Winding with the winding shore*
Robert T.S. Lowell, *The New Priest in Conception Bay* (Boston: Phillips, Sampson, 1858), quoted in: George Kapelos and Douglas Richardson, "Townscape in a tickle: Greenspond," *Canadian Antiques Collector* 10:2 (March/April 1975) 25.

the London Builder
Quoted from *Builder* 11 (April 9, 1853) 238 in: Malcolm Thurlby, "St. Patrick's Roman Catholic Church, School, and Convent in St. John's: J.J. McCarthy and Irish Gothic Revival in Newfoundland," *JSSAC* 28: 3-4 (2003) 13.

perspective view in a flat wooden case
Letters of June 6, 1853 to Bishop Mullock, in Archives of the Roman Catholic Archdiocese of Newfoundland — 104-1-7(2) and 104-1–7(5) — quoted in: Malcolm Thurlby, "St. Patrick's Roman Catholic Church, School, and Convent in St. John's: J.J. McCarthy and Irish Gothic Revival in Newfoundland," *JSSAC* 28: 3–4 (2003) 13.

87 *rude and simple; but, massive and solemn*
A. Welby Pugin, *An Apology for the Revival of Christian Architecture in England* (London: John Weale, 1843) 23 (n.13), quoted in: Thurlby, "St. Patrick's Roman Catholic Church …" 15.

as funds and material permitted
collections.ic.gc.ca/tours/stjohns/dw/sjdw_1html.

Elijah Hoole
www.lookingatbuildings.org.uk/default.asp?Document=3.S.2.2,4 (Toynbee Hall, London) and

http://www.historicplaces.ca/rep-reg/affichage-display_e.aspx?Id=2315 (George Street United, St. John's).

89 *A new wooden church … must show*
William Scott, "On Wooden Churches," *Ecclesiologist* 9 (August 1848) 19.

simply believed that architectural form
César Daly's essay in *Builder* (1864), summarized in: Collins, *Changing Ideals in Modern Architecture* 198.

Edward Shuttleworth Medley
William Frederick Vroom, *Christ Church, St.Stephen, N.B., with a Biographical Sketch of the Architect, Rev. Edward S. Medley, B.A.* (New York, 1913) 19; *Crockford's Clerical Directory*, 40th ed. (London, 1908) 973.

91 *in poor places*
William Scott, "On Wooden Churches," *Ecclesiologist* 9 (August 1848) 18.

small, plain wooden models … how it was
"Exeter Diocesan Architectural Society," *Ecclesiologist* 13 (August 1852) 293.

for our rural neighbourhoods
Charles Congdon, "On Wooden Churches," *New-York Ecclesiologist* 3 (November 1851) 182, 185.

too rigorously adhering … Sweden or
"The New-York Ecclesiologist," *Ecclesiologist* 10 (November 1849) 203 [review].

must show its real construction
Scott, "On Wooden Churches," *Ecclesiologist* 9 (August 1848) 19.

92 *Christ Church follows … tithe barn*
George L. Hersey, *High Victorian Gothic: A Study in Associationism* (Baltimore: The John's Hopkins University Press, 1972) 83–92.

94 *In the early communities*
H.M. Scott Smith, *The Historic Churches of Prince Edward Island,* 1986, updated 2d ed. (Halifax NS: SSP Publications, 2004) 12.

dropped into the matted hills
Elizabeth Bishop, "Cape Breton," quoted in: William Toye, *On Canadian Literature* (Toronto: Colombo, 2005) 25.

restore hope to dispossessed … happily
John Morgan Gray, "Thomas Douglas, Baron Daer and Shortcleuch, 5th Earl of Selkirk," *DCB* 5. 264–69.

94 *the settlers and the Island*
J.M. Bumsted, "Lord Selkirk of Prince Edward Island," *The Island Magazine* 5 (Fall-Winter 1978) 6.

96 *identified the need*
Jean M. MacLennan, "John MacLennan (McLennan)," *DCB* 5. 569–70.

97 *although a devout Baptist*
Orlo Louise Jones, "Robert Jones,"
DCB 8. 433–34.

The internal arrangements of the building
Charlottetown Patriot (October 25,
1870), quoted in: Smith, *Historic*
Churches of Prince Edward Island
105–106.

98 *numinous and mysterious … altar*
Tuck, *Gothic Dreams* (1995) 13.

At present we see only
1 Corinthians 13:12 (*Revised English*
Bible).

were to be 'thin places'
Tuck, *Gothic Dreams* (1995) 13.

masses of dark colour
Tuck, *Gothic Dreams* (1995) 20.

St. Patrick's, Grand River
Tuck, *Gothic Dreams* (1978) 84.

99 *Yes, yes, build it like Kinkora*
Smith, *The Historic Churches of Prince*
Edward Island 60–61.

although of timber … unity of nave and
Tuck, *Gothic Dreams* (1978) 84.

101 *In GOD's house every thing*
"New Churches" *Ecclesiologist* 1
(November 1841) 9–12, here 12.

an enthusiastic fiddler
Tuck, *Gothic Dreams* (1995); *see also*
Gothic Dreams (1978) 108, 110, 112

abrupt square surfaces … the sounds pro-
duced in the chancel
Tuck, *Gothic Dreams* (1995) 25–26.

101 *almost too good*
William Critchlow Harris, in an inter-
view in the Charlottetown *Examiner,*
14 March 1896, quoted in: Tuck, *Gothic*
Dreams (1995) 25–26.

QUÉBEC

104 *Architecture is the most complete*
Dom Paul Bellot, *Almanac catholique*
français pour 1933 (Paris: Libraire
Bloud & Gay, 1933) 166–67, quoted in:
Simmins, *Documents* 174–76, here 174.

peace-loving gospel
Russell Bourne, *Gods of War, Gods of*
Peace: How the Meeting of Native and
Colonial Religions Shaped Early America
(New York: Harcourt, 2002) 94.

109 *Refus Global*
Paul-Émile Borduas, "Refus Global,"
translated by Ray Ellenwood:
www.dantaylor.com/pages/refus-
global.html.

110 *Now and then we perceived*
Peter Kalm, in Adolph B. Benson (rev.
and ed.), *The America of 1750: Peter*
Kalm's Travels in North America (New
York: Dover, 1966) 415.

Saint-Pierre, Île d'Orléans
Noppen, *Les églises du Québec* 264–67;
L'Île d'Orléans (Québec: Historic
Monuments Commission of the

Province of Quebec, 1928) 199–200;
Traquair, *Old Architecture*, 137–39.

Saint-François-de-Sales, Neuville
Raymonde Gauthier, *Les tabernacles*
anciens du Québec des XVIIe, XVIIIe et
XIXe siècles (Québec: Ministère des
Affaires culturelles, 1974) 45–46, 56
and pl. 31.

withhold funds
Alan Gowans, *Church Architecture in*
New France (Toronto: University of
Toronto Press, 1955) 29–41, 116.

117 *Le Chemin du Roy*
Hélène Bourque, *Les églises et les*
chapelles de Portneuf (Portneuf QC:
2000).

wheat for the poor
Madeleine Gobeil-Trudeau, *Les*
chemins de la mémoire, tome 1, (Québec:
Les Publications du Québec, 1990) 294;
quoted in: www.patrimoine-
religieux.qc.ca/sfrasalneuf/sfrasal-
neufe.htm.

119 *sole surviving example*
Noppen, *Les églises du Québec* 150–153;
John Porter, "L'ancien baldaquin de la
chapelle du premier palais épiscopal
de Québec, à Neuville," *Les Annales*
d'histoire de l'art canadien/ Journal of
Canadian Art History, 1: no. 2 (1974)
180–200.

121 *The Place d'Armes, or Grand Parade*
Joseph Bouchette, *The British*
Dominions in North America (London:
Longman, 1832) as quoted in: Charles
P. de Volpi, *Québec: Recueil icono-*
graphique: A Pictorial Record (Toronto:
Longman, 1971) opposite pl. 77.

Cathedral of the Holy Trinity
Luc Noppen and Lucie K. Morisset, *La*
présence anglican à Québec: Holy Trinity
Cathedral (1796-1996) (Sillery: Les éditions du Septentrion, 1995) 49–55; and
www.ogs.net/cathedral/website/e-
02-site.htm; Basil F.L. Clarke, *Anglican*
Cathedrals outside the British Isles
(London: S.P.C.K., 1958) 54.

emulated James Gibbs
Terry Friedman, *James Gibbs* (New
Haven: Yale University Press, 1984) 55.

military engineers
Traquair, *Old Architecture* 94.

materials and workmanship
Quoted in: Frederick C. Würtele, "The
English Cathedral of Quebec: a mono-
graph", *Transactions of the Literary and*
Historical Society of Quebec 20 (March
1891) 77–81.

122 *to give more boldness*
Quoted in Frederick C. Würtele, "The
English Cathedral of Quebec: a mono-
graph", *Transactions of the Literary and*
Historical Society of Quebec 20 (March
1891) 77; Luc Noppen and Lucie
Morisset, *La présence anglicane à*

Québec: Holy Trinity Cathedral (1796-
1996) (Sillery: Les éditions du
Septentrion, 1995) 97.

the only stone near Québec
Quoted in Noppen and Morisset, *La*
présence anglicane à Québec 77.

123 *perfect acoustics*
Henry Roe, *Story of the First Hundred*
Years of the Diocese of Quebec (Québec:
1893) 11.

the idea was taken
Quoted in Würtele, "The English
Cathedral of Quebec" 79.

124 *In several places which we visited*
Peter Kalm, in Adolph B. Benson (rev.
and ed.), *The America of 1750: Peter*
Kalm's Travels in North America (New
York: Dover, 1966) 470.

the finest and largest there can be
Joyce Marshall (trans. and ed.), *Word*
from New France: The Selected Letters of
Marie de l'Incarnation (Toronto: Oxford
University Press, 1967) 129–30.

Ursuline Convent
Jean Trudel, *The Ursuline Chapel in*
Quebec City (Québec: Monastère des
Ursulines de Québec, 2005).

the Levasseur family dynasty
Christina Cameron, "Levasseur
Family," *TCE* 1203–1204; A.J.H.
Richardson et al., *Quebec City:*
Architects, Artisans, and Builders
(Ottawa: History Division, National
Museum of Man, 1984) 355–68.

sole surviving example
Luc Noppen and Lucie K. Morisset,
Art et architecture des églises à Québec
(Sainte-Foy QC: Publications du
Québec, 1996) 88.

127 *staunch guardian*
William Toye, *The St Lawrence*
(Toronto: Oxford University Press,
1959) 274.

128 *Saint-Jean-Baptiste*
Souvenances: St-Jean-Baptiste…un
faubourg…un clocher (n.p., 1984);
www.patrimoine-
religieux.qc.ca/sjeaque/sjeaquee.htm.

132 *large and magnificent*
Alan Gowans, *Church Architecture in*
New France (Toronto: University of
Toronto Press, 1955) 25, 41.

carpentry, sculpture, painting
Alan Gowans, *Church Architecture in*
New France (Toronto: University of
Toronto Press, 1955) 46–47.

133 *the best, if not the only*
Alan Gowans, "Claude Baillif," *DCB*
1. 75–78.

built at a later date
Luc Noppen, *Notre-Dame de Québec:*
son architecture et son rayonnement
(1647–1922) (Québec: Éditions du
Pélican, 1974) 97; Luc Noppen and
Marc Grignon, *L'art de l'architecte: three*

centuries of architectural drawing in
Québec City (Québec: Musée du
Québec/Université Laval, 1983) 49, 53,
130, 132; also F.J. Thorpe, "Gaspard-
Joseph Chaussegros de Léry," *DCB* 3.
124–28.

133 *Swedish botanist Peter Kalm*
Adolph B. Benson (rev. and ed.), *Peter
Kalm's Travels in North America* (New
York: Dover, 1966) 427, 466–67.

134 *The music never ceased*
Joyce Marshall (trans. and ed.), *Word
from New France: The Selected Letters of
Marie de l'Incarnation* (Toronto: Oxford
University Press, 1967) 316–17.

a craftsman who became an architect
Noppen and Grignon, *L'art de l'archi-
tecte* 54–58; Luc Noppen, "Jean
Baillairgé," *DCB* 5. 48–51.

François Baillairgé
David Karel, Luc Noppen and
Magella Paradis, "François Baillairgé,"
DCB 6. 24–29.

Charles Baillairgé
Christina Cameron, *Charles Baillairgé,
Architect & Engineer* (Montreal:
McGill-Queen's University Press,
1989) 72–73 and pl. 5.

135 *Sun. 25th — Christmas Day [1791]*
Elizabeth Posthuma Gwillim Simcoe,
*The Diary of Mrs. John Graves Simcoe,
Wife of the First Lieutenant-Governor of
the Province of Upper Canada, 1792–6*
(Toronto: W. Briggs, 1911) 69.

137 *Les rivières sont des chemins*
Blaise Pascal, *Pensées*, in: *Œuvres com-
plètes* (Bibliothèque de la Pléiade 34;
Paris: Gallimard, 1954) 1099.

five different churches
Beauvais and Rollin were instructed to
"refashion the ceiling [and other ele-
ments] in imitation of the one at
Marieville, construct four balconies
like those at Saint-Marc-sur-Richelieu,
fashion a pulpit and a churchwarden's
seat like those at Saint-Jean-Baptiste
de Rouville, create a candlestick for
the Paschal Candle like that at Saint-
Constant, and build pews and confessionals like those at Longueuil." See
Denyse Légaré: http://www.patri-
moinereligieux.qc.ca/stmathias/stmat
hiase.htm.

139 *Saint-Joseph-de-Beauce*
Nicole Genêt, " Ensemble institution-
nel," *Les chemins de la mémoire*, tome 1
(Québec: Publications du Québec,
1990) 428–31; Madeleine Gobeil-
Trudeau, *L'ensemble institutionnel de
Saint-Joseph de Beauce* (Québec: min-
istère de Affaires culturelles, 1984).

140 *Saint-Elzéar*
Madeleine Gobeil-Trudeau, "Église de
Saint-Elzéar et sacristie," *Les chemins
de la mémoire*, tome 1: 432–33; Groupe
Harcart, *Fabrique Saint-Elzéar de Beauce,*

Saint-Elzéar (Comté Beauce: ministère
des Affaires culturelles, 1981).

Saint-Isidore
Madeleine Gobeil-Trudeau, *Les
chemins de la mémoire*, tome 1 (Québec:
Publications du Québec, 1990) 436–37;
Groupe Harcart, *Fabrique Saint-Isidore,
Saint-Isidore, comté Dorchester* (Québec:
ministère des Affaires culturelles,
1982).

143 *The Roman liturgy*
Philippe Sylvain, "Ignace Bourget,"
DCB 11. 97.

La ville aux cent clochers
Raymond Gauthier et al., *L'architecture
de Montréal* (Montréal: Libre
Expression, 1990) 59.

144 *cradle of the English-speaking Catholic*
Gilles Lauzon and Madeline Forget,
Old Montreal: History through Heritage
(Sainte-Foy: Publications du Québec,
2003) 82.

suffered repeated alterations
Jean-Claude Marsan, *Montreal in
Evolution* (Montreal: McGill-Queen's
University Press, 1981) 99–100.

high, wide and handsome
Dimensions in Franklin Toker, *The
Church of Notre-Dame in Montreal,* 1970,
2d ed. (Montreal: McGill-Queens
University Press, 1991) 43–49, 51–52,
59. See also "The Basilica of Notre-
Dame de Montréal": www. patri-
moinereligieux.qc.ca/bndmtl/bndm-
tle.htm.

145 *the solemn tone of the organ*
B.W.A. Sleigh, *Pine Forests and
Hacmatack Clearings; or, Travel, Life and
Adventure, in the British North American
Provinces* [2d ed. (London: Bentley,
1853)] 237–38, and "Histoire de la
Semaine," *La Revue canadienne* I (June
14, 1845), quoted in: Toker, *The Church
of Notre-Dame* 60.

You expect the interior
Sleigh, *Pine Forests and Hacmatack
Clearings* 237–38, and "Histoire de la
Semaine," *La Revue canadienne* I (June
14, 1845), quoted in Toker, *The Church
of Notre-Dame* 60.

formed a few rough sketches
Quoted in: Toker, *The Church of Notre-
Dame in Montreal* 84.

146 *the most colossal auditorium in Christendom*
Pierre Vignot, *Carême de Montréal*
(Paris: Libr Victor Lecoffre, 1907) 6, 8,
quoted in: Toker, *The Church of Notre-
Dame in Montreal* 63.

148 *a quick transition*
Burke, *A Philosophical Enquiry* 103–105,
quoted in ibid. 62

instantly in an atmosphere
Henry David Thoreau, *A Yankee in
Canada, with Anti-Slavery and Reform
Papers* (Boston: Ticknor and Fields,

1866) 12–13, quoted in Toker, *The
Church of Notre-Dame* 61–62.

Victor Bourgeau
Luc Noppen, "Victor Bourgeau
(Bourgeault)," *DCB* 11. 91–94.

150 *there were 6500*
Jean-Claude Marsan, *Montreal in
Evolution* (Montreal: McGill-Queen's
University Press, 1981) 200.

eight to ten thousand
Rachel Tunnicliffe's translation, in
Charles Bourget, "The Basilica of St.
Patrick of Montréal": www.patri-
moine-religieux.ac.ca/spatmtl/
spatmtle.htm, from Raymonde
Gauthier,*Construire une église au
Québec, l'architecture religieuse avant
1939* (Montréal: Libre Expression,
1994) 107.

solid but naïve
Georges-Émile Giguère, "Felix
Martin," *DCB* 11. 587–89.

152 *too much is generally attempted*
A.W. Pugin, *The True Principles of
Pointed or Christian Architecture*
(London: John Weale, 1841) 40–41.

restraint, solidity of construction
Jean-Claude Marsan, "Foreword," in:
Ellen James, *John Ostell: Architect,
Surveyor* (Montreal; McCord Museum,
McGill University, 1985) xv.

154 *to a massive influx of destitute Irish*
Gilles Lauzon and Madeline Forget,
Old Montreal: History through Heritage
(Sainte-Foy: Publications du Québec,
2003) 166–67.

such highly emotional devotions
Sylvain, "Ignace Bourget," *DCB* 1. 98.

fine arts complex
Martin Drouin, "Les campagnes de
sauvegarde de la maison Van Horne et
du couvent des Sœurs grises ou les
questionnements d'une identité
urbaine (Montréal, 1973–1976)",
JSSAC 26: 3,4 (2001) 25–36;
www.catholicnewsagency.com/showa
rchive.php?date=2004-06-04 and
mediarelations.concordia.ca/media-
room/pressreleases/2004/06/002186.s
html.

Sainte-Brigide de Kildare
Jean-Claude Marsan, *Montreal in
Evolution* (Montreal: McGill–Queen's
University Press, 1981) 175; *Paroisse
Sainte-Brigide de Kildare: Guide pratique
pour visiter l'église* [leaflet].

Chapelle du Grand Séminaire
Jean-Paul Labelle (ed.), *Chapelle et
Crypte du Grand Séminaire de Montréal*
(Montréal : Fondation du Grand
Séminaire de Montréal, 2001) 8.

159 *We relied solely on the size and harmony*
Ernest Cormier, "Les Plans de
l'Université de Montréal," *Architecture,
Bâtiment, Construction* 2: 10 (January

1947) 29-30, quoted in: Simmins, *Documents* 166–68.

159 *the diocese of Chicoutimi*
Bergeron, *Architecture des églises* 163.
ancient Roman basilicas
Paul Racine, www.histoirequebec.qc.ca/publicat/vol12num1/v2n1_2eg.htm; Raymond Gauthier, *Construire une église au Québec. L'architecture religieuse avant 1939* (Montréal: Libre Expression, 1994).

160 *Oratoire Saint-Joseph and Brother André*
Jean-Claude Breton, o.p., *L'étrange destin d'Alfred Bessette dit frère André* (Montréal: Fides, 2004); Jean-Guy Dubuc, *Brother André* (Saint Laurent QC: Fides, 1999); Nicole Tardif-Painchaud, *Dom Bellot et l'architecture religieuse au Québec* (Québec: Presses de l'université Laval, 1978).

161 *Saint-Richard*
Bergeron, *Architecture des églises* 91–92.

163 *Première Église Évangélique Arménienne*
Bergeron, *Architecture des églises* 316–18.
Saint-Marc, La Baie
Bergeron, *Architecture des églises* 247–51.
Saint-Raphaël, Jonqière
Bergeron, *Architecture des églises* 259–62.

164 *Notre-Dame-de-Fatima, Jonqière*
Bergeron, *Architecture des églises* 286–89.
Saint-Gérard-Majella
Bergeron, *Architecture des églises* 273–78.

168 *Idleness is the enemy of the soul*
Rule of Saint Benedict; quoted in www.kansasmonks.org/RuleOfStBenedict.html.
Abbaye Saint-Benoît-du-Lac
Claude Bergeron and Geoffrey Simmins, *L'abbaye de Saint-Benoît-du-Lac et ses bâtisseurs* (Québec: Presses de l'université Laval, 1993); Kalman, *History of Canadian Architecture* 729–32; *L'abbaye de Saint-Benoît-du-Lac,* conception by Jacques Côté (rev. ed., 2001, n.p.) [pamphlet]; www.st-benoit-du-lac.com/.

170 *respected but did not imitate*
Bergeron and Simmins, *L'Abbaye de Saint-Benoît-du-Lac* 267–312, esp. 270–71.

172 *Sisters of Saint John*
See www.ssjd.ca/pioneer.html.
L'Arche
Marco Polo, "Simple Blessings," *Canadian Architect* (June 2001); Jean Vanier, *Becoming Human* (Toronto: Anansi, 1998); www.canadianarchitect.com ; www.larche.ca/en/communities/on/daybreak_richmond_hill/.

ONTARIO

178 *We thank thee for the sacrifice*
Voices United: the Hymn and Worship Book of the United Church of Canada, ed. John Ambrose (Etobicoke, Ont.: United Church Publishing House, 1999) no. 523.

180 *Sainte-Marie and the Hurons*
HAC 1, pl. 35, "The Great Lakes Basin, 1600–1653."
Barbara Heck put her brave soul
Inscription on commemorative monument, Blue Church cemetery.

182 *25 to 30 farms along the Detroit River*
Baskerville, *Ontario* 42.
granted all rights of ownership
Baskerville, *Ontario* 130.

185 *independent of the U.S.*
Noll, *History* 247
Anglican clergy… Methodist preachers
Baskerville, *Ontario* 92–95.
Ontario's population
Robert Bothwell and Norman Hillmer, "Ontario," *TCE* 1570.

186 *payment for disloyalty*
David Mills, "Rebellion Losses Bill," *TCE* 1831.
population numbers
HAC 2, pl. 20.
Ontario's social welfare system
Baskerville, *Ontario* 169.
church membership
Baskerville, *Ontario* 112–13.
Anglo-Saxon in their origins
HAC 2, pl. 52.

187 *The evolution of church architecture*
Noll, *History* 271.

188 *Jesuit missionaries circled the globe*
"Jesuits", *EB* 5: 550.
though some of the details are now disputed
Jeanie Tummon and W. Barry Gray, *Before & Beyond Sainte-Marie: 1987-1990 Excavations at the Sainte-Marie among the Hurons Site Complex (circa 1200-1990)* (Dundas: Copetown, 1995).
I wanted a church both rustic and amateur
Father John Filion, quoted at www.martyrs-shrine.com/.

193 *Every establishment of Church and State*
John Graves Simcoe, quoted in Baskerville, *Ontario* 84.
Her Majesty's Chapel of the Mohawks
McRae and Adamson, *Hallowed Walls* 10–15, especially 12; www.mohawkchapel.ca/history.html.
White Chapel, Picton
Ralph Greenhill, Ken MacPherson and Douglas Richardson, *Ontario Towns* (Ottawa: Oberon, 1974) unpaginated [21], caption to pl. 4; Patricia C. Taylor, *History of the Churches of Prince Edward County* (Picton ON: Picton Gazette Pub. Co., 1971) 144.

194 *St. Andrew's, Williamstown*
Mary J. Wilson and Eleanor MacNaughton, *History of St. Andrew's United Church at Williamstown, Ontario, 1787–1987,* 1987, 2d ed. (Williamstown: St. Andrew's United Church, 2002).

196 *Sharon Temple*
Albert Schrauwers, *Awaiting the Millenium: The Children of Peace and the Village of Hope, 1812-1889* (Toronto: University of Toronto Press, 1993), esp. chapters 2–3, 6–7.

197 *In peace I write this structure*
Mark Fram and Albert Schrauwers, *4Square* (Toronto: Coach House, 2005) 33.

199 *a secret drawer*
"The Ark Papers," Sharon Temple Study Series No. 3 (Sharon Temple, 1992).
Robert Baldwin … Louis-Hippolyte LaFontaine
Fram and Schrauwers, *4Square* 52–53.
Christ Church, Burritt's Rapids
MacRae and Adamson, *Hallowed Walls* 121.
Altona Meetinghouse
MacRae and Adamson, *Hallowed Walls* 194–95; Greenhill, MacPherson and Richardson, *Ontario Towns* unpaginated [22],
Joseph Nighswander
"Altona Mennonite Meeting House," www.pada.ca/lib/books/2/825/0.jp.
St. George's Cathedral, Kingston
Rosalind Walton and Philip Rogers, *Notes on the History of St. George's Cathedral, Kingston, Ontario* (Kingston: St. George's Cathedral, n.d.).

200 *Lord Sydenham*
P.A. Buckner, "Sydenham … ," *TCE* 2104.
St. Georges, Cathedral
Jennifer McKendry, *With Our Past before Us : Nineteenth-Century Architecture in the Kingston Area* (Toronto: University of Toronto Press, 1995) 59–68.

203 *William Coverdale*
McKendry, *With Our Past before Us* 62–66.

204 *Christian architecture is the name given*
William Hay, quoted in: William Westfall and Malcolm Thurlby, "Church Architecture and Urban Space etc.", eds. David Keene and Colin Read, *Old Ontario: Essays in Honour of J.M.S. Careless* (Toronto: Dundurn, 1990) 119.
Thomas Talbot
MacRae and Adamson, *Hallowed Walls* 114.; Alan G. Brunger, " Thomas Talbot," *DCB* 8. 857–62.

206 *St. Andrew's, Niagara-on-the-Lake*
Peter John Stokes, *Old Niagara on the Lake* (Toronto: University of Toronto Press, 1971) 9–10, 56–57.

207 *Greek Revival structures are rare*
Shannon Ricketts, Leslie Maitland and Jacqueline Hucker, *A Guide to Canadian Architectural Styles*, 1992, 2d ed. (Peterborough ON: Broadview Press, 2004) 47–53; Eric Arthur, *Toronto No Mean City*, 1964, 3d ed., rev. Stephen A. Otto. (Toronto: University of Toronto Press, 2003) 61–62, pls. 3.37, 3.38.

Cooper's plan, the Grecian Doric
MacRae and Adamson, *Hallowed Walls* 199, 202, 204.

208 *Asher Benjamin*
Greenhill, Macpherson and Richardson, *Ontario Towns* unpaginated: [viii] (Benjamin's plates), [22–23] (discussion) and caption to pl. 14.

the divil's own kist o'whustles
John S. Moir, *Enduring Witness: A History of the Presbyterian Church in Canada* (Toronto: Presbyterian Publications, 1974) 123, 133.

209 *Our Lady of Assumption, Windsor*
Yves F. Zoltvany, "Antoine Laumet, dit de Lamothe Cadillac," *DCB* 2. 351–57; Karen Stoskopf Harding, *Architecture française en Ontario: Quatre exemples marquants de l'oeuvre de nos premiers bâtisseurs* (Ottawa: Prise de Parole, 1987) 40; MacRae and Adamson, *Hallowed Walls* 130–35; "Parish History," www.assumption.rcec.london.on.ca/history.htm.

William Thomas and St. Paul's, London
Neil Einarson, "William Thomas (1799–1860), of Birmingham, Leamington Spa and Toronto," M.Phil. thesis, Department of Art, University of Essex, 1980, 202–207; Neil Einarson, "William Thomas," *DCB* 8. 872–78.

210 *French-Canadian heritage*
MacRae and Adamson, *Hallowed Walls* 18–19.

West Dumfries Wesleyan Methodist Chapel
Katherine Ashenburg, *Going to Town: Architectural Walking Tours in Southern Ontario* (Toronto: MacFarlane Walter & Ross, 1998) 89–109; Nina Perkins Chapple, *A Heritage of Stone: Buildings of the Niagara Peninsula, Fergus and Elora, Guelph, Region of Wateroo, Cambridge, Paris, Ancaster-Dundas-Flamborough, Hamilton and St. Marys* (Toronto: James Lorimer & Company, 2006) 75–85; MacRae and Adamson, *Hallowed Walls* 263, 266; *Cobblestone Buildings of Paris, Ontario* (Hamilton: Hamilton Branch of the Architectural Conservancy of Ontario, n.d. [1966]) 2.

Grace United Church
MacRae and Adamson, *Hallowed Walls* 236.

213 *Auld Kirk and Free Kirk*
Moir, *Enduring Witness: A History of the Presbyterian Church in Canada* 101.

214 *How long do they intend*
Quoted from *Hamilton Spectator* (1854) in: S.W. Vance, *St. Andrew's-St. Paul's: 1857–1957* (Hamilton: St. Paul's Church, 1957) 6.

Thomas could be proud
MacRae and Adamson, *Hallowed Walls* 149.

Arts and Crafts
Kalman, *History of Canadian Architecture* 619–20; Ricketts, Maitland and Hucker, *A Guide to Canadian Architectural Styles* 139–41.

216 *Abundant clay formed in lakes*
Bureau of Mines publication (1903) quoted in Nancy Z. Tausky and Lynne D. DiStefano, *Victorian Architecture in London and Southwestern Ontario: Symbols of Aspiration* (Toronto: University of Toronto Press, 1986) 90.

217 *tradition, construction, handcraft*
James Stevens Curl, *A Dictionary of Architecture* (Hoo, Kent: Grange, 2005) 37–38.

George F. Durand
Nancy Z. Tausky and Lynne D. DiStefano, *Victorian Architecture in London and Southwestern Ontario: Symbols of Aspiration* (Toronto: University of Toronto Press, 1986) 102, 223–36.

not recognized as architects
Geoffrey Simmins, *Ontario Association of Architects: A Centennial History, 1889–1989* (Toronto: Ontario Association of Architects, 1989) 27–41, 98–99, 103.

St. Mary's, Walkerville
Robert L. Daniels, *History of Saint Mary's Church, Walkerville* (Walkerville, 1942) 9–13, 28–33, 35.

Hiram Walker
Ronald G. Hoskins, "Hiram Walker," *DCB* 12. 1079–1081.

219 *Ralph Adams Cram*
Douglass Shand Tucci, "Ralph Adams Cram," *Macmillan Encyclopedia of Architects* 1 (New York: Free Press, 1982) 471; Douglass Shand-Tucci, *Ralph Adams Cram: Life and Architecture*, vol. 1, *Boston Bohemia, 1881–1900* (Amherst: University of Massachusetts Press, 1995) 274–75.

A thousand associations
G.H. Edgell, *The American Architecture of To-day* (New York: Charles Scribner's Sons, 1928) 203–209.

the most perfect type ever produced
Ralph Adams Cram, *Church Building: A Study of the Principles of Architecture in Their Relation to the Church* (Boston: Small, Maynard, 1901) 30.

220 *You have hunted us from every place*
Shingwaukonse, quoted in Penny Petrone (ed.), *First People, First Voices* (Toronto: University of Toronto Press, 1991) 60.

Manitoulin Island
Rhona Telford, "The Wikwemikong First Nations and the Department of Indian Affairs' Mismanagement of Petroleum Development," in Edgar-André Montigny and Lori Chambers (eds.), *Ontario Since Confederation: A Reader* (Toronto: University of Toronto Press, 2000) 40–54.

222 *Canada is decidedly not the country*
John Langton, *Early Days in Upper Canada. The Letters of John Langton* (Toronto: MacMillan, 1926) 145.

St. Thomas, Shanty Bay
MacRae and Adamson, *Hallowed Walls* 219–20.

225 *St. Andrew's Thorah Township*
MacRae and Adamson, *Hallowed Walls* 71–76.

227 *St. Peter's on the Rock*
St. Peter's-on-the-Rock, Stony Lake, Ontario: The Island Church (n.p., n.d.); Christie Bentham and Katherine Hooke, *From Burleigh to Boschink: A Community Called Stony Lake* (Toronto: Natural Heritage Books, 2000).

231 *Come, bless the Lord*
Psalm 134: 1–2 (*NRV*).

Basilique-cathèdrale Notre-Dame
Norman Pagé, *La cathédrale Notre-Dame d'Ottawa: Histoire, architecture, iconographie* (Ottawa: Presses de l'Université d'Ottawa, 1988); Norman Pagé, *Notre-Dame Basilica Cathedral* (Ottawa: Archdiocese of Ottawa, 1994).

232 *St. John the Baptist, Perth*
175 Years of Faith: The Story of the Parish of St. John the Baptist, Perth, 1823–1998 (Perth 1998).

235 *Our Lady of the Immaculate Conception,*
Kalman, *History of Canadian Architecture* 585; M. Romana and T. Collins, *The Church of Our Lady, Guelph, Ontario* (n.p., n.d.).

236 *The chapel may be said to be cozy, pretty*
Ottawa Daily Citizen (May 19, 1888) quoted in: Luc Noppen, *In the National Gallery of Canada: "One of the Most Beautiful Chapels in the Land,"* (Ottawa: National Gallery of Canada, 1988) 79.

238 *He set me down on a plain*
Ezekiel 37: 1–3 (*NRV*).

Prince Edward County
Patricia C. Taylor (ed.), *History of the Churches of Prince Edward County* (Picton: Picton Gazette, 1971); Alan R. Capon, *A Goodly Heritage, Being a*

Chronological History of the Parish of Picton (Picton: Church of Saint Mary Magdalene, 1980.

241 *iconic tableau*
Description courtesy of Shirley Ann Brown, Professor of Art History, York University, Toronto.

Toronto is a noble and promising city
[A.W.H. Rose], *The emigrant churchman in Canada*, ed. Rev. Henry Christmas, 2 vols. (London: R. Bentley, 1849) 1. 67.

Toronto's rapid growth
W.H. Smith, *Smith's Canadian Gazetteer* (Toronto: Author, 1846) 193.

a meeting house for Episcopalians
Quoted in: Eric Arthur, *Toronto, No Mean City*, 3d. ed. (Toronto: University of Toronto Press, 1986) 35.

amazing diversity of sects in Upper Canada
Sir Richard Bonnycastle, *The Canadas in 1841*, 2 vols. (London: H. Colburn, 1841) I: 183.

242 *especially in Ireland*
Douglas Scott Richardson, *Gothic Revival Architecture in Ireland*, 2 vols. (New York: Garland Publishing, 1983) 45–106.

243 *churchwarden for 35 years*
Dianne Newell, entry on William Gooderham, *DCB* 11. 358–60.

There was no Protestant church
Robertson, *Landmarks of Toronto* 4: 4

staring red brick
Mrs. [Anna] Jameson, *Winter Studies and Summer Rambles in Canada*, 3 vols. (London: Saunders and Otley, 1838) 1: 2.

Other denominations built in Toronto
Baptist: Robertson, *Landmarks of Toronto* 4: 424; Roman Catholic: MacRae and Adamson, *Hallowed Walls*; others: William Dendy, *Lost Toronto: Images of the City's Past*, rev. and updated ed. (Toronto: McClelland & Stewart, 1993), 9, 140, 148.

Henry Bowyer Lane
Stephen A. Otto and Marion Bell MacRae, "Henry Bowyer Joseph Lane," *DCB* 8. 485–87; Arthur and Otto, *Toronto, No Mean City* 80, 88, 90, 254.

Michael Power
Robert Choquette, "Michael Power," *DCB* 7. 705–706.

St. Paul's Power Street
MacRae and Adamson, *Hallowed Walls* 82–84.

St. Michael's Cathedral
Brian C. Cook, *The Voice of the Archangel Michael: 'Who is Like God?'* (Toronto: St. Michael's Cathedral, 1989) 15.

245 *Armand-François-Marie de Charbonnel*
Murray W. Nicolson and John S. Moir, Armand-François-Marie de

Charbonnel, *DCB* 12. 182–85.

he led the way himself
"Circular. Decoration of St. Michael's Cathedral." (Enclosed with a form letter, December 1858, from the Vicar General, T.M. Brugère [Archives of the Archdiocese of Toronto].)

Frederic Cumberland
Arthur and Otto, *Toronto, No Mean City* 243-44; Geoffrey Simmins, *Fred Cumberland: Building the Victorian Dream* (Toronto: University of Toronto Press, 1997).

247 *in the Gothic style*
Church (June 7, 1849) 179, quoted in Shirley Morriss with Carl Benn, "Architecture," *The Parish and Cathedral of St James'*, Toronto 1797–1997, ed. William Cooke (Toronto: St. James' Cathedral, 1998) 195.

Cumberland's design
Malcolm Thurlby, "Medieval Toronto," *Rotunda* 24, no. 4 (Spring 1992) 27–33.

richer in detail and bolder in form
Morriss, "Architecture," *Parish and Cathedral of St James'* 198, 203.

John Strachan
G.M. Craig, John Strachan, *DCB* 9. 765.

248 *William G. Storm*
Shirley G. Morriss, William George Storm, *DCB* 12. 991–94.

became a model
William Westfall, *Two Worlds: The Protestant Culture of Nineteenth Century Ontario* (Montreal: McGill-Queen's University Press, 1989) 132.

249 *I would give my ears*
Fred Cumberland to Wilmot Cumberland, October 25, 1851, quoted in: Simmins, *Fred Cumberland* 68.

251 *Anglicans almost doubled*
William Westfall, *Two Worlds: The Protestant Culture of Nineteenth Century Ontario* (Montreal: McGill-Queen's University Press, 1989) 127–29.

Edmund Burke
Angela K. Carr, "Edmund Burke," *DCB* 14. 156–58; Angela Carr, *Toronto Architect, Edmund Burke: Redefining Canadian Architecture* (Montreal: McGill-Queen's University Press, 1995) 23.

ecclesiastical amphitheatral construction
Robertson, *Landmarks of Toronto* 4. 423.

253 *Beverley Street Baptist*
Carr, "Edmund Burke," *DCB* 14. 153.

254 *Joseph Conolly was trained in Dublin*
Malcolm Thurlby, "The 'Roman Renaissance' Churches of Joseph Connolly and Arthur Holmes and their Place in Roman Catholic Church Architecture," *JSSAC* 29 (2004) 3.

St. Mary Magdalene
David Greig, *In the Fullness of Time: A History of the Church of Saint Mary Magdalene* (Toronto: Church of Saint Mary Magdalene, 1990) 2–4, 10–12.

Frank Darling
Kelly Crossman, "Frank Darling," *DCB* 15. 251–53.

instinct for Catholic worship
Eugene R. Fairweather, "Introduction," in Greig, *In the Fullness of Time* xvii.

255 *colourful vestments*
Greig, *In the Fullness of Time* 17–20.

Christ's re-united Church
Harold J. Nahabedian, "Foreword," in Greig, *In the Fullness of Time*, viii.

256 *Town planning is first and foremost*
Siegfried Giedion, *Space, Time and Architecture* (Cambridge: Harvard University Press, 3d ed., 1954) 718.

259 *They took us where they worshipped*
Prince Volodymyr's emissaries reporting back to him about Haghia Sophia in Constantinople (Istanbul), quoted in brochure, St. Elias Church, Brampton.

William Rae
www.archives.gov.on.ca/ENGLISH/exhibits/architecture/record_church.htm.

261 *Alexander C. Hutchison*
Kalman, *History of Canadian Architecture* 562–63.

262 *Sts. Cyril and Methodius*
Mykola Komar, in *50th Anniversary Sts. Cyril and Methodius Ukrainian Catholic Parish St. Catharines, Ontario* (no p. 1993) 19–20.

264 *Benjamin Brown*
Stephen A. Speisman, *The Jews of Toronto: A History to 1937* (Toronto: McClelland and Stewart, 1979) 323, n. 1.

St. George's Greek Orthodox
Peter Jeffreys, *Saint George's Greek Otthodox Church: An Architectural and Iconographic Guide* (Toronto 2000).

266 *The chief scenes of the Pachomaioi frescoes*
Peter Jeffreys, *Saint George's*, 12.

Holy Trinity Russian
V.P. Malikov, *Brief History of Holy Trinity Parish, 50th Anniversary, 1949–99*; Russian, translated by Vladislav Fedorov, November 28, 2006.

Radoslav Zuk
Walter Daschko, "Tradition and Modernity: Architecture of the Ukrainian Diaspora and Radoslav Zuk" www.ukrweekly.com/Archive/2003/520322.shtml; Alexandra Hawryluk, "Mosaics and Stained Glass: The Art of Roman Kowal" www.ukrweekly.com/Archive/2002/090226.shtml.

272 *One quit the work with more regret*
J.E.H. Macdonald, *RAIC Journal* (May-June 1925), quoted in *Saint Anne's Church, 1862–1987* (Toronto: s.n., 1987) 15.
The pictorial painting was separated
www.stannes.on.ca / Artwork.html.

274 *Architecture should enliven, ennoble*
"Foreword," *Remembering John Cresswell Parkin: An Exhibition* (Toronto: Royal Canadian Academy of Arts 1991).
No stereotyped style
The Lutheran Witness, Ontario District Edition 74 (St. Louis, October 25, 1955, No 22), quoted in: *Toronto Peetri Kirik 50* (Toronto 2006) 26.

278 *Fellowship Center Chapel*
William Fitch, *Knox Church, Toronto: Avant-Garde, Evangelical, Advancing* (Toronto: 1971) 112–18.

283 *St. Andrew's Presbyterian*
Brian Stewart, "Breathing the Spirit of Life," *Presbyterian Record* (December 2005) 28–31.

284 *Salvation Army Scarborough Citadel*
Personal communications by the architect John van Nostrand and, on behalf of the Salvation Army, by Ian Howes.

WEST

288 *Although it was the movement of settlers*
Peter C. Newman, *Caesars of the Wilderness* (Markham ON: Viking, 1987) 378.
indigenous groups were living
HAC 1, pls. 2, 14 and 17.
Maps of the mid-18th century
Hayes, *Historical Atlas* 132–35.
Bodega y Quadra and Captain James Cook
Hayes, *Historical Atlas* 156–63.
It was the North West Company
Thompson, *Prairie West* 16.
Lord Selkirk
Thompson, *Prairie West* 19–20.

290 *Marie-Anne Lagimodière*
Globe and Mail, July 15, 2006, A3.
the most intensive efforts
James Hanrahan, "Oblates of Mary Immaculate," *TCE* 1550.

291 *James Douglas*
Margaret A. Ormsby, "Sir James Douglas," *TCE* 614–15.
Church of the Holy Cross, Skatin
Barry Downs, *Sacred Places*, 96–102; collections.gc.ca/drawings/sites/site10/10facts.html, with bibliography; Mark Hume, *Globe and Mail*, July 4, 2006, A3.
Louis Riel
Thompson, *Prairie West* 38; Lewis H. Thomas, "Louis Riel," *DCB* 11. 736–52;

George F.G. Stanley, "Louis Riel," *TCE* 1870–71.

292 *Surveyors used American models*
Stanley, "Louis Riel," *TCE*) 1871; Hayes, *Historical Atlas* 213 ("The Riel Rebellion of 1869") and 216–17 ("The North-West Rebellion, 1885).
Batoche
Walter Hildebrandt, "Batoche," *TCE* 187.
hope of forming a national church
Noll, *History* 281–84.

293 *In Canada the frontier has persisted*
Hugh Keenleyside, "Recent Developments in the Canadian North," *Canadian Geographical Journal* 39 (1949), cited in William R. Morrison, *True North: The Yukon and Northwest Territories* (Toronto: Oxford University Press, 1998) 9.
The average time from the day
William R. Morrison, *True North: The Yukon and Northwest Territories* (Toronto: Oxford University Press, 1998) 45.
taken apart board by board
Bernard Flaman, "Rural Churches and Places of Worship in Saskatchewan", unpublished paper, for Historic Resources, Department of Culture, Youth and Recreation, Government of Saskatchewan.

296 *This is a vast extent of country here*
The Rev. James Evans, to Mrs. Evans, October 2, 1838, quoted in: Charlotte Gray, *Canada: A Portrait in Letters* (N.P.: Anchor, 2004) 77; first published, *Papers and Records of the Ontario Historical Society* 27 (1932) 60–63.
William Henry Taylor
L.G. Thomas, "William Henry Taylor," *DCB* 10. 673–74.

301 *This man … is one of our people*
Emile Tardif, OMI, *Saint Albert* (Edmonton: La Survivance, n.d.) 34.

303 *The moment the bells ring for church*
Edmund Hope Verney, quoted in: Charlotte Gray, *Canada: A Portrait in Letters* (Toronto: Anchor Canada, 2004) 158; cited from Allan Pritchard, *Vancouver Island Letters of Edmund Hope Verney1862-1865* (Vancouver, University of British Columbia Press, 1996) 169–73.
St. Stephen's, Saanich
Gwen and Michael Wilkey, *Symbols of Faith: The History of Saint Stephen's Church Saanichton, British Columbia* (Pat Bay: West Saanich AeroGraphic Publications, 1995); Downs, *Sacred Places* 70–76.
St. Peter's, Duncan
David R. Williams, *Pioneer Parish: The Story of St. Peter's Quamichan* (St. Peter's Quamichan,: Duncan, B. C.,

1991); Ellen Mackay, *Places of Worship in the Cowichan and Chemainus Valleys* (Victoria, B.C.: Sono Nis, 1991) 63.
The gold rush of 1858
HAC II, pl. 36.
St.Ann's, Duncan
Ellen Mackay, *Places of Worship in the Cowichan and Chemainus Valleys* (Victoria, B.C.: Sono Nis, 1991) 118–19.
Church of St. John the Divine, Yale
Historic Yale (Yale BC: Heritage, n.d.); collections.ic.gc.ca / yale / tour / index.htm; collections.ic.gc.ca / yale / tour / drstjhn.htm.

306 *First Nations girls were taught needlework*
Natasha Slik, "Yale's Ecclesiastical Textiles," *BC Historical News* 35/4 (Fall 2002) 23–25; Rachel Edwards, "Unravelling the Past," *BC Historical News* 35: 4 (Fall 2002) 20–22.
The Cariboo Road … St. Saviour's, Barkerville
HAC 2, pl. 36; Bruce Ramsey, *Barkerville: A Guide to the Fabulous Cariboo Gold Camp* (Vancouver: Mitchell, 1961) 1; *Cariboo Gold Rush* (Surrey BC: Heritage House, 1987, 1994); www.brewerplans.com/Image%20bucket/Barkerville-Church.gif
The new church now building
Quoted in Bruce Ramsey, *Barkerville: A Guide to the Fabulous Cariboo Gold Camp* (Vancouver: Mitchell, 1961) 62.
St. Anne's, Upper Similkameen Reserve
Hedley Gazette, August 20, 1914; *Gazette of the Similkameen*, July 1, 1992

308 *St. Eugene's Mission*
S.L. Thrupp, *History of Cranbrook* (1929) 109–15.
The standard of finish and the quality
Barry Downs, *Sacred Places* 138.
St. Peter's, Windermere
Fran Kimpton, "St. Peter's — The Stolen Church one hundred years old," *The Valley Echo*, September 13, 2000: 22.

310 *At first in small and then in larger groups*
Ralph Connor, *The Foreigner: a tale of Saskatchewan* (New York: Hodder & Stoughton, G.H. Doran Co., 1909) 3.
Mennonites originated
Frank H. Epp and Rodney J. Sawatsky, "Mennonites," *TCE* 1335–36 . *See also* Harry Loewen, Mennonites", in Paul Robert Magocsi, ed. *Encyclopedia of Canada's Peoples* (Toronto: University of Toronto Press, 1999) 957–74, especially 964–66.
The Mennonites then recreated
Edward M. Ledohowski, *The Heritage Landscape of the Crow Wing Study Region of Southeastern Manitoba* (Winnipeg: Historic Resources Branch, Manitoba Culture, Heritage & Tourism, 2003) 48.

310 *they are plain folk*
Paul R. Magocsi, ed., *Encyclopedia of Canada's Peoples* (Toronto: Published for the Multicultural History Society of Ontario by the University of Toronto Press, 1999)

Frelsis Church at Grund
David K. Butterfield and Maureen Devanik Butterfield, *If Walls Could Talk: Manitoba's Best Buildings Explored & Explained* (Winnipeg: Great Plains Publishing, 2000) 59.

315 *Ludger Gareau*
Laurier Gareau, "Ludger Gareau:" www.societehisto.com/Genea/Genea7.html.

Gabriel Dumont
George Woodcock, "Gabriel Dumont," *TCE* 633–34; Valerius Geist, "Bison," *TCE* 232–33.

Batoche
Deanna Christensen and Menno Fieguth, *Historic Saskatchewan* (Toronto: Oxford University Press, 1986) 46; "French and Métis Settlements," *Encyclopedia of Saskatchewan* (Regina: Canadian Plains Research Center, University of Regina, 2005) 359–60; Dave Yanko, "Batoche," *virtual saskatchewan on-line magazine* (25 September. 2006): www.virtualsk.com/current issue/batoche.html.

Byzantine Christianity of Syria
Cyril Mungo, *Byzantine Architecture* (New York: Rizzoli, 1978) chapter 9.

St. Michael's, Gardenton
John C. Lehr, "Kinship and Society in the Ukrainian Pioneer Settlement of the Canadian West," *Canadian Geographer,* 29: 3 (1985) 207–19; John C. Lehr, "Folk Architecture in Manitoba: Mennonites and Ukrainians," Society for the Study of Architecture in Canada, *Bulletin,* 11: 2 (June 1986) 4; Kalman, *History of Canadian Architecture* 512–13. David Nemirovsky, "St. Michael's Ukrainian Greek Orthodox Church (Gardenton, Manitoba, 1899)": http://home.eol.ca/~nemmer/bluesky/church/m2_gardn.html

318 *served 40 families*
Anna Maria Baran, *Ukranian Catholic Churches of Saskatchewan* ([Saskatoon 2]: Ukranian Catholic Council of Saskatchewan, 1977) 2.

Father Philip Ruh
Philip Ruh, *Missionary and Architect* (Winnipeg: Progress Printing & Publishing, 1960) 49–54; William P. Thompson, "Philip Ruh," *TCE* (2006): www.thecanadianencyclopedia.com/index.cfm?PgNm=TCE&Params=A1ARTA0010297; Borys Gengalo, "Touring

Ukrainian Ottawa 4: St. Onuphrius Ukrainian-Catholic Church": http://www.infoukes.com/ucpbaott/docs/tour4.htm; Civilization.ca, "Comuniqué," June 26, 1996: www.civilization.ca/media/show_pr_e.asp?ID=134%20

Church of the Immaculate Conception
Kalman, *History of Canadian Architecture* 734–35.

321 *Ukrainian Cultural Heritage Village*
Ukrainian Cultural Heritage Village Guide (Edmonton: Alberta Community Development, 1995).

324 *Toil and Peaceful Life*
Precepts inscribed in the meeting room of the Doukhobor Prayer Home, Veregin, Saskatchewan.

Doukhobor Community Home
Koozma J. Tarasoff, *Spirit Wrestlers: Doukhobor Pioneers' Strategies for Living* (Ottawa: Spirit Wrestlers Publishing, 2002) 385, where he rejects the term, "Prayer Home."

Peter Verigin
A.A. Donskov, "Peter Vasil'evich Verigin," *DCB* 15. 1032–36.

began selling grain
Peter Legebokoff, *Sound Heritage* 6:4 (1977) 19, quoted in: Robert Minden, *Separate from the world: meetings with Doukhobor-Canadians in British Columbia* (Vancouver: National Film Board of Canada, 1979) [9].

Doukhobors
George Woodcock and Ivan Avakumovic, *The Doukhobors* (Toronto: Oxford University Press, 1968) 19; Deanna Christensen and Menno Fieguth, *Historic Saskatchewan* (Toronto: Oxford University Press, 1986) 68; George Woodcock, "Doukhobors," *TCE* 616–17.

326 *Besedka, a* dacha *in Georgia*
Woodcock and Avakumovic, *The Doukhobors* 70; Donskov, "Verigin," *DCB* 15: 1033 ("early 1880s"); "Besedka:" Koozma J. Tarasoff, *Spirit Wrestlers: Doukhobor Pioneers' Strategies for Living* (Ottawa: Spirit Wrestlers Publishing, 2002) 272, 356.

327 *the only symbols recognized*
"The Doukhobors:" www.ualberta.ca/~jrak/doukhobors.htm.

singing a capella
Shirley Perry, "The Importance of Song in Doukhobor Life," *The Doukhobor Centenary in:* Andrew Donskov et al. (eds), *Canada: A Multi-Disciplinary Perspective on Their Unity and Diversity* (Ottawa: Slavic Research Group at the University of Ottawa, 2000) 342, 345–46.

Peter "Godly" Verigin
Donskov, "Verigin," *DCB* 15: 1034.

Hutterites
John Ryan, "Hutterites," *TCE* 1031–32.

328 *Easter is a feast of joy*
Z. Kuzelia and P. Odarchenko, "Easter," in: *Encyclopedia of Ukraine,* ed. Volodymyr Kubiiovych, 6 vols. (Toronto: University of Toronto Press, 1984–) I: [780]. encyclopediaofukraine.com/pages/E/A/Easter.htm.

330 *We are still far from having attained*
Raphael and J. Arthur Brandon, *The Open Timber Roofs of the Middle Ages* (London: David Bogue, 1849) 1.

Christ Church Cathedral
Christ Church Cathedral: A Brief History (Vancouver: Christ Church Cathedral, n.d.) 1.

332 *St. Andrew's Cathedral*
St. Andrew's Cathedral, Victoria: A Guide (Victoria: Heritage Tour Guides, 1990).

334 *St. Paul's United, Boissevain*
The United Church of Canada: St. Paul's United Church, Boissevain, Man. 1893–1943 Fiftieth Anniversary [pamphlet], [3]–[4]; *75th Anniversary, 1893–1968, St. Paul's United Church, Boissevain, Manitoba*, 3–5; *They Built for the Future: St. Paul's United Church, Boissevain, Man. 1943-1993* [leaflet]; Angela Carr, "Fields and Theatre Churches: The Non-traditional Space of Evangelism," *Architecture & ideas* no. 3 (Summer 1999) 74. Jeanne Halgren Kilde, *When Church Became Theatre: The Transformation of Evangelical Architecture and Worship in Nineteenth-Century America* (New York: Oxford University Press, 2002); Presbyterian Church in Canada, General Assembly, Committee on Church Architecture, *Designs for Village, Town and City Churches* (Toronto: Canadian Architect and Builder Press, 1893).

337 *Our Lady of Good Hope*
Janet Wright, *Church of Our Lady of Good Hope: Fort Good Hope and the Northwest Territories* (Ottawa: Parks Canada, 1986); pwnhc.learnnet.nt.ca/timeline/1850/GoodHopeChurch_1865.html.

338 *St. Jude's, Iqaluit*
www.anglicanjournal.com/news-update/100/article/iqaluits-st-judes-cathedral-unusable-due-to-fire/; www.cbc.ca/canada/north/story/2005/11/11/fire-arson-20051111.html.

340 *Our guiding principle*
Walter Gropius, *The New Architecture and the Bauhaus* (Cambridge, Mass: M.I.T. Press, 1965) 89.

342 *Cardston Temple of the Church of Jesus*
Kalman, *History of Canadian Architecture* 753–54.

344 *St. James' Vancouver*
Kalman, *History of Canadian Architecture* 716–18.

344 *St. Mary's Cathedral, Calgary*
Norman Knowles, *Winds of Change: A History of the Roman Catholic Diocese of Calgary since 1968* (Calgary: Roman Catholic Diocese of Calgary, 2004) 198–200.

347 *All architecture is shelter*
Philip Johnson, 1975 address at Columbia University, from *Philip Johnson: Writings* (Oxford University Press, 1979), quoted in: www.bsa-architects.com/articles/quotes.html.
West Vanouver modernism
Peggy Stortz, "Architectural Poetry: Incorporating the Natural Environment," www.northshore.ca.

349 *St. Mary's, Red Deer*
Lisa Rochon, *Up North* (Toronto: Key Porter, 2005) 123.

352 *I must not let technology*
Douglas Cardinal, quoted in: Simmins, *Documents* 257 (from George Melnyk, ed., *Of the Spirit* [Edmonton: NeWest Press, 1977] 113–16).
Église Précieux-Sang, Saint-Boniface
"Church of the Precious Blood, St Boniface," *AR Canada,* ed. Lance Wright, a special issue of *Architectural Review* 167: no. 999 (May 1980) 317.

354 *My epiphany occurred during a visit*
Étienne Gaboury, "Métaphores et Métamorphoses en architecture," *Cahiers franco-canadiens de l'Ouest* 3:2 (automne 1991) 184, quoted in: Faye Hellner, "Étienne Gaboury, Manitoba Modernist," *Winnipeg Modern: Architecture 1945–1975,* ed. Serena Keshavjee (Winnipeg: University of Manitoba Press, 2006) 233.
a work of genius
Carol Moore Ede, *Canadian Architecture 1960/70* (Toronto: Burns and MacEachern, 1971) 190.
Saskatchewan's most respected architect
Trevor Boddy, "Clifford Wiens." *TCE* (1988) 2304; "Clifford Wiens," *Saskatchewan Encyclopedia* (Regina: Canadian Plains Research Center, University of Regina, 2005) 102–103.
Silton Chapel
Lisa Rochon, *Up North* (Toronto: Key Porter, 2005) 111.

359 *establish a Roman Catholic mission*
Terrence J. Fay, *A History of Canadian Catholics: Gallicanism, Romanism, and Canadianism* (Montreal: McGill-Queen's University Press, 2002) 37; Robert Choquette, *The Oblate Assault on Canada's Northwest* (Ottawa: University of Ottawa Press, 1995) 81.

Cathédrale Saint-Boniface
Ruth Cawker and William Bernstein, *Contemporary Canadian Architecture,* rev. and exp. ed. (Markham ON: Fitzhenry & Whiteside, 1988) 137; Faye Hellner, "Étienne Gaboury, Manitoba Modernist," in: *Winnipeg Modern: Architecture 1945–1975,* ed. Serena Keshavjee (Winnipeg: University of Manitoba Press, 2006) 235.

362 *The approach is not by a physical*
Quoted in *Architecture of Truth: The Cistercian Abbey of Le Thoronnet in Provence photographed by Lucien Hervé and arranged with quotations and notes by Francois Cali* (London: Thames and Hudson, 1957) 21.
St. Nicholas, Winnipeg
Basil Rotoff et al., *Monuments to Faith: Ukranian Churches in Maintoba* (Winnipeg: University of Manitoba Press, 1990) 98–99; June Dutka, "St. Nicholas Ukrainian Catholic Church: Historical Highlights" www.stnicholaschurch.ca/content_pages/history/history.htm and "… Present Building" www.stnicholaschurch.ca/content_pages/history/present_building.htm.

364 *Claude-Nicolas Ledoux*
Claude-Nicolas Ledoux, *L'architecture considérée sous le rapport de l'art, des mœurs et de la législation* (Paris, 1804; repub. Paris: Lenoir, 1847).

366 *Sts. Peter and Paul, Mundare*
Lamont County: Church Capital of North America, ed. Tina Hunt, 2d ed. (Lamont, AB: Economic Development / Tourism, Lamont County, n.d.) 30–33; online at http://www.county-lamont.ab.ca/visitor/churches.htm.
St. Stephen Protomartyr, Calgary
www.ststephen-protmrtyr-calgary.ca/; www.aaa,ab,ca/pages/public/csaa/csaa-41.htm.

Changes

370 *So, after all, we did gather up his bones*
The Martyrdom of Polycarp 18, in Maxwell Staniforth (trans.), *Early Christian Writings* (Harmondsworth: Penguin, 1988) 131. Polycarp lived into old age, and was born sometime in the first century, for he was a follower of the Apostle John. The account of his death is the earliest martyrdom outside the New Testament, and the reference to treasuring martyrs' relics the earliest anywhere.

The first meetings of believers
L. Michael White, *The Social Origins of Christian Architecture,* 2 vols. (Valley Forge PA: Trinity Press International, 1997) especially 2: 123–34.

372 *Roman society was held together*
Philip A. Harland, *Associations, Synagogues, and Congregations* (Minneapolis: Fortress, 2003).
Ostia
Gustav Hermansen, *Ostia: Aspects of Roman City Life* (Edmonton: University of Alberta Press, 1982).

375 *The model for these Christian monasteries*
Peter Richardson, *Building Jewish in the Roman East* (Waco: Baylor University Press, 2004) Part 3, especially chap 9.

379 *From the late-sixth century*
Des Lavelle, *The Skellig Story: Ancient Monastic Outpost* (Dublin: O'Brien, 1993) 11–60.

380 *Missionaries began arriving in Ireland*
R.F. Foster, *The Oxford History of Ireland* (Oxford: Oxford University Press, 2001) 9–12.

381 *In 730 icons were prohibited*
EB 5:283.
provided the maximum effect
Mango, *Byzantine Architecture* 40.

383 *Romanesque architecture … fulfils*
Christian Norberg-Schulz, *Meaning in Western Architecture* (New York: Rizzoli, 1980) 91.

387 *many times the weight of the*
www.iit.edu/departments/csep/perspective/pers10_2jan91_5.html.
1643, January 1. Edward's parish,
www.williamdowsing.org/Journal.htm#_VPINDEXENTRY_19.

388 *it deeply influenced Christopher Wren*
Christian Norberg-Schulz, *Baroque Architecture* (New York: Rizzoli 1986) 192.
a Baroque system of piazzas
Christian Norberg-Schulz, *Baroque Architecture* (New York: Rizzoli 1986) 192.

390 *St. Paul's, Winchester*
Contract Record (Toronto) 5 (1 March 1894) 1; *A History of Winchester United Church: 1883–1983* (Winchester ON: 1983).

396 *Thomas Fuller and St. Stephen's*
Janet Wright, "Thomas Fuller," *TCE* 852; MacRae and Adamson, *Hallowed Walls* 159.

397 *The very principle of religious architecture*
Alain de Botton, *The Architecture of Happiness* (Toronto: McClelland & Stewart, 2006) 107–108.
Leland Bell
www.whetung.com/bell.html.

GLOSSARY
OF ARCHITECTURAL TERMS

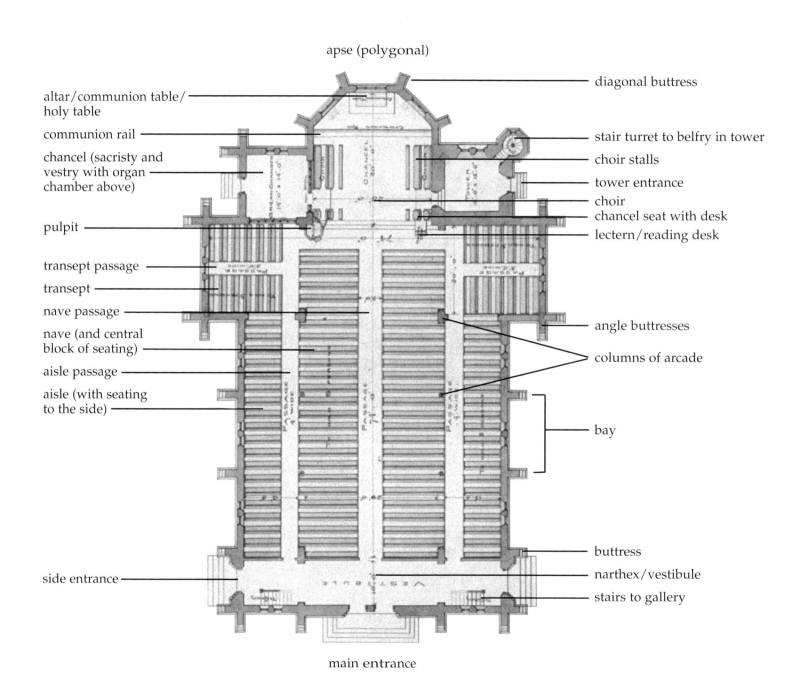

apse (polygonal)

diagonal buttress

altar/communion table/ holy table

communion rail

stair turret to belfry in tower

chancel (sacristy and vestry with organ chamber above)

choir stalls

tower entrance

choir

chancel seat with desk

pulpit

lectern/reading desk

transept passage

transept

nave passage

angle buttresses

nave (and central block of seating)

columns of arcade

aisle passage

aisle (with seating to the side)

bay

buttress

side entrance

narthex/vestibule

stairs to gallery

main entrance

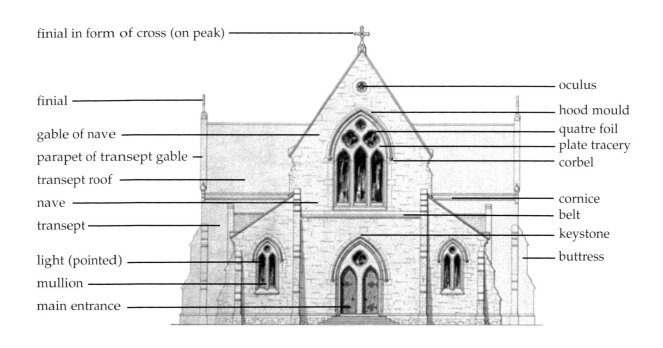

finial in form of cross (on peak)

oculus

finial

hood mould

gable of nave

quatre foil

parapet of transept gable

plate tracery

transept roof

corbel

nave

cornice

transept

belt

keystone

light (pointed)

buttress

mullion

main entrance

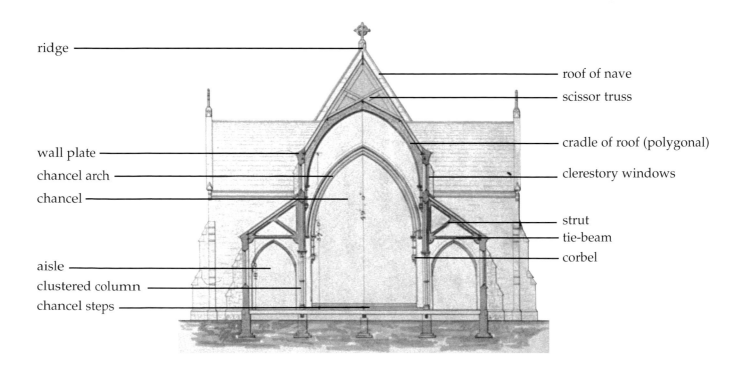

ridge

roof of nave

scissor truss

wall plate

cradle of roof (polygonal)

chancel arch

clerestory windows

chancel

strut

tie-beam

corbel

aisle

clustered column

chancel steps

This glossary is intended to provide only a brief guide to the meaning of words that may not be familiar to readers without some architectural training. There are references to photographs on the pages of this book that, we hope, will be helpful in making the meanings clear.

Readers who would like more information and a fuller definition for these and other words that appear in the text can consult any of the following works, all of which we have found most helpful; *Dictionary of Architecture* by James Stevens Curl (Hoo, Kent: Grange, 2005), *The Penguin Dictionary of Architecture and Landscape Architecture* by John Fleming, Hugh Honour and Nikolaus Pevsner (5th ed. London: Penguin, 1999) and *A Guide to Canadian Architectural Styles* by Leslie Maitland, Jacqueline Hucker and Shannon Ricketts (2nd ed. Peterborough: Broadview Press, 2004).

A

A-frame Structure framed like the letter A with steeply inclined gable roof but without sidewalls. See p. 274.

aedicule Shrine framed by columns supporting an entablative and pediment, containing a statue. See p. 152.

aisle Portion of a church parallel to but divided by columns from the nave, choir or transept. See pp. 237, 386.

Akron plan Features a consolidated liturgical centre as the focus of curved seating; Sunday school classrooms may be on a radial plan with a moveable wall system allowing all classes to be addressed from a central point. See p. 248.

alley The passage through blocks of seating in the church.

altar A table or block on which to offer a sacrifice; in Roman Catholic churches, an elevated table, often with stone top, for celebration of the mass. See p. 128.

altarpiece Sculpted or painted reredos. of wood or stone, may be narrower than the altar, or spread the width of the wall in a grand church. See p. 313.

ambulatory A passage behind the apse, originally for processional purposes. See p. 182.

amphitheatral A circular form of seating in churches, usually with rising a floor, not unlike a Roman amphitheater. See p. 335.

apse A semicircular or polygonal recess, generally housing an altar in a church; if at the west end it may house the font. See p. 101.

arcade A portion of wall carrying the structure on a range of open arches. See p. 141.

arch A curved or wedge-shaped opening in a wall. See p. 250.

architrave A structural member often made of stone, spanning the space between columns or piers. See p. 202.

ashlar Rectangular stones of equal length laid in regular horizontal courses during construction. Random ashlar is dressed stonework of varying lengths laid in even courses. See p. 342.

B

baldachin A covering or canopy over an altar or throne, often elaborate and usually carried on columns. See p. 111.

baluster A short post supporting a rail or coping, as in a staircase. See p. 54.

baptismal tank A large tank filled with water, often submerged in the floor or elevated behind an opening, used in churches practicing adult baptism. See p. 249.

baptistery A special area of a church dedicated to baptisms. See p. 354.

bargeboard A decorated board usually running along the eave in the gable. See p. 97.

barrel vault The simplest form of arched opening for a significant space — half a cylinder — supported by walls or columns on each side. See p. 386.

basilica A large rectangular building, usually with two rows of supporting columns, side aisles, apse and a higher roof over the central space (nave), with clerestory windows. See p. 386.

bay A regular structural subdivision of a church, usually marked by columns, buttresses or vaults. See p. 230.

belfry A tower, usually attached to a church, where bells are hung. See p. 21.

belt course A raised horizontal band on the façade of a church, sometimes corresponding to floor levels within the building. See p. 262.

board-and-batten A covering for frame buildings constructed of wide vertical boards, with the joints between boards covered by narrow vertical battens. See p. 38.

bond Placing bricks in a wall so that joints do not line up. See p. 246. Flemish bond is brickwork laid with alternating headers and stretchers within each course.

boss An ornamental projecting knob, usually at the intersection of ribs in a vault. See p. 230.

broach spire An octagonal spire sitting on a square tower. See p. 28.

bull's-eye *See* oculus.

buttress A pier-like projection used to support a wall or tower. See p. 242.

C

came H-shaped pieces of lead used to secure small pieces of glass in a leaded-glass window. See p. 175.

campanile An Italian-style bell tower, usually freestanding. See p. 389.

cantilever A horizontally projecting structural member without support; its stability depends on the member's strength and a dead weight at the end. See p. 275.

capital The upper portion of a column, pilaster, pier or colonnette, often ornamented. See p. 122.

cathedral An important church, usually large, with a *cathedra*, or Bishop's seat; hence a bishop's church. See p. 183.

chalice A cup used to hold the wine in the Eucharist or Lord's Supper. See p. 23.

chancel The eastern end of a liturgically oriented church containing the altar, generally reserved for the clergy and choir. See p. 40.

chapel A distinct space of worship, containing an altar. In denominations other than the established church, the name is often used for the building used for worship.

chapel of ease A freestanding chapel or place of worship within an expanding parish for those living at some distance from the church. See p. 74.

chevet A French term for the east end of a large church, including apse, ambulatory and chapels. See p. 233.

choir In a large church, the eastern portion designated for the singers, usually in stalls beyond the transepts. See p. 41.

cladding A relatively lightweight external skin of a building that covers the supporting structure.

clapboard Overlapping horizontal boards, sometimes beveled, used to clad frame buildings. See p. 55.

clearstory High windows above the nave that provide light to this central section of a basilica or large church. See p. 233.

close A courtyard or green space, often enclosed by a fence or low wall, directly around a cathedral. See p. 121.

clustered column A column composed of several shafts. See p. 7.

collar-beam A horizontal member connecting rafters or roof beams. See p. 331.

colombage A French style of timber wall construction using vertical members tied together at the sill and plate. See p. 176.

colonnette A small column.

column An upright tapering structural member (square, round or rectangular); it can be isolated or attached.

communion rail A railing that separates the chancel from the sanctuary, often the point at which the congregation participates in the Lord's Supper or Mass. See p. 113.

communion table Generally a wooden table used to hold the bread and wine for celebration of communion.

compound pier See clustered column

confessional An enclosed booth in which a priest privately hears the confession of penitent persons.

corbel A projecting block, usually of stone, either to support a structural member or, in a series with each projecting beyond the one below, to form the beginning of a vault. See p. 72.

Corinthian Slender, elegant classical order (the third of the Greek orders, fourth of the Roman orders) with a base, usually Attic, and a capital, usually with acanthus leaves and an abacus. See p. 160.

cornice The projecting section of an ornamental moulding running along the top of a wall or building. See p. 82.

crocket Leafy decorative projections at regular intervals along the upper portions of a building. See p. 68.

crop Unfolding leafy form mounted on a gable or pinnacle in Gothic style. See pp. 68, 90.

cross vault *see* groin vault

crossing The area in a cross=shaped church formed by the intersection of the nave and transepts. See p. 101.

cupola A small dome on a circular or polygonal base crowning a roof or turret. See p. 203.

D

dado A covering placed on the lower part of an interior wall from floor to waist height. See p. 321.

dentil One of a series of small blocks under the cornices of several Classical orders. See p. 202.

diagonal rib The main supports running diagonally across a bay of vaulting in Gothic architecture. See p. 333.

dome A vault with even curvature erected on a circular base or drum. See p. 162.

dormer A projection on a pitched roof, usually with its own small roof at right angles to the main roof, to permit the installation of a vertical window. See p. 396.

double-hung sash Window with two parts (sashes) hung with pulleys and weights, each part can move up and down independently. See p. 327.

double-decker A pulpit with two levels; the higher level contains a speaking and reading desk and is used by the pastor to deliver the sermon, the lower level is used by the precentor to lead the congregation in singing hymns. See p. 34.

drip-course Continuous horizontal moulding shaped to throw rainwater off a wall. See p. 246.

drum A vertical wall on a circular or polygonal plan to carry a dome or cupola, and often pierced with windows. See pp. 47, 162.

E

elevation Either the vertical faces of a building – external and internal – or the drawings of those faces projected onto a drawing surface. See p. 413.

engaged column A column that projects from but is attached to a wall. See p. 113.

entablature A horizontal member supported by a colonnade or wall. See p. 343.

F

facade The front face of a building. See p. 413.

fanlight A window, often semicircular, over a door, with radiating glazing bars in the shape of a fan. See p. 239.

fenestration The name for the pattern formed by the windows in a building's facade.

fillet A small, narrow, flat moulding, usually a plain band in a group of more decorative moldings.

finial A decorative vertical knob found at the end of a bench, gable, pinnacle or spire. See p. 33.

fluting Shallow, concave grooves running vertically on columns and pilasters. See p. 207.

foil Lobe or curve formed by flower-like cusping of a circle or an arch; the prefix (as in trefoil, quatrefoil, cinquefoil, hexafoil) indicates the number of lobes. See p. 334.

font Receptacle for baptismal water in a baptistery or church. See p. 212.

frieze The upper portion of entablature, See p. 10.

G

gable Triangular upper portion of a wall at the end of a pitched roof. See p. 36.

gallery An extra (partial) floor for seating over the narthex or aisles. See p. 126.

gingerbread Elaborate decorative carving or trim, usually under the eaves or on porches.

glue-laminated (glulam) A wooden beam, often curved, made of layers of wood glued together under pressure.

Greek cross A cross with arms of equal length (usually refers to a church plan).

H

half-timbered A timber-framed building where the spaces between the timbers are filled with stucco on laths, brick or stone.

hall church A church with aisles but no clerestory, under a continuous roof, with an interior of nearly uniform height. See p. 131.

hammer-beam A short horizontal member used in roof construction as a tie-beam but not spanning the space, effectively a bracket between the wall and roof timber. See p. 72.

header A brick or stone laid in a wall with its small end exposed.

hipped A roof that slopes away from the central point or ridge, usually the slope is the same on all sides. See p. 66.

I

iconostasis (iconostas). In Eastern-rite churches, the screen between the sanctuary and the nave, usually decorated with images (literally "place of images"). See p. 263.

J

jamb The vertical side of a window or door opening.

Jesuit plan An aisleless church plan with two transepts, in which the apse is the same width as the nave. Often referred to as a Latin cross plan. See p. 106.

K

keystone A wedge-shaped block at the crown of an arch that provides the pressure to hold the arch in place.

kneeler A low padded bench used for kneeling in church. See p. 298.

L

lancet A tall, narrow window with an uninterrupted opening. See p. 84.

lantern A structure rising above the roof usually with openings to provide light or ventilate to the interior. See p. 199.

Latin cross *See* Jesuit plan. See p. 198.

lectern A high, sloped reading surface in a church at which the Bible is read. See p. 88.

lych-gate A roofed gate at the entrance to a burial ground, often with built-in seating to accommodate pall-bearers or mourners. See p. 219.

light A glazed area in a window.

lintel A substantial beam over a door or window carrying the weight of masonry above the opening and transferring it to the side walls.

long-lot settlement French-Canadian pattern of subdivision into narrow but long strips of land at right angles to a river or road, concentrating settlers' houses in ribbons along the front of the property, near the river or road.

M

Maillou plan A simple church plan formed by a rectangle and a semicircular apse, without transepts or narrowing of the structure at the apse. See pp. 106, 389.

moulding Projecting members — horizontal, vertical or arching — of distinctive profile, according to the period, whose convexities catch the light while the concavities hold contrasting shadows.

mouchette Curved, dagger-shaped motif popular in English curvilinear tracery of the early 14th century See p. 73.

mullion A vertical post between the panes of glass in a window or the openings in a screen. See p. 43.

muntin A glazing bar in a window. See p. 327.

N

narthex the church vestibule directly behind the entrance door. See p. 319.

nave The central interior space in a basilican church between the two aisles. See p. 253.

niche A shallow ornamental recess in a wall or pier, usually for the display of sculpture. See p. 145.

O

oculus (also *œil-de-bœuf*). A circular or oval opening in wall, pediment or dome. See p. 112.

ogee (ogival) An upright double curve used in a molding, or a double S-curve used in a window opening or tracery. See p. 206.

onion-domed A pointed bulbous structure (hence onion) on the top of a tower or drum, especially common in Eastern-rite churches. See p. 294.

open seat Bench-like seating, not enclosed, in contrast to box pews.

oriented Planned so that the sanctuary lies to the East, while the far end of the nave faces West.

P

parapet A low wall or barrier at the edge of a roof or balcony. See p. 414.

pediment The gabled end of a roof in classical architecture. A broken pediment (See p. 257.), instead of running continuously, is cut to allow a varied treatment of one section.

pew A long fixed wooden bench in a church for seating of the congregation. See p. 64.

pièce-sur-pièce A method of wooden construction (also called Red River construction) using large vertical posts spaced widely apart. The gap between the posts is filled with horizontal timbers or planks mortised into the posts. See p. 299.

pier A solid, detached masonry support. See p. 377.

pilaster A shallow pier or rectangular column projecting slightly from wall. See p. 121.

plate tracery Decoratively shaped openings cut through a solid stone infilling in a window-head.

plinth The projecting base of a wall or column.

portal An imposing door or entrance, often richly decorated. See p. 360.

portico The space outside the main entrance door, roofed and often partly enclosed on the sides. See p. 202.

presbytery In Québec the name given to the housing for the priests.

prestressed concrete A method of extremely strong concrete construction that depends on putting steel rods or cables under high tension in place so they are encased by the concrete at the time of pouring. See p. 163.

processional chapel A small chapel, often located near the edge of a parish, used for minor stops in a procession to the parish church on festive occasions. See p. 105.

pulpit An elevated stand of stone or wood for use by a preacher or reader, often elaborately carved, sometimes with a sounding board above. See p. 139.

pulpitum A stone screen in a major church, cutting off the choir from the nave.

Q

quoin Decorative dressed stones at the corners of a building, usually laid with alternating large and small faces. See p. 213.

R

rafter Inclined roof members that run from the top of the wall to the ridge of the roof. See p. 304.

Récollet plan A church plan with the chancel or apse narrower than the nave, usually constructed without transepts. See p. 106.

rectory In the Anglican Church, a house for a rector.

Red River construction *See pièce-sur-pièce.*

relieving arch An arch constructed above an opening in a high wall to redistribute the weight and relieve the pressure on the opening.

reliquary A receptacle for relics.

reredos An ornamental screen behind an altar, it can be freestanding or a part of the retable. See p. 18.

retable A screen to the rear of an altar, often richly decorated or carved, including the reredos, around which it forms a frame. See p. 125.

rib A raised molding on the surface of a flat or vaulted ceiling. See p. 7.

rose-window Gothic or Gothic Revival circular window with complex tracery radiating from the centre. See p. 314.

rubble Rough unhewn stones of irregular shape, laid with large mortar joints. See p. 85.

rusticated Masonary using massive blocks, sometimes roughly cut, with deep joints, usually in the lower part of a wall. See p. 135.

S

sacristy The church vestry near the chancel to store ecclesiastical garments and utensils used in the service, sometimes used as a chapel. See p. 138.

sanctuary The part of a church around the altar or communion table that is used for liturgical ceremonies, especially in Roman Catholic, Anglican and Eastern Rite churches. In many Protestant denominations the term "sanctuary" may denote the nave or auditorium.

Solomonic column A spirally-fluted or shaped column, whose originals were thought to come from Solomon's Temple in Jerusalem. See p. 102.

sounding board A flat or shaped canopy, often decorated, constructed over a pulpit to amplify the speaker's voice. See p. 117.

spindle A turned piece of wood used as a baluster or chair leg, etc. See p. 51.

spire A tall pyramidal structure of stone or timber in a, polygonal or conical form rising from a tower or roof and terminating in a point. See p. 388.

stall Fixed seats in a chancel or choir. See p. 113.

steeple A collective term for a church tower plus its spire. See p. 388.

stretcher Bricks laid horizontally with the longest face exposed. See p. 275.

T

tabernacle A cupboard with doors for the consecrated Host in a Roman Catholic church. Originally a moveable shrine or tent for the Jewish Ark of the Covenant. See p. 102.

tie-beam A horizontal member, especially in a truss, that resists the tendency for its ends of the building to pull apart. See p. 331.

timber framing A type of construction in which the walls and partitions are framed of large wooden beams set on a foundation. The spaces between the beams are filled with other materials such as brick or plaster. See p. 33.

tracery Ornamental intersecting work in the upper part of a window, screen or panel. See p. 73.

transept The transverse arms of a cross-shaped church. See p. 118.

transom A horizontal bar of wood or stone across the top of a window or door opening, sometimes with a fanlight above.

triforium Arcaded passage facing into the nave, above the arcade and below the clerestory.

triple-decker A pulpit with three levels, the higher level with a speaking desk for the sermon, the middle for reading Scripture, the lower for the use of a precentor leading the hymns or a clerk leading responses. See p. 52.

truss A triangulated rigid frame used for spanning large spaces. See p. 271.

tunnel vault *see* barrel vault.

turret A small slender tower.

U V

vault An arched ceiling or roof made of stone, brick or concrete, often imitated in wood or plaster. See p. 84.

verge-board *see* bargeboard

vestry Room where the clergy keep vestments and put them on.

vicarage The residence of a vicar.

W X Y Z

wainscot Woodwork used to line the walls. See p. 304.

weatherboarding *see* clapboard

wheel window *see* rose window

BIBLIOGRAPHY

GENERAL

Fletcher, Banister, and Dan Cruickshank. *History of Architecture on the Comparative Method*. 20th. ed. London: Macmillan, 1996.

Jenkins, Simon. *England's Thousand Best Churches*. London: Penguin Books, 2000. [Medieval to Modern churches in England]

Norberg-Schulz, Christian. *Meaning in Architecture*. New York: Rizzoli, 1981.

Norberg-Schulz, Christian. *Genius Loci: Towards a Phenomenology of Architecture*. New York: Rizzoli, 1984.

Trachtenberg, Marvin, and Isabelle Hyman. *Architecture, from Prehistory to Postmodernity*. 1986. 2nd ed. New York. Abrams, 2002.

EARLY CHRISTIAN AND BYZANTINE

Philip A. Harland, *Associations, Synagogues, and Congregations*. Minneapolis: Fortress, 2003.

Krautheimer, Richard. *Early Christian and Byzantine Architecture*. Fourth edition. New Haven and London: Yale University Press, 1986.

MacDonald, William. *Early Christian & Byzantine Architecture*. 2d ed. New York: George Braziller, 1985.

Mango, Cyril. *Byzantine Architecture*. History of World Architecture. Re-issued, New York: Rizzoli, 1985.

Milburn, Robert. *Early Christian Art and Architecture*. Berkeley and Los Angeles: University of California Press, 1988.

Richardson, Peter. *City and Sanctuary: Religion and Architecture in the Roman Near East*. London: SCM Press, 2002.

Richardson, Peter. *Building Jewish in the Roman East*. Waco TX: Baylor University Press, 2004.

Snyder, Graydon F. *Ante Pacem: archaeological evidence of church life before Constantine*. Macon, Georgia: Mercer University Press, 2003.

White, Michael. *Social Origins of Christian Architecture*. Cambridge MA: Harvard University Press, 1996–97

MEDIEVAL

Barral i Altet, Xavier. *The Romanesque: Towns, Cathedrals and Monasteries*. Cologne: Taschen, 2001.

Busch, Harald, and Bernd Lohse ed. *Romanesque Europe*. London: Batsford, 1960.

Cox, J. Charles. *The Parish Churches of England*. 1935. 5th ed. London: B.T. Batsford, 1946–47.

Kubach, Hans Erich. *Romanesque Architecture*. Re-issued, New York: Abrams, 1975.

Stalley, Roger. *Early Medieval Architecture*. Oxford: Oxford University Press, 1999.

RENAISSANCE AND BAROQUE

Briggs, Martin S. *Puritan Architecture and Its Future*. London: Lutterworth Press, 1946.

Friedman, Terry. *James Gibbs*. New Haven: Yale University Press, 1984.

Gibbs, James. *A Book of Architecture: Containing Designs of Buildings and Ornaments*. 1728. Reprint. New York: Benjamin Blom, 1968.

Norberg-Schulz, Christian. *Baroque Architecture*. History of World Architecture; New York: Rizzoli, 1986.

Norberg-Schulz, Christian. *Late Baroque and Rococo Architecture*. History of World Architecture; New York: Rizzoli, 1980.

MODERN (mid-18th century to present)

Aldrich, Megan. *Gothic Revival*. London: Phaidon Press, 1994.

Brooks, Chris. *The Gothic Revival*. London: Phaidon Press, 1999.

Clarke, Basil F.L. *Anglican Cathedrals outside the British Isles*. London: S.P.C.K., 1958.

Cruickshank, Dan. *The National Trust/Irish Georgian Society Guide to the Georgian Buildings of Britain and Ireland*. New York: Rizzoli, 1986.

Collins, Peter. *Changing Ideals in Modern Architecture 1750-1950*. Montreal: McGill-Queen's University Press, 1965.

Curl, James Stevens. *Georgian Architecture*. Newton Abbot, Devon: David & Charles, 1993.

Giedion, Sigfried. *Space, Time and Architecture: The Growth of a New Tradition*. 1941. 5th ed. Cambridge: Harvard University Press, 1973.

Kennedy, Roger G. *American Churches*. New York: Syewart, Tabori & Chang, 1982.

Mallary, Peter T. *New England Churches & Meetinghouses, 1630–1830*. New York: Vendome Press, 1985.

Whiffen, Marcus. *Stuart and Georgian Churches: The Architecture of the Church of England outside London, 1603–1837*. London: B.T. Batsford, 1947–48.

19TH CENTURY

Cambridge Camden Society [Ecclesiological late Cambridge Camden Society from 1846]. *Ecclesiologist*. Volumes 1-29. Cambridge: 1841–45; London: 1846–68.

Clarke, Basil F.L. *Church Builders of the Nineteenth Century: A Study of the Gothic Revival in England*. London: Society for Promoting Christian Knowledge, 1938.

Dixon, Roger, and Stefan Muthesius. *Victorian Architecture*. 1978. 2nd ed. London: Thames and Hudson, 1985.

Harrison, Martin. *Victorian Stained Glass*. London: Barrie & Jenkins, 1980.

Hersey, George L. *High Victorian Gothic: A Study in Associationism*. Baltimore: John's Hopkins University Press, 1972.

Kilde, Jeanne Halgren. *When Church became Theatre: The Transformation of Evangelical Architecture and Worship in Nineteenth-Century America*. Oxford: Oxford University Press, 2002.

Medley, John *Elementary Remarks on Church Architecture*. Exeter: P.A. Hannaford, 1841.

Pugin, A. Welby. *An Apology for the Revival of Christian Architecture in England*. 1843, Reprint. Oxford: St. Barnabas Press, 1969.

Pugin, A. Welby. *The True Principles of Pointed or Christian Architecture*. 1841, Reprint. Oxford: St. Barnabas Press, 1969.

White, James F. *The Cambridge Movement: The Ecclesiologist and the Gothic Revival*. Cambridge: Cambridge University Press, 1962.

Wills, Frank. *Ancient English Ecclesiastical Architecture and Its Principles, Applied to the Wants of the Church at the Present Day*. New York: Stanford and Swords, 1850.

20TH CENTURY

Brannach, Frank. *Church Architecture: Building for a Living Faith*. Milwaukee: Bruce Publishing, 1932. [Roman Catholic churches in U.S.A.]

Bruggink, Donald J., and Carl H. Droppers. *Christ and Architecture: Building Presbyterian and Reformed Churches*. Grand Rapids: Eerdmans, 1965.

Cram, Ralph Adams. *Church Building: A Study of the Principles of Architecture in Their Relation to the Church*. Boston: Small, Maynard, 1901.

Religious Buildings for Today. An Architectural Record Book. Ed. John Knox Shear. New York: F.W. Dodge, 1957.

CANADIAN ARCHITECTURAL HISTORY

GENERAL

Brown, Shirley Ann. "Bibliography of Stained Glass Windows in Canada": www.yorku.ca/sabrown/Bibliography.html

Cawker, Ruth, and William Bernstein. *Contemporary Canadian Architecture*. Revised and expanded ed. Markham, ON: Fitzhenry & Whiteside, 1988.

Ede, Carol Moore. *Canadian Architecture1960/70*. Toronto: Burns and MacEachern, 1971.

Kalman, Harold. *Pioneer Churches*. Toronto: McClelland and Stewart, 1976.

Kalman, Harold. *A History of Canadian Architecture*. 2 vols. Toronto: Oxford University Press, 1994.

Maitland, Leslie. *Neoclassical Architecture in Canada*. Ottawa: National Historic Parks and Sites Branch, Parks Canada, Environment Canada, 1984.

Ricketts, Shannon, Leslie Maitland & Jacqueline Hucker. *A Guide to Canadian Styles*. Peterborough: Broadview, 2004.

Rochon, Lisa. *Up North Where Canada's Architecture Meets the Land*. Toronto: Key Porter, 2005.

Royal Architectural Institute of Canada. *Journal*. Vol. 33, No. 12 (December 1956). [Special issue on religious buildings.]

Simmins, Geoffrey. *Documents in Canadian Architecture*. Peterborough: Broadview Press, 1992.

ATLANTIC CANADA

Cockburn, Melville N., *A History of Greenock Church, St. Andrews, New Brunswick, from 1821 to 1906*. St. Andrews, NB: 1906.

Duffus, Allen F. et al. *Thy Dwellings Fair: Churches of Nova Scotia, 1750–1830*. Hantsport, NS: Lancelot Press, 1982.

Finley, Greg. *On Earth as it is in Heaven: Gothic Revival Churches of Victorian New Brunswick*. Fredericton: Goose Lane Editions, 1995.

John Edward FitzGerald's website, "Building the Cathedral" Hughes, Gary K. *Music of the Eye: Architectural Drawings of Canada's First City,1822-1914*. Saint John NB: New Brunswick Museum and Royal Architectural Institute of Canada, 1991. [Exhibition Catalogue]

Hyde, Susan, and Michael Bird. *Hallowed Timber: The Wooden Churches of Cape Breton*. Erin ON: Boston Mills, 1995.

McAleer, J. Philip. *A Pictorial History of the Basilica of St. Mary, Halifax, Nova Scotia*. Halifax: Technical University of Nova Scotia, 1984.

McAleer, J. Philip. *A Pictorial History of St. Paul's Anglican Church, Halifax, Nova Scotia*. Halifax: Technical University of Nova Scotia, 1993.

McBurney, Margaret, and Mary Byers. *True Newfoundlanders: Early Homes and Families of Newfoundland and Labrador*. Erin, ON: Boston Mills Press, 1997.

Smith, H.M. Scott. *The Historic Churches of Prince Edward Island*. Updated 2d ed. Halifax: SSP Publications, 2004.

Stanton, Phoebe. *The Gothic Revival & American Church Architecture: An Episode in Taste, 1840–1856*. Baltimore: Johns Hopkins University Press, 1968.

Tuck, Robert. *Churches of Nova Scotia*. Toronto: Dundurn, 2004.

Tuck, Robert C. *Gothic Dreams: The Life and Times of a Canadian Architect, William Critchlow Harris (1854–1913)*. Toronto: Dundurn, 1978.

Tuck, Robert C. *Rêves gothiques, l'architecture de William Critchlow Harris, 1854–1913; Gothic Dreams: The Architecture of William Critchlow Harris (1854–1913)*. Charlottetown: Confederation Centre Art Gallery and Museum, 1995.

Wallis, J.F., et al. (eds). *The Basilica-Cathedral of St. John Baptist, St. John's, Newfoundland, 1855-1980*. St. John's: 1980.

Watson, Robert L. *Christ Church Cathedral, Fredericton: A History*. Fredericton: Published by the Bishop and Chapter of Christ Church Cathedral, Fredericton, 1984.

QUÉBEC

Bergeron, Claude. *L'Architecture des églises du Québec 1940–1985*. Québec: Presses de l'université Laval, 1987

Bergeron, Claude, and Geoffrey Simmins. *L' Abbaye de Saint-Benoît-du-Lac et ses bâtisseurs*. Québec: Presses de l'université Laval, 1997.

Bergevin, Hélène. *Églises protestants*. Montréal: Libre Expression, 1981.

Bourque, Hélène. *Les Églises et les Chapelles de Portneuf*. Cap Santé : Regional Municipality of Portneuf, 2000.

Cameron, Christina. *Charles Baillairgé, Architect & Engineer*. Montreal: McGill-Queen's University Press, 1989.

Communauté urbaine de Montréal. *Architecture religieuse. I. Les églises. Répertoire d'architecture traditionelle sur le territoire de la Communauté urbaine de Montréal*. 1981.

Croteau, André. *Les belles églises du Québec: Montréal*. Saint-Laurent: Trécarré, 1996.

Croteau, André. *Les belles églises du Québec: Québec et la vallée du Saint-Laurent*. Saint-Laurent: Trécarré, 1996.

Gauthier, Raymonde. *Les Tabernacles anciens du Québec des XVIIe, XVIIIe et XIXe Siècles*. Québec: Ministère des Affaires culturelles, 1974.

Gauthier, Raymond, et al. *L'Architecture de Montréal*. Montréal: Libre Expression, 1990.

Gauthier, Raymond. *Construire une église au Québec: L'architecture religieuse avant 1939*. Montréal: Libre Expression, 1994.

Gowans, Alan. *Church Architecture in New France*. Toronto: University of Toronto Press, 1955.

Lauzon, Gilles, and Madeline Forget. *Old Montreal: History through Heritage*. Sainte-Foy: Les Publications du Québec, 2003.

Marsan, Jean-Claude. *Montreal in Evolution*. Montreal: McGill-Queen's University Press, 1981.

Noppen, Luc. *Les églises du Québec (1660–1850)*. Québec: Éditeur official du Québec; Montréal: Fides, 1977.

Noppen, Luc. *Notre-Dame de Québec: son architecture et son rayonnement (1647–1922)*. Québec: Éditions du Pélican, 1974.

Noppen, Luc, and Marc Grignon. *L'art de l'architecte: three centuries of architectural drawing in Québec City*. Québec: Musée du Québec/ Université Laval, 1983.

Noppen, Luc, and Lucie K. Morisset. *Art et architecture des églises à Québec*. Québec : Les Publications du Québec, 1996.

Noppen, Luc and Lucie K. Morisset. *La Présence Anglican à Québec: Holy Trinity Cathedral (1796-1996)*. Sillery: Les éditions du Septentrion, 1995.

Simpson, Patricia, and Louise Pothier. *Notre-Dame-de-Bon-Secours: A Chapel and its Neighbourhood*. Montréal: Fides, 2001.

Tardif-Plainchaud, Nicole. *Dom Bellot et l'architecture religieuse au Québec*. Québec: Presse de l'université Laval, 1978.

Toker, Franklin. *The Church of Notre-Dame in Montreal: An Architectural History*. 1970. 2d ed. Montreal: McGill-Queens University Press, 1991.

Traquair, Ramsay. *The Old Architecture of Quebec*. Toronto: Macmillan, 1947.

Trudel, Jean. *La Basilique Notre-Dame de Montréal*. 1995. Rev. ed. [Montréal]: PhotoGraphex, 2001.

Trudel, Jean. *The Ursuline Chapel in Quebec City*. Québec: Monastère des Ursulines de Québec, 2005.

ONTARIO

Angus, Margaret. *The Old Stones of Kingston*. Toronto: University of Toronto, 1966.

Arthur, Eric *Toronto, No Mean City*. 1964. 3rd ed. Revised by Stephen A. Otto. Toronto: University of Toronto Press, 2003.

Blake, Verschoyle Benson, and Ralph Greenhill. *Rural Ontario*. Toronto: University of Toronto Press, 1969.

Benn, Carl, et al. *The Parish and Cathedral of St James', Toronto, 1797–1997*. William Cooke, general ed. Toronto: Printed for the Cathedral by the University of Toronto, 1998.

Carr, Angela. *Toronto Architect, Edmund Burke: Redefining Canadian Architecture*. Montreal: McGill-Queen's University Press, 1995.

Cruickshank, Tom. *The Settler's Dream: A Pictorial History of the Older Buildings of Prince Edward County*. ed. Peter John Stokes. Picton ON: Corporation of the County of Prince Edward, 1984.

Dendy, William. *Lost Toronto: Images of the City's Past*. Revised and updated ed. Toronto: McClelland & Stewart, 1993.

Fram, Mark, and Albert Schrauwers. *4Square*. Toronto: Coach House, 2005.

Greenhill, Ralph, Ken Macpherson and Douglas Richardson. *Ontario Towns*. Toronto: Oberon, 1974.

Kidd, Martha Ann, and Louis Taylor. *Historical Sketches of Peterborough*. Peterborough: Broadview Press, 1988.

McKendry, Jennifer. *With Our Past before Us: Nineteenth-Century Architecture in the Kingston Area*. Toronto: University of Toronto Press, 1995.

MacRae, Marion, and Anthony Adamson. *Hallowed Walls: Church Architecture of Upper Canada*. Toronto: Clarke, Irwin, 1975.

Maitland, Leslie, and Louis Taylor. *Historical Sketches of Ottawa*. Peterborough: Broadview Press, 1990.

Noppen, Luc. *In the National Gallery of Canada: "One of the Most Beautiful Chapels in the Land."* Ottawa: National Gallery of Canada, 1988.

Pagé, Norman. *La cathédrale Notre-Dame d'Ottawa: Histoire, architecture, iconographie*. Ottawa: Les Presses de l'Université d'Ottawa, 1988.

Robertson, John Ross. *Landmarks of Toronto: A Collection of Historical Sketches of the Old Town of York from 1792 until 1837 and of Toronto from 1834 to 1904*. Vol. 4. Toronto: J. Ross Robertson, 1904. [Toronto churches.]

Schrauwers, Albert. *Awaiting the Millennium: The Children of Peace and the Village of Hope, 1812–1889*. Toronto: University of Toronto Press, 1993.

Simmins, Geoffrey. *Ontario Association of Architects: A Centennial History, 1889–1989*. Toronto: Ontario Association of Architects, 1989.

Simmins, Geoffrey. *Fred Cumberland: Building the Victorian Dream*. Toronto: University of Toronto Press, 1997.

Stokes, Peter John. *Old Niagara on the Lake*. Toronto: University of Toronto Press, 1971.

Tausky, Nancy Z. and Lynne D. DiStefano. *Victorian Architecture in London and Southwestern Ontario: Symbols of Aspiration*. Toronto: University of Toronto Press, 1986.

Taylor, Patricia C. *History of the Churches of Prince Edward County*. Picton: ON: Picton Gazette, 1971.

Westfall, William. *Two Worlds: The Protestant Culture of Nineteenth-Century Ontario*. Kingston: McGill-Queen's University Press, 1989.

WEST AND NORTH

Baran, Anna Maria. *Ukrainian Catholic Churches of Saskatchewan*. Trans. Christine T. Pastershank. Saskatoon: Ukrainian Catholic Council of Saskatchewan, 1977.

Butterfield, David, and Maureen Devanik Butterfield. *If Walls Could Talk: Manitoba's Best Buildings Explored & Explained.* Winnipeg: Great Plains Publications, 2000.

Butterfield, David, and Edward M. Ledohowski. *Architectural Heritage: The M[orden-] S[tanley] T[hompson-] W[inkler] Planning District.* Winnipeg: Province of Manitoba, Historic Resources Branch, Department of Culture, Heritage and Recreation, 1984.

Choquette, Robert. *The Oblate Assault on Canada's Northwest.* Ottawa: University of Ottawa Press, 1995.

Christensen, Deanna, and Menno Fieguth. *Historic Saskatchewan.* Toronto: Oxford University Press, 1986.

Downs, Barry. *Sacred Places: British Columbia's Early Churches.* Vancouver: Douglas & McIntyre, 1980

Gaboury, Étienne. *Étienne Gaboury.* Ed. Faye Hellner. Saint-Boniface MB: Editions du Blé, 2005.

Hermann, Alex. *Historic Architecture of Saskatchewan.* Regina: Focus Publishing, 1986.

Hohn, Hubert (ed.), *Byzantine Churches of Alberta.* Edmonton: Edmonton Art Gallery, 1976.

Keshavjee, Serena, ed. *Winnipeg Modern: Architecture 1945–1975.* Winnipeg: University of Manitoba Press, 2006.

Kovch-Baran, Anna Mariïa. *Ukrainian Catholic Churches of Winnipeg Eparchy.* Saskatoon: Eparchy of Winnipeg, 1991.

Ledohowski, Edward M. *The Heritage Landscape of the Crow Wing Study Region of Southeastern Manitoba.* Winnipeg: Historic Resources Branch, Manitoba Culture, Heritage & Tourism, 2003.

Mackay, Ellen. *Places of Worship in the Cowichan and Chemainus Valleys.* Victoria: Sono Nis, 1991

Rotoff, Basil, et al. *Monuments to Faith: Ukrainian Churches in Manitoba.* Winnipeg: University of Manitoba Press, 1990.

Ruh, Philip. *Missionary and Architect.* Winnipeg: Progress Printing & Publishing, 1960.

Tarasoff, Koozma J. *Spirit Wrestlers: Doukhobor Pioneers' Strategies for Living.* Ottawa: Spirit Wrestlers Publishing, 2002.

Ukrainian Cultural Heritage Village Guide. Edmonton: Alberta Community Development, 1995.

Veillette, John, and Gary White. *Early Indian Village Churches.* Vancouver: University of British Columbia Press, 1977.

Woodcock, George, and Ivan Avakumovic. *The Doukhobors.* Toronto: Oxford University Press, 1968.

Wright, Janet. *Church of Our Lady of Good Hope: Fort Good Hope and the Northwest Territories.* Ottawa: Parks Canada, 1986.

HISTORIES OF DENOMINATIONS AND ETHNIC GROUPS

Addleshaw, G.W.O., and Etchells, Frederick. *The Architectural Setting of Anglican Worship: An Inquiry into the Arrangements for Public Worship in the Church of England from the Reformation to the Present Day.* London: Faber and Faber, 1948.

Cronin, Kay. *Cross in the Wilderness.* Vancouver: Mitchell, 1960. [Oblate Missions]

Encyclopedia of Ukraine. Ed. Volodymyr Kubiiovych. 6 vols. Toronto: University of Toronto Press, 1984.

Fay, Terrence J. *A History of Canadian Catholics: Gallicanism, Romanism, and Canadianism.* Montreal: McGill-Queen's University Press, 2002.

Magocsi, Paul R. *Encyclopedia of Canada's Peoples.* Toronto: Published for the Multicultural History Society of Ontario by University of Toronto Press, 1999.

Minden, Robert. *Separate from the world: meetings with Doukhobor-Canadians in British Columbia.* Vancouver: National Film Board of Canada, 1979.

Moir, John S. *Enduring Witness: A History of the Presbyterian Church in Canada.* Toronto: Presbyterian Publications, 1974.

Noll, Mark A. *A History of Christianity in the United States and Canada.* Grand Rapids: Eerdmans, 1992.

Riendeau, Roger, et al. *An Enduring Heritage: Black Contributions to Early Ontario.* Toronto: Dundurn Press, 1984.

Schroeder, Andreas. *The Mennonoites: A Pictorial History of Their Lives in Canada.* Vancouver: Douglas & McIntyre, 1990.

STAINED GLASS

Brown, Shirley Ann. "Bibliography of Stained Glass Windows in Canada": *www.yorku.ca/sabrown/Bibliography.html*

Raguin, Virginia Chieffo. *Stained Glass: from its Origins to the Present.* New York: Harry N. Abrams, 2003.

INDEX
CANADIAN CHURCHES BY NAME

All Saints' (Anglican), 1861, McKeen's Corner NB 38, 89

All Saints' (Anglican), 1884-85, Clifton Royal NB 40

All Souls' Chapel (Anglican), 1888-89, Charlottetown PE 98, 99

Altona Meetinghouse (Mennonite), 1852-53, Markham, ON 199, 200

Assumption of the Mother of God (Ukrainian Catholic), 1906, Ashville, MB 328

Avonmore (United), 1988-90, Edmonton, AB 295

Barrington Meetinghouse, 1765, Barrington NS 50, 51

Beverley Street (Baptist), 1886-87, Toronto, ON 251, 253, 254

Black Church (United), 1849, Oro, ON 185, 222, 224

Blessed Virgin Mary (Ukrainian Catholic), 1926-27, Saint Julien, SK 294

Blue Church (Anglican), 1845, near Prescott, ON 180, 181

Bond Street Baptist, Toronto, ON 251

Bowerman's Church (Deconsecrated), 1855, Hallowell, ON 239

Carmel (United), 1886-87, Hensall, ON 216, 217

Cedars (United), 1995-96, Waterloo, ON 27

Christ Church (Anglican), 1831-32, Burritt's Rapids, ON 184, 199

Christ Church (Anglican), 1864, St. Stephen NB 69, 91, 92, 93

Christ Church (Anglican), 1873, Port Sydney, ON 226, 227

Christ Church Cathedral (Anglican), 1845-53, Fredericton NB 69, 71, 72, 73, 74, 76

Christ Church Cathedral (Anglican), 1894-95, Vancouver, BC 330, 332

Christadelphian Church (Christadelphian), 1948-49, Toronto, ON 186, 278

Church of Jesus Christ of the Latter Day Saints, Temple of (Mormon), 1913-23, Cardston, AB 340, 342

Community Church, 1861, near Grand Pré NS 33

Covenanters' Church (United), 1804-11, Grand Pré NS 33, 51, 52, 67

Cross Roads, Church at (non-denominational), 1836, Cross Roads PE 96, 97

Dominion-Chalmers (United), 1912-14, Ottawa, ON 184, 261, 262

Doukhobor Community Home, 1917-18, Veregin, SK 324, 326

Emmanuel (Baptist), 2004-05, Barrie, ON 392, 394, 397

Father Lacombe's Chapel (Roman Catholic), 1861, St. Albert, AB 300, 301

Father Pandosy's Mission (Roman Catholic), 1859-60, Kelowna, BC 290, 306

First Church (Christian Science), 1919-20, Victoria, BC 342, 343

Free Meeting House (deconsecrated), 1821, Moncton NB 66, 67

Frelsis (Lutheran), 1889, Grund, MB 310, 312, 313

Gower Street Church (United), 1894-96, St. John's NL 87

Grace (United), 1852, Niagara-on-the-Lake, ON 210, 214

Grand Séminaire de Montréal, Chapelle du (Roman Catholic), 1904-07, Montréal, QC 154, 156, 157

Granville Beach (Baptist), 1833, Granville Beach, NS, 54

Granville Centre (United Baptist), Granville Centre, NS 54

Greenock Church (Presbyterian), 1821-24, St. Andrews NB 36, 63, 64, 65, 67

Hay Bay Meetinghouse (Methodist), 1792, Napanee, ON 180, 184

Hebron, Church at (Moravian), 1830s, Hebron NL 57, 58, 59

Highlands (United), 1956-57, North Vancouver, BC 20

Holy Ascension (Russian Greek Orthodox), 1905, Sturgis, SK 16

Holy Cross (Roman Catholic), 1895-1906, Skatin, BC 291, 292

Holy Eucharist (Ukrainian Catholic), 1967, Toronto, ON 266, 268, 271

Holy Family (Roman Catholic), 2003-04, Medicine Hat, AB 364, 365, 390, 391, 393

Holy Name (Roman Catholic), 1915, Toronto, ON 256, 257

Holy Trinity (Anglican), 1854-60, Stanley Mission, SK 336

Holy Trinity (deconsecrated), 1847, Consecon, ON 239

Holy Trinity (Russian Orthodox Outside of Russia), 1922, Toronto, ON 264, 266

Holy Trinity, Cathedral of the (Anglican) 1799-1804, Québec, QC 36, 107, 108, 119, 121, 122, 123

Holy Trinity, Church of (Anglican), 1846-47, Toronto, ON 243, 254

Hopedale, Church at, 1865, Hopedale NL 57, 58, 60

Immaculate Conception (Roman Catholic), 1971-72, M'Chigeeng First Nations, ON 221

Immaculate Conception of the Blessed Virgin Mary, Cathedral of (Roman Catholic), 1954-57, Calgary, AB 344, 345

Immaculate Conception of the Virgin Mary (Ukrainian Catholic), 1930-52, Cook's Creek, MB 221, 318, 320, 328

Jarvis Street (Baptist), 1874-75, Toronto, ON 187, 216, 248, 251, 253, 254

Knox (Presbyterian), 1845, Oro, ON 185, 222, 224

Knox Fellowship Centre Chapel (Presbyterian), 1960-61, Toronto, ON 278, 279

Knox Presbyterian, 1847-48, Toronto, ON 213, 214

L'Arche Dayspring Chapel (Non-denominational), 1999, Richmond Hill, ON 168, 172, 173, 174, 175

Lady of the Lake Chapel (Roman Catholic), 1969, Silton, SK 354, 358

Little Dutch (Lutheran, Anglican), 1756, Halifax NS 46, 48, 50

Little Trinity (Anglican), 1843-44, Toronto, ON 242, 243, 253, 254

Madill (United), 1872-73, Stephenson Township, ON 226, 227

Mahone Bay (United Baptist), Mahone Bay NS 38

Malpeque (United), 1869-70, Malpeque, PE 97, 98

Martyrs Shrine (Roman Catholic), 1925-26, Midland, ON 189

Maugerville Meetinghouse (United), 1775, Sheffield, NB 68, 69

McDougall Mission (Methodist), 1862, Morley, AB 288, 300, 301

Metropolitan Community Church, 1907, Toronto, ON 26, 396

Mohawk Chapel, 1785, Brantford, ON 193, 194, 200

Monseigneur Briand, La Chapelle de (Roman Catholic), 1784-86, Québec City, QC 127, 134

Most Holy Trinity, Church of (Roman Catholic), 1833, Trinity NL 30, 78

Mount Tabor (deconsecrated), 1865-67, Milford, ON 239

Nain, Church at, 1925, Nain NL 57, 60

Nativity of the Blessed Virgin Mary (Ukrainian Catholic), 1911-12, Dobrowody, SK 318

Notre-Dame de Montréal, Basilique (Roman Catholic), 1823-29, Montréal, QC 8, 96, 143, 144, 145, 146, 147, 148, 244

Notre-Dame d'Ottawa, Basilique-Cathédrale (Roman Catholic), 1841-85, Ottawa, ON 231, 235

Notre-Dame, Basilique-Cathédrale (Roman Catholic), 1647, Québec, QC 114, 132, 133, 134, 135, 152

Notre-Dame-de-Bon-Secours, Chapelle (Roman Catholic), 1771-73, Montréal, QC 143, 144, 150

Notre-Dame-de-Fatima (Roman Catholic), 1962-63, Jonquière, QC 164, 166

Notre-Dame-de-Grâce (Roman Catholic), 1851-53, Montréal, QC 148, 152, 153

Notre-Dame-des-Victoires (Roman Catholic), 1723, Québec, QC 124

Nuestra Senora de Guadalupe, Misión Católica Latinoaméricana (Roman Catholic), 1924, Montréal, QC 160, 161

Old Colony Worship House (Mennonite), 1881, Steinbach, MB 312

Old Holy Trinity (Anglican), 1789-91, Middleton NS 54

Old Order Meetinghouse (Mennonite), 1917-18, St. Jacobs, ON 4

Omond Memorial (United), 1983, North Bay, ON 397

Oratoire Saint-Joseph (Roman Catholic), 1924-67, Montréal, QC 160, 162, 189

Our Lady of Good Hope (Roman Catholic), 1865-85, Fort Good Hope, NT 337

Our Lady of Mount Carmel (Roman Catholic), 1867, Toronto, ON 256

Our Lady of the Assumption (Roman Catholic), 1842-46, Windsor, ON 209, 210

Our Lady of the Immaculate Conception (Roman Catholic), 1876-88, Guelph, ON 182, 233, 235, 254

Our Lady of Victory (Roman Catholic), 1958-60, Inuvik, NT 338

Paris Plains (United), 1845, Paris, ON 210, 213

Pincher Creek Colony Church (Hutterite), 1945, Pincher Creek, AB 327

Port Royal Habitation, Chapel of (Roman Catholic), 1605-07, near Annapolis Royal NS 31

Port Sydney Bible Chapel (Plymouth Brethren), 2000, Port Sydney, ON 228

Précieux-Sang (Roman Catholic), 1967-68, Saint Boniface, MB 352, 353, 354

Première Église Évangélique Arménienne (Armenian Evangelical), 1966-67, Montréal, QC 163

Redeemer, Church of the (Anglican), 1878-79, Toronto, ON 283, 284

Rideau Street Convent Chapel (Roman Catholic), 1887-88, Ottawa, ON 235, 236, 237

Sacré-Coeur, Chapelle du (Roman Catholic), 1888-91, Montréal, QC 148

Sacred Heart (Roman Catholic), 1898, Greenwood, BC 306, 308

Saint-Ambroise (Roman Catholic), 1923-28, Montréal, QC 159, 160

Sainte-Anne, Chapelle (Roman Catholic), mid-18th century, Neuville, QC 117

Sainte-Anne-de-Kent (Roman Catholic), 1890, Bouctouche, NB 17

Saint-Antoine-de-Padoue (Roman Catholic), 1883-84, Batoche, SK 314, 315

Saint-Benoît-du-Lac, Abbaye de (Roman Catholic), 1994, near Austin, QC 168, 170, 171, 175

Saint-Boniface, Cathedrale de (Roman Catholic), 1859, 1906-07, 1970-72, St. Boniface, MB 20, 296, 298, 354, 359, 360, 362

Saint-Charles-Borromée (Roman Catholic), 1828-30, Charlesbourg, QC 10, 106, 127, 128, 129

Sainte-Brigide de Kildare (Roman Catholic), 1885-86, Montréal, QC 154, 156

Sainte-Famille (Roman Catholic), 1743-47, Île d'Orléans, QC 116, 117

Saint-Elzéar (Roman Catholic), 1849, Saint Elzéar, QC 140

Sainte-Marie among the Hurons (Roman Catholic), 1639-49, Midland, ON 178, 188

Sainte-Famille (Roman Catholic), 1754-58, Cap Santé, QC 118, 119

Saint-François-d'Assise (Roman Catholic), 1857-60, Beauceville, QC 138, 139

Saint-François-de-Sales (Roman Catholic), 1734-36, Île d'Orléans, QC 114

Saint-François-de-Sales (Roman Catholic), 1761-73, Neuville, QC 104, 110, 117, 118, 119

Saint-Georges (Roman Catholic), 1900-02, Saint-Georges-de-Beauce, QC 1, 140, 141

Saint-Gérard-Majella (Roman Catholic), 1961-62, Saint-Jean-sur-Richelieu, QC 164, 167, 174

Saint-Isidore (Roman Catholic), 1853-60, Dorchester, QC 14, 140

Saint-Jacques (Roman Catholic), 1823, Montréal, QC 144, 145

Saint-Jean (Roman Catholic), 1734, Île d'Orléans, QC 19, 114, 115

Saint-Jean-Baptiste (Roman Catholic), 1881-84, Québec City, QC 128, 129, 130

Saint-Jean-Baptiste, Cathédrale (Roman Catholic), 1961-62, Nicolet, QC 21, 109, 159, 174, 175

Saint-Joseph (Roman Catholic), 1835-38, Deschambault, QC 18, 119

Saint-Joseph (Roman Catholic), 1865-68, Saint-Joseph-de-Beauce, QC 139

Saint-Louis, Chapelle de (Louisbourg Fortress), 1717-58, Louisbourg NS 32

Saint-Marc (Roman Catholic), 1955-56, La Baie, QC 163, 165

Sainte-Marguerite-de-Blairfindie (Roman Catholic), 1800-01, L'Acadie, QC 138, 139

Saint-Mathias-sur-Richelieu (Roman Catholic), 1784-88, near Chambly, QC 137, 139

Saint-Pierre (Roman Catholic), 1715-19, Île d'Orléans, QC 110, 112, 113, 114, 115, 116

Saint-Pierre (Roman Catholic), 1892–93, Chéticamp NS 40

Saint-Raphaël (Roman Catholic), 1959-60, Jonquière, QC 163, 164

Saint-Richard (Roman Catholic), 1962-63, Montréal, QC 161, 163

Saints Cyril and Methodius (Ukrainian Catholic), 1944-46, St. Catherines, ON 262, 263, 266, 321

Saints Peter and Paul (Ukrainian Catholic), 1968-69, Mundare, AB 365, 366

Scarborough Citadel (Salvation Army), 1992-94, Toronto, ON 284, 285

Sharon Temple (Children of Peace), 1825-31, Sharon, ON 184, 185, 193, 196, 197, 198, 199

Sherwood Park Alliance (Christian and Missionary Alliance), 1979-81, Edmonton, AB 363, 365, 393

Shiskovichi (Ukranian Greek Orthodox), Willingdon, AB 24

Soeurs Grises, Maison mère des Chapelle (Roman Catholic), 1874-78, Montréal, QC 153, 154

St. Andrew and St. Paul, Church of (Presbyterian), 1931-32, Montréal, QC 23

St. Andrew's (Presbyterian), 1809-10, Québec City, QC 23, 127, 128

St. Andrew's (Presbyterian), 1812-13, Williamstown, ON 184, 195, 196

St. Andrew's (Presbyterian), 1831, Niagara-on-the-Lake, ON 185, 206, 207, 208, 209

St. Andrew's (Presbyterian), 1840-53, Thorah, ON 178, 185, 225

St. Andrew's (Presbyterian), 1875-76, Toronto, ON 283, 284

St. Andrew's (United), 1981-83, Toronto, ON 280, 283, 284

St. Andrew's Cathedral (Roman Catholic), 1890-92, Victoria, BC 294, 332, 333, 334

St. Andrew's-on-the-Red (Anglican), 1844-49, Lockport, MB 296, 298

St. Ann's (Roman Catholic), 1903, Duncan, BC 304

St. Anne's (Anglican), 1907-08, Toronto, ON 259, 260, 261, 272, 273, 396

St. Anne's (Roman Catholic), 1860s, Upper Similkameen, BC 306, 307

St. Anne's (Korean Roman Catholic), 1957, Calgary, AB 345

St. Anne's Chapel (Anglican), 1846-47, Fredericton NB 36, 37, 39, 74, 75, 91

St. Anselm's (Anglican), 1952-53, Vancouver, BC 295

St. Catherine's Chapel, Massey College (Non-denominational), 1962-63, Toronto, ON 187

St. Charles Mission (Roman Catholic), 1883-84, Dunvegan, AB 288, 336

St. Dunstan's Basilica (Roman Catholic), 1914-19, Charlottetown, PE 7

St. Elias (Ukrainian Catholic), 1906, Sirko, MB 328

St. Elias (Ukrainian Catholic), 1994-95, Brampton, ON 266, 268, 271

St. Eugene's Mission (Roman Catholic), 1897, near Cranbrook, BC 308

St. George the Martyr (Anglican), 1844, Toronto, ON 243

St. George's (Greek Orthodox), 1895-97, Toronto, ON 264, 266

St. George's (the Round) (Anglican), 1800-12, Halifax NS 47, 48

St. George's Cathedral (Anglican), 1825-28, Kingston, ON 35, 199, 200, 203

St. James' (Anglican), 1887, Mahone Bay NS 38

St. James' Chapel (Anglican), 1841-43, Long Reach NB 34

St. James' (Anglican), 1853, Winnipeg, MB 296, 298, 299, 300

St. James' (Anglican), 1935-37,Vancouver, BC 342, 344

St. James' Cathedral (Anglican), 1850-53, Toronto, ON 2, 152, 214, 243, 245, 247, 248, 249, 251

St. James-the-Less, Chapel of (Anglican), 1861, Toronto, ON 247, 249, 251

St. John the Baptist (Roman Catholic), 1847-48, Perth, ON 185, 232

St. John the Baptist, Basilica-Cathedral of (Roman Catholic), 1841-55, St. John's NL 80, 81, 82, 83, 87

St. John the Baptist, Cathedral of (Anglican), 1847, St. John's NL 83, 84, 85, 100

St. John the Divine (Anglican), 1863, Yale, BC 304, 306

St. John's (Anglican) 1902, North Sydney NS 100

St. John's (Anglican), 1753-58, Lunenburg NS 48

St. John's (Anglican), 1823-26, Saint John NB 36, 67, 68

St. John's (Anglican), 1953, Kingnait, NU 24, 338, 339

St. John's (Evangelical Lutheran), 1876, Mahone Bay NS 38

St. John's (Presbyterian), 1823-26, Belfast, PE 94, 95, 96

St. John's Convent Chapel (Anglican), 2003-04, Thornhill, ON 168, 172, 173, 175

St. Josaphat Cathedral (Ukranian Catholic), 1939-47, Edmonton, AB 263

St. Joseph's (Roman Catholic), 1893, Douro, ON 185, 235, 237

St. Jude's Cathedral (Anglican) (destroyed 2005), 1970-72, Iqaluit, NU 338

St. Luke's (Anglican), 1895, Newton NL 16

St. Malachy's (Roman Catholic), 1899, Kinkora, PE 99

St. Mark's (Presbyterian), 1961-63, Don Mills, ON 279, 283

St. Mary Magdalene (Anglican), 1887-90, Toronto, ON 254, 255, 396

St. Mary Magdalene (Deconsecrated), 1823-25, Picton, ON 238

St. Mary the Virgin (Anglican), 1863-64, New Maryland NB 89, 90, 91

St. Mary's (Anglican), 1790, Auburn NS 52, 53, 54

St. Mary's (Anglican), 1903-04, Windsor, ON 217, 219

St. Mary's (Roman Catholic), 1900-02, Indian River PE 98, 99, 100, 101

St. Mary's (Roman Catholic), 1965-68, Red Deer, AB 349, 352

St. Mary's Cathedral (Ukranian Catholic), 1913-14, Yorkton, SK 19

St. Mary's Cathedral-Basilica (Roman Catholic), 1820-29, Halifax NS 36

St. Michael's (Ukrainian Orthodox), 1897-99, Gardenton, MB 316, 318

St. Michael's and St. Anthony's (Roman Catholic), 1914-15, Montréal, QC 108, 159

St. Michael's Cathedral (Roman Catholic), 1845-48, Toronto, ON 209, 241, 243, 244, 245

St. Nicholas' (Ukrainian Greek Catholic), 1912, Mundare, AB 321, 322

St. Nicholas' (Anglican), 1900, near Craven, SK 293

St. Nicholas' (Ukrainian Catholic), 1964-66, Winnipeg, MB 362, 364

St. Nicolas' (Russo-Greek Orthodox), 1908, Mundare, AB 321

St. Onuphrius (Ukranian Catholic), 1915, Smoky Lake AB 318

St. Patrick's (Roman Catholic), 1836-44, Grand River PE 98

St. Patrick's (Roman Catholic), 1843-47, Montréal, QC 148, 150, 151, 152, 209

St. Patrick's (Roman Catholic), 1864-81, St. John's NL 86, 87

St. Patrick's (Roman Catholic), 1866-73, Ottawa, ON 234, 235

St. Paul's (Anglican), 1895, Charlottetown PE 101

St. Paul's (Anglican), 1750-63, Halifax NS 36, 42, 44, 45, 46, 51, 54

St. Paul's (Anglican), 1844-46, London, ON 185, 209, 210, 212, 213, 243

St. Paul's (Anglican), 1849, Wikwemikong, ON 220

St. Paul's (Anglican), 1866, Esquimalt, BC 303

St. Paul's (Anglican), 1892-93, Trinity NL 30

St. Paul's (Presbyterian), 1854-57, Hamilton, ON 214, 215

St. Paul's (Presbyterian), 1895, Winchester, ON 390

St. Paul's (United), 1893, Boissevain, MB 334, 335

St. Paul's Basilica (Roman Catholic), 1887-89, Toronto, ON 252, 253, 254

St. Peter's (Anglican), 1874-76, Duncan, BC 303, 304

St. Peter's (Anglican), 1887, Windermere, BC 308

St. Peter's (Roman Catholic), 1887, near Cranbrook, BC 24

St. Peter's (Roman Catholic), 1941, Kugaaruk, NU 338, 339

St. Peter's Estonian (Evangelical Lutheran), 1954-55, Toronto, ON 274, 276

St. Peter's, Cathedral (Anglican), 1867-69, Charlottetown, PE 98, 99

St. Peter's-on-the-Rock (Non-denominational), 1912-15, Stoney Lake, ON 227, 228

St. Pius X (Roman Catholic), 1954, Toronto, ON 256, 257

St. Saviour's (Anglican), 1869-70, Barkerville, BC 291, 306

St. Simon's (Anglican), 1900, Whitehorse, YK 337

St. Stephen Protomartyr (Ukrainian Catholic), 1978-82, Calgary, AB 366

St. Stephen's (Anglican), 1857, Greenspond, NL 37, 86

St. Stephen's (Anglican), 1820, Chambly, QC 138, 139

St. Stephen's (Anglican), 1862, Saanich, BC 303

St. Stephen-in-the-Fields (Anglican), 1857-58, Toronto, ON 393, 396

St. Thomas (Anglican), 1822, St. Thomas, ON 204, 206

St. Thomas' (Anglican), 1869-70, Brooklin, ON 182

St. Thomas' (Anglican), 1834-36, St. John's NL 78, 80

St. Thomas' (Anglican), 1838-41, Shanty Bay, ON 185, 222

St. Vladimir's (Ukrainian Greek Orthodox), 1934, Mundare, AB 321, 322

Trinity (Presbyterian), 2002-03, Oro, ON 391, 393

Trinity (United), 1862, Mahone Bay NS 38

Union Church (non-denominational), 1914-15, Sturgeon Point, ON 228, 229

Unitarian Church, 1964, Vancouver, BC 347, 348, 349

United Baptist, 1864-65, St. Andrews NB 54, 69

Unity Church of Truth, Toronto, ON 278

Ursulines, La Chapelle des (Roman Catholic), 1730, Québec City, QC 124, 126, 127, 134

Walkerton (Baptist), 1883, Walkerton, ON 214, 216, 217

Wellington Meetinghouse (deconsecrated), 1885, Wellington, ON 238, 239

Wesleyan Methodist, 1875, Toronto, ON 216

West Ellesmere (United), 1957, Toronto, ON 277

West Vancouver (Baptist), 1966-67, Vancouver, BC 163, 347, 349

Westminister Abbey (Roman Catholic), 1953-82, Mission, BC 168, 171, 172

White Chapel (United), 1809-11, Picton, ON 193, 195

INDEX
CANADIAN CHURCHES BY LOCATION

ALBERTA

Calgary, Immaculate Conception of the Blessed Virgin Mary, Cathedral of (Roman Catholic) 1954-57, 344, 345

Calgary, St. Anne's (Roman Catholic), 1957, 345

Calgary, St. Stephen Protomartyr (Ukrainian Catholic), 1978-82, 366

Cardston, Church of Jesus Christ of the Latter Day Saints, Temple of (Mormon), 1913-23, 340, 342

Dunvegan, St. Charles Mission (Roman Catholic), 1883-85, 288, 336

Edmonton, Avonmore (United), 1988-90, 295

Edmonton, Sherwood Park (Christian and Missionary Alliance), 1979-81, 363, 365, 393

Edmonton, St. Josaphat (Ukranian Catholic), 1939-47, 263

Medicine Hat, Holy Family (Roman Catholic), 2003-04, 364, 365, 390, 391, 393

Morley, McDougall Mission (Methodist), 1862, 288, 300, 301

Mundarc, St. Nicholas' (Ukrainian Greek Catholic), 1912, 321, 322

Mundare, St. Nicolas' (Russo-Greek Orthodox), 1908, 321

Mundare, St. Vladimir's (Ukrainian Greek Orthodox), 1934, 321, 322

Mundare, Saints. Peter and Paul (Ukrainian Catholic), 1968-69, 365, 366

Pincher Creek, Pincher Creek (Hutterite), 1945, 327

Red Deer, St. Mary's (Roman Catholic), 1965-68, 349, 352

St. Albert, Father Lacombe's Chapel (Roman Catholic), 1861, 300, 301

Willingdon, Shiskovichi (Ukranian Greek Orthodox) 24

BRITISH COLUMBIA

Barkerville, St. Saviour's (Anglican), 1869-70, 291, 306

Cranbrook, near, St. Peter's (Roman Catholic), 1887, 24

Cranbrook, near, St. Eugene's Mission (Roman Catholic), 1897, 308

Duncan, St. Ann's (Roman Catholic), 1903, 304

Duncan, St. Peter's (Anglican), 1874-76, 303, 304

Esquimalt, St. Paul's (Anglican), 1866, 303

Greenwood, Sacred Heart (Roman Catholic), 1898, 306, 308

Kelowna, Father Pandosy's Mission (Roman Catholic), 1859-60, 290, 306

Mission, Westminister Abbey Church (Roman Catholic), 1953-82, 168, 171, 172

North Vancouver, Highlands (United), 1956-57, 20

Saanich, St. Stephen's (Anglican), 1862, 303

Skatin, Holy Cross (Roman Catholic), 1895-1906, 291, 292

Upper Similkameen, St. Anne's (Roman Catholic), 1860s, 306, 307

Vancouver, Christ Church Cathedral (Anglican), 1894-95, 330, 332

Vancouver, St. Anselm's (Anglican), 1952-53, 295

Vancouver, St. James' (Anglican), 1935-37, 342, 344

Vancouver, Unitarian Church, 1964, 347, 348, 349

Vancouver, West Vancouver (Baptist), 1966-67, 163, 347, 349

Victoria, First Church (Christian Science), 1919-20, 342, 343

Victoria, St. Andrew's Cathedral (Roman Catholic), 1890-92, 294, 332, 333, 334

Windermere, St. Peter's (Anglican), 1887, 308

Yale, St. John the Divine (Anglican), 1863, 304, 306

MANITOBA

Ashville, Assumption of the Mother of God (Ukrainian Catholic), 1906, 328

Boissevain, St. Paul's (United), 1893, 334, 335

Cook's Creek, Immaculate Conception of the Virgin Mary (Ukrainian Catholic), 1930-52, 318, 320, 328

Gardenton, St. Michael's (Ukrainian Orthodox), 1897-99, 316, 318

Grund, Frelsis (Lutheran), 1889, 310, 312, 313

Lockport, St. Andrew's-on-the-Red (Anglican), 1844-49, 296, 298

Saint Boniface, Précieux-Sang (Roman Catholic), 1967-68, 352, 353, 354

Sirko, St. Elias (Ukrainian Catholic), 1906, 328

St. Boniface, Saint-Boniface, Cathédrale de (Roman Catholic), 1839, 1906-07, 1970-72, 296, 298, 354, 359, 360, 362

Steinbach, Old Colony Worship House (Mennonite), 1881, 312

Winnipeg, St. James' (Anglican), 1853, 296, 298, 299, 300

Winnipeg, St. Nicholas' (Ukrainian Catholic), 1964-66, 362, 364

NEW BRUNSWICK

Bouctouche, Sainte-Anne-de-Kent (Roman Catholic), 1890, 17

Clifton Royal, All Saints' (Anglican), 1884-85, 40

Fredericton, Christ Church Cathedral (Anglican), 1845-53, 69, 71, 72, 73, 74, 76

Fredericton, St. Anne's Chapel (Anglican), 1846-47, 36, 37, 39, 74, 75, 91

Long Reach, St. James Chapel (Anglican), 1841-43, 34

McKeen's Corner, All Saints' (Anglican), 1861, 38, 89

Moncton, Free Meeting House (deconsecrated), 1821, 66, 67

New Maryland, St. Mary the Virgin, Church of (Anglican), 1863-64, 89, 90, 91

Saint John, St. John's (Anglican), 1823-26, 36, 67, 68

Sheffield, Maugerville Meetinghouse (United), 1775, 68, 69

St. Andrew's, Greenock Church (Presbyterian), 1821-24, 36, 63, 64, 65, 67

St. Andrew's, (United Baptist), 1864-65, 54, 69

St. Stephen, Christ Church (Anglican), 1864, 69, 91, 92, 93

NEWFOUNDLAND AND LABRADOR

Greenspond, St. Stephen's (Anglican) 1857, 37, 86

Hebron, Church at (Moravian), 1830s 57, 58, 59

Hopedale, Church at (Moravian) 1865, 57, 58, 60

Nain, Church at (Moravian) 1925, 57, 60

Newtown, St. Luke's (Anglican), 1895, 16

St. John's, Gower Street (United), 1894-96, 87

St. John's, St. John the Baptist, Basilica-Cathedral of (Roman Catholic), 1841-55, 80, 81, 83, 87

St. John's, St. John the Baptist, Cathedral of (Anglican), 1847, 83, 84, 85, 100

St. John's, St. Patrick's (Roman Catholic), 1864-81, 86, 87

St. John's, St. Thomas' (Anglican), 1834-36, 78, 80

Trinity, Most Holy Trinity, Church of the (Roman Catholic), 1833, 30, 78

Trinity, St. Paul's (Anglican), 1892-93, 30

NORTHWEST TERRITORIES

Fort Good Hope, Our Lady of Good Hope (Roman Catholic), 1865-85, 337

Inuvik, Our Lady of Victory (Roman Catholic), 1958-60, 338

NOVA SCOTIA

Annapolis Royal (near), Port Royal Habitation, Chapel of, 1605-07, 31

Auburn, St. Mary's (Anglican), 1790, 52, 53, 54

Barrington, Barrington Meetinghouse, 1765, 50, 51

Chéticamp, Saint-Pierre (Roman Catholic), 1892–93, 40

Grand Pré (near), Community Church, 1861, 33

Grand Pré, Covenanters' Church (United), 1804-11, 33, 51, 52, 67

Granville Beach, Granville Beach Baptist, 1833, 54

Granville Centre, Granville Centre Church (United Baptist), 54

Halifax, Little Dutch (Lutheran, Anglican), 1756, 46, 48, 50

Halifax, St. George's (the Round) (Anglican), 1800-12, 47, 48

Halifax, St. Mary's Cathedral-Basilica (Roman Catholic), 1820-29, 36

Halifax, St. Paul's (Anglican), 1750-63, 36, 42, 44, 45, 46, 51, 54

Louisbourg, Saint-Louis, Chapelle de (Louisbourg Fortress), 1717-58, 32

Lunenburg, St. John's (Anglican), 1753-58, 48

Mahone Bay, Mahone Bay United Baptist, 38

Mahone Bay, St. James' (Anglican), 1887, 38

Mahone Bay, St. John's (Evangelical Lutheran), 1876, 38

Mahone Bay, Trinity (United), 1862, 38

Middleton, Old Holy Trinity (Anglican), 1789-91, 54

North Sydney, St. John's (Anglican), 1902, 100

NUNAVUT

Iqaluit, St. Jude's Cathedral (Anglican) (destroyed 2005), 1970-72, 295, 338

Kingnait, St. John's (Anglican), 1953, 338, 339

Kugaaruk, St. Peter's (Roman Catholic), 1941, 338

ONTARIO

Barrie, Emmanuel (Baptist), 2004-05, 392, 394, 397

Brampton, St. Elias (Ukrainian Catholic), 1994-95, 266, 268, 271

Brantford, Mohawk Chapel, 1785, 193, 194, 200

Brooklin, St. Thomas' (Anglican), 1869-70, 182

Burritt's Rapids, Christ Church (Anglican), 1831-32, 184, 199

Consecon, Holy Trinity (deconsecrated), 1847, 239

Don Mills, St. Mark's (Presbyterian), 1961-63, 279, 283

Douro, St. Joseph's (Roman Catholic), 1893, 185, 235, 237

Guelph, Our Lady of the Immaculate Conception (Roman Catholic), 1876-88, 182, 233, 235, 254

Hallowell, Bowerman's Church (deconsecrated), 1855, 239

Hamilton, St. Paul's (Presbyterian), 1854-57, 214, 215

Hensall, Carmel (United), 1886-87, 216, 217

Kingston, St. George's Cathedral (Anglican), 1825-28, 35, 199, 200, 203

London, St. Paul's (Anglican), 1844-46, 185, 209, 210, 212, 213, 243

M'Chigeeng First Nations, Immaculate Conception (Roman Catholic), 1971-72, 221

Markham, Altona Meetinghouse (Mennonite), 1852-53, 199, 200

Midland, Martyrs Shrine (Roman Catholic), 1925-26, 189

Midland, Sainte-Marie among the Hurons (Roman Catholic), 1639-49, 178, 188

Milford, Mount Tabor (deconsecrated), 1865-67, 239

Napanee, Hay Bay Meetinghouse (Methodist), 1792, 180, 184

Niagara-on-the-Lake, Grace (United), 1852, 210, 214

Niagara-on-the-Lake, St. Andrew's (Presbyterian), 1831, 185, 206, 207, 208, 209

North Bay, Omond Memorial (United), 1983, 397

Oro, Black Church (United), 1849, 185, 222, 224

Oro, Knox (Presbyterian), 1845, 185, 222, 224

Oro, Trinity (Presbyterian), 2002-03, 391, 393

Ottawa, Basilique-Cathédrale Notre-Dame d'Ottawa (Roman Catholic), 1841-85, 231, 235

Ottawa, Dominion-Chalmers (United), 1912-14, 184, 261, 262

Ottawa, Rideau Street Convent Chapel (Roman Catholic), 1887-88, 235, 236, 237

Ottawa, St. Patrick's (Roman Catholic), 1866-73, 234, 235

Paris, Paris Plains (United), 1845, 210, 213

Perth, St. John the Baptist (Roman Catholic), 1847-48, 185, 232

Picton, St. Mary Magdalene (deconsecrated), 1823-25, 238

Picton, White Chapel (United), 1809-11, 193, 195

Port Sydney, Christ Church (Anglican), 1873, 226, 227

Port Sydney, Port Sydney Bible Chapel (Plymouth Brethren), 2000, 228

Prescott, near, Blue Church (Anglican), 1845, 180, 181

Richmond Hill, L'Arche Dayspring Chapel (non-denominational), 1999, 168, 172, 173, 174, 175

Shanty Bay, St. Thomas' (Anglican), 1838-41, 185, 222

Sharon, Sharon Temple (Children of Peace), 1825-31, 184, 185, 193, 196, 197, 198, 199

Sheguiandah First Nations, St. Andrew's (Anglican), 1886, 220, 221

St. Catherines, Saints Cyril and Methodius (Ukrainian Catholic), 1944-46, 262, 263, 266, 321

St. Jacobs, Old Order Meetinghouse (Mennonite), 1917-18, 4

St. Thomas, St. Thomas (Anglican), 1822, 204, 206

Stephenson Township, Madill Church (United), 1872-73, 226, 227

Stoney Lake, St. Peter's-on-the-Rock (non-denominational), 1912-15, 227, 228

Sturgeon Point, Union Church (non-denominational), 1914-15, 228, 229

Thorah, St. Andrew's (Presbyterian), 1840-53, 178, 185, 225

Thornhill, St. John's Convent Chapel (Anglican), 2003-04, 168, 172, 173, 175

Toronto, Beverley Street (Baptist), 1886-87, 251, 253, 254

Toronto, Bond Street (Baptist), 251

Toronto, Christadelphians Church (Christadelphian), 1948-49, 186, 278

Toronto, Holy Eucharist (Ukrainian Catholic), 1967, 266, 268, 271

Toronto, Holy Name (Roman Catholic), 1915, 256, 257

Toronto, Holy Trinity (Russian Orthodox Outside of Russia), 1922, 264, 266

Toronto, Holy Trinity, Church of the (Anglican), 1846-47, 243, 254

Toronto, Jarvis Street (Baptist), 1874-75, 187, 216, 248, 251, 252, 253, 254

Toronto, Knox Fellowship Centre Chapel (Presbyterian), 1960-61, 278, 279

Toronto, Knox (Presbyterian), 1847-48, 213, 214

Toronto, Little Trinity (Anglican), 1843-44, 242, 243, 253, 254

Toronto, Metropolitan Community Church, 1907, 26, 396

Toronto, Our Lady of Mount Carmel (Roman Catholic), 1867, 256

Toronto, Redeemer, Church of the (Anglican), 1878-79, 283, 284

Toronto, Scarborough Citadel (Salvation Army), 1992-94, 284, 285

Toronto, St. Andrew's (United), 1981-83, 280, 283, 284

Toronto, St. Andrew's Presbyterian, 1875-76, 283, 284

Toronto, St. Anne's (Anglican), 1907-08, 259, 260, 261, 272, 273, 396

Toronto, St. Catherine's Chapel (non-denominational), 1961-63, 187

Toronto, St. George the Martyr (Anglican), 1844, 243

Toronto, St. George's (Greek Orthodox), 1895-97, 264, 266

Toronto, St. James' Cathedral (Anglican), 1850-53, 2, 152, 214, 243, 245, 247, 248, 249, 251

Toronto, St. James-the-Less, Chapel of (Anglican), 1861, 247, 249, 251

Toronto, St. Mary Magdalene (Anglican), 1887-90, 254, 255, 396

Toronto, St. Michael's Cathedral (Roman Catholic), 1845-48, 209, 241, 243, 244, 245

Toronto, St. Paul's Basilica (Roman Catholic), 1887-89, 252, 253, 254

Toronto, St. Peter's Estonian (Evangelical Lutheran), 1954-55, 274, 276

Toronto, St. Pius X (Roman Catholic), 1954, 256, 257

Toronto, St. Stephen-in-the-Fields (Anglican), 1857-58, 393, 396

Toronto, Unity Church of Truth, 278

Toronto, Wesleyan Methodist Church, 1875, 216

Toronto, West Ellesmere (United), 1957, 277

Walkerton, Walkerton Baptist, 1883, 214, 216, 217

Waterloo, Cedars, 1995–96, 27

Wellington, Wellington Meetinghouse (deconsecrated), 1885, 238, 239

Wikwemikong, St. Paul's (Anglican), 1849, 220

Williamstown, St. Andrew's (Presbyterian), 1812-13, 184, 195, 196

Winchester, St. Paul's (Presbyterian), 1895, 390

Windsor, Our Lady of the Assumption (Roman Catholic), 1842-46, 209, 210

Windsor, St. Mary's (Anglican), 1903-04, 217, 219

PRINCE EDWARD ISLAND

Belfast, St. John's (Presbyterian), 1823-26, 94, 95, 96

Charlottetown, All Souls' Chapel (Anglican), 1888-89, 98, 99

Charlottetown, St. Dunstan's Bascilica (Roman Catholic), 1914-19, 7

Charlottetown, St. Paul's (Anglican), 1895, 101

Charlottetown, St. Peter's, Cathedral (Anglican), 1867-69, 98, 99

Cross Roads, Cross Roads, Church at (non-denominational), 1836, 96, 97

Grand River, St. Patrick's (Roman Catholic), 1836-44, 98

Indian River, St. Mary's (Roman Catholic), 1900-02, 98, 99, 100, 101

Kinkora, St. Malachy's (Roman Catholic), 1899, 99

Malpeque, Malpeque United, 1869-70, 97, 98

QUÉBEC

Austin, near, Abbaye de Saint-Benoît-du-Lac (Roman Catholic), 1994, 168, 170, 171, 175

Beauceville, Saint-François-d'Assise (Roman Catholic), 1857-60, 138, 139

Cap Santé, Sainte-Famille (Roman Catholic), 1754-58, 118, 119

Chambly, near, Saint-Mathias-sur-Richelieu (Roman Catholic), 1784-88, 137, 139

Chambly, St. Stephen's (Anglican), 1820, 138, 139

Charlesbourg, Saint-Charles-Borromée (Roman Catholic), 1828-30, 10, 106, 127, 128, 129

Deschambault, Saint-Joseph (Roman Catholic), 1835-38, 119

Dorchester, Saint-Isidore (Roman Catholic), 1853-60, 140

Gatineau, St. Onuphrius (Ukranian Catholic), 1915, 318

Île d'Orléans, Sainte-Famille (Roman Catholic), 1743-47, 116, 117

Île d'Orléans, Saint-François-de-Sales (Roman Catholic), 1734-36, 114

Île d'Orléans, Saint-Jean (Roman Catholic), 1734, 114, 115

Île d'Orléans, Saint-Pierre (Roman Catholic), 1715-19, 110, 112, 113, 114, 115, 116

Jonquière, Notre-Dame-de-Fatima (Roman Catholic), 1962-63, 164, 166

Jonquière, Saint-Raphaël (Roman Catholic), 1959-60, 163, 164

L'Acadie, Sainte-Marguerite-de-Blairfindie (Roman Catholic), 1800-01, 138, 139

La Baie, Saint-Marc (Roman Catholic), 1955-56, 163, 165

Montréal, Grand Séminaire de Montréal, Chapelle du (Roman Catholic), 1904-07, 154, 156, 157

Montréal, Notre-Dame-de-Grâce (Roman Catholic), 1851-53, 148, 152, 153

Montréal, Notre-Dame de Montréal, Basilique (Roman Catholic), 1823-29, 8, 96, 143, 144, 145, 146, 147, 148, 244

Montréal, Notre-Dame-de-Bon-Secours, Chapelle (Roman Catholic), 1771-73, 143, 144, 150

Montréal, Nuestra Senora de Guadalupe, Misión Católica Latinoamericana (Roman Catholic), 1924, 160, 161

Montréal, Oratoire Saint-Joseph (Roman Catholic), 1924-67, 160, 162, 189

Montréal, Première Église Évangélique Arménienne (Armenian Evangelical), 1966-67, 163

Montréal, Sacré-Coeur, Chapelle du (Roman Catholic), 1888-91, 148

Montréal, Saint-Ambroise (Roman Catholic), 1923-28, 159, 160

Montréal, Sainte-Brigide de Kildare (Roman Catholic), 1885-86, 154, 156

Montréal, Saint-Jacques (Roman Catholic), 1823, 144, 145

Montréal, Saint-Richard (Roman Catholic), 1962-63, 161, 163

Montréal, St. Andrew and St. Paul, Church of (Presbyterian), 1931-32, 23

Montréal, St. Michael's and St. Anthony's (Roman Catholic), 1914-15, 108, 159

Montréal, St. Patrick's (Roman Catholic), 1843-47, 148, 150, 151, 152, 209

Montréal, Soeurs Grises, Chapelle Maison mère des (Roman Catholic), 1874-78, 153, 154

Neuville, Saint-Anne, Chapelle (Roman Catholic), mid-18th century, 117

Neuville, Saint-François-de-Sales (Roman Catholic), 1761-73, 104, 110, 117, 118, 119

Nicolet, Saint-Jean-Baptiste, Cathédrale (Roman Catholic), 1961-62, 109, 159, 174, 175

Québec City, Monseigneur Briand, La Chapelle de (Roman Catholic), 1784-86, 127, 134

Québec City, Holy Trinity, Cathedral of the (Anglican) 1799-1804, 36, 107, 108, 119, 121, 122, 123

Québec City, Notre-Dame, Basilique-Cathédrale (Roman Catholic), 1647, 132, 133, 134, 135

Québec City, Notre-Dame-des-Victoires (Roman Catholic), 1723, 124

Québec City, Saint-Jean-Baptiste (Roman Catholic), 1881-84, 128, 129, 130

Québec City, St. Andrew's (Presbyterian), 1809-10, 127, 128

Québec City, Ursulines, La Chapelle des (Roman Catholic), 1730, 124, 126, 127, 134

Saint-Elzéar, Saint-Elzéar (Roman Catholic), 1849, 140

Saint-Georges-de-Beauce, Saint-Georges (Roman Catholic), 1900-02, 1, 140, 141

Saint-Jean-sur-Richelieu, Saint-Gérard-Majella (Roman Catholic), 1961-62, 164, 167, 174

Saint-Joseph-de-Beauce, Saint-Joseph (Roman Catholic), 1865-68, 139, 140

SASKATCHEWAN

Batoche, Saint-Antoine-de-Padoue (Roman Catholic), 1883-84, 314, 315

Craven, near, St. Nicholas' (Anglican), 1900, 293

Dobrowody, Nativity of the Blessed Virgin Mary (Ukrainian Catholic), 1911-12, 318

Saint Julien, Blessed Virgin Mary (Ukrainian Catholic), 1926-27, 294

Silton, Lady of the Lake Chapel (Roman Catholic), 1969, 354, 358

Stanley Mission, Holy Trinity (Anglican), 1854-60, 336

Sturgis, Holy Ascension (Russian Greek Orthodox), 1905, 16

Veregin, Doukhobor Community Home, 1917-18, 324, 326

YUKON

Whitehorse, St. Simon's (Anglican), 1900, 337

Yorkton, St. Mary's Cathedral (Ukranian Catholic), 1913-14, 19

INDEX
CANADIAN CHURCHES BY DENOMINATION

ANGLICAN

All Saints', 1861, McKeen's Corner NB 38, 89
All Saints', 1884-85, Clifton Royal NB 40
All Souls' Chapel, 1888-89, Charlottetown PE 98 - 99
Blue Church, 1845, near Prescott, ON 180, 181
Christ Church Cathedral, 1845-53, Fredericton NB 69, 71, 72, 73, 74, 76
Christ Church Cathedral, 1894-95, Vancouver, BC 330, 332
Christ Church, 1831-32, Burritt's Rapids, ON 184, 199
Christ Church, 1864, St. Stephen NB 69, 91, 92, 93
Christ Church, 1873, Port Sydney, ON 226, 227
Holy Trinity, 1854-60, Stanley Mission, SK 336
Holy Trinity, Cathedral of the, 1799-1804, Québec City, QC 36, 107, 108, 119, 121, 122, 123
Holy Trinity, Church of the , 1846-47, Toronto, ON 243, 254
Little Dutch Church, 1756, Halifax NS 46, 48, 50
Little Trinity, 1843-44, Toronto, ON 242, 243, 253, 254
Mohawk Chapel, 1785, Brantford, ON 193, 194, 200
Old Holy Trinity, 1789-91, Middleton NS 54
Redeemer, Church of the, 1878-79, Toronto, ON 283, 284
St. Andrew's, 1886, Sheguiandah First Nations, ON 220, 221
St. Andrew's-on-the-Red, 1844-49, Lockport, MB 296, 298
St. Anne's Chapel, 1846-47, Fredericton NB 36, 37, 39, 74, 75, 91
St. Anne's, 1907-08, Toronto, ON 259, 260, 261, 272, 273, 396
St. Anselm's, 1952-53, Vancouver, BC 295
St. George the Martyr, 1844, Toronto, ON 243
St. George's (the Round), 1800-12, Halifax NS 47, 48
St. George's Cathedral, 1825-28, Kingston, ON 35, 199, 200, 203
St. James' Anglican, 1887, Mahone Bay NS 38
St. James' Chapel, 1841-43, Long Reach NB 34
St. James' Cathedral, 1850-53, Toronto, ON 2, 152, 214, 243, 245, 247, 248, 249, 251
St. James', 1853, Winnipeg, MB 296, 298, 299, 300
St. James', 1935-37,Vancouver, BC 342, 344
St. James-the-Less, Chapel of, 1861, Toronto, ON 247, 249, 251
St. John the Baptist, Cathedral of, 1847, St. John's NL 82, 83, 84, 85, 100

St. John the Divine, 1863, Yale, BC 304, 306
St. John's Convent Chapel, 2003-04, Thornhill, ON 168, 172, 173, 175
St. John's, 1902 North Sydney, NS 100
St. John's, 1753-58, Lunenburg NS 48
St. John's, 1823-26, Saint John NB 36, 67, 68
St. John's, 1953, Kingnait, NU 338, 339
St. Jude's Cathedral (destroyed 2005), 1970-72, Iqaluit, NU 338
St. Luke's, 1895, Newtown, NF 16
St. Mary Magdalene, 1887-90, Toronto, ON 254, 255, 396
St. Mary the Virgin, Church of, 1863-64, New Maryland NB 89, 90, 91
St. Mary's, 1790, Auburn NS 52, 53, 54
St. Mary's, 1903-04, Windsor, ON 217, 219
St. Nicholas', 1900, near Craven, SK 293
St. Paul's 1892-93, Trinity NL 30
St. Paul's, 1750-63, Halifax NS 36, 42, 44, 45, 46, 51, 54
St. Paul's, 1844-46, London, ON 185, 209, 210, 212, 213, 243
St. Paul's, 1849, Wikwemikong, ON 220
St. Paul's, 1866, Esquimalt, BC 303
St. Paul's, 1895, Charlottetown, PE 101
St. Peter's, 1874-76, Duncan, BC 303, 304
St. Peter's, 1887, Windermere, BC 308
St. Peter's, Cathedral, 1867-69, Charlottetown, PE 98, 99
St. Saviour's, 1869-70, Barkerville, BC 291, 306
St. Simon's, 1900, Whitehorse, YK 337
St. Stephen's, 1820, Chambly, QC 138, 139
St. Stephen's, 1857, Greenspond NL 37, 86
St. Stephen's, 1862, Saanich, BC 303
St. Stephen-in-the-Fields, 1857-58, Toronto, ON 393, 396
St. Thomas, 1822, St. Thomas, ON 204, 206
St. Thomas, 1869-70, Brooklin, ON 182
St. Thomas', 1834-36, St. John's NL 78, 80
St. Thomas', 1838-41, Shanty Bay, ON 185, 222
see also
Barrington Meetinghouse, 1765, Barrington NS 50, 51
Free Meeting House, 1821, Moncton NB 66, 67
Holy Trinity, 1847, Consecon, ON 239
St. Mary Magdalene, 1823-25, Picton, ON 238
St. Paul's Presbyterian, 1854-57, Hamilton, ON 214, 215

ARMENIAN EVANGELICAL

Première Église Évangélique Arménienne, 1966-67, Montréal, QC 163

BAPTIST

Beverley Street, 1886-87, Toronto, ON 251, 253, 254
Bond Street, Toronto, ON 251
Emmanuel, 2004-05, Barrie, ON 392, 394, 397
Granville Beach, 1833, Granville Beach, NS 54
Granville Center, Granville Center, NS 54
Jarvis Street, 1874-75, Toronto, ON 187, 216, 248, 251, 252, 253, 254
Mahone Bay, Mahone Bay, NS 38
United Baptist, 1864-65, St. Andrews, NB 54, 69
Walkerton, 1883, Walkerton, ON 214, 216, 217
West Vancouver, 1966-67, Vancouver, BC 163, 347, 349
see also
Barrington Meetinghouse, 1765, Barrington NS 50, 51
Cross Roads, Church at, 1836, Cross Roads PE 96, 97
Free Meeting House, 1821, Moncton NB 66, 67

CHRISTADELPHIAN

Christadelphian Church, 1948-49, Toronto, ON 186, 278

CHRISTIAN AND MISSIONARY ALLIANCE

Sherwood Park, 1979-81, Edmonton, AB 363, 365, 393

CHRISTIAN SCIENCE

First Church, 1919-20, Victoria, BC 342, 343

CONGREGATIONALIST

Barrington Meetinghouse, 1765, Barrington NS 50, 51
Covenanters' Church, 1804-11, Grand Pré NS 33, 51, 52, 67
Maugerville Meetinghouse, 1775, Sheffield, NB 68, 69

DOUKHOBOR

Doukhobor Community Home, 1917-18, Veregin, SK 324, 326

EASTERN RITE

GREEK ORTHODOX
St. George's, 1895-97, Toronto, ON 264, 266
RUSSIAN ORTHODOX
Holy Trinity (Russian Orthodox Outside of Russia), 1922, Toronto, ON 264, 266
RUSSO-GREEK ORTHODOX
Holy Ascension, 1905, Sturgis, SK 16
St. Nicolas', 1908, Mundare, AB 321

UKRAINIAN CATHOLIC
Assumption of the Mother of God, 1906, Ashville, MB 328
Blessed Virgin Mary, 1926-27, Saint Julien, SK 294
Holy Eucharist, 1967, Toronto, ON 266, 268, 271
Immaculate Conception of the Virgin Mary, 1930-52, Cook's Creek, MB 318, 320, 328
Nativity of the Blessed Virgin Mary, 1911-12, Dobrowody, SK 318
Saints Cyril and Methodius, 1944-46, St. Catherines, ON 262, 263, 266, 321
Saints Peter and Paul, 1968-69, Mundare, AB 365, 3668
St. Elias, 1906, Sirko, MB 328
St. Elias, 1994-95, Brampton, ON 266, 268, 271
St. Josaphat, 1939-47, Edmonton, AB 263
St. Mary's Cathedral, 1913-14, Yorkton, SK 19
St. Nicholas', 1964-66, Winnipeg, MB 362, 364
St. Onuprius, 1915, Gatineau, QC (Smoky Lake, AB) 318
St. Stephen Protomartyr, 1978-82, Calgary, AB 366

UKRAINIAN GREEK CATHOLIC
St. Nicholas Ukrainian Greek Catholic Church, 1912, Mundare, AB 321, 322

UKRAINIAN ORTHODOX
St. Michael's, 1897-99, Gardenton, MB 316, 318

UKRAINIAN GREEK ORTHODOX
Shiskovichi, Willingdon, AB 24
St. Vladimir's (Ukrainian Greek Orthodox), 1934, Mundare, AB 321, 322

HUTTERITE
Pincher Creek Colony Church, 1945, Pincher Creek, AB 327

LUTHERAN
Frelsis, 1889, Grund, MB 310, 312, 313
St. John's (Evangelical Lutheran), 1876, Mahone Bay NS 38
St. Peter's Estonian, 1954-55, Toronto, ON 274, 276
see also
Little Dutch Church, 1756, Halifax NS 46, 48, 50

MENNONITE
Altona Meetinghouse, 1852-53, Markham, ON 199, 200
Old Colony Worship House, 1881, Steinbach, MB 312
Old Order Meetinghouse, 1917-18, St. Jacobs. ON 4

METHODIST
Black Church, 1849, Oro, ON 185, 222, 224
Bowerman's Church, 1855, Hallowell, ON 239
Hay Bay Meetinghouse, 1792, Napanee, ON 180, 184

Gower Street, 1894-96, St. John's NL 87
Grace United Church, 1852, Niagara-on-the-Lake, ON 210, 213, 214
Madill Church, 1872-73, Stephenson Township, ON 226, 227
McDougall Mission, 1862, Morley, AB 288, 300, 301
Mount Tabor, 1865-67, Milford, ON 239
Paris Plains United, 1845, Paris, ON 185, 210, 213
St. Andrew's, 1981-83, Toronto, ON 280, 283
Wesleyan Methodist Church, 1875, Toronto, ON 216
West Dumfries Chapel, 1845, Paris, ON 210, 213
White Chapel, 1809-11, Picton, ON 184, 193, 195
see also
Barrington Meetinghouse, 1765, Barrington NS 50, 51
Free Meeting House, 1821, Moncton NB 66, 67

METROPOLITAN COMMUNITY
Metropolitan Community Church, 1907, Toronto, ON 26, 396

MORAVIAN BRETHREN
Hebron, Church at, 1830s, Hebron NL 57, 58, 59
Nain, Church at, 1925, Nain NL 57, 60
Hopedale, Church at, 1865, Hopedale NL 57, 58, 60

MORMON
Church of Jesus Christ of the Latter Day Saints, Temple of, 1913-23, Cardston, AB 340, 342

NON-DENOMINATIONAL
Barrington Meetinghouse, 1765, Barrington NS 50, 51
Community church, 1861, near Grand Pré NS 33
Cross Roads, Church at, 1836, Cross Roads PE 96, 97
L'Arche Dayspring Chapel, 1999, Richmond Hill, ON 168, 172, 173, 174, 175
St. Catherine's Chapel, 1962-63, Toronto, ON 187
St. Peter's-on-the-Rock, 1912-15, Stoney Lake, ON 227, 228
Union Church, 1914-15, Sturgeon Point, ON 228, 229

PLYMOUTH BRETHREN
Port Sydney Bible Chapel (Plymouth Brethren), 2000, Port Sydney, ON 228

PRESBYTERIAN
Greenock Church, 1821-24, St. Andrews NB 36, 63, 64, 65, 67
Knox, 1845, Oro, ON 185, 222, 224
Knox Fellowship Centre Chapel, 1960-61,

Toronto, ON 278, 279
Knox, 1847-48, Toronto, ON 213, 214
St. Andrew's, 1875-76, Toronto, ON 283, 284
St. Andrew's, 1809-10, Québec City, QC 127, 128
St. Andrew's, 1812-13, Williamstown, ON 184, 195, 196
St. Andrew's, 1831, Niagara-on-the-Lake, ON 185, 206, 207, 208, 209
St. Andrew's, 1840-53, Thorah, ON 178, 185, 225
St. Andrew and St. Paul, Church of, 1931-32, Montréal, QC 23
St. John's, 1823-26, Belfast PE 94, 95, 96
St. Mark's, 1961-63, Don Mills, ON 279, 283
St. Paul's, 1854-57, Hamilton, ON 214, 215
St. Paul's, 1895, Winchester, ON 390
Trinity, 2002-03, Oro, ON 391, 393
see also
Barrington Meetinghouse, 1765, Barrington NS 50, 51
Carmel, 1886-87, Hensall, ON 216, 217
Covenanters', 1804-11, Grand Pré NS 33, 51, 52, 67
Dominion-Chalmers, 1912-14, Ottawa, ON 184, 261, 262
Free Meeting House, 1821, Moncton NB 66, 67
Grace, 1852, Niagara-on-the-Lake, ON 210, 214
Malpeque, 1869-70, Malpeque PE 97, 98
St. Andrew's, 1840-53, Thorah, ON 178
St. Andrew's, 1981-83, Toronto, ON 280, 283
Trinity, 1862, Mahone Bay NS 38

QUAKER (CHILDREN OF PEACE)
Sharon Temple, 1825-31, Sharon, ON 184, 185, 193, 196, 197, 198, 199
see also
Barrington Meetinghouse, 1765, Barrington NS 50, 51
Wellington Meetinghouse, 1885, Wellington, ON 238, 239

ROMAN CATHOLIC
Father Lacombe's Chapel, 1861, St. Albert, AB 300, 301
Father Pandosy's Mission, 1859-60, Kelowna, BC 290, 306
Grand Séminaire de Montréal, Chapelle du, 1904-07, Montréal, QC 154, 156, 157
Holy Cross, 1895-1906, Skatin, BC 291, 292
Holy Family, 2003-04, Medicine Hat, AB 364, 365, 390, 391, 393
Holy Name, 1915, Toronto, ON 256, 257
Immaculate Conception, 1971-72, M'Chigeeng First Nations, ON 221
Immaculate Conception of the Blessed Virgin Mary, Cathedral of, 1954-57, Calgary, AB 344, 345
Lady of the Lake Chapel, 1969, Silton, SK 354, 358

Martyrs Shrine, 1925-26, Midland, ON 189

Monseigneur Briand, La Chapelle de, 1784-86, Québec City, QC 127, 134

Most Holy Trinity, Church of the, 1833, Trinity NL 30, 78

Notre-Dame de Montréal, Basilique 1823-29, Montréal, QC 8, 96, 143, 144, 145, 146, 147, 148, 244

Notre-Dame d'Ottawa, Basilique-Cathédrale, 1841-85, Ottawa, ON 231, 235

Notre-Dame, Basilique-Cathédrale, 1647, Québec City, QC 114, 132, 133, 134, 135, 152

Notre-Dame-de-Bon-Secours, Chapelle, 1771-73, Montréal, QC 143, 144, 150

Notre-Dame-de-Fatima, 1962-63, Jonquière, QC 164, 166

Notre-Dame-de-Grâce, 1851-53, Montréal, QC 148, 152, 153

Notre-Dame-des-Victoires, 1723, Québec City, QC 124

Nuestra Senora de Guadalupe, Misión Católica Latinoaméricana , 1924, Montréal, QC 160, 161

Oratoire Saint-Joseph, 1924-67, Montréal, QC 160, 162, 189

Our Lady of Good Hope, 1865-85, Fort Good Hope, NT 337

Our Lady of Mount Carmel, 1867, Toronto, ON 256

Our Lady of the Assumption, 1842-46, Windsor, ON 209, 210

Our Lady of the Immaculate Conception, 1876-88, Guelph, ON 182, 233, 235, 254

Our Lady of Victory, 1958-60, Inuvik, NT 338

Port Royal Habitation, Chapel of 1605-07, near Annapolis Royal NS 31

Précieux-Sang, 1967-68, Saint Boniface, MB 352, 353, 354

Rideau Street Convent Chapel, 1887-88, Ottawa, ON 235, 236, 237

Sacré-Coeur, Chapelle du, 1888-91, Montréal, QC 148

Sacred Heart, 1898, Greenwood, BC 306, 308

Saint-Benoît-du-Lac, Abbaye de, 1994, near Austin, QC 168, 170, 171, 175

Saint-Ambroise, 1923-28, Montréal, QC 159, 160

Saint-Anne, Chapelle, mid-18th century, Neuville, QC 117

Sainte-Anne-de-Kent, 1890, Bouctouche, NB 17

Saint-Antoine-de-Padoue, 1883-84, Batoche, SK 314, 315

Saint-Boniface, Cathedrale de, 1839, 1906-07, 1970-72, St. Boniface, MB 296, 298, 354, 359, 360, 362

Saint-Charles-Borromée, 1828-30, Charlesbourg, QC 10, 106, 127, 128, 129

Sainte-Brigide de Kildare, 1885-86, Montréal, QC 154, 156

St. Dunstan's Basilica, 1914-19, Charlottetown, PE 7

Sainte-Famille, 1743-47, Île d'Orléans, QC 116, 117

Saint-Elzéar, 1849, Saint Elzéar, QC 140

Sainte-Marie among the Hurons, 1639-49, Midland, ON 178, 188

Saint-Famille, 1754-58, Cap Santé, QC 118, 119

Saint-François-d'Assise, 1857-60, Beauceville, QC 138, 139

Saint-François-de-Sales, 1734-36, Île d'Orléans, QC 114

Saint-François-de-Sales, 1761-73, Neuville, QC 104, 110, 117, 118, 119

Saint-Georges, 1900-02, Saint-George-de-Beauce, QC 1, 140, 141

Saint-Gérard-Majella, 1961-62, Saint-Jean-sur-Richelieu, QC 164, 167, 174

Saint-Isidore, 1853-60, Dorchester, QC 140

Saint-Jacques, 1823, Montréal, QC 144, 145

Saint-Jean, 1734, Île d'Orléans, QC 114, 115

Saint-Jean-Baptiste, 1881-84, Québec City, QC 128, 129, 130

Saint-Jean-Baptiste, Cathédrale, 1961-62, Nicolet, QC 109, 159, 174, 175

Saint-Joseph, 1835-38, Deschambault, QC 119

Saint-Joseph, 1865-68, Saint-Joseph-de-Beauce, QC 139, 140

Saint-Louis, Chapelle de (Louisbourg Fortress), 1717-58, Louisbourg NS 32

Saint-Marc, 1955-56, La Baie, QC 163, 165

Sainte-Marguerite-de-Blairfindie, 1800-01, L'Acadie, QC 138, 139

Saint-Mathias-sur-Richelieu, 1784-88, near Chambly, QC 137, 139

Saint-Pierre, 1715-19, Île d'Orléans, QC 110, 112, 113, 114, 115, 116

Saint-Pierre, 1892– 93, Chéticamp NS 40

Saint-Raphaël, 1959-60, Jonquière, QC 163, 164

Saint-Richard, 1962-63, Montréal, QC 161, 163

St. Andrew's Cathedral, 1890-92, Victoria, BC 294, 332, 333, 334

St. Ann's, 1903, Duncan, BC 304

St. Anne's, 1860s, Upper Similkameen, BC 306, 307

St. Anne's (Korean), 1957, Calgary, AB 345

St. Charles Mission, 1883-84, Dunvegan, AB 288, 336

St. Eugene's Mission, 1897, near Cranbrooke, BC 308

St. John the Baptist, 1847-48, Perth, ON 185, 232

St. John the Baptist, Basilica-Cathedral of, 1841-55, St. John's NL 80, 81, 82, 83, 87

St. Joseph's, 1893, Douro, ON 185, 235, 237

St. Malechy's, 1899, Kinkora, PE 99

St. Mary's Cathedral-Basilica, 1820-29, Halifax NS 36

St. Mary's, 1900-02, Indian River PE 98, 99, 100, 101

St. Mary's, 1965-68, Red Deer, AB 349, 352

St. Michael's and St. Anthony's, 1914-15, Montréal, QC 108, 159

St. Michael's Cathedral, 1845-48, Toronto, ON 243, 244, 245

St. Patrick's, 1836-44, Grand River PE 98

St. Patrick's, 1843-47, Montréal, QC 148, 150, 151, 152, 209

St. Patrick's, 1864-81, St. John's NL 86, 87

St. Patrick's, 1866-73, Ottawa, ON 234, 235

St. Paul's Basilica, 1887-89, Toronto, ON 252, 253, 254

St. Peter's, 1887, near Cranbrook, BC 24

St. Peter's, 1941, Kugaaruk, NU 338

St. Pius X, 1954, Toronto, ON 256, 257

Soeurs Grises, Maison mere des, Chapelle, 1874-78, Montréal, QC 153, 154

Ursulines, La Chapelle des, 1730, Québec City, QC 124, 126, 127, 134

Westminister Abbey, 1953-82, Mission, BC 168, 171, 172

see also

Free Meeting House (deconsecrated), 1821, Moncton NB 66, 67

Première Église Évangélique Arménienne, 1966-67, Montréal, QC 163

SALVATION ARMY

Scarborough Citadel, 1992-94, Toronto, ON 284, 285

SEVENTH-DAY ADVENTIST

see Free Meeting House, 1821, Moncton NB 66, 67

UNITARIAN

Unitarian Church, 1964, Vancouver, BC 347, 348, 349

Unity Church of Truth, Toronto, ON 278

UNITED

Avonmore, 1988-90, Edmonton, AB 295

Black Church, 1849, Oro, ON 185, 222, 224

Carmel, 1886-87, Hensall, ON 216, 217

Cedars, 1995-96, Waterloo, ON 27

Covenanters', 1804-11, Grand Pré NS 33, 51, 52, 67

Dominion-Chalmers, 1912-14, Ottawa, ON 184, 261, 262

Gower Street, 1894-96, St. John's NL 87

Grace, 1852, Niagara-on-the-Lake, ON 210, 214

Highlands, 1956-57, North Vancouver, BC 20

Madill, 1872-73, Stephenson Township, ON 226, 227

Malpeque, 1869-70, Malpeque PE 97, 98

Maugerville Meetinghouse, 1775, Sheffield, NB 68, 69

Omond Memorial, 1983, North Bay, ON 397

Paris Plains, 1845, Paris, ON 185, 210, 213

St. Andrew's, 1981-83, Toronto, ON 280, 283, 284

St. Paul's, 1893, Boissevain, MB 334, 335

Trinity United, 1862, Mahone Bay NS 38

West Ellesmere, 1957, Toronto, ON 277

White Chapel, 1809-11, Picton, ON 193, 195

see also

Bowerman's Church, 1855, Hallowell, ON 239

Mount Tabor, 1865-67, Milford, ON 239

GENERAL INDEX

Acadians, 32, 33, 40, 51, 99, 117
Ackerman, Robert, 256
acoustics, 101, 123, 146, 253, 261, 390
*An Act for the Building of Additional Churches
  in Populous Parishes* (1818), 68
Adam style, 67
Aesthetic Movement, 98
Affleck, Desbarats, Dimakopoulos,
  Lebensold, Sise, 167
Akron plan, 26, 251, 334, 389, 390–92, 396
Alan of Walsingham, 382
Alberta, 292, 293, 300–301, 315, 344–45,
349–52
    Eastern-rite churches in, 321–22
    Hutterites in, 327
    megachurches in, 363–65, 390, 391, 393
    Mormons in, 340–41
Alberti, Leon Battista, 121–22
Alexander II (of Russia), 312
All Hallows School (Yale, BC), 306
Alline, Henry, 54
altars, 104, 113, 114, 124, 143, 154
Amish, 310
Anderson, John, 196
André, Brother (Alfred Bessette), 160–61
Andrew, Father (Holy Trinity Monastery), 266
Anglicans, 187, 344, 387. *See also* Church of
  England
    in Atlantic Canada, 35, 67, 80
    in North and West, 293, 336, 338, 344
    in Ontario, 185, 200, 241, 251
    in Québec, 108, 121–23, 139
Anthemius of Tralles, 380, 381
L'Arche, 172–73
Architectural Magazine, 82
architecture, 210, 217
    design elements in, 23–24
    practice of, 393
Arnold, Benedict, 137
Arnoldi, King, 234, 235
Art Deco, 160, 344
Arts and Crafts style, 214, 217
artwork (church), 24
    First Nations, 333, 334, 338
    by Group of Seven, 259, 260, 272–73
    painting, 189, 266
    sculpture, 75–76, 83
Atlantic Canada, 31–32, 35–36. *See also*
    specific provinces
Augustines de la miséricorde de Jésus, 104
Baccerini, 145

Bach, Michael, 274
Baillairgé, Charles, 128, 129, 134
Baillairgé, François, 112
    church buildings by, 106, 116, 119
    interiors by, 104, 118, 133, 134
    school of, 104, 110, 112, 118
Baillairgé, Jean, 117, 133, 134
Baillairgé, Pierre-Florent, 129
Baillairgé, Thomas, 10, 112, 129, 134, 140
    influence, 127–28
Baillif, Claude, 133
balconies, 48
baldachins, 104, 110, 117–19, 134, 387
Baldwin, Robert, 186, 199
Bank of Montreal (Montréal), 157
Baptist Convention of Ontario and Québec,
  187
Baptists, 187, 251, 349.
    in Atlantic Canada, 35–36, 54, 67, 97
barns, 91, 92
Baroque period, 385, 387–89
Baroque Revival
    Gibbsian, 36, 243, 256
    in Québec, 113–14, 127–29, 134, 139–40,
        148, 152, 160
Basilian Fathers, 366
basilicas, 372–75. *See also* cathedrals
    in Atlantic Canada, 74, 81–83
    Baroque, 387, 389
    early Christian, 378–79
    medieval, 381–82
    minor, 148–50, 209, 254
    in Ontario, 209, 231, 248, 252–54, 256
    in Québec, 132–35, 148–50
Bates, Maxwell, 344–45
Batoche, Battle of (1885), 314, 315
Bawlf, Cooper & Associates, 333
Bayard, Major, 54
Beaugrand-Champagne, Aristide, 108, 159
beauty, 80–81
Beauvais, René, 137
Beer family (Exeter), 76
Bell, Joseph, 68
Bell, Leland, 221, 399
Bell, M.C. Farrar, 193
Bellot, Paul, 109, 159, 161, 162, 168, 170
bell towers, 321, 328–29, 391
Benedictines, 168
Benjamin, Asher, 64, 208
Beresford, A.J.B., 72
Berlinguet, François-Xavier, 139

Berlinguet, Louis-Thomas, 115
Bernard of Clairvaux, Saint, 362
Bernini, Gianlorenzo, 387, 388
Bessette, Alfred (Brother André), 160–61
Beth Jacob Synagogue (Toronto), 264
Bethune, John, 195
Bishop, Elizabeth, 94
Blackfoot, 300
blacks, 32, 182, 222–25, 243
Blomfield, Arthur, 254
Bodega y Quadra, Juan Francisco, 288
Boivin, Charles, 178, 188
Bonnycastle, Richard, 241
Borduas, Paul-Émile, 109, 159
Boreskie, Michael, 364, 390
Bostra (Bosra) Cathedral (Syria) 379
Boughton, Levi, 210, 213
Bouillon, Georges, 231, 235–36, 237
Boullée, Étienne, 364
Bourgeau, Victor, 143, 145, 148, 153, 154
Bourgeoys, Saint Marguerite, 143
Bourget, Ignace, 153, 154
Bouriché, Henri, 143, 148
Bourne, Adolphus, 107
Bowen, R.J., 337
Bowerman, Mrs. Thomas, 239
Bramante, Donato, 381, 387
Brant, Joseph (Thayendanegea), 35, 193
Brant, Molly, 200
Brébeuf, Saint Jean de, 180, 188
Bredin, Hautry, 239
Breen, Russell, 151
Briand, Jean-Olivier, 127
brick, 216
    bichromatic, 253, 391, 396
    construction, 87, 387
    mud (cob), 222, 370–71
    polychrome, 82, 168, 216, 243, 262, 264
    ancient, 372, 375
    Gothic, 381, 385
    in Ontario, 184, 186–87, 199–200, 204–17,
        238–47, 251, 253–55, 257–68, 274,
        277–79, 285, 390–92
    in Québec, 108, 170–173
    in West, 293, 295, 332–35, 343–45, 348–54,
        363, 365–66, 390–91
British. *See* English
British Columbia, 291, 303–8, 327, 330–34,
342–44, 347–49. *See also* Vancouver Island
British North America Act (1867), 108
Brown, Benjamin, 266

Brown, Bernard, 363, 364
Brown, Brisley and Brown, 175
Brown, Carolyn Whitney, 173
Brûlé, Étienne, 178
Brunelleschi, Filippo, 387
Bryson, John, 127, 128
Builder, 86
Bukovina, 316
Burdett-Coutts, Angela, 303
Burke, Edmund (British statesman), 80–81, 148
Burke, Edmund (Canadian architect), 216, 217, 251
Burke and Horwood, 259
Burpee, William, 69
Burton, Harold W., 340
Butterfield, William, 38, 71, 73, 76, 89, 91, 216
Byzantine Revival, 381, 390
    in Ontario, 184, 259–72
    in Québec, 108, 126, 160
    in West, 315, 366
Byzantium, 376

Cabot, John, 31
Cadillac, Antoine Laumet, 208
Calatrava, Santiago de, 243
Calvinists, 51
Cambridge Camden Society, 71
Canadian Pacific Railway (CPR), 308
Cape Breton Island (NS), 31, 32–33
Cardinal, Douglas, 294, 349–54, 393
Carew, John Edward, 83
Carmichael, Franklin, 272
Carpenter, R.C., 38
Cartier, Jacques, 31, 104
Cassidy, Jim and John, 227
Cassilis, John, 63
cathedrals
    Anglican, 108, 121–23, 200–203, 210
    in Atlantic Canada, 71–76, 81–85
    Baroque, 387, 388
    early Christian, 375, 377, 379
    medieval, 382, 383–84
    in North, 337, 338
    in Ontario, 200–203, 210, 231, 243–44
    in Québec, 108, 121–23, 132–35
    Roman Catholic, 231, 243–44, 344–45, 354, 359–62
    in West, 295, 296, 330–34, 344–45, 354, 359–62
Catherine the Great (of Russia), 312
ceilings, 100–101, 123
Chalmers, Thomas, 213
Champlain, Samuel de, 31, 104, 137, 178, 188
chapels, 132, 354, 385
    in Atlantic Canada, 32, 98, 99
    of ease, 74, 78, 249–51
    funerary, 247, 249–51
    in Ontario, 187, 193, 228, 235–36, 278–79
    processional, 105, 117
    in Québec, 127, 132, 143, 148, 172–73
    in West, 354, 358

Charbonnel, Armand-François-Marie de, 245
Charland, Jean-Paul, 159, 175
Charlemagne, 382
Charles II (of England), 388
Chauchetière, Claude, 105
Chaudière River, 139–40
Chaussegros de Léry, Gaspard, 133
Children of Peace, 185, 196–99
Christian and Missionary Alliance, 365
Christianity, 76, 370, 397
    Eastern-rite, 315–23, 328–29, 381
Christian Scientists, 342
Christopherson, Sigurdur, 312
Chrysostomos, Brother (Mount Athos Monastery), 266
churches, 23. *See also* chapels; megachurches
    air rights sales by, 283, 284
    attendance at, 187, 277
    Byzantine, 376–81
    and change, 24–26, 36, 187, 277, 280–85, 396
    closings of, 238–39, 393
    for cottagers, 227–28
    Eastern-rite, 321–22, 362
    evangelical, 393, 396
    hall, 244
    houses as, 370–72
    medieval, 381
    mission, 288, 337–38
    modifications to, 387
    monastery, 170
    new roles, 238–39, 280–85, 393
    in New World, 389–91
    origins, 370–76
    pilgrimage, 382
    Romanesque, 381–82
    seating in, 39, 46, 91, 140, 152, 298
    shared, 280, 283
    suburban, 365, 393, 396–97
    synagogues as, 264–66
    worship in, 24, 59–60, 76
Church Missionary Society, 298, 336
Church of England, 36, 54, 76, 389. *See also* Anglicans
Church of Scotland, 36, 63, 195, 213. *See also* Presbyterians
Church of the Holy Nativity (Bethlehem) 375, 380
Church of the Holy Sepulchre (England) 382
Church of the Holy Sepulchre (Jerusalem) 382
church plans, 106
    Akron-type, 26, 251, 334, 389, 390–92, 396
    amphitheatral, 251–52, 334, 393
    Greek-cross, 200, 259, 263, 268, 315, 363
    Jesuit (Latin-cross), 106, 112, 116, 119, 138, 161, 165, 172, 332, 382
    Maillou, 106, 138, 389
    Récollet, 106, 114–15, 117, 118
    Scottish (T-shaped), 127, 128
church union, 292. *See also* United Church of Canada

Classicism, 80, 370, 381, 385, 387. *See also* Neoclassical style
    in Nova Scotia, 46–48
    in Ontario, 185, 200, 254
    in West, 342, 343, 362
Clayton & Bell, 91
Clinch, John, 30
cob (mud brick), 222, 370–71
Cochrane, Thomas, 78
Cockran, William, 298
colour schemes, 148, 170, 232, 253, 254, 334
Commercial Bank of the Midland District (Toronto), 243
Commissioner's Gothic, 68
communal buildings, 57–59. *See also* Doukhobors; Hutterites
Concordia University (Montréal), 154
concrete construction, 161–65, 352, 364
    with brick, 160–61, 167–68, 259–61, 343
    early Christian, 380–81
    in Ontario, 285
    in Québec, 108–9, 159–68, 172
    in West, 320–21, 328, 343–44, 352, 354, 363–64
    with wood, 353–55, 358
Confederation, 35, 108
Conger, Stephen, 195
Congregationalists, 50, 51, 68–69. *See also* United Church of Canada
Connolly, Joseph, 182, 233, 235, 252, 254
Constantine the Great, 372, 375, 376–80
convents, 172, 235
Cook, James, 288
Coome, Hannah Grier, 172
Cooper, James, 207
Corbusier. *See* Le Corbusier (Charles Édouard Jeanneret)
Cormier, Ernest, 109, 159–60, 161, 163
Cornwallis, Edward, 42, 44
Côté, Claude, 168, 170, 175
Côté, Paul-Marie, 163, 164, 165–66
Cottingham, Lewis Nockalls, 245
Counter-Reformation, 385, 387, 389
Covenanters. *See* Scottish Free Church
Coventry Cathedral (UK), 354
Cram, Goodhue and Ferguson, 217, 219
Cram, Ralph Adams, 219
Crandall, Joseph, 67
Cree, 300
crockets, 68
Cromwell, Oliver, 385
Crowfoot, 301
Crusaders, 381, 382
Cumberland, Frederic, 214, 245–49
Cumberland and Ridout, 247
Cumberland and Storm, 247, 249
Cunningham, John, 68

Daly, César, 89
Daprato Studios, 129
Darby, John Nelson, 228

Darling, Charles, 254
Darling, Frank, 254
Darling, Frank, Jr., 254–55
Daudelin, Charles, 148
David, Louis-Basile, 116, 117
Davidson, John, 209
Deconstructionism, 187
Delaere, Achille, 315
Demers, Modeste, 304
De Morin & Le Borgne, 152
Desgagné, Léonce, 164, 166
Des Groseilliers, Médard Chouart, 178–80
Designs for Village, Town and City Churches,
    334
Desnoyers, Mercure & Associés, 153
Dion, Louis and Francis, 139
Doan, Ebenezer and John, 193, 197
Dobrolige, Vadym, 321, 322
domes, 162. *See also* Byzantine Revival;
    churches, Eastern-rite
Douglas, James, 291
Doukhobors (Union of Spiritual
    Communities of Christ), 292, 324–27
Downing, A.J., 69
Dowsing, Will, 387
Duban, F.J., 148
Dubois, M., 148
Duhamel, Joseph-Thomas, 231
Dumont, Gabriel, 292, 315
Durham Cathedral (England) 382
Dunham, George Foote, 343
Duomo (Sena Cathedral, Italy) 385
Dura Europos, 370, 371
Durand, George F., 216, 217
Dutch, 104–6, 107

Early English style, 74, 84
Ecclesiological Society, 19, 37, 76, 91
Ecclesiologist, The, 19, 71, 80, 83, 84, 91
ecclesiology, 36–39, 71, 74–76, 89, 182, 185
eclecticism, 19–20, 129
École des arts et métiers (Québec), 132–33
École des beaux-arts (Paris), 154, 157, 359
Edgell, G.H., 219
education, 186, 256
Edward, Duke of Kent, 46
Edward VI (of England), 385
Elizabeth I (of England), 385
Elken, Ants, 274, 276
Elliott, Charles, 333, 334
Elliott, Robert, 209, 210
Ely Cathedral (England) 382
Ely, Reginald, 385
Émond, Pierre, 113, 114, 127
English, 68
    architectural influence, 106, 108, 127, 235,
        237
    and Atlantic Canada, 31, 32, 33
    in Ontario, 181, 185
    vs. French, 107–8, 134
Enoch Turner Schoolhouse (Toronto), 243

Erickson, Arthur, 330
Estonians, 274–76
Europeans, 104–6, 288. *See also specific*
    nationalities
Evangelical Fellowship of Canada, 187
Excelsior Glass Company, 175
Exeter Diocesan Architectural Society, 71
expressionism, 20

fan vaults, 237
Feaster, William, 200
Federal style, 208
Fedorov, Vladislav, 266
Feild, Edward, 78, 84
Fennell, Roger, 228
Ferguson, Frank, 219
Feschuk, Ivan, 294
Filion, John M., 188, 189
Finley, Gregg, 69
Finsterer, Jean-Georges, 138, 139
Finsterer, Louis-Daniel, 139
First Nations, 30. *See also specific peoples*
    art by, 333, 334, 338
    in Atlantic Canada, 33, 35
    in British Columbia, 304, 306, 307
    Europeans and, 104–6
    influence on church design, 220–21, 294,
        304, 352
    in North and West, 288, 291, 315, 337
    in Ontario, 180, 182
Flavelle, Clara Ellsworth and Joseph, 228
Fleming, Michael Anthony, 81, 82, 83
Fort Good Hope (NT), 293
Fraser, Simon, 288
Free Church of Scotland, 51, 213
French. *See also* New France
    in Atlantic Canada, 31–32
    in Ontario, 182, 195, 208–9
    vs. English, 107–8, 134
Frérot, François, 210
frescoes, 266, 373
Frost, Shepherd Johnson, 66, 67
Fuller, Thomas, 396
Fuller and Laver, 235
fur trade, 290, 293, 300

Gaboury, Étienne J., 294, 352–54, 360–62, 393
Gagnon, Yves, 114
Galicia, 316
Gallarus Oratory (Ireland) 379, 380
Galt, John, 235
Gareau, Ludger, 314, 315
Gåthe, Asbjørn, 171, 172
George II (of England), 56–57
George III (of England), 123, 128
Georgian style, 36, 204, 209, 210, 298. *See also*
    Neo-Georgian style
    in Atlantic Canada, 51, 78, 96, 97
Germans, 46, 48
Gerson, Wolfgang, 347, 348
Giacomo della Porta, 387

Gibbs, James, 36, 42, 46, 67, 108, 134, 388, 389
    Book of Architecture, 36, 44, 46, 63, 67, 121,
        388–89
    St. Martin-in-the-Fields, 46, 63, 67, 121–23,
        128, 389
    St. Mary-le-Strand, 256, 389
Giguère, Georges-Émile, 151
Gillis, D.J., 99
Gilmore, George, 51
Giroux, Raphaël, 399
glulam construction, 274, 277, 295, 353–55
gold rushes, 291, 304, 306
Gomez, Esteban, 31
Gooderham, William and Harriet, 243
Gooderham & Worts, 243
Goodhue, Bertram Grosvenor, 219
Gothic period, 382, 383–85
Gothic Revival, 19–20, 39, 97, 210. *See also*
Gothic Revival styles
    in Atlantic Canada, 34, 36–40, 67–68, 69,
        71–74, 96
    in Newfoundland and Labrador, 33, 78–80
    in Ontario, 185, 193, 199, 204–6, 209–10,
        227, 231–32, 235, 238–55, 283
    in Québec, 108, 130, 143–45, 148, 150
    in West, 298, 310, 313, 330–35, 344–45
Gothic Revival styles
    Canadian, 209
    Carpenter, 39, 48, 97–98, 221
    Decorated, 84–85, 214, 243–47
    French, 100
    Georgian, 204
    Irish, 87
    Modern (Collegiate), 76, 86, 219
    Perpendicular, 67–68, 75, 242
    Rational, 89–93, 182
    Stripped, 94
    Victorian, 78, 212
Gray, John Morgan, 94
Gray, John Wilson, 278
Greek Revival, 206–7
Greenberg, Robert, 266–68, 271
Green Blankstein Russell, 363, 364
Grey Nuns. *See* Sisters of Charity
Grondin, Jean G., 114
Grouard, Émile, 288, 336–37
Group of Seven, 259, 260, 272–73
Gua, Pierre du, 31
Guiet, Jean, 178, 188
Guillot, Jean-Baptiste, 140
Gundry & Langley, 182, 396

Hadfield, Matthew E., 76
Haghia Sophia (Istanbul) 380, 381
Hall, William, 121, 122
Hallgrimsson, Byring, 310, 312, 313
Handy, Ted, 392
Hanganu, Dan S., 168–72
Harris, Robert, 98
Harris, William Critchlow, 38, 39, 40, 98,
    99–101

Haufschild, Lutz, 171–72
Hay, William, 85
Hayward, John, 71
Hébert, Louis-Philippe, 148
Hébert, Philippe, 231
Heck, Barbara, 180
Helena, Saint, 372
Hennepin, Louis, 180
Henri, Pierre, 338, 339
Henry VI (of England), 385
Henry VII (of England), 385
Henry VIII (of England), 385
Hiscocks, Henry, 255
historicism, 19–20, 36
Hodgson, George, 98
Hogan, John, 83
Holmes, Arthur W., 252, 256, 257
Holy Blossom Synagogue (Toronto), 264
Hoole, Elijah, 87
Hope, Thomas, 82
Hopkins, John William, 238
Horn, David, 280
housebarns, 312
house-churches, 370–72
Houston, James, 338
Howard, John, 243, 249
Howland, Ford, 259
Hudson, Henry, 178
Hudson's Bay Company (HBC), 290, 291, 296,
    298, 339, 359
Hughes, William, 47
humanism, 385, 387
Hunt, Robert, 336
Hurons, 180–81, 188, 208–9
Hus, Jan, 57
Husson, Auguste, 288, 336
Hutchison, Alexander C., 184, 261–62
Hutter, Jakob, 327
Hutterites, 292, 327

Icelanders, 292, 310, 312–13
icons, 316, 381
Île Royale. See Cape Breton Island (NS)
Île Saint-Jean. See Prince Edward Island
immigrants, 222, 389
    in Ontario, 185, 186, 222, 237, 266, 274
    in Québec, 108, 109
Inglis, Charles, 54
Ingrand, Max, 159, 174
International Style, 20, 159, 186, 364
Inuit, 57, 59, 338, 339
Irish
    in Atlantic Canada, 33, 36, 51, 81, 86
    in Ontario, 185, 235, 237, 244
    in Québec, 108, 150, 154
Iroquois, 106, 132, 180–82, 188
Isidorus of Miletus, 380, 381
Islam, 375
Italianate style, 210, 213, 214, 222

Jackson, John, 33–35
Jameson, Anna, 243
Japanese-Canadians, 308
Jesuits (Society of Jesus), 104, 387
    church plans, 106, 112, 116, 119
    in Ontario, 180–81, 188, 208
Jews, 372. See also Judaism; synagogues
Jodoin, Lamarre, Pratt & Associates, 148
John Paul II (Pope), 150
Johnson, Lloyd, 67
Johnson, Pauline, 193
Johnson, William, 200
Jolliet, Louis, 178–80
Jones, Benjamin, 254
Jones, Jacobine, 172, 173
Jones, Robert, 94, 97
Jonsson, Kristjan, 312
Judaism, 370, 375. See also Jews; synagogues
Justinian I (of Byzantium), 375, 379, 380–81

Kahn, Albert, 219
Kalm, Peter, 133–34
Kalmykova, Luker'ia, 326
Karapoulos workshop, 266
Kay, John, 196
Keenleyside, Hugh, 293
Kekot, Wasyl, 316
Kempe, C.E., 85
Kimpton, Rufus, 308
King's College Chapel (England) 385
Kough, Patrick, 78, 80
Kruth, Ferdinand, 57, 59

Labrador. See Newfoundland and Labrador
Lacombe, Albert, 300, 301
LaFontaine, Louis-Hippolyte, 186, 199
Lagimodière, Marie-Anne, 290
Lalement, Gabriel, 188
Lane, Henry Bowyer, 242, 243
Langley, Henry, 244, 248, 251, 254
Langley and Burke, 216, 217, 248, 251, 253
Langley and Howland, 259
L'Anse aux Meadows (NF), 30
Lapierre, Louis-J., 163
L'Arche, 172–73
La Richardie, Armand de, 208
Larocque, Maurice, 338
La Salle, René-Robert Cavelier de, 178
Lassus, J.B., 148
Lau, Kim, 363
Laud, William, 385
Laurent, Father (Toronto priest), 256
Laval, François de, 106–7, 110, 127, 132
Laver, Augustus, 234, 235
La Vérendrye family, 180
Le Corbusier (Charles Édouard Jeanneret),
    159, 164, 352, 354
Ledoux, Claude-Nicolas, 364
Leprohon, Alcibiade, 153, 154
Levasseur, Pierre-Noël, 124–27, 129
Levasseur family, 118, 119, 124

Levitsky, Myron, 266, 268
Lipinski, Peter, 321, 322
Lobko, Joe, 173, 174
log construction
    in Ontario, 222, 224, 226, 227
    in West, 288–90, 292–93, 306, 316, 321, 328,
        336–37
Loring, Frances, 272, 273
Louisbourg (NS), 31–32, 42, 46
Lount, Samuel, 185
Lowell, Robert, 86
Lowery, Edward, and Son, 334–35
Loyalists. See also United Empire Loyalists
    in Atlantic Canada, 32–33, 36, 52
    in New Brunswick, 63, 68–69
    in Ontario, 181–84, 193, 195, 200
    in Québec, 139
Loyola, Ignatius, 387
Lussier, Denis L., 354
Lutherans, 312–13
lych-gates, 219

Macaulay, Angus, 94–96
Macaulay, William, 238
MacDonald, J.E.H., 272, 273
Macdonald, John A., 235
Macdonell, Miles, 359
Macdonnell, Alexander, 235
Mackenzie, Alexander, 195, 288
Mackenzie, A.W. and M.A., 227
MacLean, Alexander, 67
MacLennan, John, 96
Maderno, Carlo, 388
Madill, John, 226
Maillou, Jean-Baptiste, 389
Majella, Saint Gérard, 164
Mallandain, Edward, 303, 304
Malouin, Gérard, 109, 159, 175
Manitoba, 291–92, 296–300, 310–13, 315,
    334–35, 352–64
    Eastern-rite churches in, 316–21, 328, 362
Manitoulin Island (ON), 220–21
Marchand, Jean-Omer, 152, 153, 154, 156, 157,
    359–61
Margaret (of Scotland), 139
Marie de l'Incarnation, Saint, 104, 124, 127,
    134
Martin, Arthur, 272
Martin, Félix, 150, 151
Mary I (of England), 385
Matthews, William, 53, 54
Mauger, Joshua, 68
May, Fred, 221
Mayer and Company, Munich, 2, 235, 245
McCarthy, James Joseph, 86–87, 254
McCauley, David, 391
McDonagh, John, 232
McDougall, George, 288, 300, 301
McDougall, John, 301
McGill family (Toronto), 244
McKim, Mead & White, 157

McMaster, Susan Moulton and William, 251
McMaster University, 187
McMillan Long, 366
McRae, Duncan, 298
medieval style, 36, 78, 212, 233, 235, 237. *See
also* Gothic Revival
Medley, Edward Shuttleworth, 38, 39, 89–93
Medley, John, 34, 36–39, 71–74, 76, 89, 91
meetinghouses, 46, 312
    in Atlantic Canada, 48–50, 51, 66, 68–69
    in Ontario, 196, 199, 222, 238–39
meetinghouse style
    in Atlantic Canada, 44, 48, 54, 67
    in Ontario, 193–95, 206, 208, 224–25, 279
megachurches, 187, 390–93, 397
Meloche, François-Xavier-Édouard, 144
memorials, 375
Mennonites, 199, 292, 310, 312
Mesnard, Albert, 144, 148, 153, 332, 333
Metcezev, Alex, 266
Methodists. *See also* United Church of Canada
    in Atlantic Canada, 35, 67
    in Ontario, 185, 241–43, 251
    in West, 290, 301, 334
Métis, 291–92, 298, 299, 313–15
Michelangelo, 387
Mi'kmaq, 97, 98
Milan Cathedral (Italy) 383
Mirvish, David and Ed, 284
missionaries, 33–35, 67, 106. *See also specific
    orders;* churches, mission
    Anglican, 200, 290, 303
    early Christian, 380
    Methodist, 300, 301
    Moravian, 56–60
    in North, 293
    in Ontario, 180, 186, 188, 200, 208, 220
    in Québec, 104
    Roman Catholic, 51, 104, 290, 304
    in West, 288, 290, 292, 298, 300–301, 303–4,
        359
Mitson, David, 193
Modernism, 20, 340–66. *See also* International
    Style
    beginnings, 340–45
    in Ontario, 186, 187, 266, 274–79, 391, 392
    in Québec, 109, 159–68
    in West, 294, 340–66
Mohawks, 35, 193, 200
Moiseiwitsch, Tanya, 187
monasteries, 168–75, 370, 375–76, 378, 379–80
Montcalm, Marquis de, 108
Montgomery & Sisam, 173, 175
Moore, William, 195
Moravian (United) Brethren, 56–57, 59, 310
Morden, James, 54
Morin, Pierre-Louis, 150
Mormons (Church of Jesus Christ of Latter
    Day Saints), 292, 340–41
Morrison, John, 178, 225
Morrison, William, 293

Mosteller, Sue, 172
Mountain, Jacob, 121, 238
Mudry, Arthur, 347
Murdoch, James, 51
music, 59–60, 208

Napier, William H.E., 296
native peoples. *See specific peoples;* First
    Nations
Neale, John Mason, 74–75
Neoclassical style, 34
    in Ontario, 199–200, 206, 225, 231
    in Québec, 113–114, 119, 127–28, 134, 140,
        160
Neo-Georgian style, 195, 199, 200
New Brunswick, 31, 32, 34, 35, 63–76
    wood construction in, 34, 37, 65, 89–93
New England (US), 42, 54, 65, 106
    architectural influence, 36, 39–40, 44–46,
        50, 51
    settlers from, 50, 51, 68
Newfoundland and Labrador, 30–31, 33–35,
    56–60, 78–87
    Irish in, 33, 81, 86
New France, 104–7, 124, 137, 178–81, 387
Niagara region (ON), 206–8, 210, 213–14,
    262–63
Nicaea, councils of, 376, 381
Nicholson, Peter, 207–8
Nickerson, Joshua, 50
Niemeyer, Oscar, 159
Nitchuk, Alex, 363, 364
Noble, Seth, 68
Norse, 30–31
North, 293, 336–39
Northgrave, Paul, 283
North West Company, 195, 288, 290, 293, 336,
    337, 359
North-West Rebellion (1885), 292, 301, 314,
    315
Northwest Territories, 293, 337–38
Nouwen, Henri, 172
Nova Scotia, 31, 32, 35, 42, 46, 52
    wood construction in, 31, 42–54
Nowakowski, F., 318
Nunavut, 293, 338–39

Oblates of Mary Immaculate, 231
    churches of, 308, 314, 315
    in North, 337–38, 339
    in West, 288, 290– 291, 300, 306– 307, 315,
        336
O'Brien, E.G., 222
O'Connell, Daniel, 81
Odelin and Mallioux, 138
O'Donel, James Louis, 81
O'Donnell, James, 8, 143, 144, 145, 148
Olekshy, Eugene, 365, 366
Olga, Saint, 322
O'Mahony, Timothy, 254
Ontario, 178–81, 185, 187, 238, 390. *See also*

specific cities and regions
    architectural influences in, 195, 235, 237
    megachurches in, 392, 393
    Modernism in, 186, 187, 266, 274–79, 391,
        392
    Niagara region, 206–8, 213–14, 262–63
    southwestern, 204–6, 208–10
Ontario Association of Architects, 217
Orléans, Île d', 110–17
O'Shea, J.P., 152
Ostell, John, 151–52
Osterrath, José, 175
Ouellet, David, 40, 117, 124, 126, 127, 141

Pachomaioi, 266
paintings, 189, 266. *See also specific artists*
Palladio, Andrea, 46–48
    Palladian style, 83, 121–22, 252, 387
Pandosy, Charles, 290, 306
Pantheon (Rome), 387
Paquet, André, 112–14, 119, 128
Parent, Léandre, 140
Parent, Lucien, 161, 162
Paris, Treaty of
    1763, 31, 108, 181
    1783, 181–82
Pariseau, Philippe, 231
Parkin, Edmund T., 186
Parkin, John B., 186, 278, 279
Parkin, John C., 274
Partridge, David, 228
Patry, Michel, 140
Paul, Tim, 334
Peachy, Joseph-Ferdinand, 127, 128–30, 139
Pentecostals, 187
Perrault, Claude, 128
Perrault, Henri-Maurice, 144, 148, 153, 261,
    332, 333
Petitot, Émile, 337–38
pews/benches, 39, 46, 91, 140, 152, 298
Picturesque style, 182, 212, 253, 332–34
pièce-sur-pièce construction, 105, 299–300, 314,
    315
Piranesi, Giambattista 387
Pius VI (Pope), 81
Plessis, Joseph-Octave, 144, 359
Plymouth Brethren, 228
Poitier, Pierre, 208
Poitras, Pierre, 196
Poitras & Martin, 156
polychromy, 82, 148
    in brick, 82, 168, 216, 243, 253, 262, 264
    in Ontario, 243, 262, 264
Pope, Hyrum C., 340
Post-Modernism, 187
Power, Joseph, 200, 203
Power, Michael, 243, 244
Pre-Raphaelite Movement, 91
Presbyterians. *See also* Church of Scotland;
    United Church of Canada
    in Atlantic Canada, 35, 51, 67

in Ontario, 185, 241, 251
in Québec, 108, 127
in West, 290
Prince, Thomas, 42
Prince Edward Island, 31, 32, 35, 94–101
processions, 134. *See also* chapels,
    processional
Protestants, 251, 390. *See also specific*
    denominations; Reformation
Provencher, Joseph-Norbert, 359
Pugin, A.W., 84, 86, 100–101, 150, 152
    writings, 76, 87, 100
pulpits, 8, 10, 124, 139, 209
    double-decker, 34, 64, 67, 195
    triple-decker, 52
Purcell, James, 83, 84

Qalaat Samaan (Syria) 378
Quakers, 50, 196, 238–39, 324
Qumran 370
Québec, 109, 137, 185. *See also specific cities*
    and regions; New France
    architectural influence of, 299–300, 304
    architectural influences in, 106, 108, 127
    Chemin du Roy, 117–19
    English in, 107–8
    French régime in, 104–7, 110–19
    Irish in, 108, 150, 154
    regional styles, 124–34
Quévillon, Louis-Amable, 118, 137, 139, 140,
    144
Quiblier, Joseph, 150
Quintal and Morin, 154, 156

Radisson, Pierre-Esprit, 178–80
Rae, William, 255, 259, 272
Raikes, Robert, 389
Rams, Hans, 173, 174, 175
Rationalism, 89
Rebellion Losses Bill (1849), 186
Rebellion of 1837, 108, 185, 199
Récollets, 104, 180
    church plans, 106, 114–15, 117, 118
Red River Colony, 290, 291, 293, 296
Red River construction. *See pièce-sur-pièce*
    construction
Red River Rebellion (1869–70), 291–92, 313
Reformation, 385, 387, 389. *See also*
    Protestants
Reform Movement, 185–86, 199
Reichel, L.T., 59, 60
religion, 23, 51, 186, 256
    changes in, 187, 277, 280–85
    freedom of, 51, 54, 81, 108, 312
    in Québec, 108, 109
Renaissance, 385, 387
Renaissance style, 129, 130
retables, 113, 114, 124–27, 148
La revue canadienne, 145–50
Reynard, James M., 291, 306
Richards, Jackson John, 143–44

Richardson, Henry Hobson, 253–54
Richardsonian Romanesque, 261
Richelieu River (QC), 137
Ridout, Thomas, Jr., 247
Ridout, Thomas Gibbs, 247. *See also*
    Cumberland and Ridout
Riel, Louis, 291–92. *See also* North-West
    Rebellion; Red River Rebellion
Rigali, Michele, 129
Robe, William, 121–23
Robertson, John Ross, 251
Robillard, Antoine, 231
Robillard, Maurice, 161, 163
Robinson, Peter, 237
Rochileaux, François-Xavier, 196
Rochon, Flavien, 231
Rochon, Jean, 175
Rococo style, 134
Rogers, Thomas, 200, 203
Rollin, Paul, 137
Roman Catholics, 231–37. *See also* Counter-
    Reformation
    in Atlantic Canada, 35, 36, 67, 81, 99
    Irish, 108, 185
    in North, 293, 336
    in Ontario, 185, 243
    in Québec, 108, 109, 139
Romanesque Revival, 261, 360
    in Atlantic Canada, 81–83, 87
    in Ontario, 210, 213, 222, 251, 254, 259–61,
        263–64, 272, 283–84
    in Québec, 150, 153, 154
Romanticism, 80–81
Rousselot, Benjamin-Victor, 143, 148
Ruggles, Captain, 54
Ruh, Philip, 262, 263, 318–21
Rundbogenstil, 82
Ruskin, John, 150, 210–13, 214, 243

Saarinen, Eliel, 345
Saguenay region (QC), 162–63
Sahuri, Hutchinson, Brzezinski, 364, 390
St. John's Rehabilitation Hospital (Montréal),
    172
St. Martin-in-the-Fields (London, UK), 46, 63,
    67, 121–22, 128
St. Mary's, Snettisham (UK), 71–72, 74, 75
St. Matthew's (Duddeston, UK), 210
Saint-Charles, Joseph, 157
Sainte-Chapelle (Paris), 148
Sainte-Trinité (Paris), 129, 130
Saint-Gelais, Evans, 164
Saint-Michel, Jean-Baptiste, 140
Saint-Sernin in Toulouse (France) 382
Salisbury Cathedral (England) 385
Salvation Army, 284
Sanders, George, 303
Santa Costanza (Rome) 378, 387
Sant'Ambrogio Basilica (Milan), 82
Saskatchewan, 292, 313–15, 318, 324–27, 336,
    354, 358

Schinkel, Karl Friedrich, 81
Schmalz, Timothy, 364, 391
Schmidt, Ole Jörgen, 81–82
Scots
    in Atlantic Canada, 51, 94–96
    in Canada, 108, 127, 185, 213, 214, 225, 296
    church designs of, 108, 127, 128
Scott, Adrian Gilbert, 342, 344
Scott, Christopher, 64–65, 67
Scott, George Gilbert, 84–85
Scott, George Gilbert, Jr., 85
Scott, John Oldrid, 85
Scott, William, 91
Second Vatican Council (1962–65), 109, 114,
    354, 364
Séguin, Jean, 337
Selkirk, Thomas Douglas, Earl of, 94, 290, 359
Seven Years' War, 107–8, 181
Sharp and Thompson, 342, 344
Shields, T.T., 187
Shim, Brigitte, 187
Short, Richard, 44
shrines, 189
Shwaykivsky, Pylyp, 294
Siddall, John Wilson, 264
Siena Cathedral (Italy) 385
Sifton, Clifford, 324
Simcoe, Elizabeth, 135
Simcoe, John Graves, 184, 193
Simeon Sylites, Saint, 376, 378
Simon, Charles, 280
Simone da Orsegnigo, 383
Simpson, A.B., 365
Simpson, Douglas C., 295
Sisters of Charity (Grey Nuns), 148, 153–54
Sisters of St. John the Divine, 172
Six Nations Confederacy, 193, 200
Skey, Lawrence, 259, 272
Sleigh, B.W.A., 145
Smith, John, 194
Smith, W.H., 241
Smith and Gemmell, 283
Society for the Propagation of the Gospel in
    Foreign Parts (SPG), 33–35, 200, 243, 298
Society of Friends, 239. *See also* Quakers
Society of Jesus. *See* Jesuits
Sons of Freedom, 327
Spence, Basil, 354
Spencer, Aubrey, 83
Sproule, Robert, 133
stained glass
    in Atlantic Canada, 73, 76, 91, 93
    in Ontario, 241, 245, 276
    in Québec, 152, 159, 171–72, 174–75
    in West, 354, 362
Stalker, G.F., 390–91
Stanley, K.C., 295
St. Catherine's Monastery (Egypt) 378, 379
St. John Lateran (Rome) 375, 378
St. Paul's Cathedral (England) 387, 388
St. Peter's Basilica (Rome) 387

St. Simon Stylites, Monastery of (Syria) 376, 378
Sts. Sergius, Bacchus and Leontius (Bosra) 377
steel construction, 170
    in Ontario, 257, 259–61, 280
    in Québec, 170, 171
    in West, 348, 360, 363–64
stencilling, 234, 235
Stephen of Aila, 378
stone construction
    early Christian, 370–82
    medieval, 383–85
    in New Brunswick, 36, 39, 67–68, 71–76
    in Newfoundland and Labrador, 81–87
    in North, 338, 339
    in Nova Scotia, 32, 40
    in Ontario, 178, 182, 189, 195–96, 200–203, 210, 213–15, 217, 219, 225, 228, 231–39, 243–52, 257, 264, 283, 392
    in Prince Edward Island, 98, 99
    in Québec, 104, 106, 110–59, 170
    Renaissance, 387
    in West, 293, 295, 296, 330–31, 340–44, 359–60
    and wood construction, 98, 99–101
Stoneys, 301
Storm, William G., 248, 283–84. *See also* Cumberland and Storm
Strachan, John, 247–48
Street, George Edmund, 254
Stroud, John, 254
Stuart, John (missionary), 35, 193, 199–200
Stuart, John (archaeologist/architect), 206–7
style, 16–20, 36. *See also specific styles*
Sublime, 80–81, 134, 148
Suchaçev, Igor, 263, 266
Sulpicians, 144, 148, 150, 153
Sunday schools, 26, 389–91
Sveinson, Arni, 310, 312, 313
Swaine, Elijah, 50
Sydenham, Lord, 200
symbolism, 72, 74–75, 98
synagogues, 264–66, 280, 370, 372

Taché, Antonin, 359
Talbot, Thomas, 204
Taylor, William Henry, 298
Telizyn, Emile, 363
Thayendanegea (Joseph Brant), 35, 193
Theophilos, Brother (Mount Athos Monastery), 266
Therry, Éric de, 109, 159
Thévenot, Étienne, 241, 245
Theyanoguin, 35
Thom, Ron, 187, 295, 338
Thomas, John, 245
Thomas, William, 209–10, 212–15, 241, 243–45
Thompson, David, 195, 288
Thoreau, Henry David, 148
timber construction, 51

in Ontario, 178, 180, 188, 193, 197
    in West, 299, 303–8, 312
Tolstoy, Leo, 324
towers, 68. *See also* bell towers
Tractarians, 71
Travisanutto, Giovanni, 363
Tremblay, Fernand, 164
Trudeau, Pierre Elliott, 148
Tuchak, Ivan, 294
Tudor Revival, 235
Tully, Kivas, 208
Tutty, William, 44

Ukrainians, 292, 315–23, 328–29, 364, 365
United Brethren. *See* Moravian (United) Brethren
United Church of Canada, 40, 187, 261–62
United Empire Loyalists, 52, 108, 182–84. *See also* Loyalists
United States. *See* New England
Université de Montréal, 160
University of Toronto, 186, 187, 279
Upper Canada College (Toronto), 217
urban planning, 256–57
Ursulines, 104, 387
Utrecht, Treaty of (1713), 31, 107, 181

Vancouver Island, 290–91, 303–4, 332–34, 342
van de Velde, Franz, 338, 339
Vanier, Jean, 172
Vannier, Paul, 168
van Nostrand, John, 284
Varley, F.H., 272, 273
Vatican II. *See* Second Vatican Council
Venne, Alphonse, 160, 162
Verigin, Peter Vasil'evich, 324–26, 327
Vermonet, A., 235
Verrazzano, Giovanni da, 31
Verrier, Étienne, 31–32
Verville, Jean-François, 32
Viau, Dalbé, 160, 162
Victorian style
    Gothic, 78, 212
    High, 99, 251
    Late, 212, 330–35
Vignot, Pierre, 146
Viollet-le-Duc, Eugène Emmanuel, 241
Vladimir, Saint, 322
Voltaire, 36

Wailes, William, 73, 76
Walker, Hiram, 217–19
War of 1812, 184–85, 206, 222
Warrington, William, 76
Watts, Richard, 35
Webb, Benjamin, 74–75
Wells Cathedral (England) 382, 383
Wesley, Charles, 60
Wesleyan Missions, 300, 301
West. *See also specific provinces*
    pre-Confederation, 296–301

Québec influence in, 299–300, 304
    settlement of, 290–92, 310–27
West Coast, 293. *See also* British Columbia
Wickenden, C.O., 330
Wickson, A. Frank, 228, 229
Wiens, Clifford, 354, 358
Wilby, Ernest, 219
Willan, Healey, 254, 255
Wills, Frank, 36, 37, 71–74, 75–76
Willson, David, 185, 193, 196–99
Wilson, John, 194
windows, 84, 174, 219. *See also* stained glass
Wiswall, John, 54
Wix, Edward, 78, 80
Wolfe, James, 107–8
Women's Christian Temperance Union, 186
wood construction, 36, 91. *See also* log construction; timber construction
    balloon-frame, 328
    board-and-batten, 39–40, 69, 182, 291
    cabinetry/woodworking in, 52, 54, 67, 140
    clapboard, 40, 54
    glulam, 274, 277, 295, 353–55
    in New Brunswick, 34, 36, 38, 63–67, 89–93
    in Newfoundland and Labrador, 30, 33, 37, 78–80
    in North, 338, 339
    in Nova Scotia, 31, 36, 40, 42–54
    in Ontario, 181, 182, 193–99, 220–29, 268, 271
    pièce-sur-pièce, 105, 299–300, 314, 315
    in Prince Edward Island, 94–101
    in Québec, 36, 105, 132, 148, 156, 163, 173
    stone construction and, 39, 98, 99–101
    in West, 288, 291–95, 303–19, 322, 324–27, 347–48
    woods used in, 65, 229
Worts, James, 243
Wren, Christopher, 44–46, 387, 388–89
Wright, Frank Lloyd, 340–44
Wright, John, 303
Wyandottes, 208
Wyle, Florence, 272, 273

Yanishewski, Yarema, 322
Young, Thomas, 243
Youville, Saint Marguerite d', 148, 154
Yukon, 293, 337

Zabolotny, Paul, 318
Zadorozny, Vasyl', 294
Zeidler, Eberhard, 276–77
Zinzendorf, Nikolaus Ludwig, Count von, 57, 59
Zuk, Radoslav, 266, 268, 366

PHOTO CREDITS

T = Top, M = Middle, B = Bottom,
R = Right, L = Left, C = Centre

Front Cover: John de Visser
Back Cover: John de Visser

John de Visser: 1, 4, 7, 8, 10, 14, 16, 17, 19 T, 20, 21, 22, 23, 24, 25, 28-29, 31, 32, 33 L, 34, 38-39, 41, 43, 45, 46, 47 L, 49, 50, 51 T, 52 R, 53, 54, 55, 56-57, 58, 60, 61, 62, 64, 65, 66, 68, 69 L, 73, 75, 79, 80 R, 81, 82, 83, 84, 85, 86 R, 88, 90, 91, 92, 94, 95, 96 BL R, 97, 99, 100, 101 T, 102-103, 108, 109, 111, 112 R, 113 B, 116 T, 117, 118, 119, 120, 123, 125, 126, 127, 128, 129, 130, 136, 138 TR B, 139, 140, 141, 142, 144, 145, 146-147, 149, 150, 150-151, 152 R, 157, 162 TR BR, 163 L, 167, 171 T, 174 B, 176-177, 179, 181, 182, 183, 184, 187, 190-191, 194 R, 195, 196, 200, 201, 202, 206 B, 208, 209, 212, 213, 215, 217, 225, 228, 230, 232, 233, 234 R, 235, 237, 238 R, 239, 242, 243, 244, 245, 246, 248 R, 250, 251 B, 252 R, 253, 257, 260, 262, 263, 265, 266, 270, 271 L, 275, 276 R, 278, 279 L, 286-287, 289, 290 R, 291, 294, 295, 298 T, 299, 300, 301 T, 302, 304 R, 305, 306, 307, 309, 311, 312 T, 313, 314, 316 R, 317, 318, 319 T, 320 T, 325, 328, 331, 332 R, 333 B, 340, 337, 338, 339, 341, 342, 343 B, 344, 348, 350-351, 352, 353 T, 354, 355, 356, 357, 359 T, 361 TL B, 364, 365, 366, 367, 391, 392, 394-395

Douglas Richardson: 37, 38, 40, 47 R, 69 R, 72, 74, 80 L, 86 L, 87, 96 TL, 98, 105 R, 152 L, 154, 155, 156, 205, 207 L, 210, 211, 214 R, 216, 218, 219 B, 249, 254, 255, 264, 267, 293, 298 B, 312 B, 316 L, 320 B, 326, 335 TL B, 358, 361 TR, 362, 390 M, 396 R

Peter Richardson: 18, 19 B, 26, 27, 106 R, 112 L, 113 T, 114, 115, 116 B, 122, 131, 134, 138 TL, 148, 158, 160, 161, 162 L, 163 R, 164, 165 L, 166 R, 169, 170, 172, 173 R, 174 T, 175 TL TR, 180, 186, 188, 189, 194 L, 195 L, 199, 220, 221, 223, 224, 226, 229, 234 L, 238 L, 261, 268, 269, 276 L, 277, 279 R, 290 L, 301 B, 304 L, 308, 321, 324, 327, 332 L, 334, 345 R, 349 B, 363 L, 368-369, 373, 374, 375 R, 376, 377, 378, 379, 380, 381, 382, 383, 384, 385, 390 T B, 396 L

OTHER CONTRIBUTORS:

Arban, Tom: 173 L, 175 B

Architectural Unit, Department of Culture, Heritage and Tourism, Province of Manitoba: 329

Archives of Ontario: 203, 206 T, 248 L, 251 T, 256; Horwood Collection: 247 L

Bell, Leland: 397

Blue Guide Rome, with permission: 375 L

Braun, Willi: 363 R

Castle Photographic Service; with permission from the Nova Scotia Archives and Records Management: 44

Canadian Centre for Architecture, Montréal: 386

Cram, R.A, *Substance of Gothic*: 219

Destrubé Photography: 333 T, 343 T

Division des archives, Université de Montréal. Collection Adine Baby-Thompson (P0059). FG152. *View of the Place d'Armes, Québec 1832. – Canada: Adolphus Bourne, 1874*: 107

Fram, Mark and Albert Schrauwers: *An introduction to the Sharon Temple National Historic Site, to the Children of Peace who made it, and to their place in the history of Canada before Canada*, Toronto: Coach House Books, 2005: 198

Harland, Philip: 372 T

Hines, Sherman: 70

Holdsworth, Patricia: 359 B

Jensen, Debra: 371 T

Ledohowski, Ed: 335 TR

Library and Archives Canada: 296-297; National Map Collection: 207 R

MacRae, Marion and Anthony Adamson, *Hallowed Walls: church architecture of Upper Canada*. 1975: 214 L, 252 L

Monastère des Ursulines de Québec: 189

Musée de la civilisation, fonds d'archives du Séminaire de Québec. *Plan d'Église par Mr Jean Maillou*. Jean Maillou. Vers 1715. Jacques Lessard, photographer: 389

National Monuments Record, English Heritage: 77

Neufeldt, Ron: 345 L

Pugin, A.W. *Present State of Ecclesiastical Architecture in England*, 1843: 76

Paris, Michael: 346, 349 T

Paulette, Claude: 132 T

Regehr, Henry: 2, 192, 197, 240, 258, 272, 273, 280

Richardson, Jonathan: 227

Rollmann, Hans: 59

Seding, Volker, photographer; with permission from John Van Nostraud of Architects Alliance, Toronto: 284, 285

St. Anne's Church Fredericton, NB: 36

Ukrainian Cultural Heritage Village, Edmonton, AB; courtesy of Arnold Grandt: 322, 323

University of Calgary, Libraries and Cultural Resources: Cathedral of the Arctic, Ron Thom fonds, Canadian Architectural Archives: 336

University of Toronto, University College: 133

University of Toronto, Thomas Fisher Rare Book Library: 35, 153, 388

Drawings courtesy of Fowler Bauld & Mitchell Ltd., Architecture: 47 B

Illustrations by Imagineering Media Services Inc.: 33 R, 51 B, 52 L, 101 B, 105 L, 106 L, 132 B, 165 R, 166 L, 171 B, 217 L, 271 R, 292, 319 B, 353 B, 371 B, 372 B, 377 B, 387

DEDICATION

Over the past two-and-a-half years or so
it has been my distinct privilege and great pleasure to travel the length and
breadth of this country to photograph between three and four hundred
churches of which about 250 are in this book.

These churches run the gamut from the very old (in Canadian terms) to the
brand new, from the traditional to the very modern, from the sadly abandoned
to some tragically disfigured by fire. And, of course, from the grand and
majestic to the modest, little ones, many of them standing all alone in a field
somewhere but all of them lovingly kept and maintained.

When one travels this country from east to west perhaps the most fascinating
aspect of the trip is how our history, young as it is when compared with the
"Old World," becomes younger and younger as you move west. The oldest
churches in the east date to the 18th century. The oldest Ukrainian church in
Manitoba was finished in 1899. And going ever farther west and north, in
many cases the oldest church was built in living memory!

I am grateful to everyone along the way who graciously opened doors
and turned on the lights. I hope that I have "kept the faith."

— *John de Visser*